ELDER LAW

The West Legal Studies Series

Your options keep growing with West Legal Studies

Each year our list continues to offer you more options for every area of the law to meet your course or on-the-job reference requirements. We now have over 140 titles from which to choose in the following areas:

Administrative Law
Alternative Dispute Resolution
Bankruptcy
Business Organizations/Corporations
Civil Litigation and Procedure
CLA Exam Preparation
Client Accounting
Computer in the Law Office
Constitutional Law
Contract Law
Criminal Law and Procedure
Document Preparation
Environmental Law
Ethics

Family Law
Federal Taxation
Intellectual Property
Introduction to Law
Introduction to Paralegalism
Law Office Management
Law Office Procedures
Legal Research, Writing, and Analysis
Legal Terminology
Paralegal Employment
Real Estate Law
Reference Materials
Torts and Personal Injury Law
Will, Trusts, and Estate Administration

You will find unparalleled, practical support

Each text is augmented by instructor and student supplements to ensure the best learning experience possible. We also offer custom publishing and other benefits such as West's Student Achievement Award. In addition, our sales representatives are ready to provide you with dependable service.

We want to hear from you

Our best contributions for improving the quality of our books and instructional materials is feedback from the people who use them. If you have a question, concern, or observation about any of our materials, or you have a product proposal or manuscript, we want to hear from you. Please contact your local representative or write us at the following address:

West Legal Studies, 3 Columbia Circle, P.O. Box 15015, Albany, NY 12212-5015

For additional information point your browser at

www.westlegalstudies.com

ELDER LAW

Jeffrey A. Helewitz, J.D.

WEST

THOMSON LEARNING™

Australia   Canada   Mexico   Singapore   Spain   United Kingdom   United States

WEST LEGAL STUDIES

Elder Law
Jeffrey A. Helewitz, J.D.

Business Unit Director:
Susan L. Simpfenderfer

Executive Editor:
Marlene McHugh Pratt

Acquisitions Editor:
Joan M. Gill

Editorial Assistant:
Lisa Flatley

Executive Marketing Manager:
Donna J. Lewis

Channel Manager:
Nigar Hale

Executive Production Manager:
Wendy A. Troeger

Production Editor:
Betty L. Dickson

Cover Designer:
Dutton and Sherman Design

Cover Image:
Digital Imagery © copyright 2000
PhotoDisc, Inc.

For permission to use material from this text or product, contact us by
Tel (800) 730-2214
Fax (800) 730-2215
www.thomsonrights.com

Library of Congress Cataloging-in-Publication Data
Helewitz, Jeffrey A.
    Elder law / Jeffrey Helewitz.
        p. cm.
    Includes index.
    ISBN 0-7668-1371-1
    1. Aged—Legal status, laws, etc.—United States. 2. Legal assistants—United States—Handbooks, manuals, etc. I. Title.
KF390.A4 H45 2000
346.7301'3—dc21   00-043414

NOTICE TO THE READER

CONTENTS

CHAPTER 6   Estate Planning   225

CHAPTER 7   Elder Abuse   269

PREFACE

It is a statistical reality that the average American is rapidly approaching what has euphemistically been referred to as the "Golden Years." As more and more people fall into the category of "elderly," the law and the legal profession will become increasingly concerned with the legal needs of this ever-expanding segment of the population. *Elder Law* was written to address the legal community's need to become familiar with the law that affects the elderly in this country.

The purpose of *Elder Law* is to help the lawyer, legal assistant, and anyone whose vocation or avocation brings them into contact with older Americans. An understanding of the laws that directly affect the elderly is imperative if one is to provide appropriate legal advice—to any client, as all clients will eventually fall into the category of the elderly. *Elder Law* analyzes the legal, ethical, and social problems of the elderly, and provides, in a simple, easy-to-read format, a comprehensive overview of the most important laws affecting the elderly today. Furthermore, the text gives the reader a resource guide of agencies and associations that can provide additional information and assistance for the elderly client.

Elder Law is the most complete and comprehensive text on the market regarding this subject for the legal assistant. No other text available meets this specific need in a manner that is appropriate for legal professionals. *Elder Law* is designed specifically for the legal assistant and professional, to provide a complete yet comprehensible guide to the world of elder law, one of the fastest growing areas of law in the country.

ORGANIZATION OF *ELDER LAW*

The text is divided into eight chapters and is structured to be compatible with any school-established method of course instruction. Most importantly, the text is written in a manner that is comprehensible to paralegal students; its goal is to demystify elder law for legal assistants.

Each of the eight chapters has a similar format. Every chapter begins with an introduction that outlines the basic principles covered in the body of the chapter. The chapters are arranged to take the student through all of the most important aspects of the law that relates to the elderly client. Each chapter provides numerous examples of the principles discussed, taken from ordinary, everyday situations, as well as those typically encountered in a legal practice. In this fashion the examples help the student understand the law from a practical standpoint. Each chapter includes a summary that concisely recapitulates the subject matter covered.

Unlike most texts, which merely provide lists of the terms used in the chapters, *Elder Law* provides definitions of key terms in the margin where those terms are first used in text. This running glossary, along with key terms lists and a cumulative glossary at the end of the book, reinforces the chapter terminology in students' mind. Each chapter further provides edited judicial decisions, germane to the chapter's content, that highlight the law discussed in the body of the chapter. Every chapter concludes with a set of exercise problems designed to test the student's knowledge of the basic concepts discussed in the chapter.

SUPPLEMENTAL TEACHING AND LEARNING MATERIALS

An instructors' manual will be provided for *Elder Law*. The manual includes:

- Sample course syllabi
- Chapter outlines
- Teaching suggestions
- Answers to text exercises and questions
- Sample exams in various formats

ABOUT THE AUTHOR

Jeffrey A. Helewitz received his J.D. and LL.M. degrees from Georgetown University Law Center and an M.B.A. (Finance) from New York University. He has worked for the National Office of the Internal Revenue Service and has been in private practice for several years. He is the author of a dozen texts designed for paralegals and lawyers, as well as numerous articles and a forthcoming casebook. He has taught at several paralegal institutions in the New York area, has lectured for the

New York County Lawyers' Association C.L.E. program, and is an Adjunct Professor of Law at both C.U.N.Y. School of Law and Touro College Law Center.

ACKNOWLEDGMENTS

I would like to thank all the people at West Legal Studies whose kind assistance and encouragement in the preparation of this text is greatly appreciated.

The comments and suggestions of the following reviewers are greatly appreciated:

Mardy Chaplin
    Cuyahoga Community College

Deborah Howard
    University of Evansville

Nancy Jakubowski
    Warren County Community College

Diana D'Amico Juettner
    Mercy College

Deborah Kukowski
    Moorhead State University

Alvin L. McDonald
    Mew Mexico State University

Barbara Paul
    Community College of Philadelphia

Julia O. Tryk
    Cuyahoga Community College

I realize that I am not perfect, and that all texts can be improved. If you or your students have suggestions on how this text can be improved, please write to me, care of the publisher, so that *Elder Law* can be made an even better book in the future. I look forward to your comments.

JEFFREY A. HELEWITZ

WHAT IS ELDER LAW?

CHAPTER OUTLINE _____

Introduction

Psychological and Social Aspects of
an Aging Society

Ethical Considerations of Elder Law

INTRODUCTION

The term **elder law** has been applied to a body of legal rights and obligations that affect persons who have attained a "certain age," even though there are very few actual laws directed principally for the elderly. The aging pattern of American society is changing, and a greater number of people (both actually and by percentage) are living longer, fuller, more active lives. Many legal principles that had rarely applied to the elderly (because few people lived long enough to come within their purviews) are now part and parcel of many Americans' existences. The legal needs of the elderly were specifically addressed for the first time (excluding Social Security) only in the mid-1960s, and it has only been in the last few decades that a legal specialty in the area has arisen. This text highlights and addresses some of the laws and issues of specific importance to the elderly. However, the reader should remember that elder law, like property law, is merely a "bundle of rights" that are applied to persons as they arrive at a specified chronological age.

elder law Area of law concerned with the legal problems of persons deemed to be elderly.

Definition of *Elder*

To identify the legal rights and obligations that affect older Americans, one must define what is meant by the term **elder**. According to the American Athletic Union, competitive swimmers are considered

elder Anyone over a certain age; not universally defined by the law.

1

"masters" once they have attained the age of 25. Most teenagers believe that any person over the age of 30 cannot be trusted, because of those advanced years. The Age Discrimination in Employment Act applies to persons over the age of 40, and the American Association of Retired Persons solicits a prospective member on his or her 50th birthday. Social Security retirement benefits begin at age 62, whereas the author's grandmother adhered to the notion that life only begins at 80. Consequently, age, or being elderly, is both a state of mind and a legal classification, depending on the particular right under scrutiny.

The reason that elder law can be viewed as a bundle of rights rather than a specific legal concept is because neither society nor the legislatures have been able to provide a precise, all-encompassing definition of the term *elder*. Therefore, the definition of *elder* is a somewhat nebulous notion, to be applied depending on the particular facts and circumstances of a given situation.

The Older Americans Act of 1965

In the mid-1960s, along with other civil rights legislation, the federal government passed the **Older Americans Act of 1965**, 42 U.S.C. § 3001 *et seq.,* the first civil rights law specifically addressing the older American. Historically, this statute can be considered the start of the concept of elder law. This legislation, which is very general, was designed to promote, *inter alia,* the following:

- an adequate income during retirement

- the best possible physical and mental health care for persons as they age

- methods to enable older Americans to obtain and maintain adequate housing

- full restorative services for older persons who require institutional care

- employment opportunities regardless of the worker's or applicant's age

- retirement with health and dignity, including meaningful social and civic involvement

- prohibitions against abuse and neglect of the elderly.

Older Americans Act of 1965 First federal statute specifically addressing the needs of the elderly.

The statute contains more platitudes than specific and enforceable rights, but it provided the starting point for a consideration of the needs that affect Americans as they age.

To apply and implement the principles enunciated in this act, the President's Council on Aging was established, headed by an appointed

Commissioner on Aging. In 1992 the Commissioner on Aging was re-placed by an Assistant Secretary for Aging, meaning that the concerns of elderly Americans had thereby become a part of the permanent exec-utive government. In 1998, pursuant to Executive Order 11022, the Presidential Council on Aging was abolished.

The Older Americans Act did not specifically define *older Americans,* but it did provide the impetus for all of the specific legislation that fol-lowed. Those follow-up laws were designed to implement the concepts stated in the statute and to codify the recognition that specific legal concerns affect aging persons.

PSYCHOLOGICAL AND SOCIAL ASPECTS OF AN AGING SOCIETY

Americans are living longer than they ever have in history. According to governmental statistics, the fastest growing percentage of the popu-lation for the decade 1990–2000 consisted of persons between the ages of 90 and 95. Furthermore, the current life expectancy for a person who is 65 years of age in the year 2000 is 81, while a person born in the millennium has an average life expectancy of 86. This ever-lengthening aging pattern of American society has necessitated a reevaluation of the psychological and social aspects of getting older.

Why are more Americans living longer? The answer can be extrapo-lated from various life statistics:

1. Since the middle of the 20th century, the birth rate has been higher than ever before, not necessarily in numbers of births but in the number of infants who attain adulthood, because of improved medical and general health care.

2. There is an increased life expectancy resulting from medical advances. Many illnesses that had historically been fatal have now either been eradicated or been made manageable by medi-cation or other forms of health care.

3. Many people have delayed child-bearing because of the ever-increasing number of women in the workforce who wish to pursue and establish a career before starting a family. Hav-ing children later in life keeps the parents active at older ages.

All of the foregoing have caused a tremendous reevaluation of what it means to be old in American society. Once again, according to gov-ernment statistics, by the year 2010, 39 percent of the population will be over the age of 65—a percentage that will increase to 69 percent by the year 2030. Most amazingly, by 2050 10 percent of the American population will be over the age of 85. The elderly, once perceived to be a small minority of the population, may soon become the majority.

A person's chronological age, however, is merely one aspect of the aging pattern. Generally, as a person ages, three specific areas of concern must be addressed:

1. The *functional capacity* of the individual: Can the person still maintain an active and independent lifestyle, or have the physical aspects of the aging process limited the person's ability to cope with daily life functions?

2. The *social involvement* of the individual: As family move away and friends retire or die, is the person capable and desirous of interacting with others, or does the person become more and more isolated?

3. The *physical and mental health* of the individual: As the body changes over time, what are the effects of the slowing-down of general physical and metal processes?

All these factors contribute to a person's *physiological age,* which is determined by the interaction of both chronological age and intrinsic capacity. Depending on these factors, a person may consider himself or herself, or may be considered, elderly or merely not young.

Example

For the past several years, a woman in her eighties has run in the Boston Marathon. At an interview, the woman stated that she only started running when she was in her seventies. After she retired and her husband died, she spent more and more time at home. Her daughter, a young sprig in her fifties, was concerned about her and advised her to get out of the house more. The woman started walking around a pond in her neighborhood that was a favorite trail for runners; after a few months of seeing people run past her, she started a slow jog around the pond. Living in the Boston area, she became intrigued with participating in the marathon, and was accepted because of her age. At the time of the interview she had been participating in the Boston marathon for several years. The interviewer asked the woman what her daughter thought now, and the woman said that her daughter thought she was crazy and that at her age she should rest and slow down. People have preconceived notions of what the elderly can, or should, do!

A person's ability to cope with age is dependent not only on the person's physical well-being, but also on the perceptions the person and others have about what the person can do. Because of better health care, and the fact that the elderly are surrounded by more contemporaries than ever before, people are maintaining active and dynamic lifestyles well into their nineties.

Example

Al Hirschfeld, the well-known theatrical caricaturist for the *New York Times* and other publications, who is in his nineties, still works, as well as drives his own car, maintains his own house, and leads an active social life. This raises eyebrows in some circles where such activities are perceived to be beyond the abilities of octogenarians.

Independence and Dependence

One of the major concerns of people as they age is their ability to maintain independent lifestyles. Years ago, when American families were less peripatetic, generations would live together, each segment providing specific services for the family unit. As more and more American families become mobile, fewer and fewer households remain multigenerational, and people no longer live and die in a limited geographical location. The consequences of this moving pattern means that more people are living on their own as they age.

Example

In 1910 a couple immigrated to the United States from Russia. They settled in New York and eventually bought their own house. They had two children who grew up, married, and bought houses within three blocks of their parents' house. When the children had children, the couple moved in and provided child care, and the three generations lived together in the same household in the same community where they grew up.

Example

In 1950 a couple immigrated to the United States from the Soviet Union. They settled in New York and eventually bought a house there. They had two children. One child married and moved to Tucson, Arizona; the other child accepted a job offer in Seattle, Washington. The couple rarely see their grandchildren, and have now decided to retire to Florida to be with their friends in a retirement community.

A primary concern as people age is their ability to maintain some **autonomy** in their lives, being able to live on their own without assistance. Provided that the person is healthy, both physically and mentally, this has become a necessity as well as a desire, as opportunities

autonomy The ability to make decisions for oneself.

to live with families and relations become scarcer. However, to maintain a independent lifestyle, the person must have adequate financial resources, reasonable housing, and access to health care.

Example

A man in his eighties lives on his own in a house he bought 50 years ago. The man's main sources of income are Social Security benefits, a small pension, and interest on a small savings account. When the plumbing freezes and cracks, causing floods in the basement and first floor, the man slips and breaks his hip. If he is to continue living on his own, the man needs financial assistance to repair the pipes and pay medical bills and needs physical assistance until his hip heals.

Physical Limitations

One of the major factors that determines whether a person can live on his or her own is the physical limitations that occur as the person ages. Statistically, as a body matures it becomes subject to both chronic and acute physical ailments. A **chronic ailment** is continuous, persistent, and incapable of being cured, such as arthritis, osteoporosis, senile dementia, and Alzheimer's disease (the most typical chronic problems afflicting the elderly).

Example

An elderly woman wants to live on her own in the apartment she has occupied for more than 50 years. The woman suffers from severe arthritis in her fingers, and now finds it difficult to open jars and cans, and has trouble doing housework. To continue to live on her own, the woman needs some limited housekeeping assistance.

Acute ailments, in contrast, are temporary conditions that usually result from traumatic circumstances such as a broken leg or a severe bout of flu. These types of problems, provided that they do not escalate into a chronic problem such as loss of mobility if the bone does not heal properly, have only short-term effects on the person's ability to maintain his or her independence.

chronic ailment
Continuous and persistent physical problem that cannot be cured.

acute ailment
Physical problem of a temporary nature.

Example

An elderly woman catches a bad cold after she leaves her window open all night. Although she runs a fever and is ill for several days, this is an acute condition that only temporarily interferes with her lifestyle.

In addition to chronic and acute physical problems, there is a general and unavoidable decline in physical ability as a body ages, resulting in muscle loss, memory loss, and slowed physical and mental reactions. However, this does not mean that a person cannot still be active and healthy, and many Americans actually become more active as they age, even testing higher on physical stress and strength tests than sedentary 20-somethings. Physical aging merely places certain limitations on an active and involved lifestyle, rather than making it impossible.

ETHICAL CONSIDERATIONS OF ELDER LAW

Because more Americans are living longer, attention is now being paid to the legal, emotional, and physical needs of our aging society. Problems that did not exist 100 years ago, because of limited longevity, have now become the daily concerns of an increasing segment of the population. To meet these needs, American society must be willing and able to address the specific needs of the elderly, particularly in the areas of health care, housing, legal rights, and personal decision making.

Access to Health Care

Access to health care covers two broad concerns: the financial ability of the individual to obtain adequate health care and the ability of the individual to make informed decisions regarding his or her health care.

In addition to private insurance policies, the federal government provides some financial assistance to the elderly to help secure health care. The primary governmental health care program is **Medicare**, which is a form of federal health insurance that covers all citizens and lawful permanent residents who are over the age of 65 or who receive Social Security benefits. The Medicare program (discussed in detail in Chapter 2) provides health care coverage after the recipient has met a standard **deductible**, an amount that the participant himself or herself must pay for health services. However, the Medicare program does not provide complete coverage; after a certain number of payments have been made, the individual is responsible for **co-payments**, a portion of the medical bill for which Social Security will not repay the recipient. Because Medicare is not all-inclusive, many individuals maintain supplemental medical insurance to cover the portions of health care bills that are not met by Medicare. For persons with very low incomes, as established by statute, the federal government does provide **Medicaid** to cover most medical needs, including medications and health care

Medicare Federally funded health insurance for persons who receive Social Security benefits.

deductible Percentage of a medical bill for which the patient remains responsible and must pay before insurance coverage takes over.

co-payment Portion of a medical bill that is not reimbursed or covered by insurance and remains the responsibility of the patient.

Medicaid Federally funded program providing medical care to low-income persons.

appliances such as wheelchairs and crutches. However, some individuals' income is too high to qualify for Medicaid, but their income and assets are too low to enable them to purchase their own private health insurance; thus, their medical needs may not be met purely because of finances. (See Exhibit 1-1.) Is it ethical for a responsible society to expect or demand that its elderly citizens spend their life savings just to acquire basic health care?

EXHIBIT 1-1

Percentages of Persons Age 65+ in Poverty	
All Elderly	12.0%
Men	7.6%
Women	15.4%
White	10.1%
Black	33.8%
Hispanic	22.5%
Men Living Alone	16.5%
Women Living Alone	26.5%

Source: U.S. Bureau of the Census, "Current Population Reports," Series P-60, No. 175.

Example

An elderly man suffers from severe asthma. His only income is derived from Social Security and a small pension, and he owns his own home. He does not qualify for Medicaid because of his financial resources, but his income is too low for him to afford supplemental medical insurance premiums. The nature and quality of his health care are limited by his financial situation.

Patient Self-Determination Act
Federal statute requiring Medicare and Medicaid recipients to be given written statements regarding their health care rights.

Even if the financial aspect of a person's health care is provided for, it is still necessary for the individual to be able to make informed choices as to the type of medical treatment he or she is to receive. Pursuant to the **Patient Self-Determination Act**, 42 U.S.C. § 1395cc(f), every Medicare and Medicaid recipient must be given written information regarding the nature and extent of his or her condition and suggested treatment, so that the patient can make an informed decision with respect to his or her care. However, to make an informed decision, the individual must be mentally competent to make such decisions. Pursuant to case law, a person's competency to make a health care decision must be shown by "clear and convincing evidence" (*see In* *re Westchester County Medical Center* at the end of this chapter). Whenever an individual enters into certain types of arrangements known as **advance directives**, the person's mental competence comes into question. There are three types of advance directives:

1. health care proxies
2. living wills
3. do-not-resuscitate (DNR) orders or directives.

Even though these arrangements are directives that give the ultimate decision-making power to someone other than the patient, the patient's mental ability at the time he or she executed such an instrument must be proven before the directives can be given effect.

A **health care proxy** is a legal instrument in which an individual nominates another person to make health care decisions for the individual should he or she become incapable of speaking for himself or herself.

Example

A woman is about to undergo surgery. Several weeks prior to the operation, she goes to an attorney's office to sign a health care proxy in favor of her sister, which was drawn up by the attorney's paralegal. After surgery, the woman falls into a coma. The sister, as the health care proxy, is now authorized to make decisions regarding the woman's treatment, *provided* the woman was competent to execute the proxy in the first place.

A **living will** is an instrument executed by an individual indicating the person's wishes with respect to life support systems and organ donation should the individual become unable to speak for himself or herself.

A **do-not-resuscitate directive** is a document by which the signatory states that he or she does not wish to be resuscitated or maintained on life support systems should he or she become incompetent. Unlike a health care proxy, living wills and do-not-resuscitate orders indicate the individual's wishes but do not authorize another person to make these decisions; consequently, it is up to the hospital, the physician, and the court to implement these documents.

Example

Under the direction of an attorney, a man executes a living will (drafted by the attorney's legal assistant) in which he indicates that he does not wish to be maintained on life support equipment should he become incapacitated. The man suffers a stroke, is placed in a religiously affiliated hospital, and eventually slips into a coma. The man's daughter wishes the

advance directive Document that expresses the future health care wishes of the signatory.

health care proxy Legal document authorizing someone other than the principal to make heath care decisions for the principal should the principal become incapable of speaking for himself or herself.

living will Document indicating the signatory's wishes with respect to life support should the signatory become incompetent.

do-not-resuscitate (DNR) directive Document indicating that the signatory does not wish to be resuscitated or maintained on life support equipment.

living will to take effect, but the hospital refuses. It is now up to a court and judicial interpretation to determine whether the man's wishes will be given effect.

Example

A woman executes a DNR order because she has a fear of being kept alive like a vegetable for years. She is in an accident several years after the order is signed, and her chances of survival are minimal. Her daughter wishes the DNR order to be given effect, but her son does not. The DNR order only indicates the woman's state of mind when it was executed, not her current wishes, so the hospital may not give it effect.

Because the human body deteriorates over time, the necessity of access to appropriate health care becomes a more pressing and urgent problem.

Access to Housing

As noted earlier, more and more elderly persons are now living on their own, and their ability to maintain their homes or to continue to pay rent becomes both a financial and a physical issue. Even if an individual is healthy, financial resources may become limited as the person retires and leaves the workforce. Numerous federal, state, and local statutes specifically address the housing needs of the elderly (see Chapter 4) by providing rent maintenance, public assistance for low-cost housing, and low-interest loans to maintain and repair residences. Also, the federal government provides funding for construction and rehabilitation of residences specifically designed for the elderly, so as to provide adequate housing for the older population.

Example

An elderly couple has been living in their house for more than 30 years. The roof is in need of repair, but they do not have capital resources to expend on the work. They are able to get a low-interest loan to cover the roof repair cost and thereby continue to remain in their home.

Many retirement and health care communities have come into existence specifically because a growing percentage of the population is aging and in need of some form of assisted living. If families are no longer able or willing to care for their elderly relations who are physically unable to live alone, it becomes the responsibility of society at large to see that the housing needs of this segment of the population are taken care of.

Access to Legal Counsel

At some point all individuals need the advice and skills of an attorney. As more and more people live longer, this need for legal assistance becomes more likely. However, even though the need for legal counsel may exist, the problems associated with access to such counsel change as a person ages. There are two main concerns with providing adequate legal services to the elderly: funding and the specialized skills necessary to advise this particular group.

Because many elderly persons are living on reduced or limited incomes, the cost of obtaining legal counsel becomes a primary factor in asserting or defending rights. Only limited government funding is available for **public interest law clinics** such as Legal Aid, Public Defenders, and law school clinical programs; a set income and asset limit is enforced for those who seek these organizations' services. Therefore, even though an elderly person has relatively low income and resources, he or she may still be precluded from obtaining public legal services if his or her finances exceed the statutory income and resource limitations established by the government.

> *Example*
>
> An elderly woman wishes to obtain some estate planning advice. She has a moderate income and owns her own home. She cannot afford the several hundred dollars per hour a private attorney would charge for such work, but her finances make her ineligible for clinical assistance.

Many law firms and bar associations provide **pro bono legal services** (free legal counseling provided for qualifying individuals), but, once again, a person's income may place him or her beyond the reach of these services, or the type of problem the person has may not be within the scope of the legal services the attorney is offering.

Recently, many individuals have availed themselves of **alternative dispute resolution**, such as arbitration or mediation, in which they can represent themselves in a quasi-legal setting that is more cost- and time-effective than the regular judicial process. However, the individual's mental capacity and legal knowledge may severely limit the effectiveness of these alternatives.

> *Example*
>
> An elderly couple is having a problem with a contractor they hired to make some repairs on their home. The contract specified arbitration in the case of a dispute, which the couple favored because of cost-effectiveness. However, at the arbitration the contractor was represented by counsel and the couple had no idea what they were supposed to do. They could not afford

public interest law clinic Government-funded office providing legal services to low-income persons.

pro bono legal services Free legal services provided by law offices and bar associations to low-income individuals.

alternative dispute resolution Non-judicial method of resolving legal problems, such as arbitration or mediation.

to hire their own lawyer. Because they could not present their case effectively, the arbitrator found in favor of the contractor.

Many legal problems of the elderly require specialized skill and in-depth knowledge of the cases and statutes that affect the rights and obligations of older persons. In 1974, pursuant to a general omnibus bill, an **Area Agency on Aging** was created by the Legal Services Corporation to provide specialized legal services for the elderly. Since then, many law offices have evolved practices geared specifically to address the legal problems of older Americans. As more and more Americans age, the need for this specialized area of knowledge becomes increasingly pressing.

Competency

One of the primary ethical considerations of anyone dealing with the elderly is the elderly person's mental **competency**; legally, the person's ability under the law to make decisions for himself or herself. There is, of course, a distinction between legal incompetence and mere eccentricity or idiosyncrasy; therefore, when a legal professional agrees to represent a client, the professional must determine whether the client is legally capable of making his or her own decisions.

Example

An elderly woman comes to an attorney's office for advice. She likes to talk to flowers and birds, wears unusual clothing, and sits in lotus position in the lawyer's office. Is she incompetent or merely eccentric?

Area Agency on Aging Division of the Legal Services Corporation, specializing in the needs of the elderly.

competency The legal ability to make decisions for oneself.

guardianship Court authorization for someone to act on behalf of an incompetent.

conservatorship Court authorization to have one person make decisions for another who is deemed incompetent.

Many times elderly persons are accompanied by family members or friends when they seek legal advice, and it is the responsibility of the law office to determine exactly who is the client. If a person is under **guardianship** or **conservatorship** (see Chapter 4), a court has authorized someone to act on behalf of that individual because the individual has been deemed legally incapable of handling his or her own affairs. The client then is the guardian or the conservator. If the elderly individual is merely being accompanied to the office, the elderly individual is the client. If the attorney believes that the individual cannot legally make decisions for himself or herself, the attorney should refuse to represent the individual. The attorney cannot be directed by an accompanying family member until a court has authorized the family member to act on the elderly relative's behalf. One of the most important functions that an elder law legal assistant can perform, in a nonlegal capacity, is to evaluate (by observation and impression) the general competence of an elderly client, to determine whether guardianship might be appropriate.

Another ethical problem that might arise with respect to representing a competent elderly individual is the possibility that the elderly person is being unduly influenced by a family member in reaching certain legal decisions. In this instance, the **undue influence** could negate the elderly individual's actions. It is the responsibility of the law office to make sure both that the elderly client is competent and that he or she is not acting under any duress or coercion from younger family members.

Example

An elderly man comes to a lawyer's office with his son to have a will drawn up. The elderly man is competent, and indicates that he wants to leave the bulk of his estate to his son, cutting off his daughter whom he says does not love him. Is this the result of the daughter's indifference to the man, or the son's undue influence over the father?

CHAPTER REVIEW

The term elder law encompasses all legal, ethical, social, and psychological rights, duties, and problems attendant to a person's chronological age. Because older Americans represent an ever-increasing percentage of the total population, greater emphasis is being placed on the needs of the elderly, especially because the elderly are not acting as society has traditionally assumed the elderly would act.

Older Americans are still active, social beings, many of whom continue to work well into their eighties and maintain active physical and social lives. The caricature of the "disco grandma" of the 1970s has become the ordinary spectacle of elderly couples jogging in the park.

Unfortunately, not all older Americans are capable of fending for themselves, either financially or physically, and it has increasingly become the responsibility of society at large to make sure that older persons who need assistance are provided with adequate care. Many public interest groups have emerged since the mid-1960s specifically to address the concerns of the aging population: the American Association of Retired Persons (AARP), the National Council of Senior Citizens (NCSC), the Gray Panthers, the National Alliance of Senior Citizens (NASC), and the National Association of Retired Federal Employees (NARFE); a new field of law has evolved, specifically concerned with persons over a "certain age."

A new term, **generational justice**, has come into use to refer to the rights of the younger population, who are now called upon to pay for

undue influence
Using a confidential relationship to influence another person's actions in an unwarranted manner.

generational justice
Younger generations paying for the needs of older generations.

the needs of the older population through Social Security and other government transfer payments funded by the taxes imposed on the working young. What was once a limited problem for a few individuals who were primarily supported, both financially and emotionally, by families and private institutions, has now become a national concern, especially as more and more persons fall into the category of the elderly.

The legal assistant involved in an elder law practice performs many functions for the client, not all of which are legal in nature. The elder law paralegal is responsible for eliciting information from the client and making the client comfortable and informed with respect to the legal representation. In many instances, because of their close client contact, legal assistants may be the first to be aware of the client's legal (or social) needs. This societal function of the legal assistant in an elder law practice cannot be too strongly stressed.

The remainder of this text examines the most frequently encountered legal and social problems affecting the elderly in today's society.

KEY TERMS

acute ailment

advance directive

alternative dispute resolution

Area Agency on Aging

autonomy

chronic ailment

competency

conservatorship

co-payment

deductible

do-not-resuscitate directive

elder

elder law

generational justice

guardianship

health care proxy

living will

Medicaid

Medicare

Older Americans Act of 1965

Patient Self-Determination Act

pro bono legal services

public interest law clinic

undue influence

EXERCISES

1. Develop a questionnaire that a law office could use to determine an elderly client's legal needs.

2. Develop a list of resources in your area that provide assistance to the elderly.

3. List the various factors that should be used to determine a person's competency.

4. Discuss the implications of generational justice and how it may affect the passage of legislation directed to assisting the elderly.

5. Survey your friends, relations, and acquaintances who would be considered elderly to ascertain what they consider to be their most pressing legal, social, and physical concerns.

EDITED JUDICIAL DECISIONS

In re Storar
52 N.Y.2d 363, 438 N.Y.S.2d 266 (1981)

In these two cases the guardians of incompetent patients objected to the continued use of medical treatments or measures to prolong the lives of the patients who were diagnosed as fatally ill with no reasonable chance of recovery. In *Matter of Eichner,* Brother Fox, an 83-year-old member of the Society of Mary, was being maintained by a respirator in a permanent vegetative state. The local director of the society applied to have the respirator removed on the ground that it was against the patient's wishes as expressed prior to his becoming incompetent. In *Matter of Storar,* a State official applied for permission to administer blood transfusions to a profoundly retarded 52-year-old man with terminal cancer of the bladder. The patient's mother, who was also his legal guardian, refused consent on the ground that the transfusions would only prolong his discomfort and would be against his wishes if he were competent. In each case the courts below have found that the measures should have been discontinued.

The orders of the lower courts were stayed and the treatments continued pending appeals to the Appellate Division and this court. Nevertheless both of the patients have died, thus rendering these particular controversies moot. However, the underlying issues are of public importance, are recurring in other courts throughout the State and, as these cases illustrate, are likely to escape full appellate review even when the appeals have been expedited. Under those circumstances we may, and often have, addressed the issues despite the mootness (see, e.g., *Matter of Oliver v Postel, 30 NY2d 171, 177–178; Matter of Westchester Rockland Newspapers v Leggett, 48 NY2d 430, 436–437*), particularly when, as here, the controlling principles have not been previously identified and discussed by this court (cf. *Matter of Hearst Corp. v Clyne, 50 NY2d 707*).

It should be emphasized though, that any guidance we may provide for future cases is necessarily limited. Unlike the Legislature, the courts are neither equipped nor empowered to prescribe substantive or procedural rules for all, most, or even the more common contingencies. Our role, especially in matters as sensitive as these, is limited to resolving the issues raised by facts presented in particular cases.

On the records we have concluded that the order should be reversed in the *Storar* case. In the *Eichner* case the order should be modified and resolved on a narrower ground than relied on by the Appellate Division.

THE EICHNER CASE

For over 66 years Brother Joseph Fox was a member of the Society of Mary, a Catholic religious order which, among other things, operates Chaminade High School in Mineola. In 1970 Brother Fox retired to Chaminade where he resided with the religious members of the school's staff and continued to perform limited duties. In late summer of 1979 he sustained a hernia while moving some flower tubs on a roof garden at the school. He was then 83 years old and, except for the hernia, was found to be in excellent health. His doctor recommended an operation to correct the condition and Brother Fox agreed.

While the operation was being performed on October 1, 1979 he suffered cardiac arrest, with resulting loss of oxygen to the brain and substantial brain damage. He lost the ability to breathe spontaneously and was placed on a respirator which maintained him in a vegetative state. The attending physicians informed Father Philip Eichner, who was the president of Chaminade and the director of the society at the school, that there was no reasonable chance of recovery and that Brother Fox would die in that state.

After retaining two neurosurgeons who confirmed the diagnosis, Father Eichner requested the hospital to remove the respirator. The hospital, however, refused to do so without court authorization. Father Eichner then applied, pursuant to article 78 of the Mental Hygiene Law, to be appointed committee of the person and property of Brother Fox, with authority to direct removal of the respirator. The application was supported by the patient's 10 nieces and nephews, his only surviving relatives. The court appointed a guardian ad litem and directed that notice be served on various parties, including the District Attorney.

At the hearing the District Attorney opposed the application and called medical experts to show that there might be some improvement in the patient's condition. All the experts agreed, however, that there was no reasonable likelihood that Brother Fox would ever emerge from the vegetative coma or recover his cognitive powers.

There was also evidence, submitted by the petitioner, that before the operation rendered him incompetent the patient had made it known that under these circumstances he would want a respirator removed. Brother Fox had first expressed this view in 1976 when the Chaminade community discussed the moral implications of the celebrated Karen Ann Quinlan case, in which the parents of a 19-year-old New Jersey girl who was in a vegetative coma requested the hospital to remove the respirator (see *Matter of Quinlan, 137 NJ Super 227,* revd *70 NJ 10,* cert den sub nom. *Garger v New Jersey, 429 U.S. 922*). These were formal discussions prompted by Chaminade's mission to teach and promulgate Catholic moral principles. At that time it was noted that the Pope had stated that Catholic principles permitted the termination of extraordinary life support systems when there is no reasonable hope for the patient's recovery and that church officials in New Jersey had concluded that use of the respirator in the *Quinlan* case constituted an extraordinary measure under the circumstances. Brother Fox expressed agreement with those views and stated that he would not want any of this "extraordinary business" done for him under those circumstances. Several years later, and only a couple of months before his final hospitalization, Brother Fox again stated that he would not want his life prolonged by such measures if his condition were hopeless.

In a thoughtful and comprehensive opinion, Mr. Justice Robert C. Meade at the Supreme Court held that under the circumstances Brother Fox would have a common-law right to decline treatment and that his wishes, expressed prior to becoming incompetent, should be honored. The court noted that the evidence of his stated opposition to use of a respirator to maintain him in a vegetative state was "unchallenged at every turn and unimpeachable in its sincerity."

The Appellate Division modified in an exhaustive and wide-ranging opinion by Presiding Justice Milton A. Mollen. The court held that the patient's right to decline treatment was not only guaranteed by the common law but by the Constitution as well. It also found that this right should not be lost when a patient becomes incompetent and, if a patient has not made his wishes known while competent as Brother Fox had done, an appropriate person should be appointed to express the right on his behalf by use of "substituted judgment." The court went on to establish an elaborate set of procedures to be followed by doctors, hospitals, family members, parties and the courts before future applications of this nature may be entertained or granted.

THE STORAR CASE

John Storar was profoundly retarded with a mental age of about 18 months. At the time of this proceeding he was 52 years old and a resident of the Newark Development Center, a State facility, which had been his home since the age of 5. His closest relative was his mother, a 77-year-old widow who resided near the facility. He was her only child and she visited him almost daily.

In 1979 physicians at the center noticed blood in his urine and asked his mother for permission to conduct diagnostic tests. She initially refused but after discussions with the center's staff gave her consent. The tests, completed in July, 1979, revealed that he had cancer of the bladder. It was recommended that he receive radiation therapy at a hospital in Rochester. When the hospital refused to administer the treatment without the consent of a legal guardian, Mrs. Storar applied to the court and was appointed guardian of her son's person and property in August, 1979. With her consent he received radiation therapy for six weeks, after which the disease was found to be in remission.

However in March, 1980 blood was again observed in his urine. The lesions in his bladder were cauterized in an unsuccessful effort to stop the bleeding. At that point his physician diagnosed the cancer as terminal, concluding that after using all medical and surgical means then available, the patient would nevertheless die from the disease.

In May the physicians at the center asked his mother for permission to administer blood transfusions. She initially refused but the following day withdrew her objection. For several weeks John Storar received blood transfusions when needed. However, on June 19 his mother requested that the transfusions be discontinued.

The director of the center then brought this proceeding, pursuant to section 33.03 of the Mental Hygiene Law, seeking authorization to continue the transfusions, claiming that without them "death would occur within weeks." Mrs. Storar cross-petitioned for an order prohibiting the transfusions, and named the District Attorney as a party. The court appointed a guardian ad litem and signed an order temporarily permitting the transfusions to continue, pending the determination of the proceeding.

At the hearing in September the court heard testimony from various witnesses including Mrs. Storar, several employees at the center, and seven medical experts. All the experts concurred that John Storar had irreversible cancer of the bladder, which by then had spread to his lungs and perhaps other organs, with a very limited life span, generally estimated to be between 3 and 6 months. They also agreed that he had an infant's mentality and was unable to comprehend his predicament or to make a reasoned choice of treatment. In addition, there was no dispute over the fact that he was continuously losing blood.

The medical records show that at the time of the hearing, he required two units of blood every 8 to 15 days. The staff physicians explained that the transfusions were necessary to replace the blood lost. Without them there would be insufficient oxygen in the patient's blood stream. To compensate for this loss, his heart would have to work harder and he would breathe more rapidly, which created a strain and was very tiresome. He became lethargic and they feared he would eventually bleed to death. They observed that after the transfusions he had more energy. He was able to resume most of his usual activities—feeding himself, showering, taking walks and running—including some mischievous ones, such as stealing cigarette butts and attempting to eat them.

It was conceded that John Storar found the transfusions disagreeable. He was also distressed by the blood and blood clots in his urine which apparently increased immediately after a transfusion. He could not comprehend the purpose of the transfusions and on one or two occasions had displayed some initial resistance. To eliminate his apprehension he was given a sedative approximately one hour before a transfusion. He also received regular doses of narcotics to alleviate the pain associated with the disease.

On the other hand several experts testified that there was support in the medical community for the view that, at this stage, transfusions may only prolong suffering and that treatment could properly be limited to administering pain killers. Mrs. Storar testified that she wanted the transfusions discontinued because she only wanted her son to be comfortable. She admitted that no one had ever explained to her what might happen to him if the transfusions were stopped. She also stated that she was not "sure" whether he might die sooner if the blood was not replaced and was unable to determine whether he wanted to live. However, in view of the fact that he obviously disliked the transfusions and tried to avoid them, she believed that he would want them discontinued.

The court held that the center's application for permission to continue the transfusions should be denied. It was noted that John Storar's fatal illness had not affected his limited mental ability. He remained alert and carried on many of his usual activities. However, the court emphasized that the transfusions could not cure the disease, involved some pain and that the patient submitted to them reluctantly. The court held that a person has a right to determine what will be done with his own body and, when he is incompetent, this right may be exercised by another on his behalf. In this case, the court found that John Storar's mother was the person in the best position to determine what he would want and that she "wants his suffering to stop and believes that he would want this also."

The Appellate Division affirmed in a brief memorandum.

I

In the Eichner case the Supreme Court properly granted the petition. At common law, as Cardozo noted, every person "of adult years and sound mind has a right to determine what should be done with his own body; and a surgeon who performs an operation without his patient's consent commits an assault, for which he is liable in damages * * *. This is true except in cases of emergency where the patient is unconscious and where it is necessary to operate before consent can be obtained" (*Schloendorff v Society of N.Y. Hosp., 211 NY 125, 129-130;* see, also, *Pearl v Lesnick, 20 AD2d 761,* affd *19 NY2d 590; Garzione v Vassar Bros. Hosp., 36 AD2d 390,* affd *30 NY2d 857;* 2 Harper and James, Law of Torts, 61 [1968 Supp]; Patient's Right to Refuse Treatment Allegedly Necessary to Sustain Life, Ann., *93 ALR 3d 67*). Even in emergencies, however, it is held that consent will not be implied if the patient has previously stated that he would not consent (Restatement, Torts 2d, § 62, Illustration 5; Powell, Consent to Operative Procedures, *21 Md L Rev 189, 199;* Bryn, Compulsory Life Saving Treatment for the Competent Adult, *44 Fordham L Rev 1, 15, n 64*). The basic right of a patient to control the course of his medical treatment has been recognized by the Legislature (see Public Health Law, §§ 2504, 2805-d; CPLR 4401-a).

Father Eichner urges that this right is also guaranteed by the Constitution, as an aspect of the right to privacy. Although several courts have so held (see, e.g., *Matter of Quinlan, 70 NJ 10,* supra; *Superintendent of Belchertown State School v Saikewicz, 373 Mass 728*), this is a disputed question (see, e.g., Bryn, op. cit., pp 5–9), which the Supreme Court has repeatedly declined to consider (see Note, The "Living Will": The Right to Death With Dignity?, 26 Case Western Reserve L Rev 485, 501, n 76; see, also, *Garger v New Jersey, 429 U.S. 922,* supra). Neither do we reach that question in this case because the relief granted to the petitioner, Eichner, is adequately supported by common-law principles.

The District Attorney urges that the patient's right to decline medical treatment is outweighed by important State interests when the treatment is necessary to preserve the patient's life. We recognize that under certain circumstances the common-law right may have to yield to superior State interests, as it would even if it were constitutionally based (*Roe v Wade, 410 U.S. 113, 154–155; Doe v Bolton, 410 U.S. 179*). The State has a legitimate interest in protecting the lives of its citizens. It may require that they submit to medical procedures in order to eliminate a health threat to the community (see, e.g., *Jacobson v Massachusetts, 197 U.S. 11*). It may, by statute, prohibit them from engaging in specified activities, including medical procedures which are inherently hazardous to their lives (*Roe v Wade, supra, pp 150, 154*). In this State, however, there is no statute which prohibits a patient from declining necessary medical treatment or a doctor from honoring the patient's decision. To the extent that existing statutory and decisional law manifests the State's interest on this subject, they consistently support the right of the competent adult to make his own decision by imposing civil liability on those who perform medical treatment without consent, although the treatment may be beneficial or even necessary to preserve the patient's life (see, e.g., *Schloendorff v Society of N.Y. Hosp., 211 NY 125*, supra; *Matter of Erickson v Dilgard, 44 Misc 2d 27; Matter of Melideo, 88 Misc 2d 974*; Public Health Law, §§ 2504, 2805-d; CPLR 4401-a). The current law identifies the patient's right to determine the course of his own medical treatment as paramount to what might otherwise be the doctor's obligation to provide needed medical care. A State which imposes civil liability on a doctor if he violates the patient's right cannot also hold him criminally responsible if he respects that right. Thus a doctor cannot be held to have violated his legal or professional responsibilities when he honors the right of a competent adult patient to decline medical treatment.

The District Attorney also urges that whatever right the patient may have is entirely personal and may not be exercised by any third party once the patient becomes incompetent. He notes that although a court may appoint a guardian to manage an incompetent's financial affairs and to supervise his person, some rights have been held to be too personal to be exercised by an incompetent's representative (see, e.g., *Mainzer v Avril, 108 Misc 230, 232; Matter of Barletta, 2 Misc 2 135, 139; Matter of Rasmussen, 147 Misc 564, 566*; cf. *Matter of Buttonow, 23 NY2d 385, 394; Matter of Hills, 264 NY 349, 354*; 44 CJS, Insane Persons, § 49; 27 NY Jur, Incompetent Persons, § 81). He argues that a right to decline lifesaving treatment conflicts with the patient's fundamental and constitutionally guaranteed right to life (US Const, 14th Amdt) and to permit a third party to choose between the two means, in effect, that the right to life is lost once the patient becomes incompetent. Finally he urges that if a patient's right to decline medical treatment survives his incompetency, it must yield to the State's overriding interest in prohibiting one person from causing the death of another, as is evidenced by the homicide laws.

The District Attorney's arguments underscore the very sensitive nature of the question as to whether, in case of incompetency, a decision to discontinue life sustaining medical treatment may be made by some one other than the patient (see, also, Kamisar, Some Non-Religious Views Against Proposed "Mercy-Killing" Legislation, *42 Minn L Rev 969*; Collester, Death, Dying and the Law: A Prosecutorial View of the Quinlan Case, *30 Rutgers L Rev 304*). However, that issue is not presented in this case because here Brother Fox made the decision for himself before he became incompetent. The Supreme Court and the Appellate Division found that the evidence on this point, as well as proof of the patient's subsequent incompetency and chances of recovery was "clear and convincing." We agree that this is the appropriate burden of proof and that the evidence in the record satisfies this standard.

Although this is a civil case in which a preponderance of the evidence is generally deemed sufficient, the District Attorney urges that the highest burden of proof beyond a reasonable doubt should be required when granting the relief may result in the patient's death. But that burden, traditionally reserved for criminal cases where involuntary loss of liberty and possible stigmatization are at issue (*Addington v Texas, 441 U.S. 418, 428*), is inappropriate in cases where the purpose of granting the relief is to give effect to an individual's right by carrying out his stated intentions. However, we agree with the courts below that the highest standard applicable to civil cases should be required. There is more involved here than a typical dispute between private litigants over a sum of money. Where particularly important personal interests are at stake, clear and convincing evidence should be required (*Addington v Texas, supra, p 424*). It is constitutionally required in cases of involuntary civil commitments (*Addington v Texas, supra*) and we have recognized the need for the higher standard in exceptional civil matters (see, e.g., *Ross v Food Specialties, 6 NY2d 336; Amend v Hurley, 293 NY 587; Porter v Commercial Cas. Ins. Co., 292 NY 176*). Clear and convincing proof should also be required in cases where it is claimed that a person, now incompetent, left instructions to terminate life sustaining procedures when there is no hope of recovery. This standard serves to "impress the factfinder with the importance of the decision" (*Addington v Texas, 441 U.S. 418, 427, supra*) and it " 'forbids relief whenever the evidence is loose, equivocal or contradictory' " (*Backer Mgt. Corp. v Acme Quilting Co., 46 NY2d 211, 220*).

In this case the proof was compelling. There was no suggestion that the witnesses who testified for the petitioner had any motive other than to see that Brother Fox'[s] stated wishes were respected. The finding that he carefully reflected on the subject, expressed his views and concluded not to have his life prolonged by medical means if there were no hope of recovery is supported by his religious beliefs and is not inconsistent with his life of unselfish religious devotion. These were obviously solemn pronouncements and not casual remarks made at some social gathering, nor can it be said that he was too young to realize or feel the consequences of his statements (cf. *Matter of Quinlan, 70 NJ 10, supra*). That this was a persistent commitment is evidenced by the fact that he

reiterated the decision but two months before his final hospitalization. There was, of course, no need to speculate as to whether he would want this particular medical procedure to be discontinued under these circumstances. What occurred to him was identical to what happened in the Karen Ann Quinlan case, which had originally prompted his decision. In sum, the evidence clearly and convincingly shows that Brother Fox did not want to be maintained in a vegetative coma by use of a respirator.

II

In the *Storar* case, of course, we do not have any proof of that nature. John Storar was never competent at any time in his life. He was always totally incapable of understanding or making a reasoned decision about medical treatment. Thus it is unrealistic to attempt to determine whether he would want to continue potentially life prolonging treatment if he were competent. As one of the experts testified at the hearing, that would be similar to asking whether "if it snowed all summer would it then be winter?" Mentally John Storar was an infant and that is the only realistic way to assess his rights in this litigation (see Bryn, op. cit., p 24, n 107). Thus this case bears only superficial similarities to *Eichner* and the determination must proceed from different principles.

A parent or guardian has a right to consent to medical treatment on behalf of an infant (Public Health Law, § 2504, subd 2). The parent, however, may not deprive a child of lifesaving treatment, however well intentioned (*Matter of Sampson, 29 NY2d 900; Matter of Vasko, 238 App Div 128; Matter of Santos v Goldstein , 16 AD2d 755, mot for lv to app dsmd 12 NY2d 642; cf. Matter of Hofbauer, 47 NY2d 648*). Even when the parents' decision to decline necessary treatment is based on constitutional grounds, such as religious beliefs, it must yield to the State's interests, as parens patriae, in protecting the health and welfare of the child (*Matter of Sampson, supra; Jehovah's Witnesses v King County Hosp. Unit, 390 U.S. 598, affg 278 F Supp 488; People ex rel. Wallace v Labrenz, 411 Ill 618, cert den 344 U.S. 824*; Power of Public Authorities to Order Medical Care for A Child Over Objection of Parent or Guardian, Ann., *30 ALR 2d 1138; cf. Prince v Massachusetts, 321 U.S. 158*). Of course it is not for the courts to determine the most "effective" treatment when the parents have chosen among reasonable alternatives (*Matter of Hofbauer, 47 NY2d 648,* supra). But the courts may not permit a parent to deny a child all treatment for a condition which threatens his life (compare *Custody of A Minor, 375 Mass 733,* with *Matter of Hofbauer, supra, p 656*). The case of a child who may bleed to death because of the parents' refusal to authorize a blood transfusion presents the classic example (*Jehovah's Witnesses v King County Hosp., supra; Matter of Sampson, supra*).

In the Storar case there is the additional complication of two threats to his life. There was cancer of the bladder which was incurable and would in all probability claim his life. There was also the related loss of blood which posed the risk of an earlier death, but which, at least at the time of the hearing, could be replaced by transfusions. Thus, as one of the experts noted, the transfusions were analogous to food—they would not cure the cancer, but they could eliminate the risk of death from another treatable cause. Of course, John Storar did not like them, as might be expected of one with an infant's mentality. But the evidence convincingly shows that the transfusions did not involve excessive pain and that without them his mental and physical abilities would not be maintained at the usual level. With the transfusions on the other hand, he was essentially the same as he was before except of course he had a fatal illness which would ultimately claim his life. Thus, on the record, we have concluded that the application for permission to continue the transfusions should have been granted. Although we understand and respect his mother's despair, as we respect the beliefs of those who oppose transfusions on religious grounds, a court should not in the circumstances of this case allow an incompetent patient to bleed to death because someone, even someone as close as a parent or sibling, feels that this is best for one with an incurable disease.

In conclusion we note that it has been suggested by the District Attorney in the Eichner case that these applications do not present a justiciable controversy; that they call for innovations in the law, both substantive and procedural, which should be left to the Legislature, subject only to review by the courts for compliance with constitutional requirements (see, also, *Matter of President & Directors of Georgetown Coll, 3 F2d 1000, 1010, 1015* [Burger, J., dissenting]; Sharpe & Hargest, Lifesaving Treatment for Unwilling Patients, *36 Fordham L Rev 695;* Note, *77 Harv L Rev 1539*). We, of course, cannot alter statutory responsibility but we can declare the rights and obligations of the parties under existing law. In fact the District Attorney does not contend that the courts can never rule upon the legality of such activities but suggests that the courts should wait for the parties to act before considering whether there is any civil or criminal liability. However, responsible parties who wish to comply with the law, in cases where the legal consequence of the contemplated action is uncertain, need not act at their peril (*New York Public Interest Research Group v Carey, 42 NY2d 527, 530*). Nor is it inappropriate for those charged with the care of incompetent persons to apply to the courts for a ruling on the propriety of conduct which might seriously affect their charges.

We emphasize, however, that any such procedure is optional. Neither the common law nor existing statutes require persons generally to seek prior court assessment of conduct which may subject them to civil and criminal liability. If it is desirable to enlarge the role of the courts in cases involving discontinuance of life sustaining treatment for incompetents by establishing, as the Appellate Division suggested in the Eichner case, a mandatory procedure of successive approvals by physicians, hospital personnel, relatives and the courts, the change should come from the Legislature.

Accordingly, the order of the Appellate Division should be reversed, without costs, in the Storar case and modified, without costs, in the Eichner case by deleting everything but the authorization to the petitioner to discontinue use of the respirator.

In re Westchester County Medical Center
72 N.Y.2d 517, 534 N.Y.S.2d 886 (1988)

Mary O'Connor is an elderly hospital patient who, as a result of several strokes, is mentally incompetent and unable to obtain food or drink without medical assistance. In this dispute between her daughters and the hospital the question is whether the hospital should be permitted to insert a nasogastric tube to provide her with sustenance or whether, instead, such medical intervention should be precluded and she should be allowed to die because, prior to becoming incompetent, she made several statements to the effect that she did not want to be a burden to anyone and would not want to live or be kept alive by artificial means if she were unable to care for herself.

The hospital has applied for court authorization to insert the nasogastric tube. The patient's daughters object claiming that it is contrary to her "expressed wishes," although they conceded at the hearing that they do not know whether their mother would want to decline this procedure under these circumstances, particularly if it would produce a painful death. The trial court denied the hospital's application, concluding that it was contrary to the patient's wishes. The Appellate Division affirmed, with two Justices dissenting. The hospital has appealed by leave of the Appellate Division which also granted a stay permitting the patient to be fed intravenously while this appeal is pending.

We have concluded that the order of the Appellate Division should be reversed and the hospital's petition granted. On this record there is not clear and convincing proof that the patient had made a firm and settled commitment, while competent, to decline this type of medical assistance under circumstances such as these.

The patient is a 77-year-old widow with two children, Helen and Joan, both of whom are practical nurses. After her husband's death in 1967 she lived alone in her apartment in the New York City area where she was employed in hospital administration. In 1983 she retired from her job after 20 years service.

Over the years a number of her close relatives died of cancer. Her husband died of brain cancer. The last two of her nine brothers died of cancer, one in 1975 and the other in 1977. During their final years she regularly visited them in the hospital and cared for them when they were home. In November 1984, after being informed that her stepmother had died of cancer in Florida, Mrs. O'Connor had an attack of congestive heart failure and was hospitalized. She was released from the hospital in December 1984.

In July of the following year she suffered the first of a series of strokes causing brain damage and related disabilities which rendered her unable to care for herself. She became passive, could only carry on limited conversations, and could not walk, eat, dress or care for her bodily needs without assistance from others. Upon her release from the hospital in August 1985, Mrs. O'Connor resided with her daughter Helen who, together with Joan and another woman, provided her with full-time care.

In December 1987, Mrs. O'Connor had a second major stroke causing additional physical and mental disabilities. She became unresponsive and unable to stand or feed herself. She had to be spoon-fed by others. Her gag reflex was also impaired, as a result of which she experienced difficulty swallowing and thus could eat only pureed foods. In this condition her daughters found that they could no longer care for her at home and, when she left the hospital in February 1988, she was transferred to the Ruth Taylor Institute (the Institute), a long-term geriatric care facility associated with the Westchester County Medical Center (the hospital). In conjunction with this transfer, her daughters submitted a document signed by both of them, to be included in her medical file, stating that their mother had expressed the wish in many conversations that "no artificial life support be started or maintained in order to continue to sustain her life," and that they wanted this request to be honored.

During the initial part of her stay at the Institute the staff found Mrs. O'Connor was cooperative, capable of sitting in a chair and interacting with her surroundings. However, in June her condition deteriorated. She became "stup[o]rous, virtually not responsive" and developed a fever. On June 20, 1988, she was transferred from the Institute to the hospital.

At the hospital it was determined that she was suffering from dehydration, sepsis and probably pneumonia. The hospital staff also found that she had lost her gag reflex, making it impossible for her to swallow food or liquids without medical assistance. She showed marked improvement after receiving fluids, limited nourishment and antibiotics intravenously. Within a few days she became alert, able to follow simple commands and respond verbally to simple questions. However her inability to swallow persisted and her physician, Dr. Sivak, determined that a nasogastric tube should be used to provide more substantial nourishment. When Mrs. O'Connor's daughters objected to this procedure, the matter was brought before the hospital's ethics committee which found that it would be inappropriate to withhold this treatment under the circumstances.

On July 15, the hospital commenced this proceeding by order to show cause seeking court authorization to use the nasogastric tube, claiming that without this relief Mrs. O'Connor would die of thirst and starvation within a few weeks. In an opposing affidavit her daughters stated that this was against their mother's expressed wishes because before becoming incompetent, she had repeatedly stated that she did not want her life prolonged by artificial means if she was unable to care for herself. They noted the number of relatives she had comforted during prolonged final illnesses and urged that the effect of her statements should be evaluated against that background.

The hearing on the petition began on July 19 and concluded on July 21. Two medical experts testified regarding Mrs. O'Connor's condition: Dr. Sivak for the hospital and Dr. Wasserman for the respondents. With respect to the patient's statements concerning life-sustaining measures the respondents themselves both testified and called one additional witness, James Lampasso.

The treating physician, Dr. Sivak, testified that Mrs. O'Connor was suffering from multi-infarct dementia as a result of the strokes. This condition substantially impaired her cognitive ability but she was not in a coma or vegetative state. She was conscious, and capable of responding to simple questions or requests sometimes by squeezing the questioner's hand and sometimes verbally. She was also able to respond to noxious stimuli, such as a needle prick, and in fact was sensitive to "even minimal discomfort," although she was not experiencing pain in her present condition. When asked how she felt she usually responded "fine," "all right" or "ok." The treating physician also testified that her mental awareness had improved at the hospital and that she might become more alert in the future. In fact during the latest examination conducted that morning, in response to the doctor's request she had attempted to sit up and had been able to roll over on her side so that he could examine her lungs. However, Dr. Sivak stated that she is unable to comprehend complex questions, such as those dealing with her medical treatment, and doubted that she would ever regain significant mental capacity because the brain damage was substantial and irreparable.

The doctor stated that Mrs. O'Connor was presently receiving nourishment exclusively through intravenous feeding. However, this procedure was inadequate for long-term use because it does not provide sufficient nutrients and the veins tend to deteriorate. He testified that intravenous feeding is used as a temporary measure which generally must be discontinued within several weeks. He noted that these difficulties could be overcome with a gastric tube connected to the patient's digestive tract through her nose or abdomen. This procedure would provide adequate nutrients and could cause only transient discomfort at the time of insertion. Since the patient's condition is otherwise fairly stable, this procedure would preserve her life for several months, perhaps several years. If the procedure were not employed and the intravenous methods could no longer be used or were otherwise discontinued, she would die of thirst and starvation within 7 to 10 days. The doctor stated that death from starvation and especially thirst, was a painful way to die and that Mrs. O'Connor would, therefore, experience extreme, intense discomfort since she is conscious, alert, capable of feeling pain, and sensitive to even mild discomfort.

The respondents' expert Dr. Wasserman, a neurologist, agreed essentially with Dr. Sivak's evaluation and prognosis. In his opinion, however, Mrs. O'Connor would not experience pain if permitted to die of thirst and starvation. Because of the extensive brain damage she had suffered, the doctor did not "think she would react as you or I would under the circumstances" but would simply become more lethargic, unresponsive and would ultimately die. If she experienced pain he believed she could be given pain killers to alleviate it. He conceded, however, that he could not be "medically certain" that she would not suffer because he had never had a patient, or heard of one, dying after being deprived of food and water. Thus he candidly admitted: "I guess we don't know."

Interestingly, Dr. Wasserman also admitted that during his examination, which occurred just before the close of the hearing, the patient exhibited further improvement in her condition. He found that she was generally able to respond to simple commands, such as a request to move her arm or foot. He also noted that she was able to state her name, seemed to be aware of where she was, and responded to questions about 50 or 60% of the time, although her speech was slow and halting and her responses were not always appropriate. Most significantly, she was able to converse in short sentences of two or three words which, he noted, she had not been able to do since her admission to the hospital. He also observed that she had a gag reflex. Although he did not know whether Mrs. O'Connor would be able to use it to eat, he recognized the possibility that she might.

Neither of the doctors had known Mrs. O'Connor before she became incompetent and thus knew nothing of her attitudes toward the use of life-sustaining measures. The respondents' first witness on this point was James Lampasso, a former co-worker and longtime friend of Mrs. O'Connor. He was also acquainted with other members of the family and presently worked with the patient's daughter Helen at a local hospital. He testified that his first discussion with Mrs. O'Connor concerning artificial means of prolonging life occurred about 1969. At that time his father, who was dying of cancer, informed him that he would not want to continue life by any artificial method if he had lost his dignity because he could no longer control his normal bodily functions. The witness said that when he told Mrs. O'Connor of this she agreed wholeheartedly and said: "I would never want to be a burden on anyone and I would never want to lose my dignity before I passed away." He noted that she was a "very religious woman" who "felt that nature should take its course and not use further artificial means." They had similar conversations on two or three occasions between 1969 and 1973. During these discussions Mrs. O'Connor variously stated that it is "monstrous" to keep someone alive by using "machinery, things like that" when they are "not going to get better"; that she would never want to be in the same situation as her husband and Mr. Lampasso's father and that people who are "suffering very badly" should be allowed to die.

Mrs. O'Connor's daughter Helen testified that her mother informed her on several occasions that if she became ill and was unable to care for herself she would not want her life to be sustained artificially. The first discussion occurred after her husband was hospitalized with cancer in 1967. At that time Mrs. O'Connor said that she never wanted to be in a similar situation and that she would not want to go on living if she could not "take care of herself and make her own decisions." The last discussion occurred after Mrs. O'Connor's stepmother died of cancer and Mrs. O'Connor was hospitalized for a heart attack: "My mother said that she was very glad to be home, very glad to be out of the hospital and [hoped] she would never have to be back in one again and would never want any sort of intervention [or] any sort of life support systems to maintain or prolong her life." Mrs. O'Connor's other daughter, Joan, essentially adopted her sister's testimony. She described her mother's statements on this subject as less solemn pronouncements: "it was brought up when we were together, at times when in conversations you start something, you know, maybe the news was on and maybe that was the topic that was brought up and that's how it came about."

However, all three of these witnesses also agreed that Mrs. O'Connor had never discussed providing food or water with medical assistance, nor had she ever said that she would adhere to her view and decline medical treatment "by artificial means" if that would produce a painful death. When Helen was asked what choice her mother would make under those circumstances she admitted that she did not know. Her sister Joan agreed, noting that this had never been discussed, "unfortunately, no."

At the conclusion of the hearing the daughters submitted a counterclaim seeking an order directing the hospital to also discontinue the intravenous feeding.

As noted the trial court denied the hospital's petition and granted the counterclaim concluding that Mrs. O'Connor's "past expressions plainly covered any form of life-prolonging treatment." The Appellate Division affirmed noting that requiring greater specificity would impose an undue burden on those seeking to avoid life-prolonging treatment.

II

It has long been the common-law rule in this State that a person has the right to decline medical treatment, even lifesaving treatment, absent an overriding State interest (*Schloendorff v Society of N.Y Hosp., 211 NY 125, 129-130*). In 1981, we held, in two companion cases, that a hospital or medical facility must respect this right even when a patient becomes incompetent, if while competent, the patient stated that he or she did not want certain procedures to be employed under specified circumstances (*Matter of Storar and Matter of Eichner v Dillon, 52 NY2d 363*). In *Storar*, involving a retarded adult suffering from terminal

cancer, who needed blood transfusions to keep him from bleeding to death, we declined to direct termination of the treatment because it was impossible to determine what his wish would have been were he competent and it would be improper for a court to substitute its judgment for the unascertainable wish of the patient. Commenting on this latter principle in a subsequent case we noted that the right to decline treatment is personal and, under existing law in this State, could not be exercised by a third party when the patient is unable to do so (*People v Eulo, 63 NY2d 341*).

In contrast to the patient in *Storar*, the patient in *Eichner* had been competent and capable of expressing his will before he was silenced by illness. In those circumstances, we concluded that it would be appropriate for the court to intervene and direct the termination of artificial life supports, in accordance with the patient's wishes, because it was established by "clear and convincing evidence" that the patient would have so directed if he were competent and able to communicate (*52 NY2d, at 379, supra; see also, Matter of Delio v Westchester County Med. Center, 129 AD2d 1; Addington v Texas, 441 U.S. 418, 424*). We selected the "clear and convincing evidence" standard in *Eichner* because it "'[impresses] the factfinder with the importance of the decision' * * * and it 'forbids relief whenever the evidence is loose, equivocal or contradictory' " (*Matter of Storar, supra, at 379*). Nothing less than unequivocal proof will suffice when the decision to terminate life supports is at issue.

In *Eichner*, we had no difficulty finding "clear and convincing" evidence of the patient's wishes. Brother Fox, the patient in *Eichner*, was a member of a religious order who had conscientiously discussed his moral and personal views concerning the use of a respirator on persons in a vegetative state. The conclusion that "he carefully reflected on the subject * * * [was] supported by his religious beliefs and [was] not inconsistent with his life of unselfish religious devotion." (*Id., at 379-380.*) Further, his expressions were "solemn pronouncements and not casual remarks made at some social gathering, nor [could] it be said that he was too young to realize or feel the consequences of his statements" (*id., at 380*). Indeed, because the facts in Brother Fox's case were so clear, we had no need to elaborate upon the kind of showing necessary to satisfy the "clear and convincing" standard.

The facts in this case present a much closer question and require us to explore in more detail the application of that standard in this context. It would, of course, be unrealistic for us to attempt to establish a rigid set of guidelines to be used in all cases requiring an evaluation of a now-incompetent patient's previously expressed wishes. The number and variety of situations in which the problem of terminating artificial life supports arises preclude any attempt to anticipate all of the possible permutations. However, this case, as well as our prior decisions, suggest some basic principles which may be used in determining whether the proof "clearly and convincingly" evinces an intention by the patient to reject life prolonged artificially by medical means.

III

At the outset, since the inquiry in New York is limited to ascertaining and then effectuating the patient's expressed wishes, our focus must always be on what the patient would say if asked today whether the treatment in issue should be terminated. However, we can never be completely certain of the answer to our question, since the inquiry assumes that the patient is no longer able to express his or her wishes. Most often, therefore, the inquiry turns on interpretation of statements on the subject made by the patient in the past. This exercise presents inherent problems.

For example, there always exists the possibility that, despite his or her clear expressions in the past, the patient has since changed his or her mind. And, as Judge Simons in his dissenting opinion correctly points out, human beings are incapable of perfect foresight. Thus, almost inevitably, the medical circumstances in the mind of the patient at the time the statements were made will not coincide perfectly with those which give rise to the need for the inquiry. In addition, there

exists the danger that the statements were made without the reflection and resolve that would be brought to bear on the issue if the patient were presently capable of making the decision.

But the existence of these problems does not lead inevitably to the conclusion that we should abandon the inquiry entirely and adopt as guideposts the objective factors used in the so-called "substituted judgment" approach (see, *Brophy v New England Sinai Hosp., 398 Mass 417, 429-440, 497 NE2d 626*). That approach remains unacceptable because it is inconsistent with our fundamental commitment to the notion that no person or court should substitute its judgment as to what would be an acceptable quality of life for another (*People v Eulo, supra, at 357*). Consequently, we adhere to the view that, despite its pitfalls and inevitable uncertainties, the inquiry must always be narrowed to the patient's expressed intent, with every effort made to minimize the opportunity for error.

Every person has a right to life, and no one should be denied essential medical care unless the evidence clearly and convincingly shows that the patient intended to decline the treatment under some particular circumstances (*Matter of Storar, supra, at 379*). This is a demanding standard, the most rigorous burden of proof in civil cases (id.). It is appropriate here because if an error occurs it should be made on the side of life.

Viewed in that light, the "clear and convincing" evidence standard requires proof sufficient to persuade the trier of fact that the patient held a firm and settled commitment to the termination of life supports under the circumstances like those presented. As a threshold matter, the trier of fact must be convinced, as far as is humanly possible, that the strength of the individual's beliefs and the durability of the individual's commitment to those beliefs (see, *Matter of Eichner, supra, at 380*) makes a recent change of heart unlikely. The persistence of the individual's statements, the seriousness with which those statements were made and the inferences, if any, that may be drawn from the surrounding circumstances are among the factors which should be considered.

The ideal situation is one in which the patient's wishes were expressed in some form of a writing, perhaps a "living will," while he or she was still competent. The existence of a writing suggests the author's seriousness of purpose and ensures that the court is not being asked to make a life-or-death decision based upon casual remarks. Further, a person who has troubled to set forth his or her wishes in a writing is more likely than one who has not to make sure that any subsequent changes of heart are adequately expressed, either in a new writing or through clear statements to relatives and friends. In contrast, a person whose expressions of intention were limited to oral statements may not as fully appreciate the need to "rescind" those statements after a change of heart.

Of course, a requirement of a written expression in every case would be unrealistic. Further, it would unfairly penalize those who lack the skills to place their feelings in writing. For that reason, we must always remain open to applications such as this, which are based upon the repeated oral expressions of the patient. In this case, however, the application must ultimately fail, because it does not meet the foregoing criteria.

Although Mrs. O'Connor's statements about her desire to decline life-saving treatments were repeated over a number of years, there is nothing, other than speculation, to persuade the fact finder that her expressions were more than immediate reactions to the unsettling experience of seeing or hearing of another's unnecessarily prolonged death. Her comments—that she would never want to lose her dignity before she passed away, that nature should be permitted to take its course, that it is "monstrous" to use life-support machinery—are, in fact, no different than those that many of us might make after witnessing an agonizing death. Similarly, her statements to the effect that she would not want to be a burden to anyone are the type of statements that older people frequently, almost invariably, make. If such statements were routinely held to be clear and convincing proof of a general intent to decline all medical treatment once incompetency sets in, few nursing home patients would ever receive life-sustaining medical treatment in the future. The aged and infirm would be placed at grave risk if the law uniformly but unrealistically treated the expression of such sentiments as a calm and deliberate resolve to decline all life-sustaining medical assistance once the speaker is silenced by mental disability. That Mrs. O'Connor made similar statements over a long period of time, does not, by itself, transform them from the type of comments that are often made casually into the type of statements that demonstrate a seriousness of purpose necessary to satisfy the "clear and convincing evidence" standard.

We do not mean to suggest that, to be effective, a patient's expressed desire to decline treatment must specify a precise condition and a particular treatment. We recognize that human beings are not capable of foreseeing either their own medical condition or advances in medical technology. Nevertheless, it is relevant to the fundamental question—the patient's desires—to consider whether the infirmities she was concerned with and the procedures she eschewed are qualitatively different than those now presented. Not that the exact nature of her condition would be dispositive in this analysis—it is but another element to be considered in the context of determining whether her pronouncement made on some previous occasion bears relevance to her present condition.

Thus, it is appropriate for us to consider the circumstances in which Mrs. O'Connor made the statements and to compare them with those which presently prevail.

Her statements with respect to declining artificial means of life support were generally prompted by her experience with persons suffering terminal illnesses, particularly cancer. However, Mrs. O'Connor does not have a terminal illness, except in the sense that she is aged and infirm. Neither is she in a coma nor vegetative state. She is awake and conscious; she can feel pain, responds to simple commands, can carry on limited conversations, and is not experiencing any pain. She is simply an elderly person who as a result of several strokes suffers certain disabilities, including an inability to feed herself or eat in a normal manner. She is in a stable condition and if properly nourished will remain in that condition unless some other medical problem arises. Because of her age and general physical condition, her life expectancy is not great. But that is true of many nursing home patients. The key thing that sets her apart—though there are likely thousands like her—is her inability to eat or obtain nourishment without medical assistance.

It is true, of course, that in her present condition she cannot care for herself or survive without medical assistance and that she has stated that she never wanted to be a burden and would not want to live, or be kept alive "artificially" if she could not care for herself. But no one contends, and it should not be assumed, that she contemplated declining medical assistance when her prognosis was uncertain. Here both medical experts agreed that she will never regain sufficient mental ability to care for herself, but it is not clear from the record that the loss of her gag reflex is permanent and that she will never be able to obtain food and drink without medical assistance.

The record also shows that throughout her life Mrs. O'Connor was an independent woman who found it distasteful to be dependent on others. Unfortunately, she has been unable to care for herself for several years. As a result of her first stroke in July 1985, she has required full-time care, and following her latest stroke in December of 1987, she had to be spoon-fed until her gag reflex completely failed in June of this year. No one contends that the assistance she received up to that point violated her wishes, although there is little question that she would not have survived without this constant attention from others, including some medical professionals. The only change in her condition is the loss of her gag reflex, and the consequent need for medical assistance in eating, which is said to be contrary to her desires.

In sum, on this record it cannot be said that Mrs. O'Connor elected to die under circumstances such as these. Even her daughters, who undoubtedly know her wishes better than anyone, are earnestly trying to carry them out, and whose motives we believe to be of the highest and most loving kind, candidly admit that they do not know what she would do, or what she would want done under these circumstances.

Accordingly the order of the Appellate Division should be reversed, the petition granted and counterclaim dismissed, without costs.

HEALTH CARE AND THE ELDERLY

INTRODUCTION

Concerns over one's physical and mental well-being are not limited to any special age group. All persons want to lead healthy and meaningful lives. However, it is a physiological fact that as the human body ages there is a continual process of slowing down: muscles weaken, bones become brittle, memory fails, eyesight and hearing diminish, and so forth. Although some physical decline is unavoidable as part of the human condition, total deterioration is not preordained. Consequently, as the body matures, getting appropriate care to maintain a healthy lifestyle becomes an ever-increasing concern.

With escalating costs for medical care, and a proliferation of health-related services being created, all Americans, not just the elderly, are faced with making two distinct decisions: which type of health care is best suited for the individual, and how health care decisions are to be made if the person becomes incapacitated. Once these decisions have been reached, the method of financing the desired health care becomes of paramount importance.

The legal assistant working in a law office that is involved with elder law will be concerned with assisting the elderly client to obtain the most appropriate health care possible. By analyzing various health insurance contracts, preparing applications for Medicare and Medicaid, filing claims and appeals, and assisting the attorney in any court representation, the paralegal will help acquire necessary health services for the client.

This chapter focuses on the health care concerns of the elderly, most specifically highlighting programs that exist to aid the elderly patient in obtaining medical care.

Types of Health Care Available

Unlike most developed countries of the world, the United States does not have a universal health care system to provide medical care to its citizens and lawful permanent residents. Hence, each individual must select from the various services available, making the decision based on cost and the nature of the medical aid required.

Most Americans still receive their primary health care from private physicians, who either charge the patient directly or are reimbursed for the care they provide through the patient's private health insurance program. Many employed Americans receive some form of health care coverage as part of an employee benefit package, and are only responsible for reduced premiums and co-payments for the portion of care that is not covered by the terms of the policy.

Example

An individual has been suffering with a skin rash for the past week and so makes an appointment with a doctor for a checkup. The doctor bills the patient, who then files a claim with her insurer who is liable for 80 percent of the doctor's bill. The 20 percent of the bill that is not covered, by the terms of the insurance policy, remains the personal responsibility of the patient as a co-payment.

A distinct advantage of private health insurance is that persons so covered are likely to receive preventative health care, because most of the cost is covered by the terms of the policy, and thus expense does not deter them from seeking medical aid. If an individual must pay for the entire cost of a doctor's visit personally, it is statistically more likely that the person will not use preventative care and will seek medical care only in an emergency.

health maintenance organization (HMO)
A managed health care provider.

Over the past two decades, there has been a tremendous growth in **health maintenance organizations (HMOs)** as a method of minimizing health care costs. Persons who belong to an HMO are typically required to use only physicians and related health care professionals who are associated with the HMO to which the insured subscribes. Basically, all health care costs are covered by the individual's premium payments; however, some problems have been associated with HMO health care decisions being made on a cost-effectiveness basis rather than on a health-related basis.

Example

A person maintains a health insurance policy that provides coverage at a specified HMO. The insured has been suffering from extreme shortness of breath and goes to the HMO for a checkup. The doctor examines the insured and believes that she is all right. Although certain tests may be advisable, the doctor does not recommend them, so that the HMO's cost will stay low. The patient does not have to pay for the visit, because it is covered under the terms of the insurance policy; consequently, the fewer tests and the shorter the visit, the more money the HMO makes.

For persons who are unable to afford the premiums for a private insurance policy (an alarming number of Americans fall into this category), primary health care is typically provided by a low-cost medical clinic or a hospital emergency room. Because of the high cost of medical care, persons who fall into this category usually seek medical assistance only in extreme situations.

Example

An individual who does not receive health care benefits at his job cannot afford to maintain health care coverage because of the cost of the premiums. He has been experiencing shortness of breath but cannot afford to visit a physician. Three weeks after he first notices the condition, he experiences severe chest pains and goes to a hospital emergency room, where he is diagnosed as having a mild heart attack. The cost of the emergency room visit and attendant care is the individual's personal responsibility.

Individuals who are entitled to Social Security benefits are also entitled to be enrolled in the federal Medicare program. This program, a form of nationally funded health insurance, provides basic health care coverage for these qualifying individuals. Every elderly citizen and lawful permanent resident is covered by Medicare.

Example

A 70-year-old man on Social Security is experiencing shortness of breath. He visits his physician for a diagnosis. The cost of the visit is borne by his Medicare coverage.

For low-income individuals and the disabled, regardless of age, a form of federal medical coverage is available under the Medicaid program. Medicaid benefits are not based on Social Security benefits, but are available to all persons regardless of age whose income and resources fall below a specified level determined by the federal government and each individual state.

Example

A low-income single mother who is unable to work has applied for and received Medicaid assistance. When her infant runs a fever, she takes him to a doctor, whose fees are paid by the government under the provisions of Medicaid.

Persons who require constant medical care may have to decide to reside in a nursing home facility. These facilities are licensed by the state governments and their costs may be covered by one of the federal programs. Nursing homes are health care living facilities.

Example

An elderly woman is suffering from Alzheimer's disease and can no longer care for herself. Her family places her in a nursing home where she receives 24-hour medical care.

Finally, people who are suffering from a terminal illness and who have a short life expectancy may elect to spend their last days in a **hospice**, a medical facility designed to care exclusively for the terminally ill. The cost of such care may be covered by private insurance or government programs.

Example

An elderly man has been diagnosed with cancer and has a three-month life expectancy. He has no immediate family and so is placed in a hospice to receive the care he will need until his death.

The Decision-Making Process

As can be seen, many health care alternatives are available. Cost factors aside, the primary concern is the person's ability to make a decision with respect to the type and nature of the treatment and care he or she will receive. Although this decision-making process is a concern for all individuals, when one is dealing with the elderly this is a special concern because of the possibility that the person may lack the capacity to give informed consent to treatment and care. Both legal and health

hospice Facility designed to provide care to the terminally ill.

care professionals must be alert to anything that might interfere with a person's legal ability to make an informed decision regarding his or her health care.

Example

An elderly client is discussing his estate plan with his attorney and the attorney's paralegal and expresses concern over his quixotic and failing memory. The client also indicates that he will be entering the hospital in a few days for back surgery. The attorney and the paralegal are concerned that the client may not be able to make a competent decision with respect to his health care because of his failing memory.

To assist individuals in reaching appropriate health care decisions, various laws have been enacted to protect patients' rights with respect to obtaining effective medical care. These alternatives are discussed in the following section.

HEALTH CARE DECISION MAKING

A person's ability to make health care decisions is based both on the amount of information he or she has at his or her disposal and his or her legal competence to make an informed decision.

Informed Consent

It has long been established under the common law that all patients have the right to determine their own medical treatment, including the right to refuse to submit to a particular treatment, provided that the individual is legally competent to make such choices. To be able to make such decisions, the person must be able to comprehend the nature and severity of his or her condition and the consequences of accepting or refusing a particular treatment. Furthermore, a person's competence to make health care decisions is separate and distinct from the person's legal ability to make decisions in other areas of his or her life, such as managing his or her finances.

Example

An elderly woman has been diagnosed with breast cancer. Her doctor advises a radical mastectomy, but the woman prefers to try alternative, less invasive, procedures. The woman is legally competent and even though her wishes are totally contrary to her physician's advice, she is entitled to determine her own course of treatment.

However, to make an informed health care decision, the individual must be aware of all factors that could influence the decision-making process. In 1991 the federal government passed the Patient Self-Determination Act, 42 U.S.C. § 1395cc, which requires all Medicare and Medicaid provider organizations, including HMOs, nursing homes, and hospices, to give all individuals who are receiving medical care from the organization complete information regarding the patient's rights with respect to health care decisions. This information must be in writing and be given to the patient before the person begins receiving health care. The patient's medical record must document any health care decision that the patient has made. The content of the written information, as well as its format, is left up to state regulation. However, because all Medicare and Medicaid providers must adhere to this directive, all elderly patients are required to be informed of their rights relating to health care decision making.

Example

A Medicare recipient is entering the hospital for a bypass operation. Upon admission the patient is required to receive written information detailing the patient's rights as to decisions about the health care treatment the patient may receive.

Conservatorship

If a person lacks the legal capacity to make such decisions for himself or herself, a court of competent jurisdiction may place that person under conservatorship. A **conservator** is a court-appointed individual who is charged with making decisions on behalf of a person who is deemed incompetent for physical or mental reasons. Conservators, or **guardians**, fall into four general categories:

conservator (guardian) Person designated by a court to manage another person's estate and/or property.

guardian of the estate Court-appointed representative who is responsible for administering the property of an incompetent.

1. **Guardian of the estate.** This guardian is appointed solely to protect the property of another individual, and the guardian's powers are limited to financial decisions.

Example

An elderly man has started giving away large sums of money to strangers. His children apply to the court to be appointed guardians of his property, stating that their father's mental ability has deteriorated. If approved by the court, the children can be appointed to manage their father's money, but the father is still legally competent to make his own health care decisions.

---

2. **Guardian of the person**. This guardian is appointed to make decisions affecting another person's physical well-being.

   Example _____

   An elderly woman is diagnosed with Alzheimer's disease and her daughter seeks a court appointment to become her mother's guardian of the person. In this instance the daughter is the one who is legally competent to make health care decisions for her mother.

---

3. **Plenary guardian**. A plenary guardian is appointed by the court to oversee another person's person *and* property.
4. **Limited guardian**. As the name indicates, this form of guardianship is for only limited and specific purposes as specified by a court order.

   Example _____

   An elderly man has been diagnosed with the beginning stages of Parkinson's disease. At present he is still clear-headed, but is becoming slightly muddled in his speaking and memory. His daughter seeks legal advice and the attorney recommends guardianship. The legal assistant drafts and files the appropriate documents for the court. The court approves the application and appoints the daughter as a limited guardian, meaning that she will make decisions on behalf of her father *only to the extent* necessary to compensate for his declining abilities.

In many circumstances family members are reluctant to go to court to be formally appointed as guardians, but will make health care decisions on behalf of an ailing family member informally. These decisions are often totally without legal authority, unless the matter has been statutorily addressed by the state, and the health care professional should be wary of following such informal directives.

If an individual makes a health care decision when competent and then becomes incompetent for any reason, the person has the right to have that health care decision carried out, *provided* that it can be proven by "clear and convincing" evidence that the person was competent and adequately informed when the original decision was reached. However, these situations generally result in a legal battle. To avoid such situations, the law permits a competent person to make health care decisions prospectively in the form of a health care directive.

guardian of the person Court-appointed representative who is responsible for making decisions regarding the physical care of an incompetent.

plenary guardian Court-appointed representative who is responsible for overseeing another person's person *and* property.

limited guardian Court-appointed representative charged with making decisions in a limited area for an incompetent.

Example

An elderly woman, faced with surgery, executes a do-not-resuscitate order prepared by a paralegal under the direction of an attorney, in case she falls into a coma and must be maintained on life support systems. The situation she feared occurs, and her family wishes her to be kept alive on life support; however, the woman's advance directive can prevail.

Health Care Proxies

To avoid problems that may arise when a competent person becomes incapacitated and legally incapable of speaking for himself or herself with respect to health care decisions, all jurisdictions permit certain advance directives to be executed by competent individuals. *Advance directive* is a generic term used to cover documents that indicate a person's future health care wishes. The most common form of an advance directive is a health care proxy.

A *health care proxy* is a power of attorney in which an individual, known as the *principal*, authorizes another person to make health care decisions on the principal's behalf should the principal become incapable of speaking for himself or herself. All jurisdictions provide for health care proxies, usually under the state mental hygiene, mental health, or public health law, and the forms and procedures that must be followed are dictated by each jurisdiction. If a person who has executed a valid health care proxy becomes incompetent, the proxy is already authorized to make health care decisions on the principal's behalf. If the principal is under conservatorship, a guardian may execute a health care proxy on behalf of the principal.

Example

As part of her estate plan, an elderly woman executes a health care proxy, drafted by a paralegal under a lawyer's direction, appointing her son to make any health care decision for her should she become incompetent. Several weeks later the woman is hit by a car and goes into a coma. Pursuant to the health care proxy, the woman's son is now authorized to make decisions regarding his mother's health care treatment until she comes out of the coma and can act on her own behalf.

Terminal Situations

Several forms of advance directives have been created to cover situations in which the individual is terminally ill or injured.

Do-Not-Resuscitate Orders

Do-not-resuscitate (DNR) orders, which are legally effective only if permitted under state law, allow competent persons to execute documents stating that they do not wish to be resuscitated if it is medically determined that resuscitation will only act to keep the person alive for a short period of time prior to ultimate death. DNR orders have only limited application, and may be ordered even for persons who lack capacity if judicially sought by close relatives. DNR orders are effective only for terminally ill persons.

Example

An elderly woman has fallen into a coma and is suffering from a terminal illness. She has never executed a health care proxy. Her husband seeks legal advice, and the attorney and paralegal draft a DNR order. The husband then goes to court to have the order approved, to avoid an extreme burden from his wife's medical condition in a situation in which she is going to die anyway. The court may grant the husband's petition if it believes it is in the best interests of the incapacitated wife not to have to go through the trauma of resuscitation only to face ultimate death.

Living Will

A *living will* is a statement executed by a person who is competent indicating the person's wishes with respect to life support assistance and medical treatment in case the person becomes incapacitated. Living wills differ from health care proxies in that, with a living will, the individual has not authorized anyone to act on his or her behalf, but has simply indicated his or her wishes with respect to medical treatment. Although valid, many jurisdictions view living wills as rebuttable indications of a person's intentions and they may not be given effect by physicians, hospitals, or courts. However, living wills may be used as evidence of a person's intent with respect to health care decisions.

Example

A woman executes a living will in which she indicates that, should she become incompetent, she does not wish to be maintained on life support systems. Three years later she is in a train accident and is rushed to a religiously affiliated hospital. Her grandson shows the hospital the living will, but the hospital refuses to honor it because it is contrary to the hospital's religious principles. The grandson goes to court to have the living will given effect. The court, however, views the living will as evidence of the woman's state of mind three years ago. Although it indicates that intent, it can be rebutted by more recent evidence of the woman's current state of mind.

As previously stated, a person does have the right to refuse treatment the consequences of which may result in death. Although there is a common-law right to die, in many instances a court may order treatment for a terminally ill patient if it can be determined that the interests of the state in maintaining life override the individual's decision to die. As a general principle, the law always favors life, and there are many ethical concerns with respect to permitting a person to die. Furthermore, anyone who knowingly and intentionally assists a person in terminating life, even if the individual is terminally ill, may be liable to judicial prosecution (see Chapter 8).

Example

A physician believes that he has an ethical responsibility to help a patient who is terminally ill and in severe pain to end the patient's life. The doctor assists the patient in committing suicide. The doctor may be culpable for homicide. There is a difference between refusing life-saving treatment and actively seeking death.

MEDICARE

The Medicare program was created in 1965 as an amendment to the Social Security Act, 42 U.S.C. § 1395 *et seq.*, and it operates as a federally funded health insurance policy for qualifying individuals. The program is designed to work with private health care facilities so that an individual can seek medical treatment privately but have the cost, or a portion thereof, reimbursed by the federal government. The Medicare program is administered under the auspices of the **Health Care Finance Administration (HCFA)** under the Department of Health and Human Services. Medicare contracts with private organizations to process charges filed by covered individuals. These privately contracted facilities are known as *fiscal intermediaries*. HCFA publishes a manual to explain its claims and benefit policies and procedures.

There are four main areas of focus with respect to understanding Medicare:

Health Care Finance Administration (HCFA) Federal agency that administers government health care programs.

1. who is eligible to receive Medicare
2. how one enrolls for Medicare coverage
3. what medical treatment is covered by Medicare
4. how one appeals an adverse decision respecting a Medicare claim for benefits.

Eligibility

Any individual who is entitled to receive Social Security benefits (see Chapter 3), who is either 65 years of age or who has been disabled for a period of not less than 24 months, is automatically eligible to receive Medicare. Unlike Medicaid (discussed later in this chapter), coverage is not based on a person's income or assets. Furthermore, government employees and persons who are entitled to railroad retirement or disability benefits are also eligible for Medicare. If an individual is over the age of 65 but is not otherwise eligible, he or she may still receive Medicare if he or she pays a premium for the coverage.

Example

A man has retired from his job after 45 years of employment. He is now 65 years old and entitled to receive Social Security retirement benefits. Because he is eligible for Social Security and is 65 years of age, he is automatically eligible for Medicare.

Example

A 34-year-old woman is severely injured in a car accident and is now permanently disabled. The accident occurred 20 months ago. The woman is not yet entitled to receive Medicare. At the start of the 25th month of her disability, she may begin to receive Medicare benefits.

Example

A 70-year-old woman has never worked. For most of her life she was supported by her family and then by her husband, who did not work but lived on the income from a small trust fund. This woman is not entitled to receive Social Security benefits, which are based on employment. However, because she is over the age of 65, she may pay a premium to the government to be covered by Medicare.

Enrollment

Medicare coverage is divided into two sections, Part A and Part B. Part A coverage is automatic when one applies for Social Security or railroad retirement benefits; Part B provides optional coverage which the individual may elect either to take or to decline. Part A requires no premium payment from the individual, whereas Part B requires a minimal premium payment. Also, as stated earlier, individuals who are over the age of 65 but who do not qualify for Social Security or railroad retirement benefits may also apply for Medicare coverage.

Enrollment for Medicare coverage is divided into three defined periods.

Initial Enrollment Period

The **initial enrollment period** is defined as the three months before and the three months immediately following the day on which the individual would be eligible to receive Social Security benefits. If the person applies 3 months before attaining the age of 65, Medicare coverage will commence on the first day of the first month of the person's 65th birthday. If the individual does not enroll either before or after his or her 65th birthday, coverage starts on the first day of the first month following the enrollment.

Example

Two months before her sixty-fifth birthday (March 23), a woman applies for Medicare coverage. On March 1 her coverage will begin. Her twin sister also turns 65 on March 23 but does not enroll for Medicare coverage until April 3. Her Medicare coverage will start on May 1.

General Enrollment Period

The first three months of every calendar year is called the **general enrollment period**, during which time any person who has failed to enroll in Medicare during his or her initial enrollment period may apply for coverage. For Part A coverage, an individual may enroll at any time, and the coverage will be retroactive for a six-month period if the individual pays a premium for such retroactive coverage. For persons who enroll during this period, coverage starts on July 1. Part B coverage, if not applied for during the initial enrollment period, can only be applied for during the general enrollment period, and a surcharge of 10 percent may be added to the premium for such Part B enrollment unless the individual qualifies as working elderly (see next section).

Example

A 67-year-old man opted out of Part B coverage when he first enrolled for Medicare on his 65th birthday, but now he wishes to have such coverage. During the general enrollment period he may enroll for Part B coverage, which will be retroactive for 6 months, but he must pay a 10 percent surcharge on his Part B premium.

Special Enrollment Period

For individuals who continue to work after their 65th birthday, known as the *working elderly*, and who have been covered by their **employer group health plan (EGHP)**, a **special enrollment period** was enacted in 1980. For these persons, the enrollment period begins on the first day of the first month after the employer group health plan stops, and

---

initial enrollment period   Period during which an eligible person can enroll in Medicare.

general enrollment period   Yearly period during which persons may enroll in Medicare Part B if they did not do so during their initial enrollment period.

employer group health plan (EGHP)   Health insurance coverage maintained by an employer.

special enrollment period   Time period during which the working elderly can enroll in Medicare.

terminates seven months later. If the person does not enroll during this period, he or she may be subject to a surcharge, and may enroll only during the general enrollment period.

Example

A paralegal continues to work for the legal department of her company until her 70th birthday and is covered by her employer group health insurance for 6 months after her retirement. For this working elderly woman, her special enrollment period starts on the first day of the seventh month after her retirement (when her EGHP coverage stops) and ends seven months later.

Note that employers are prohibited from covering their older employees, who would qualify for Medicare, under a different health insurance plan than their other employees. Furthermore, employers who employ fewer than 20 persons are exempt from this statute.

Be alert to the fact that an individual may enroll in Part A coverage at any time. Failure to enroll in Part B coverage, though, can delay such coverage and subject the individual to a 10 percent surcharge for each year that he or she failed to enroll.

Coverage and Exclusions

As stated earlier, Medicare coverage is divided into Part A and Part B. Generally, Part A covers inpatient hospital care and is funded by tax dollars. Part B covers medical care and services, outpatient and some home care, and some medical equipment; it is funded by monthly premiums paid by the recipient. Medicare coverage is not intended for preventative or custodial care; to be covered, medical services prescribed must be "reasonable and recovery must be likely."

Part A Coverage

Hospital Care: Part A covers the following hospital care:

1–60 days	Full coverage less a deductible. A *deductible* is the amount the recipient must pay for care before coverage begins.
61–90 days	Medicare pays 75 percent of the care and the recipient must pay 25 percent of the cost as a co-payment.
More than 90 days	The Medicare recipient is entitled to 60 lifetime reserve days for his or her entire life, and is subject to a co-payment for this period as well.

Medicare coverage for hospital care includes all hospital-prescribed services except for those that are considered luxuries (such as rental of a television), but it does not include the cost of the doctor's services, which are billed to the patient. Such doctor's bills are covered by Medicare Part B.

Example

A Medicare recipient is in an accident and is placed in the hospital for 19 days. After the recipient meets a deductible, all other hospital services, such as the cost of the room, medicine, nursing care, and so forth are paid for by Medicare. The bills for the surgeon and the anesthesiologist must be paid by the patient individually unless the patient has Part B coverage.

To be covered, the hospital stay must be medically necessary.

Rehabilitation: Part A will also cover inpatient rehabilitation services, provided the following requirements are met:

- A physician certifies that such rehabilitation is necessary
- The rehabilitation hospital must be a Medicare facility
- The patient must require intensive rehabilitation
- The rehabilitation must be designed to enable the patient to function independently
- The care must be both reasonable and necessary and not available at a lower cost outside of the hospital setting.

Example

An elderly man falls and breaks his leg, which necessitates hip replacement surgery. After the surgery the man requires intensive rehabilitation services to enable him to walk again. This rehabilitation would probably be covered by Part A.

Example

An elderly woman falls and breaks her arm, and her care requires a hospital stay. Her arm must be kept immobilized with metal pins and traction until the bone heals. After the pins are removed, the woman requires some therapy to regain full use of her arm. This rehabilitation could be handled on an outpatient basis and probably would not be covered by Part A, but might be covered by some other type of insurance.

Skilled Nursing Facility Coverage: Medicare Part A will pay for skilled nursing facility care only if required after a recipient has been in a hospital for three consecutive days; it will not cover nursing care not preceded by a hospital stay. Part A will pay for the first 20 days of such care, and then will pay a portion of such care for an additional 80 days, with a requisite recipient co-payment. To receive this coverage,

- A physician must certify that skilled nursing facility care is needed
- The recipient must have been in the hospital for a minimum of three days prior to such care
- The recipient must require daily care
- The daily care the recipient requires must be available only at a nursing care facility.

Example

A Medicare recipient suffers a stroke and is put in a hospital for five days. The man will need constant daily care for several weeks, including daily medication, until recovery. In this instance Medicare Part A may cover the cost of skilled nursing facility care.

Home Health Care: Medicare Part A will cover home health care for an unlimited period of time, with no deductible or co-payment, provided the following criteria are met:

- A physician signs a specified plan of care for the recipient
- The recipient is confined at home
- The recipient needs nursing care on a periodic basis
- The home health care is provided by a Medicare provider.

Example

The elderly stroke victim from the preceding example has now recovered enough to go home, but he cannot walk and is confined to a wheelchair. He requires injections three times a day, as well as other nursing care. In this instance Medicare Part A would probably cover the cost of such home health care.

The home health care services provided by Medicare Part A include therapy, limited social services, home nursing care, and the use of a home health aide.

Hospice Care: Hospice care is not designed for rehabilitation, but is dedicated exclusively to care of the terminally ill. To qualify for

Medicare hospice coverage, the recipient must opt out of all other Medicare coverage, which terminates his or her right to coverage for any treatments outside of the hospice setting. If the individual is incompetent, such election may be made by the person legally authorized to make such decisions for the recipient. To qualify, the individual must be certified by a physician as being terminally ill with a life expectancy of six months or less.

Example

An elderly man has been diagnosed with liver, lung, and kidney cancer and has been given three months to live. The man decides to end his days in a hospice, and opts out of his other Medicare coverage so that he can be placed in a Medicare-certified hospice to die.

To be covered, the hospice care must be contained in a master care plan certified by the physician, including all care and medication the patient is to receive.

Part B Coverage

The following services are covered under Medicare Part B:

1. Physician's services
2. Services furnished incident to a doctor's services that cannot be self-administered
3. Diagnostic tests
4. X-ray and radium therapy
5. Surgical devices
6. Durable medical equipment
7. Prosthetic devices
8. Braces, trusses, and eyewear
9. Ambulance services
10. Outpatient surgical and hospital services
11. Physical, occupational, and speech therapy
12. Comprehensive outpatient rehabilitation facility (CORF) services
13. Health clinic services
14. Dialysis
15. Ambulatory surgical center services
16. Antigen and blood-clotting factors
17. Certain vaccinations

18. HMO services
19. Mammography and Pap smear services
20. Certified psychological services
21. Therapeutic molded shoes for diabetics.

Part B coverage is optional. Since the early 1970s, eligible individuals who receive Social Security benefits and who elect Part B coverage have had their premium payments automatically deducted from their Social Security checks. Unless the person specifically opts out of Part B coverage, he or she is automatically enrolled when he or she becomes entitled to Part A coverage.

Under Part B, Medicare pays for 80 percent of the approved charges for the listed services, and the recipient is responsible for the remaining 20 percent. One of the problems associated with Part B coverage involves Medicare's determination of "approved" charges.

Example

A physician authorizes an MRI for a patient and bills $1,500 for the test. Medicare states that a charge of only $700 is appropriate for an MRI. Who is responsible for the other $800?

A physician may agree to an **assignment**, whereby the physician agrees to accept the Medicare determination and the patient is billed only for the 20 percent co-payment Medicare Part B will not cover. If the physician does not accept assignment, the patient will be responsible for the entire bill not covered by Part B.

Example

A physician does not accept assignment and submits a bill for $100 for some diagnostic tests. Medicare only approves a charge of $50 and pays the physician $40. The patient must pay the doctor the remaining $60. However, if the physician accepts Medicare Part B assignment and Medicare only approves a charge of $50 and pays the doctor $40, the patient need only pay the doctor the remaining $10 of the approved charge.

HMOs

Because of the extraordinary cost of health care, many individuals have opted for managed health care under the umbrella of a health maintenance organization (HMO). Medicare does provide for HMO care, but to receive such coverage the recipient must elect **managed care** and opt out of other Medicare coverage not provided by the HMO.

assignment Under Medicare, a physician's agreement to accept whatever payment Medicare provides.

managed care Health care rendered through an HMO arrangement.

There are two types of Medicare HMOs: risk HMOs and cost-basis HMOs.

Risk HMO: This category of Medicare HMO must provide all services and supplies covered under Part A and Part B, except for hospice care, to all individuals residing in the HMO's geographic area. Persons who enroll in a **risk HMO** are not subject to deductible and co-payment charges, but the HMO itself may require a premium or membership fee which is the responsibility of the individual enrollee. A risk HMO enrollee may only receive care at the specified HMO.

Cost-Basis HMO: Enrollees in this category of HMO may receive treatment at the specified HMO or at some other facility, and are not locked in to just one location. Some services that are provided as general services by risk HMOs may be separately charged to the **cost-basis HMO** enrollee, but the cost-basis HMO enrollee has more flexibility in the types and nature of treatment he or she receives.

Appealing Decisions

Appeals of denials of Medicare benefits or enrollment are made either to the Social Security Administration or the Railroad Retirement Board. The legal assistant in an elder law practice will be involved in preparing these appeals, which follow specific procedures.

Part A Appeals

1. After the initial determination in which the claim is denied, the recipient must make a written request for reconsideration within 60 days of the denial, unless good cause can be shown why an extension of the time limit should be granted.
2. Inpatient benefits are entitled to an expedited review, which must be made within three working days of the request for reconsideration.
3. If the reconsideration results in an affirmation of the denial, the claimant is entitled to an administrative hearing before an administrative law judge (ALJ), provided that there is at least $100 in controversy for hospice or home health care or $200 in controversy for hospital care; the request for the administrative hearing must be made within 60 days of affirmation of the denial unless an extension is granted for good cause. Statistically, recipients have an 80 percent success rate at this level.
4. If the ALJ affirms the reconsideration, the claimant may have the ALJ's decision reviewed by the Social Security Appeals

risk HMO   Managed care that provides all services to enrollees in its geographic area.

cost-basis HMO   Form of managed care in which the insured may use various facilities but must pay a small fee for each service received.

Council if such request is made within 60 days of the ALJ's decision.

5. If still unsatisfied, the claimant may seek judicial review in federal court if there is at least $1,000 in controversy for hospice or home health care or $2,000 in controversy for hospital care. A peer review organization (PRO) must review claims for hospital care before such claims can be filed for judicial review. The pleadings must be filed in federal court within 60 days of the final arbitration decision.

Part B Appeals

1. To seek review of denial of a Part B benefit, the claimant must first receive an explanation of Medicare benefits (EOMB) prepared by the Medicare carrier. The request for review must be made within 6 months of the denial and is permitted only if the amount in controversy is at least $100, either singly or in the aggregate.

2. The claimant is entitled to a **fair hearing** before a carrier hearing officer, and the claimant may be represented by counsel.

3. If the claimant does not receive a favorable decision from the carrier hearing officer, the claimant may request review before an ALJ, provided that such request is made within 60 days of the carrier hearing officer's decision and the amount in controversy is at least $500.

4. If the claimant is still dissatisfied with the ALJ's decision, review may be sought in the federal courts if the amount in controversy is at least $1,000 and the pleadings are filed with 60 days of the ALJ's decision.

Prospective Payment System

Because of the tremendous drain on Medicare resources caused by ever-increasing medical care costs (see Exhibit 2-1), since October 1, 1983, the government has utilized a program called the *Prospective Payment System (PPS)*, in which a hospital is paid a prospective amount for each Medicare patient. If the patient remains in the hospital for a longer period than that contemplated by the prospective payment, the hospital bears the additional cost. The program raises several ethical questions with respect to the value of the health care the recipient receives. It is more cost-effective for the hospital to discharge the patient as soon as possible, even if the patient has not received complete or adequate treatment, because the hospital can then retain the extra payment that has already been received. Conversely, for hospitals that do

fair hearing   Administrative hearing to which a Medicaid recipient is entitled if benefits are denied.

EXHIBIT 2-1

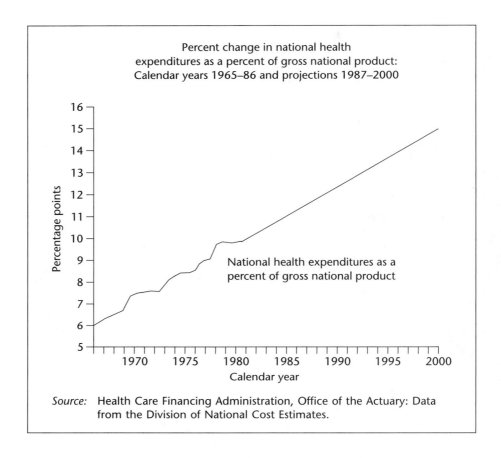

Percent change in national health
expenditures as a percent of gross national product:
Calendar years 1965–86 and projections 1987–2000

National health expenditures as a
percent of gross national product

Source: Health Care Financing Administration, Office of the Actuary: Data
from the Division of National Cost Estimates.

not participate in the PPS, it may be more financially advantageous to
keep a person in the hospital, even if the patient no longer requires inpatient care, to receive additional fees. These questions about the PPS
program only highlight the problem of providing appropriate health
care for the elderly in this country.

MEDICAID

Along with Medicare, in 1965 Congress passed Medicaid legislation,
42 U.S.C. § 1396, which established a joint federal/state program
designed to provide health care coverage to low-income individuals.
Whereas Medicare applies to the elderly and disabled regardless of
income or assets, Medicaid only applies to individuals who meet its
income and assets requirements.

The Medicaid program guidelines are established by the federal government, but each state designs its own program format, meaning that the operation of the program may vary greatly from state to state. Consequently, the legal assistant must review the program of each jurisdiction to determine an individual's rights and obligations under Medicaid.

Major changes affecting Medicaid were passed in 1993 pursuant to the **Omnibus Budget Reconciliation Act (OBRA)**, Pub. L. No. 103-66, which became effective on September 1, 1994. For persons who were already receiving Medicaid prior to the operational date, the previous rules remain effective, whereas persons who became eligible after September 1,1994, are subject to the new guidelines. The differences between the two sets of regulations are discussed, where appropriate, throughout this section.

Coverage and Eligibility

All United States citizens, lawful permanent residents of the United States, and aliens who are residing in the United States under color of law may be eligible to receive Medicaid. Residing in the country "under color of law" means that the alien entered the United States with a presumably lawful visa, although the alien may be subject to removal proceedings for various violations of the immigration law.

Example _____

A citizen of Bolivia entered the United States pursuant to a valid student visa. The time of stay permitted under the visa has expired, but the Bolivian has remained in the country. Although this person has violated the terms of the visa requiring departure by a specified date, the alien is in the United States under "color of law" until his status is discovered by the Immigration and Naturalization Service.

_____

To qualify for Medicaid benefits, the individual must be resident in the state when he or she applies for such coverage, and must meet certain financial tests. Because Medicaid is designed exclusively for low-income individuals and families, income and asset guidelines have been established. These guidelines may vary from state to state, and the legal assistant must examine each jurisdiction's laws. Some typical guidelines include:

1. The individual is entitled to receive Medicare Part A.
2. The person's income is beneath the established poverty level.
3. The person's resources do not exceed the SSI resource levels ($4,000 for individuals, $6,000 for a couple, etc.).

Omnibus Budget Reconciliation Act (OBRA) Federal statute, enacted in 1993, that affects Medicaid recipients.

Furthermore, in many states any person who receives Supplemental Security Income (SSI) is automatically eligible for Medicaid.

Example

An individual is disabled and can only work part-time. His total monthly income is $400, and all of his assets total only $2,500. This person would qualify to receive Medicaid under its financial limitations and under his state's guidelines.

If the applicant's income is equal to 100–110 percent of the poverty level or the applicant's resources exceed twice the SSI resource level, Medicaid will only pay for the applicant's Medicare Part B coverage under the Specified Low Income Medicaid Benefit Program (SLIMB). Otherwise, Medicaid provides the recipient with the following services:

1. *Community medical services*, which include physicians' services, outpatient and clinic services, lab and x-ray charges, rehabilitation services, transportation to receive medical treatment, and medical supplies.
2. *Home care services*, which include nursing, home health aid services, therapy, personal care aid services, and long-term home health care.
3. *Institutional care*, which includes care in hospitals, nursing homes, and other medical facilities.

In 1991 Medicaid implemented a program known as the **Medical Assistance Utilization Threshold Program (MUTS)**, which imposes limitations on the number of visits and services the recipient may receive each year. The purpose of the program was to limit unnecessary use of outpatient services, to keep the cost of Medicaid down. The limitations imposed under MUTS are:

- 10 physician visits
- 40 pharmacy items
- 18 laboratory tests
- 3 dental clinic services
- 40 mental health clinic services.

Medical Assistance Utilization Threshold Program (MUTS)
Federal program designed to limit the use of Medicaid benefits.

Pursuant to MUTS, the elderly, blind, or disabled are not subject to any limitations for managed care services, hemodialysis, or prior authorized services. Furthermore, a Medicaid provider may also provide "emergency" services that are not subject to these limitations.

If an individual is nearing his or her threshold limitations, Medicaid will alert the person of such fact to allow the individual the opportunity to make an override application. An **override application**, which is completed by the individual's physician, requests additional services because of medical necessity. Also, if an individual has a chronic condition that requires treatment beyond the limitations, the person may apply for an exemption from MUTS.

---

*Example*_____

An elderly man suffers from severe diabetes and arthritis, both of which are chronic conditions, and he requires frequent medical care to keep these problems in check. He and his physician file an application for an exemption from the MUTS limitations, which will probably be granted.

In another cost-saving measure, in 1993 Medicaid attempted implementation of a co-payment requirement, mandating that most eligible Medicaid recipients contribute a small portion to their medical care. Currently, this measure is being challenged in the courts and so full implementation has been delayed. Under this program, the Medicaid provider is responsible for collecting the co-payment from the Medicaid recipient, but the provider is prohibited from denying treatment to any recipient who is unable to make the co-payment.

---

*Example*_____

A Medicaid recipient has received treatment from a provider who has requested the recipient to make a co-payment. The recipient does not have the funds for such co-payment. The doctor cannot refuse further treatment to the recipient just because the recipient cannot meet the co-payment.

Applications to receive Medicaid are made through the state agency authorized to administer the program, following the procedure established by the individual state. The elder law paralegal may be called upon to assist the attorney and the client in preparing and filing these applications.

Exempt Assets

Because Medicaid is designed for low-income persons, to receive Medicaid benefits an applicant must demonstrate that his or her income and resources fall within the Medicaid financial limitations.

For purposes of determining the applicant's income level, all income, whether earned or unearned, is included in the computation.

override application
Request for additional care over and above that permitted pursuant to MUTS.

However, for all SSI applicants, the following items are not calculated as part of the applicant's available income:

- Income used to pay health insurance premiums, including Medicare Part B payments
- Interest from a burial fund
- Reparation payments
- The first $20 of monthly household income
- Contributions of goods or services from persons who are not legally responsible for the applicant, known as "in-kind" support
- Restitution payments made to Japanese Americans and Aleuts
- Agent Orange payments

In determining the amount of the applicant's employment-related income, the first $65 of earned income per month is exempt, and only one-half of the balance is considered as income for determining Medicaid eligibility.

Example

A disabled individual who applies for Medicaid has the following income resources:

- Income, earned from a part-time job, of $500 per month
- Food contributed to him by his cousin, valued at $200 per month
- $10 monthly interest income on a bank account he maintains as his burial fund.

Every month he pays $45 for his Medicare Part B coverage. His income for determining Medicaid eligibility is $172.50: $500 - 65 \times \frac{1}{2} - 45$; all other income is exempt.

---

surplus income Income above the limit to qualify for Medicaid.

spend-down program Method whereby a person divests himself or herself of assets in order to qualify for Medicaid.

The Medicaid recipient is required to use all funds available to him or her for medical care. Consequently, the recipient cannot refuse any gift or bequest because it would destroy his or her Medicaid eligibility. If the recipient is the claimant in a personal injury lawsuit, Medicaid will impose a lien on any amount the recipient is awarded for medical treatment, and the remainder of any recovery is deemed income to the recipient.

If an individual would otherwise be eligible to receive Medicaid except for the fact that the person's income exceeds the Medicaid limitations, that person may still receive Medicaid benefits if, in any month, the person's medical expenses exceed the amount of income that is above the Medicaid income ceiling. This is known as the **surplus income** or **spend-down program**.

Example

A woman qualifies for Medicaid except for the fact that her monthly income exceeds the Medicaid limitation by $50. Each month that her medical bills exceed this $50 excess, she would qualify for Medicaid coverage.

The other financial test that a Medicaid applicant must meet, in addition to income levels, concerns the amount of assets or resources at the applicant's disposal. Any asset that is actually available to the applicant that can be sold or used for medical treatment, unless deemed to be an exempt asset, is calculated to determine the applicant's financial eligibility.

Typical exempt resources include:

- the applicant's homestead and surrounding land

- personal property, such as clothes and furniture, including a car

- life insurance policies with a cash surrender value not exceeding $1,500 (if the cash surrender value exceeds $1,500, the amount of the excess is included as part of the applicant's available resources)

- a separate burial fund not exceeding $1,500

- German and Austrian reparation payments

Note that the list of exempt resources may vary from state to state, so the legal assistant must examine each state's laws.

In addition to the preceding, if the applicant is disabled, a supplemental needs trust established for his or her benefit will not be included in the determination of the person's assets, provided that the following requirements are met:

- The beneficiary is disabled

- The trust was established before the beneficiary attained the age of 65

- The trust was established by a parent, grandparent, legal guardian, or a court

- The trust provides that at the death of the beneficiary the state will receive reimbursement from the trust assets for all Medicaid benefits provided on behalf of the beneficiary.

A *supplemental needs trust* is one in which income is distributed on behalf of the beneficiary only when the beneficiary's medical expenses exceed his or her medical coverage.

Example _____

A child was born with severe birth defects due to the malpractice of the doctor and the hospital when the child was born. The child and the child's parents are awarded a multimillion-dollar judgment for their pain and suffering. The parents use these funds to establish a supplemental needs trust (created by an attorney assisted by a paralegal) for the benefit of their child, who is not yet 10 years old. The value of the trust is not considered in determining the child's eligibility for Medicaid.

Protecting a Spouse's Assets

In determining an applicant's financial eligibility for Medicaid, the applicant's total resources, including that of the applicant's spouse, may be considered. Under federal law, all jointly held property is deemed to belong to the applicant for the purpose of determining eligibility, even though many states consider that only half of such property is owned by each joint tenant if the joint tenants are married. Consequently, most marital property may be included to determine an applicant's assets. The only property of an applicant's spouse that will be protected is the homestead and personal property individually owned by the spouse.

Example _____

The wife of a Medicaid applicant inherits $10,000 from her aunt. Because the property was inherited by the wife in her individual capacity, this property may be exempt from Medicaid calculations. However, if the wife places the money in a joint account with her husband, the entire $10,000 is considered part of the husband's accessible assets.

Transferring Assets

To meet the Medicaid resource test, many individuals attempt to divest themselves of their assets. Medicaid places no limitation on a person simply spending his or her excess assets (assuming that he or she receives fair market value for property sold) in order to come within the Medicaid financial limitations. Also, an attorney and the attorney's staff, if performing under the attorney's direction, may be held criminally liable for advising a client to "spend down" just to meet Medicaid limitations. However, if the individual transfers property to another person to divest himself or herself of property to qualify for Medicaid, Medicaid imposes certain tests to determine the validity of the transfers. The rules with respect to such transfers changed in 1993 pursuant to OBRA, and are examined separately here.

Transfers Before August 10, 1993

For the purpose of determining the applicant's financial eligibility, Medicaid will review all property transfers made by the applicant and/or the applicant's spouse within 30 months of making the application. This is known as the **look-back period**. The applicant is required to furnish Medicaid with all financial documents for the period, although Medicaid only reviews transfers of nonexempt property.

If Medicaid determines that the applicant has transferred funds within the look-back period, a period of ineligibility for receiving service will be imposed as a penalty. The formula used to determine the period of ineligibility is made by reference to the dollar value of the transfers divided by the average monthly cost of Medicaid services, but in no event will the period of ineligibility exceed 30 months from the date of the transfer.

Transfers After August 10, 1993

The new rules under OBRA apply only to applications or reapplications made on or after August 11, 1993. Under the new rules, penalties are imposed for transferring income as well as assets (the older rules only referred to asset transfers). The look-back period for these transfers is now 36 months, and a separate look-back period of 60 months has been established for transfers involving trusts. However, the new rules cannot be applied prior to August 11, 1993. Furthermore, under the new guidelines the penalty period is unlimited, whereas previously it could not exceed 30 months.

Exempt Transfers

Certain transfers made within the look-back period are exempt for the purpose of calculating either assets or penalty periods. Such exempt transfers include:

- transfers for fair market value

- transfers for purposes other than receiving Medicaid; this requires a showing of need to make the transfers

- transfers to a blind or disabled child of any age

- interspousal transfers

If the applicant can demonstrate that undue hardship would result from imposition of a penalty period, the penalty period can be waived. To qualify for the exemption, the individual must be otherwise eligible for Medicaid, must be unable to obtain other medical coverage without Medicaid, and must show that he or she has attempted to recover the

look-back period
Period of time the government will review to determine whether an applicant has improperly divested himself or herself of property to become entitled to receive Medicaid.

transferred asset, which may require the applicant to institute a lawsuit against the transferee. The attorney and the paralegal may become involved in litigation at this point. For transfers occurring after August 11, 1993, if the applicant recovers the transferred asset, the penalty period incurred because of the transfer will be canceled.

There is a special rule regarding transfers of the applicant's homestead. Even though the homestead is deemed exempt property, if the applicant transferred the homestead on or after October 1, 1989, a penalty period will be imposed unless the transfer was made to:

- the applicant's spouse
- the applicant's child who is either less than 21 years of age or blind or disabled
- the applicant's sibling who has a property interest in the residence
- the applicant's nondisabled child who has lived in the house for at least two years prior to the transfer and who has provided care to the applicant

Certain other rules apply to transfers of property made by the applicant's spouse, and special rules exist with respect to benefit determination for married couples, one or both of whom are applying for Medicaid. Severe penalties may be imposed for transfers made to the applicant's spouse, and full financial disclosure must be made regarding the couple's income and resources to determine Medicaid eligibility.

Appealing Medicaid Decisions

The right to receive Medicaid assistance was determined to be a property right by the United States Supreme Court in *Goldberg v. Kelly*, 397 U.S. 254 (1970). Thus, an individual may not be deprived of such right without due process of law. Due process requires that the applicant receive written notice of any Medicaid action, detailing the reasons why such action is being taken. The legal assistant may be called upon to aid the attorney in preparing Medicaid appeals.

A Medicaid recipient has the right to continue receiving Medicaid benefits if the recipient made a request for a fair hearing within 60 days of receiving written notice of a denial of benefits. Such benefits will continue until a determination is made at the conclusion of the fair hearing.

The request for a fair hearing, which is an administrative review of the adverse decision, must be made in writing within 60 days of receiving notice of a denial of benefits. The time limit may be extended upon a showing of good cause. The claimant has the right to be represented at the hearing and has the right to review all files relating to the claim.

If an application for Medicaid was not acted on within 30 days (60 days if it concerns a disability) and the delay is not due to the fault of the claimant, the nonaction is deemed to be a denial, which gives the claimant the right to appeal.

The fair hearing is conducted before an administrative law judge, who must render a decision in writing. If the decision of the ALJ is adverse, the claimant may seek judicial review in state court by filing with the court within 120 days of receiving the adverse decision.

For low-income individuals, Medicaid provides an additional way to receive appropriate health care, and many elderly Americans on limited incomes do fall within the financial requirements to receive Medicaid benefits. However, it should be noted that many older persons transfer assets as part of an estate plan (see Chapter 6), and they may find that such transfers affect their Medicaid eligibility. Furthermore, Medicaid can impose a lien on the estate of a deceased Medicaid recipient to be reimbursed for benefits paid on the deceased recipient's behalf.

HEALTH INSURANCE

Because of the ever-increasing cost of health care, many persons acquire private health insurance to reduce their out-of-pocket medical expenses. Even persons who are covered by Medicare may have additional insurance to cover costs not reimbursed by Medicare Part A or Part B. Furthermore, many older Americans do not qualify for the Medicare or Medicaid benefits and thus must provide for their own health maintenance.

Types of Insurance

Health insurance falls into a few simple categories: policies that provide coverage for specified health care; **supplemental insurance** that pays for health care not covered by other programs or policies; and disability and accident insurance that covers injuries that result in short- or long-term disabilities. The decision with respect to the appropriate policy for an individual is totally dependent on the particular facts of the individual's history.

supplemental insurance Health care coverage designed to provide benefits for care not covered by other policies or programs.

Example

A woman is covered by Medicare Part A and has further elected to pay for Part B coverage. However, because Medicare does not pay for 100 percent of her health care costs, she also maintains private insurance that provides supplemental benefits to cover the portion of her health care not covered by Medicare.

Example

A man works as a long-distance truck driver. Because of the potential for accidents, he maintains an accident and disability insurance policy. If he should have an accident, or become disabled due to an accident, the insurance company will pay him a contractually determined amount to defray the costs of his health care and his loss of income.

Example

A couple are each over the age of 50 and are self-employed. Because they do not yet qualify for Medicare, they maintain private health insurance to cover the cost of their medical care.

Terms and Conditions

Health insurance is a private contract between the insurer and the insured, and consequently the specific terms and conditions of policies will vary. The elder law legal assistant must examine each clause of the contract to determine the client's rights and obligations under the coverage. Many employers and organizations offer employees and members the opportunity to participate in a group health insurance policy, under which the insurer agrees to accept smaller premium payments for each member because of the large number of persons being covered by the policy. A *premium* is the periodic payment made by the insured to the insurer as the consideration for the coverage specified in the policy. Most insurance policies specify the maximum lifetime amount that the insurer will pay out for the insured's medical care, and further specify the amount of the insured's deductible and co-payment responsibilities. A *deductible* is the specified amount of the insured's medical bills each year for which the insured is personally liable before the insurance coverage takes effect. The insured must pay this amount before the insurer begins to pay for the health care. A *co-payment* is a specified percentage of the amount billed by the health care provider that remains the individual responsibility of the insured.

Example

A 50-year-old woman is employed by a large corporation as a paralegal. Under the terms of her employment, she may participate in the company's group health insurance plan by paying $100 per month to receive health coverage. If she were to purchase the same policy on her own as a private individual, the insurer would charge her $500 per month as her premium. It is more cost-effective for her to maintain her policy as a group member.

Example

A man has a health insurance policy with a $1,000 deductible. Each year he must pay the first thousand dollars of his health care costs; after that specified amount has been met, the insurance company will start providing benefits.

Example

A man's health insurance policy provides that, after a certain limit has been reached, the insurer will only pay 80 percent of the insured's health care; the insured must pay the remaining 20 percent himself. This 20 percent constitutes the insured's co-payment.

It is important that the legal assistant read all of the provisions of each individual policy to determine what health care services and supplies are covered by the insurance. Because an insurance policy is a contract, only those items specified in the policy are subject to the insured's claims.

Filing Claims

As stated previously, health insurance is subject to private contractual arrangements between the insured and the insurance company. Although every state regulates the insurance companies operating within its jurisdiction, aside from state-mandated basic due process requirements, each company has its own policies and procedures with respect to filing claims. The insurance company is required to provide each insured individual with a written statement detailing the procedures that must be followed to file claims, and the individual must follow those procedures to receive the insurance benefit.

Example

Under the terms of an insurance contract, the insured is required to pay the physician for his or her services and then submit a copy of the physician's bill, with evidence of payment, to the insurance company, which will then send a check for the covered services to the insured. Under this arrangement, the insured will receive reimbursement from the insurer only if he or she first pays the physician.

HMOs

As previously discussed, HMOs are a form of managed health care that has become increasingly prominent over the past two decades. Pursuant to these types of arrangements, the insured is required to receive all medical services from the HMO, for which he or she pays nothing or just a nominal charge beyond the premium. The insured's premium payment covers the cost of almost all medical care.

Problems have arisen with HMOs, especially with respect to the nature of the care the participant receives. Because basically all treatment is prepaid by the premium, the determination of the type of treatment a patient may receive includes a definite cost-factor element—the less treatment, the more profit for the HMO. There have been many claims, some substantiated and some unsubstantiated, that this cost-saving factor has resulted in severe injuries or death for participants who did not receive the care their conditions demanded because the HMO was more concerned with costs than care. Furthermore, many HMOs require that the participant receive treatment only at a specified center, meaning that if travel to the center becomes difficult the participant must pay individually for medical care he or she receives elsewhere.

On the benefit side, HMO coverage is generally less expensive than other forms of private health insurance. Because almost all services are prepaid, participants are statistically more likely to seek and receive preventative care, because it does not cost extra.

Example

A couple in their late fifties maintains private health insurance. The husband has a general health insurance policy, whereas the wife participates in an HMO. The husband seeks medical care only when he is very ill, because he is responsible for a deductible and a co-payment. The wife goes to her HMO whenever she feels ill, because her cost is only $5 per visit pursuant to her HMO health insurance policy.

Supplemental Insurance

Medi-gap insurance Form of supplemental insurance designed to provide payment for items not covered by Medicare.

open enrollment General period during which a person may enroll for Medicare.

long-term care insurance Form of health insurance that provides benefits for extended health care.

Because health insurance companies are regulated by state statutes, the legal assistant must scrutinize each jurisdiction's law to determine the specific rights and obligations in a given situation. However, because of the gap between Medicare coverage and actual medical costs, many insurance companies offer what is generally termed *supplemental insurance*, which falls into two broad categories:

1. Medicare supplemental insurance (Medi-gap)
2. long-term care insurance.

Medi-gap insurance is designed to cover all amounts not covered by Medicare Part A and Part B. Because Medicare is operated by the state and federal governments, each state mandates an **open enrollment** period each year during which all eligible Medicare recipients can apply for this coverage. **Long-term care insurance** is designed to cover nursing home and other extended hospital treatment beyond the period covered by Medicare and other insurance policies. Such a policy will specify the number of months of coverage and, once again, each state sets the number of months that should be covered. In New York, for example, the number of months of long-term care is 24.

NURSING HOMES

Nursing homes are not old-age homes or retirement communities to which people go when they retire or reach a certain age in order to be surrounded by similarly situated or aged persons. Rather, nursing homes are health care facilities designed to provide long-term care for persons (regardless of age) who do not need hospital care but who cannot manage their health care unsupervised in a home setting.

Nursing homes are regulated by state law and, since 1987, by federal statute pursuant to the provisions of the **Nursing Home Reform Act (NHRA)**, 42 U.S.C. § 1396r. Many elderly individuals must go to a nursing home either after a stay in the hospital for a severe illness or condition or for long-term care because of a serious chronic medical condition.

Finding a Nursing Home

More than 40,000 nursing homes are licensed in this country, but finding one that is appropriate for a given individual presents several problems. First of all, pursuant to statute, nursing homes are not required to admit persons who are mentally ill or severely retarded, which already excludes a segment of the population who might need such care but who are not required by law to be served. If these persons are to receive nursing home care, a facility that agrees to admit them must be located.

Some nursing homes are willing to accept Medicaid recipients, but some will only accept persons who will cover the cost of their care personally. Consequently, if an individual is a Medicaid recipient, only Medicaid-certified nursing homes are available for his or her care. Furthermore, because Medicare will pay for only a portion of nursing home care, if the individual requires long-term care he or she must have sufficient funds or adequate supplemental insurance to cover the costs, which are quite high.

If a patient requires specific nursing care, the home must be able or willing to provide such specialized treatment. Because each facility is different, finding a facility that can provide the special treatment and

nursing home
Health care facility designed for long-term care for persons who do not need to be in a hospital but who cannot manage their health care on their own.

Nursing Home Reform Act (NHRA)
Federal statute affecting the rights of nursing home patients.

has the appropriate equipment is another consideration in locating an appropriate nursing home.

Every nursing home has its own policies and procedures with respect to the transfer and discharge of residents, and it must be determined prior to entry that the facility's policies meet the needs of the individual patient. If the home has a policy of keeping residents for only a stated period of time, but the individual *may* require more extended care, it might be prudent to locate a different facility, whose policies are determined by the care required rather than by time limitations.

Finally, as with most residence decisions, one of the primary factors is the location of the facility. How close is the home to the resident's own home, friends, and family? Is it in a location that will enable the resident's family to make regular visits? Is the home in an area that is familiar to the patient and relatively safe and quiet? All of these factors must be considered when deciding on a nursing home facility.

Nursing Home Contracts

Both state and federal law prohibit discrimination in the provision of accommodations at nursing homes, and state law typically regulates the operation of facilities deemed to be nursing homes. Be aware that facilities designed simply to provide housing to the elderly, and which do not provide medical care, are not nursing homes but adult living facilities (discussed in Chapter 4).

The individual's rights and obligations with respect to nursing home living are governed by the terms of the specific contract between the facility and the resident. However, the law does not require a nursing home to accept Medicaid patients, so low-income individuals may have to seek out certified Medicaid facilities. Furthermore, federal law prohibits a facility from requiring a third-party guarantee to cover the cost of staying in a nursing home. Consequently, one of the primary factors, after the nature and the quality of the care provided, is the cost to the resident of staying in the facility. Nursing homes are allowed to require a deposit for the prospective stay, which will be used to defray the cost of the resident's care.

The specific terms and conditions depend on the individual contract, and are beyond the scope of this text. However, the legal assistant must be prepared to aid the attorney in analyzing the client's rights and obligations under the contract and in explaining the consequences and requirements of the contract to the client.

Example

An elderly woman on Medicaid has been in the hospital and now requires several weeks of nursing home care. The first few facilities her family located do not accept Medicaid patients. The family must continue to search until they find a Medicaid-certified nursing home.

Example

An elderly Islamic woman needs nursing home care. The optimal facility to provide the care she needs refuses to accept her because of her religion. This is a violation of federal and state law, and the facility must accept the patient.

Waiting Lists

Each nursing home is required to establish a written admission policy that meets the requirements of federal and state antidiscrimination laws. Furthermore, access to nursing home care may be limited, unless privately financed, to individuals who satisfy various medical criteria indicating that they require medical care that cannot be met by less expensive means.

Nursing homes may establish waiting list procedures because of the demand on the facilities' beds, and applicants for admission are required to be notified of these bed reservation procedures. Most state laws mandate that a nursing home hold a patient's bed for a specified period of time if the patient must be removed from the home to a hospital for medical care.

Example

An elderly man has been in a New York nursing home for five weeks. Then his ulcers erupt and he must be taken to a hospital for emergency treatment. Under New York law, the man's bed must be held for him for a period of up to 15 days, so that he will have a place to go after the hospital stay.

Every nursing home resident must be under the care of a physician who retains primary responsibility for the patient's care. The physician must be affiliated with the facility in the same way that a physician must be affiliated with a hospital.

Residents are evaluated at the time of admission, and a course of care is determined in conjunction with the resident's primary care physician. The resident has the right to participate in determining his or her treatment, provided that the resident is competent (see Chapter 1). The resident also has the right to refuse any specific treatment or medication, and must be permitted to review his or her own medical records.

NHRA mandates that physical restraints may be used on a resident only under very unusual circumstances, and only after alternative methods have been tried and found to be ineffective. Unless it is an emergency, physical restraints may be used only with the patient's consent, and are permitted only to protect the health, safety, and welfare of the patient, other residents, and facility staff. Additionally, the use of physical restraints must be ordered in the resident's health care diagnostic plan.

Example

An elderly woman who is confined to a wheelchair has lost motor control. As a consequence, she has started falling out of her chair. To protect her from injury resulting from such falls, the nursing home straps her into the chair. This physical restraint would probably be appropriate under these circumstances, but the restraint must be applied according to physician's orders in the woman's health care plan.

Additionally, NHRA mandates that *chemical restraints*—drugs used to control behavior—may be administered only with the approval of the physician, and only for legitimate medical reasons. The use of such medication must be indicated on the patient's diagnostic health care plan.

Example

A resident of a nursing home who has been diagnosed with bipolar disorder alternates between extreme depression and extreme joy. To moderate his behavior, and to prevent him from injuring himself during the periods of depression, the facility administers certain drugs with the physician's approval. This would be an appropriate use of chemical restraints.

Pursuant to the Nursing Home Reform Act (NHRA), 42 U.S.C. § 1395l, a nursing home resident can be transferred to a different facility or discharged only if certain requirements are met:

1. The transfer or discharge to a different facility is necessary for the resident's welfare
2. The resident's health has improved so that he or she no longer needs nursing home care
3. The health or safety of the other residents would be at risk if the resident remained
4. The resident has not paid for his or her stay
5. The facility ceases operation.

The law applies to all transfers between facilities, though not to transfers between rooms within a single facility, regardless of whether the facility is governmentally or privately funded. The rationale behind enactment of the law was to reduce the stress associated with the involuntary transfer of nursing home patients. The patient or the patient's legal guardian must be consulted before any transfer or discharge.

Example

An elderly woman has been at a nursing home facility for a considerable period of time and her health has so improved that she can be discharged. She has become attached to the facility and does not want to leave; because of her health improvement, however, the facility has the right to discharge her.

Remember that every state regulates nursing homes within its jurisdiction and has its own laws with respect to the rights and treatment of patients, in addition to the federal statutes. The legal assistant must review the specifics of his or her own state law. Nursing homes are generally evaluated by state agencies on an annual basis to assure that they are meeting all federal and state standards.

Residents' Bill of Rights

Pursuant to the NHRA, all nursing home residents have the following rights:

1. The right to receive a written statement of one's legal rights when entering a nursing home facility
2. The right to receive a written statement of fees, charges, and services
3. The right to receive care in a manner that preserves personal dignity, self-determination, and the basic quality of life
4. The right to privacy
5. The right to manage one's own finances
6. The right to receive visitors at reasonable hours
7. The right for visitors to have reasonable access to the resident
8. The right to participate in resident and family groups
9. The right to be free from abuse and neglect
10. The right of confidentiality
11. The right to present grievances to the facility's management
12. The right to examine one's medical records and to participate in determining treatment.

FINANCING HEALTH CARE

One of the most commonly discussed concerns of the elderly is their ability to finance the health care necessitated by the physical and mental changes that occur as a body ages. Most of the methods of financing such care were discussed earlier, but they are summarized here.

Insurance

Many older Americans do not qualify for Medicare or Medicaid, and therefore remain personally responsible for the cost of their health care. To meet these potential financial obligations, many persons maintain private health insurance coverage, which may vary from an overall, major medical health insurance policy; to supplemental insurance for care not covered by Medicare or Medicaid; to long-term insurance in case the insured requires extensive, extended medical care. Several factors must be considered when deciding on a particular insurance policy:

1. The cost of the premium. Private health insurance premiums can be quite high, and therefore many individuals try to find a group that they can join to acquire group health insurance, which typically has lower premiums.

2. The amount of the deductible. All health insurance policies include a deductible, a specified dollar amount of health care costs that the insured must pay for personally each year before the insurance benefits take over. Generally, the smaller the deductible, the higher the premium.

3. The amount of the co-payments. Co-payments represent the portion of the health care costs for which the individual remains personally responsible; it is usually the portion for which a person acquires supplemental health insurance coverage.

4. Managed care. Health insurance that provides for managed care (usually through an HMO) is typically less expensive, but the care may be limited to a particular facility or specified types of treatment.

Government Benefits

For all individuals who are entitled to Social Security retirement or disability benefits, the government provides a government health insurance policy under the provisions of Medicare Part A and Part B. Part A only covers certain hospital and health care facility services. If the individual wishes more coverage, he or she can elect Part B coverage, which applies to specified physician and diagnostic treatment—but the government charges a premium for such coverage. Low-income individuals who meet specified financial tests are entitled to receive Medicaid. which provides greater health care coverage than Medicare, and these individuals are also permitted to maintain limited private health insurance coverage within Medicaid guidelines.

Viatical Settlements

Viatical settlement refers to the sale of a life insurance policy to a individual or institution that will pay the insured a lump sum in return for being named the beneficiary under the policy. The insured may then use this lump sum for medical treatment, although such use is not required.

Typically, for an insured to avail himself or herself of a viatical agreement, the following criteria must be met:

1. The insured must be terminally ill with a life expectancy of no more than two years.
2. The policy must have been in effect for at least two years prior to the viatical settlement.
3. The policy must be assignable.
4. The insured must obtain releases from all beneficiaries.
5. The insured must release all medical records to the purchaser.
6. The insured and the purchaser must enter into a written agreement.

As of January 1, 1997, the proceeds that the insured receives from a viatical settlement are not subject to federal income tax, but each state determines the taxability of such payments for state income tax purposes. To fall within the federal tax exemption, the viatical purchaser must be a **qualified viatical settlement company**, which is a person or company who regularly purchases or takes assignment of life insurance policies of the terminally ill and is licensed by the state in which the insured lives, or meets the requirements established by the **Viatical Settlement Model Act.**

Another option that is similar to the viatical settlement is known as an **accelerated death benefit**. The insured receives a portion of the face value of the life insurance policy from the original insurer, and the remaining face value stays in effect for the benefit of the named beneficiaries upon the insured's death. Also, under certain life insurance policies, an insured may have the right to borrow against the policy, which thereby acts as an additional source of funds that may be used for medical care should such financial need arise.

viatical settlement Agreement whereby a terminally ill insured person accepts a lump sum from a purchaser who becomes the beneficiary of the insured's life insurance policy.

qualified viatical settlement company Person or company that is licensed by a state or meets the requirements of the Viatical Settlement Model Act; payments received by the insured from such companies exempt from federal income tax.

Viatical Settlement Model Act Model act designed to regulate viatical settlements.

accelerated death benefit Portion of the face value of a life insurance policy paid to the insured, the remainder of the face value remaining in effect for the named beneficiaries.

Taxes

Income taxes levied by the government are the source of funds for the government benefit programs, such as Medicare and Medicaid, that enable many Americans to receive medical care. This is a form of federal health insurance premium payment and the primary source of most Americans' health care coverage.

Also, employers are given a tax break, in the form of an expense deduction from taxable income, for premiums they pay for health insurance for the benefit of employees. In this fashion the government encourages employers to maintain private health insurance to assure that working Americans are able to access adequate health care.

ETHICAL CONSIDERATIONS

Access to health care is one of the primary challenges for older Americans today. The United States is virtually the only industrialized nation that does not provide universal health care for its citizens and lawful residents, and even the benefits that are provided by federal programs tend to be designed to meet immediate medical problems rather than to provide preventative care.

To reduce the cost of medical care, the government has been attempting to limit the number and nature of the treatment patients receive under federal programs, which can have the effect of denying appropriate care to needy individuals. Furthermore, programs such as the Medicaid Prospective Payment System may have the effect of denying treatment to patients so that the provider can make a profit.

Even though the law permits a person to transfer assets in order to qualify for benefits, the law also imposes criminal sanctions if the attorney alerts his or her client to this aspect of the law. The law thus penalizes the legal professional for advising a client as to the provisions of the law. Query: Can this situation be logically and ethically supported?

The premium rates for private health insurance rise dramatically each year, and many Americans find themselves unable to afford costly private policies. For the elderly, groups such as the American Association of Retired Persons (AARP) offer group insurance to keep premium costs down (available to Americans over the age of 50), but even such reduced premiums may be beyond the reach of elderly persons on very limited incomes.

The unwillingness to provide adequate health care at financially reasonable rates typifies the modern American attitude of younger generations with respect to the elderly. The ethical and moral implications of these choices will only become more obvious as the population continues to age.

CHAPTER REVIEW

There are two important considerations with respect to health care for the elderly: the person's ability to make a competent health care decision and the person's ability to finance the health care he or she has decided upon.

All information required by law to be given to an individual, so that he or she may make an informed decision with respect to the nature or extent of the care he or she will receive, is rendered meaningless if the person lacks the mental ability to comprehend the information or make such decisions. If a person is not legally competent to decide health care matters personally, the court may appoint a guardian for the individual, legally authorized to make such decisions for the incompetent person, or the individual may execute an advance directive at a time when he or she is deemed legally competent to execute such documents. Health care proxies are usually given effect, because they appoint someone to make decisions on behalf of a person who can no longer speak for himself or herself. However, living wills and do-not-resuscitate orders are only evidence of intent and may not be honored.

Two primary sources are used to finance health care: government transfer payments and private insurance policies. The government payments take the form of Medicare for all Social Security retirement and disability benefits recipients (retirees over the age of 65), and Medicaid benefits for persons who qualify under strict financial limitation requirements. For persons who do not qualify for either form of governmental medical care, private insurance companies offer various forms of health insurance to finance health care costs.

The legal assistant will be called upon to assist the attorney in preparing all applications for governmental health benefits and, if the benefits are denied, to assist in the appeals process, including potential court litigation. The elder law paralegal will also be required to review health care contracts to determine client rights and obligations thereunder.

KEY TERMS

accelerated death benefit

assignment

conservator

cost-basis HMO

employer group health plan
(EGHP)

fair hearing

general enrollment period

guardian

guardian of the estate

guardian of the person

Health Care Finance
Administration (HCFA)

health maintenance organization
(HMO)

hospice

initial enrollment period

limited guardian

long-term care insurance

look-back period

managed care

Medical Assistance Utilization
Threshold Program (MUTS)

Medi-gap insurance

nursing home

Nursing Home Reform Act
(NHRA)

Omnibus Budget Reconciliation
Act (OBRA)

open enrollment

override application

plenary guardian

qualified viatical settlement
company

risk HMO

special enrollment period

spend-down program

supplemental insurance

surplus income

viatical settlement

Viatical Settlement Model Act

EXERCISES

1. Obtain a copy of a health insurance contract and analyze its provisions.

2. Draft a health care proxy and a living will.

3. Obtain a copy of a nursing home contract and analyze its provisions.

4. What is your opinion of the managed care system? Draft a model statute that could be used to determine an insured's managed-care rights and obligations.

5. Check your state statutes for regulations regarding nursing homes. What, if any, changes would you make to the regulation of such entities? Explain.

EDITED JUDICIAL DECISIONS

Duggan v. Bowen
691 F. Supp. 1487 (D.D.C. 1988)

Introduction

This case involves a challenge to the Department of Health and Human Services' ("HHS") administration of the Medicare home health care program. Plaintiffs take issue with the agency's interpretation and application of the "part-time or intermittent" care provision. I agree with plaintiffs that defendants' policy is contrary to the plain language of the Medicare Act and was promulgated in violation of the procedures required by the Administrative Procedure Act. Appropriate relief requires the certification of a nationwide class, the issuance of a declaratory order and the imposition of an injunction against further implementation of the challenged policy.

The named plaintiffs are seventeen elderly and sick Medicare patients, an association of home health care agencies, National Association for Home Care ("NAHC"), individual home health care agencies, and several members of Congress. They have brought this lawsuit on behalf of a nationwide class of elderly Medicare patients whom they claim are being injured by HHS' unlawful restriction of home health care coverage.

Plaintiffs lodge two separate but related causes of action. First, plaintiffs assert that HHS is using an unlawfully narrow definition of "part-time or intermittent care"—especially at the initial coverage determination stage of the four-step Medicare reimbursement process-to deny home health care benefits to deserving patients. Second, plaintiffs charge that HHS "has abdicated its legal responsibility and thwarted the Medicare statute by delegating primary decision making authority to private fiscal intermediaries without adequate supervision or regulatory mandate." Complaint at 6.

Plaintiffs contend that the upshot of their first cause of action is the unfair denial of benefits to a large class of elderly patients—especially those that lack the financial means, physical and emotional strength and tenacity to pursue an appeal of an initial declination of coverage. They claim that the prime product of HHS' wrongful delegation of authority to private intermediaries is a standardless system of ad hoc decision making which leads to irrational, contradictory and unexplained home health care coverage determinations. Complaint at 6.

For their part, defendants contend that "plaintiffs raise vague, abstract, overbroad, premature and conflicting claims . . ." and "fail to present a specific, concrete controversy appropriate for resolution by this Court." Defendants' Motion to Dismiss at 1. Defendants have interposed the usual procedural defenses in order to stop plaintiffs from receiving a hearing on the merits. For instance, defendants maintain that none of the plaintiffs has standing, that plaintiffs' claims are not ripe for adjudication, that this court lacks subject matter jurisdiction to review plaintiffs' claims, and that plaintiffs' claims are moot. Defendants also contest plaintiffs' charges on the merits.

Plaintiffs' causes of action are in very different procedural postures. Plaintiffs' "part-time or intermittent" care claim has been the subject of extensive briefing, a bench trial and several oral arguments. It is ripe for judgment. On the other hand, the broader "wrongful delegation" claim has now been stayed (before the completion of discovery) pursuant to the joint motion of the parties. See Order, May 16, 1988. Hence, this Memorandum Opinion and Order will focus exclusively on plaintiffs' part time or intermittent care claim; it constitutes my Findings of Fact and Conclusions of Law pursuant to Fed. R. Civ. P. 52(a).

At stake in this case are fundamental issues of judicial review, administrative law, statutory interpretation and most importantly, the access of elderly, sick and needy individuals to much-needed medical care.

OVERVIEW

A. The Medicare Program and the Home Health Benefit

The Medicare program, established by Title XVIII of the Social Security Act, *42 U.S.C. §§ 1395 et seq.*, is a system of health insurance for the aged and disabled. See generally Social Security Amendments of 1965, Pub. L. No. 89-97, Title I, 79 Stat. 286 (1965). It is administered by HHS through the Health Care Financing Administration ("HCFA"). The Medicare program consists of two basic parts. Medicare Part A provides coverage for the costs incurred by eligible beneficiaries for hospital care, extended care and home health care. See generally *42 U.S.C. §§ 1395c to 1395i-2.* Medicare Part B is a voluntary program in which eligible beneficiaries who pay a monthly premium are entitled to reimbursement for physicians' and other medical services. See generally *42 U.S.C. §§ 1395j-1395w.*

This case involves Medicare Part A. Services are provided under Part A by home health agencies ("HHAs") which enter into agreements with the Secretary to provide health care to persons eligible for Medicare. HHAs provide Part A services in patients' homes rather than in an institutional setting for two principal reasons—first, home services are more humane, and secondly, they are more economical. Home health services include: part-time or intermittent nursing care provided by or under the supervision of a registered nurse; physical, occupational or speech therapy; medical social services under the direction of a physician; and part-time or intermittent services of a home health aide. See *42 U.S.C. § 1395x(m).*

Under the Medicare Act a beneficiary must meet certain conditions to receive home health care coverage. The patient must need skilled care while "confined to his home." *42 U.S.C. § 1395f(a)(2)(C).* The care must be medically "reasonable and necessary." *42 U.S.C. § 1395y(a)(1)(A).* In addition, Medicare coverage for home health care is limited to the "part-time or intermittent" care of a nurse and/or a home health aide. *42 U.S.C. § 1395x(m)(1) and (4).*

Plaintiffs and defendants agree that the "part-time or intermittent" care requirement is derived from the statutory definition of "home health services." The legislative history makes it clear that Congress intended the part-time or intermittent requirement to exclude more or less full-time care. The relevant House and Senate Reports provide an identical description of home health care covered by Medicare:

> Covered Service.—The proposed post-hospital home health payment would meet the cost of part-time or intermittent nursing services, physical occupational, and speech therapy, and other related home health services furnished by visiting nurse agencies, hospital based home health programs and similar agencies. More or less full-time nursing care would not be paid for under the home health benefits provision.

See H.R. Rep. No. 213, 89th Cong. 1st Sess. 29 (1965) and S. Rep. No. 404, 89th Cong., 1st Sess. 32 (1965) (emphasis added).

The rationale for such an exclusion was simple: full time care generally would be provided more humanely and economically in an institutional setting. The dispute between the parties centers on what care is "part-time or intermittent" and hence appropriately rendered in the home, and what care is "full-time" and hence better provided in an institutional setting. Succinctly stated, plaintiffs have a different conception of what care qualifies as "part-time or intermittent" from that of defendants. The answer to this dispute, as discussed below, is found in the legislative history and the plain language and structure of the Medicare Act.

B. The Administrative Process

Pursuant to his responsibility to determine benefits claims under Medicare Part A "in accordance with regulations prescribed by him," *42 U.S.C. § 1395ff(a)*, the Secretary of HHS has delegated much of the day-to-day administration of the Medicare Part A program to private fiscal intermediaries. The Secretary has also issued regulations which provide that private intermediaries—typically insurance companies—make the initial determination as to whether a particular service is covered by Medicare Part A. The Secretary had contracted with 47 different private intermediaries at the start of 1987, but was ordered by Congress to reduce the number of regional intermediaries to no more than ten by July 1, 1987. See Deficit Reduction Act of 1984, Pub. L. No. 98-369, § 2326(b) (codified at *42 U.S.C. § 1395h(e)(4)).*

The beneficiary has the right to appeal the private intermediary's initial coverage determination to the HCFA. The beneficiary has the right to pursue his or her appeal, if refused by the HCFA, before an Administrative Law Judge (ALJ), and ultimately to HHS' highest administrative appeals forum, the Appeals Council. Finally, if the beneficiary's claim exceeds $1,000, he or she has the right to judicial review of the Secretary's final decision in the same manner as is provided in 42 U.S.C. § 405(g) for social security claimants. See *42 U.S.C. § 1395ff(b)(2); 42 C.F.R. § 405.730; 20 C.F.R. §§ 404.981, 422.210.*

The Procedural History of this Litigation

This lawsuit was filed by plaintiffs on February 17, 1987. They filed a motion for partial summary judgment regarding their claim that defendants' definition of "part time or intermittent care" was erroneous. After the motion was fully briefed, I held a hearing on July 1, 1987.

At that hearing, plaintiffs contended that HHS' "part time or intermittent" care policy is applied substantially more restrictively, in effect requiring a Medicare patient to demonstrate a need for both "part time and intermittent care." By merging those two separate concepts, plaintiffs contended, HHS unduly restricts eligibility for home health coverage. In addition, plaintiffs claimed that defendants' policy mandates that "daily" services provided more than four times a week be excluded from Medicare home health care coverage because such services are not "intermittent" or "part-time." Defendants considered home health care in excess of four days per week to be "daily" care. According to plaintiffs, the bottom line effect of defendants' interpretation of the "part time or intermittent care" requirement was that HHS did not cover home health aide services if they were

required more than four days a week-regardless of the number of hours per day the Medicare patient needed such care.

Defendants took issue with the accuracy of plaintiffs' description of their policies and alleged that plaintiffs misunderstood their policy. Transcript at 27 and 31 ("They're mischaracterizing what the policy actually is."). According to defendants:

> Defendants' policy on intermittent or part-time home health care is a long-standing one. It's been in effect in its present substance since 1966. ... It doesn't say what plaintiffs claim it does.

Id. at 28. Defendants' counsel adamantly insisted at this initial hearing that HHS' policy has been unchanged since 1966 and that HHS' current policy did not include any "rule of thumb" that intermediaries should deny home health care benefits to those (otherwise eligible) individuals needing services more than four days per week. After this hearing, seizing on the apparent possibility that this lawsuit arose from their misunderstanding of defendants' policies, plaintiffs proposed the following stipulation:

> The Medicare Act provides for part-time or intermittent skilled nursing and home health aide services. See *42 U.S.C. § 1395x(m)(1), (4).*
> Skilled nursing and home health aide services are covered under Medicare as long as they are part-time in nature, regardless of how many days per week they are medically necessary.

See Proposed Stipulated Partial Summary Judgment. Defendants rejected this proposal. It is thus clear to me that defendants have not been forthcoming about their position despite their protestations that they have no policy which would preclude such an interpretation.

Accordingly, based on the foregoing, and after reviewing the parties' briefs and the oral argument, I came to the conclusion that material issues of fact needed to be resolved in order to decide the "part-time or intermittent" care issue. In particular, I found that Defendants' Statement of Genuine Issues set forth crucial factual issues which had to be settled. According to defendants, the following assertions made by plaintiffs were actually disputed issues of fact which were material to resolving plaintiffs' motion for partial summary judgment:

1. That "defendants' policy mandates care in excess of four times per week is to be considered 'daily' care."
2. That "defendants' policy, with a limited exception for short-term services generally of a 2–3 week period, excludes 'daily' care from Medicare home health coverage."
3. That "defendants' policy mandates that a Medicare patient demonstrate a need for part-time and intermittent care."
4. That the Appeals Council "has ruled that 'part-time' daily home health aide services are covered without limitation occasioned by defendants' intermittent care policy."

Defendants' Statement of Genuine Issues (filed May 1, 1987); see also Plaintiffs' Memorandum in Support of Proposed Findings of Fact and Conclusions of Law at 3–4. Defendants contended that none of these assertions were true. Because these vigorously contested factual issues went right to the heart of plaintiffs' claims, I issued an Order scheduling an evidentiary hearing to consider HHS' policy regarding "part-time" or "intermittent" care. See Order, November 20, 1987 at 3.

The evidentiary hearing was held on February 3, 1988. The plaintiffs presented six witnesses, including Thomas Hoyer, the Director of the Division of Provider Services Coverage Policy in the Bureau of Eligibility and Reimbursement Coverage in HCFA (and the individual in HHS primarily responsible for the policies at issue). Plaintiffs submitted 29 exhibits into evidence, including the affidavits of several home health care providers. Defendants did not present any witnesses, but they submitted four exhibits, including three excerpts from administrative materials and information regarding the denial of coverage of one of the named plaintiffs (Lorraine Lis). After the hearing, the parties submitted post-trial briefs and proposed findings of fact and conclusions of law. A final oral argument was held on March 31, 1988.

Upon consideration of the full record of this case, including the testimony and exhibits offered at the evidentiary hearing, the post trial briefs and the closing oral argument, I enter the following findings of fact and conclusions of law.

FINDINGS OF FACT

A. The Evolution of the Part-time or Intermittent Care Policy

1. The Medicare Act was enacted by Congress in 1965 to provide eligible elderly and disabled persons access to necessary health services such as the home health care services at issue in this case. Eligible Medicare beneficiaries are entitled to home health care services including "part-time or intermittent" skilled nursing care and "part-time or intermittent" home health aide care. *42 U.S.C. § 1395x(m)(1,4).* See supra, pp. 5–6, n.3. Congress has not changed the governing statutory language since the Act's passage.

2. The only published regulations dealing with home health care essentially track the statutory language by providing for "part-time or intermittent" care. See *42 C.F.R. § 409.40 (1987).*

3. The bulk of defendants' policy statements regarding the home health care benefit are found in manuals and transmittals. None of these policies has been subject to public notice and comment.

4. The principal home health care manuals are entitled Health Insurance Manual ("HIM")-11 and HIM-13. See Hoyer Deposition (Plaintiffs' Exhibit 1) at 13–14. The relevant coverage criteria in these two manuals are essentially the same, and hereafter I will refer solely to HIM-11.

5. The first version of HIM-11 provided that:

> Part-time or intermittent care is usually services for a few hours a day several times a week. Occasionally, service for a full day may be provided for a short period when, because of unusual circumstances, neither the alternative of part-time care nor hospitalization is feasible.

HIM-11 § 205.1, at 14 (1966) (Plaintiff's Exhibit 3); see also Defendant's Post-Hearing Brief at 3.

6. In mid-1966, defendants' predecessors proposed regulations for public notice and comment. They provided, in relevant part:

c. Definition of part-time or intermittent.

Most patients will require service a few hours a day, several times a week. Some may require longer service on one day than on other days and such adjustments are to be encouraged. Occasionally, service for a full day may need to be provided for a short time when, because of unusual circumstances, neither the alternative or part-time care nor hospitalization is feasible.

31 Fed. Reg. 7143, 7145 (May 14, 1966) (proposed to be codified as new 20 C.F.R. § 405.1224(c)) (Plaintiffs' Exhibit 3); see also Defendants' Post-Hearing Brief at 3, n.3. The final regulation provided a substantively similar definition for "part-time or intermittent." *33 Fed. Reg. 12,090, 12,093* (Aug. 27, 1968) (codified at 20 C.F.R. § 405.1224(c)) (Plaintiffs' Exhibit 4); see also Defendants' Post-Hearing Brief at 3, n.3.

7. HEW deleted this definition of "part-time or intermittent care" from its regulations in 1971. See Fed. Reg. 18,696 (Sept. 18, 1971). Defendants have offered no explanation for this action. There are currently no published regulations defining "part-time or intermittent care."

8. In 1968, HEW issued a transmittal which stated that: "Part-time or intermittent home health aide services are defined to permit up to 20 hours of service in each week and up to 4 hours of home health aide care in a day (which may constitute one or more visits)." Plaintiffs' Exhibit 6 (March 29, 1968 letter from Thomas M. Tierney, Director, Bureau of Health Insurance, to Merritt W. Jacoby, Blue Cross Association, setting forth interim operating guideline). An attachment to the "Tierney letter" indicated that the transmittal did not establish limits, but rather, set forth guidelines. According to Tierney, "there are some situations where longer periods of service can be justified." Id.

9. In 1975, HEW issued a revised version of HIM-II which reflected the Tierney letter and other transmittals issued during the late 1960s and early 1970s. It provided, in relevant part, as follows:

206.6   Part-Time or Intermittent Services.—

Part-time or intermittent services of professional personnel and home health aides is usually service for a few hours a day several times a week. Occasionally, more service, i.e., 8 hours may be provided for a limited period when the physician recommends and, when because of unusual circumstances, neither the alternative of part-time care nor institutionalization is feasible … .

Home health aide visits usually will be provided two or three times a week for several hours. Thus, most agencies average 20 hours or less a week for the Medicare case load. This average reflects the planning and flexibility needed to provide up to 8 hours a day, 5 days a week, for a few very ill patients who need extensive care and have no family member present during the day.

In recognition of the span of normal practice followed in home care, reimbursement may ordinarily be made for up to 100 hours a month of home health aide service assuming no question exists regarding the coverage status of such services. By the same token, on an intermittent basis, service for up to 8 hours a day, 5 days a week, may be provided when medically necessary due to unusual circumstances, e.g., the patient has just returned from the hospital and must be oriented, along with his family, to various aspects of home care; the patient's condition is terminal; or he has suffered a relapse.

HIM-11 § 206.6 (Plaintiffs' Exhibit 8) (emphasis added).

10. Hence, prior to 1980, defendants' predecessors imposed no limits on the number of days a week an otherwise eligible beneficiary could receive home health services. See Hoyer Testimony, Transcript at 16. For instance, the agency would reimburse a patient for twenty hours of care rendered over the course of a week even if such care was provided on each of the seven days of the week. See Hoyer Testimony, Transcript at 29–32; Plaintiffs' Exhibit 6. Such care, although "daily" and therefore not "intermittent," would be eligible for coverage under the "part-time" prong of the statutory provision. On the other hand, services needed more than eight hours per day were considered full-time and not part-time in nature. The central and prevailing theme common to the

pre-1980 regulatory statements was to distinguish between full-time care and part-time services.

11. In a May 1981 transmittal, HHS deleted the part of the HIM-II instruction which stated that "most agencies average 20 hours or less a week for the Medicare case load and that reimbursement could be made for up to 100 hours a month of home health services, since these figures were being erroneously applied in cases where less service was needed." Plaintiffs' Exhibit 9. The 1981 transmittal did not impose any hourly ceilings on services nor did it alter the prior 100 hours of services per month guideline. Rather, it stressed the need to make a case-by-case determination of whether a patient needed certain services. Hoyer Deposition (Plaintiffs' Exhibit 1) at 36–37.

12. In June 1984, HCFA issued a transmittal given nationwide effect which provided that "daily skilled nursing care of an indefinite duration will not be considered to meet the intermittent requirement and such services are not covered under the Medicare home health benefit." Plaintiffs' Exhibit 12. A few months later, defendants instructed all Medicare fiscal intermediaries that "Medicare coverage for daily home health aide services are subject to the same intermittent guidelines as skilled nursing care." See Plaintiffs' Exhibit 13 (Transmittal dated November 20, 1984). The effect of these transmittals was to restrict Medicare coverage of home health services. This was a drastic change from prior requirements.

13. In a November 14, 1986 letter, defendants further significantly restricted coverage of home health services. In that letter, which is the central document of this litigation, Robert Streimer, the Acting Director of the Bureau of Eligibility, Reimbursement and Coverage, responded to questions raised on behalf of all ten regional fiscal intermediaries about the concept of "daily" by stating:

> You indicated that whether the term ["daily"] is defined as 5 days or 7 days makes a tremendous difference in both whether beneficiaries qualify for home health services and in the nature of the skilled nursing and home health services available to them. ...

> ... we expect that daily would be defined as 5 days per week in most localities. ... We believe that it is appropriate to define "daily" as 5 days per week. Therefore, care which is ordered 5, 6 or 7 days per week would be considered "daily" care within the context of the Q and A discussion of "intermittent."

"Streimer Letter" to Mary Townsend, Manager, Department of Operations, Blue Cross and Blue Shield Association (Plaintiffs' Exhibit 14). Although in form an informal "transmittal," Mr. Streimer's new interpretation of the term "daily" is in effect a determination of defendants. Moreover, his interpretation represented a marked substantive break with the agency's past understanding and application of this crucial term. The rigid and narrow definition of "daily" set forth by Mr. Streimer is inconsistent with the agency's longstanding interpretation of the home health care benefit and contrary to law and congressional intent.

14. Mr. Hoyer's testimony confirmed and amplified the Streimer letter. See Transcript at 18, 35–37. Although his testimony was at times contradictory, when his statements are considered in conjunction with plaintiffs' exhibits, it is clear that plaintiffs' characterization of the agency's policies is accurate. As plaintiffs contended throughout these proceedings, defendants' current policy regarding "part-time and intermittent care" is as follows:

> a. Defendants define part-time to include anything less than eight hours of services in any given day regardless of the number of visits in a given day. Hoyer Testimony, Transcript at 18, 35.

> b. The agency considers care to be intermittent only if it is not "daily."

> c. Since November 14, 1986, the date of the Streimer letter, defendants have defined "daily" to be five, six or seven days a week. Intermittent care is therefore limited to care that is rendered in one, two, three or four days per week. Hoyer Testimony, Transcript at 18–20, 26, 36; Plaintiffs' Exhibit 14 at 2; Plaintiffs' Exhibit 15.

d. Even if the amount of care rendered is only four or five hours per week, if it is administered during five separate days it is not eligible for coverage under defendants' policy. Because such care is "daily" and hence not "intermittent," it is ineligible. Id.

e. Defendants' policy therefore denies Medicare coverage, for instance, to individuals needing five or six hours of care per week if it is needed at the rate of one hour for each of five or six days. In contrast, an individual needing seven hours of care a day for four days per week is eligible for coverage.

The bottom line is that defendants' interpretation of the terms "daily," "part-time" and "intermittent" can result in coverage for people needing as much as 28 hours of care in a week yet deny coverage to a person needing as little as five or six hours of care per week. Hoyer Testimony, Transcript at 14; see also Hoyer Deposition (Plaintiffs' Exhibit 1) at 69–73.

f. Defendants interpret the disjunctive statutory phrase "part-time or intermittent" care as if it were written "part-time and intermittent" care. They only provide coverage if a patient meets both criteria. See Hoyer Testimony, Transcript at 24, 41, 42; see also Deposition of Stanton J. Collins, Jr., Associate Regional Administrator for Health Standards and Quality, Boston Regional Office of HCFA (Plaintiffs' Exhibit 16) at 39–43.

g. Hence, defendants require care to be both part-time (less than eight hours per day) and intermittent (four or less days per week) for individuals to receive the home health care benefit.

15. The administrative standards represented by the Streimer letter and Mr. Hoyer's testimony are significantly more restrictive than the guidelines that prevailed since the program's inception in 1966. Many individuals presently being denied coverage for home health care services would have been covered under the agency's earlier interpretations of the "part-time or intermittent" care requirement.

16. Defendants' current home health care policy conflicts not only with the plain meaning of the statute and Congress' intent to provide part-time home health care coverage for those individuals who did not need to be institutionalized but also with the regulatory standards established in the 1960s and 1970s.

B. The Application and Consequences of Defendants' New Policy

17. Defendants' new part-time or intermittent care policy has the force of law. It binds the fiscal intermediaries who make all initial coverage determinations and reconsideration decisions. While defendants' counsel has characterized HCFA directives to fiscal intermediaries as nonbinding, Mr. Hoyer candidly admitted HCFA's expectation that fiscal intermediaries would follow HCFA transmittals. See e.g. Hoyer Deposition (Plaintiffs' Exhibit 1) at 55. Failure to adhere to agency transmittals could result in the termination of the federal contract under which an intermediary is hired. Hoyer Testimony, transcript at 48. In practical terms, fiscal intermediaries cannot ignore agency transmittals. Id.

Actual experience indicates that the fiscal intermediaries have followed the policy outlined in the Streimer letter apparently without deviation. Plaintiffs have submitted into evidence numerous examples of fiscal intermediary denials in conformity with the Streimer letter and the policies outlined by Mr. Hoyer. See e.g. Testimony of Edward Dale, Director of Legal Assistance to Medicare Patients, for Connecticut Legal Services, Transcript at 91–92 ("any time a patient required ... five or more days a week of nursing services, part-time nursing services or part-time home health aide services ... they will be uniformly denied on the basis of HCFA's interpretation of the intermittency requirement ..."); see also Plaintiffs' Exhibits 18–29 (collecting examples of fiscal intermediary denials of coverage on the basis of the challenged policy; also collecting affidavits from home health care providers attesting to effect of agency's policy; listing numerous concrete individual examples of how the policy has cut off part-time care).

I find that the individual cases of, for instance, Anna Mazzola, Lorraine Lis, Katherine Duggan, and the cases outlined in the affidavits of health care providers (Plaintiffs' Exhibits 21–29), are credible and provide powerful and conclusive evidence that the Streimer letter and other HHS transmittals have been uniformly applied with the force of law. Those materials present the stories of many individuals who have been denied coverage for plainly part-time home health care because such care was needed more than four days per week. See e.g. Affidavit of Ms. Josephine Sienkiewicz, R.N., M.S.N. (Plaintiffs' Exhibit 22). Ms. Sienkiewicz, the Director of Friends Home Health Care, a nonprofit home health agency in New Jersey, discusses the cases of Mr. Harold Galbraith, Ms. Antoinette Roberson, Ms. Helen Fenton and Mr. Stephen Karandovski, among others, all of whom would have been covered under defendants' part-time and intermittent care policy during the 1960s and 1970s, but who have been denied coverage by fiscal intermediaries pursuant to the Streimer letter and other recent transmittals.

The case of one of her patients, Mr. Galbraith, is particularly instructive. He is a paraplegic who has a history of severe skin ulcers and also requires a foley catheter. He requires the services of a home health aide for one hour per day five days a week to supplement his once or twice-weekly skilled nursing care. The aide only spends five hours per week helping Mr. Galbraith. With the help of the aide Mr. Galbraith has managed to use a wheelchair and has achieved some independence at his home and has avoided going to an institution. Defendants have denied coverage for the aide services for the stated reason that the services are not part-time or intermittent.

There can be no doubt that such services previously would have been eligible for coverage. Defendants' present policies, typified by the Streimer letter, have foreclosed such coverage.

Despite my request that they search for such evidence, defendants have provided no examples of a fiscal intermediary acting contrary to the challenged policies. I therefore find that various HCFA transmittals, including the Streimer letter and Plaintiffs' Exhibits 12 and 15, function to prohibit fiscal intermediaries from allowing payment for part-time home health care which is needed more than four days a week (for an indefinite term).

18. The evidence indicates that if a Medicare beneficiary appeals the denial of coverage for part-time daily health services to an administrative law judge ("ALJ"), the beneficiary will almost always obtain a favorable ruling from the ALJ. The ALJs almost uniformly conclude that part-time, daily home health services are covered by Medicare. Hoyer Testimony, Transcript at 49–50; Dale Testimony, Transcript at 83–87 (reporting "18 for 18" record on such ALJ cases involving the "part-time or intermittent" care requirement); Plaintiffs' Exhibits 18–21, 29 (collecting successful cases).

19. Furthermore, the Appeals Council has ruled that part-time home health services are covered without limitation on how many days per week they are provided. The Appeals Council has therefore construed the relevant statutory provision in direct contravention to defendants' recent transmittals. See e.g., Dale Testimony, Transcript at 85; Collins Deposition (Plaintiffs' Exhibit 16) at 36–39. Defendants have not altered or apparently even reconsidered their policy since the Appeals Council's rulings. Rather, defendants have blatantly ignored the Appeals Council's ruling and it is clear that without the intervention of this court, defendants will continue to interpret the law according to the Streimer letter and in clear defiance of the administrative adjudications.

20. Defendants' refusal to implement the Appeals Council's interpretation of the "part-time or intermittent" care requirement and their continued adherence to the challenged policies is having a devastating impact on those individuals who are unable, because of their age, infirmities, isolation or other reasons to appeal an adverse claim determination. As Mr. Hoyer admitted, the effect of defendants' refusal to acquiesce in the rulings of either the ALJs or the Appeals Council (or to pay any attention to the havoc being wrought on home health care providers and beneficiaries) is that individuals must continuously appeal to ALJs to obtain their deserved benefits. Those that have insufficient energy or resources to appeal simply

fall by the wayside. See generally Dale Testimony, Transcript at 83–88.

21. Even for those who are capable of appealing an adverse decision, a victorious appeal does not safeguard a beneficiary from future denials. Defendants do not give prospective effect to ALJ decisions rejecting their "part-time or intermittent" care policy. As a result, many individuals who have successfully appealed an initial denial to an ALJ are needlessly forced to repeat such appeals. The experiences of Anna Mazzola, Lorraine Lis and Katherine Duggan typify this problem. See e.g. Plaintiffs' Exhibit 20 (collection of ALJ decisions favorable to Anna Mazzola); see also Dale Testimony, Transcript at 83–86 (describing series of successful appeals by Ms. Mazzola followed inevitably by another denial by her fiscal intermediary of coverage for part-time or intermittent services; patient eventually died after her fourth successful appeal—at her death she was owed reimbursement for services for which her family paid because Medicare had refused payment).

22. Defendants' challenged policy has caused irreparable harm to many Medicare beneficiaries. Because defendants are unwilling to provide part-time daily home health services, many people needlessly have been forced to make the cruel choice between foregoing needed care or submitting to institutionalization in a nursing home or hospital. For many of these people, such a choice hurts both them and the public Treasury. Institutionalization of these people in a hospital or nursing home costs substantially more than would coverage of a home health aide—yet such institutionalization is harmful to both the patient and his or her family.

The testimony of the lead plaintiff's 83-year-old husband, Mr. William Duggan, and the corroborating testimony of Ms. Mary Faye Verville, Executive Director of Goldcoast Home Health Services, the nonprofit home health care agency that served the Duggans, vividly portrays the irreparable harm that can be caused by defendants' challenged policy. Mrs. Duggan was diagnosed as having Alzheimer's disease and needed skilled nursing care twice a month to service a foley catheter and to care for urinary tract infections. Verville Testimony, transcript at 126–27. She also needed the help of a home health aide six days a week for an hour and a half a day. Id. at 126–28. She received such services beginning in April, 1981. The aide provided personal care, bathing, female hygiene, skin care, range of motion and assistance in getting going for the day after the care had been completed. Id. Because Mr. Duggan has cardiac problems, the home health aide was essential. Id. Without it, Mrs. Duggan would have had no choice but to enter a nursing home. Duggan Testimony, Transcript at 134-36. With it, she was able to remain at home. Id.

Defendants covered the Duggans' home health aide services for six days a week until June 30, 1986. See Plaintiffs' Exhibit 18. The Duggans abruptly were denied coverage for the services of their home health aide during the month of July, 1986 because their fiscal intermediary claimed the care was not "part-time or intermittent" in nature—even though "the actual services received by [the Duggans] ... were similar in nature to those as had been previously rendered" for the past five years. Plaintiffs' Exhibit 18; see also Verville Testimony, Transcript at 128. The coverage denial caused the Duggans emotional and financial distress. The denial of coverage for these vital services also would have necessitated the institutionalization of Ms. Duggan, and her concomitant separation from Mr. Duggan, had not a generous benefactor fortunately intervened. The Duggans appealed the denial to an ALJ and prevailed at an administrative hearing—a year later. See Plaintiffs' Exhibit 18; Verville Testimony, Transcript at 129 30. Without the intervention of the benefactor, Mrs. Duggan either would have had to forego medically necessary services because she could not afford it, or she would have had to have been institutionalized. Had she foregone medically necessary care, she would have been at risk of adverse medical consequences.

The case of Mrs. Judy Wilson of Binghamton, New York, outlined in the Affidavit of Elaine Petrozello, Reimbursement Coordinator, Twin Tier Home Health, (Plaintiffs' Exhibit 25), corroborates the Duggans' story and provides further insight into the effects of defendants' policy. Mrs. Wilson has a severe degenerative disorder which has left her bedbound. See Plaintiffs' Exhibit 25; Plaintiffs' Memorandum in Support of Proposed Findings of Fact and Conclusions of Law at 2. While her husband works and her children attend school, she requires the attention of a home health aide. Id. She receives care one and a half hours per day, five days a week. Id. She has been denied coverage for these 6.5 hours because her home health services are provided more than four days a week. Id. Mrs. Wilson has been forced to forego home health services. The home health aides she has been able to pay for out of her own funds are poorly trained and are inadequate to meet her needs. Id. She has been and continues to be irreparably harmed by the challenged policy.

In her case, moreover, application of defendants' part-time or intermittent care policy has resulted in the total termination of her benefits because her needs allegedly exceed permissible limits. Id. In other words, defendants do not cover four days of services and separately deny the excess; they totally deny coverage. At a minimum, even accepting, arguendo, the parameters of defendants' challenged policy, Mrs. Wilson should receive coverage for four days of services each week. This plaintiff has been harmed to a degree well beyond the typical irreparable harm that is caused by defendants' policy. The government shall take steps to remedy this situation and must insure that others are not treated in such an inequitable manner. See also Plaintiffs' Exhibit 25 (describing case of Ms. Julia Brennan, an 86 year old female with Multiple Sclerosis, who was totally denied home health care coverage for 6.5 hours a week of home health care and cannot afford to finance replacement services).

Plaintiffs therefore have submitted extensive evidence that defendants' policy is having a widespread effect on Medicare beneficiaries who need part-time care more than four days a week. Defendants have submitted nothing to the contrary. I credit Mr. Duggan's testimony. I similarly credit Ms. Verville's testimony. I find the experience of the Duggans, Mrs. Wilson, and the experiences of the other individuals described in the evidentiary submissions representative of the experience of many other individuals similarly situated. Because of defendants' policy regarding part-time or intermittent care, they have been irreparably harmed. The upshot is that many patients have entered nursing homes and other institutions as an alternative to less costly home care. Testimony of Linda Gilmore, Executive Director, Chaves County Home Health Services, Transcript at 123. Others have overstayed in hospitals. Id. Others have foregone necessary care. Id. Still others may have given up the fight out of frustration. As a result, the government may have been improperly enriched on the backs of those in society who are the most vulnerable to being overreached.

23. Moreover, the lengthy process of obtaining a fair determination before an ALJ, coupled with defendants' policy of denying prospective effect to ALJ rulings exacerbates the physiological, emotional and financial implications for individuals denied coverage because of defendants' policy.

C. Class Action Findings

24. There are numerous elderly and disabled beneficiaries living throughout the United States who have been or will be denied Medicare coverage for part-time home health care services required more than four days a week. Dale Testimony, Transcript at 83.

The evidence submitted by plaintiffs resolves beyond any doubt that a large number of people have been denied coverage because of defendants' challenged part-time or intermittent care policy. See Plaintiffs' Exhibits 18–29 (discussing numerous cases around the country). Based on their submissions, it is apparent that thousands of people are affected by defendants' policy. Aside from legal arguments that would eradicate the "class," altogether, defendants have not provided me with anything that would suggest the policy affects a manageable number of people.

25. These people are typically old, infirm or disabled and in need of medically necessary care. See e.g. Testimony of Gloria Morris, mother of

Medicare beneficiary Anna Mazzola (see Plaintiffs' Exhibit 20), Transcript at 109 (Ms. Mazzola is a paraplegic and unable to attend judicial proceedings); Verville Testimony, Transcript at 126 (describing Mrs. Duggan's condition). They are often isolated and without ready access to legal assistance. Id. They are usually without the resources or the will to mount independently a "federal agency.["] Because they are scattered throughout the United States, it is impossible for these people to join in this action individually. Dale Testimony, Transcript at 91–92.

26. Defendants have adopted a policy of applying adjudicative rulings only to the individual named parties. Defendants' policy of "nonacquiescence" is articulated in the Home Health Agency Manual:

> A policy of the Supreme Court of the United States is unqualifiedly binding and is a precedent for all similar cases. A decision of a lower Federal Court is binding only for that case. Although other courts within the territorial jurisdiction of the court rendering the decision may use it as a precedent in similar cases, each case must be filed and an individual court decision made.

HIM-13 § 3788 (Exhibit 1 to Plaintiffs' Motion for Class Certification, filed April 3, 1987).

Hence, Medicare beneficiaries other than the named plaintiffs will be vulnerable to continued irreparable harm if a class is not certified.

CONCLUSIONS OF LAW

A. Class Certification

The first issue before me is whether to certify a plaintiff class. Plaintiffs have asked me to certify a class "consisting of all persons whose claims to reimbursement under Medicare have been or will be denied by defendants or their agents on the ground that the provided services did not constitute part-time and/or intermittent care." See Proposed Order attached to Plaintiffs' Motion for Class Certification. Certification of a class generally along the lines requested by plaintiffs is appropriate.

The plaintiffs certainly satisfy the three requirements for class certification pursuant to Fed. R.

Civ. P. 23(b)(2). First, joinder of all class members would be impracticable. Secondly, the individual claims are sufficiently similar to make a class action appropriate. Thirdly, "the party opposing the class has acted or refused to act on grounds generally applicable to the class, thereby making appropriate final injunctive relief or corresponding declaratory relief with respect to the class as a whole . ..." Fed. R. Civ. P. 23(b)(2). Indeed, the actions by HHS in the cases presented to me has been reprehensible. It is the most blatant form of stonewalling that an agency can engage in and the Secretary should certainly take all steps to prevent this from happening again.

1. Joinder of all Plaintiffs Would be Impracticable

The evidence submitted by plaintiffs reveals that individuals who have been denied coverage because of defendants' challenged policy are widely dispersed and numerous. See generally Plaintiffs' Exhibits 18–29; Findings of Fact paras. 17–26 (describing dozens of individuals affected by defendants' policy). The numerosity requirement is plainly satisfied.

2. The Claims Raised Are Sufficiently Similar to Make a Class Action an Efficient Litigation Mechanism

Fed. R. Civ. P. 23 also requires that: there be questions of law or fact common to the class; that the claims of the class representatives be typical of the claims of the class; and that the representative parties will fairly and adequately protect the interests of the class. See Fed. R. Civ. P. 23(a). A shorthand way of combining these three requirements is to ask whether a class action would serve as an efficient method of litigating the issues in the case. See *McCarthy v. Kleindienst, 239 App. D.C. 247, 741 F.2d 1406, 1410–11 (D.C. Cir. 1984)* (citing *General Telephone Co. of the Southwest v. Falcon, 457 U.S. 147, 157 n.13, 72 L. Ed. 2d 740, 102 S. Ct. 2364 (1982)*).

A common question of law, namely the procedural and substantive legality of defendants' part-time or intermittent care policy, is shared by all those denied care by defendants' challenged policy. All affected individuals share a common interest in having the policy invalidated and halting harmful denials of home health care benefits that are inconsistent with statutory law and HHS' mandate. The named plaintiffs and those who have been discussed in their exhibits as representative of the class, are both typical and capable of adequately representing the interests of the class. The issues raised are discrete and narrow and require no development of a factual record for any given patient, and thus are particularly well suited for determination by a class action. Defendants' opposition to class certification is largely irrelevant to the core issues at stake here. Defendants contend that because each plaintiff requires an individualized administrative review before he or she can obtain a reversal of a denial of benefits, their claims are insufficiently similar to make a class action appropriate. Defendants misconstrue the focus of plaintiffs' claims. Plaintiffs do not seek the reversal of individual benefit determinations. Rather, plaintiffs are attacking the legitimacy of the underlying policy. They are attacking the unwillingness or inability of defendants to scrap a policy contrary to law that has been determined to be so in numerous individual case adjudications. Indeed, it is only through the vehicle of a class action that meaningful relief can be obtained by those needy and elderly citizens who can hardly any longer stand up to the defendant's insensitive and improper tactics.

Judge Jackson of this court recently ordered class certification in a similar HHS case involving a class of plaintiffs seeking a nationwide policy change rather than the award of benefits to each individual. His analysis is directly applicable here:

> There can be no doubt that these cases present common questions of law, appropriately handled in the context of a class action ... . [P]laintiff ... does not request an adjudication of individual class members' entitlement to benefits. Rather she seeks only a determination of the validity of certain administrative regulations and policies which themselves determine eligibility when applied to specific cases. As a result, factual variations are of minimal importance, the class claim

being controlled solely by common questions of law.

Pratt v. Heckler, 629 F. Supp. 1496, 1503, reconsideration denied sub nom. Pratt v. Bowen, 642 F. Supp. 883, 885–87 (D.D.C. 1986).

Plaintiffs' concerns can be addressed without dealing with the specific merits of any one plaintiff's case—except insofar as that plaintiff's case represents evidence of an unlawful pattern or practice of the agency. Alleged factual differences in plaintiffs' claims are therefore irrelevant. Plaintiffs' shared interest in eliminating HHS policies that are contrary to law is sufficient for class certification.

3. HHS' Actions Affect the Entire Class

I find that HHS "has acted or refused to act on grounds generally applicable to the class, thereby making appropriate final injunctive relief or corresponding declaratory relief with respect to the class as a whole." See Fed. R. Civ. P. 23(b)(2). Plaintiffs are complaining about HHS' conduct across the entire nation. Relief for an individual plaintiff or a group of plaintiffs would not serve to help other individuals not part of this court action.

Defendants' strenuous objections to class certification in this case, combined with defendants' repeated contention that this court only has jurisdiction over those individual plaintiffs who have exhausted their administrative remedies, makes me concerned that defendants will not alter their underlying policies unless I certify a nationwide class. This concern is exacerbated by defendants' policy of "non-acquiescence," which condemns worthy plaintiffs to litigate the same issues again and again. Home health care benefits must go to all eligible patients—not just those with inexhaustible intestinal fortitude.

In fact, this case presents compelling special reasons beyond judicial efficiency for certifying a plaintiff class. These plaintiffs are elderly and sick Medicare patients. See Findings of Fact paras. 17–26. Many of them are dependent on the receipt of Medicare home health benefits to obtain necessary medical care. Id. Plaintiffs' age and infirmities, make them particularly vulnerable to errors in the administrative process. Id. An erroneous determination that a patient's home health care is not eligible for reimbursement will often have a devastating psychological and physical impact on an aged, sick and poor patient. Id. Many of the patients who are initially denied Medicare reimbursement by a financial intermediary lack the tenacity, finances and energy to pursue an appeal through the administrative process. Id.; see Complaint at para. 17 ("... many beneficiaries, for reasons of age, health, fear or unawareness of their legal rights, cannot appeal from these initial denials."). The individual's right to an administrative appeal is not a cure-all for what plaintiffs claim ails defendants' part-time or intermittent care policy.

For the foregoing reasons, I certify a nationwide class "consisting of all persons whose claims to reimbursement under Medicare for home health care services have been or will be denied by defendants or their agents based on defendants' unlawful 'part-time or intermittent care' policy interpretation." In addition, I reserve the right to amend the definition of the class—and to add additional classes or sub-classes—if the "wrongful delegation" aspect of this litigation develops.

B. Jurisdiction [discussion omitted]

C. Standing, Ripeness and Mootness [discussion omitted]

D. The Standard of Judicial Review [discussion omitted]

CONCLUSION

For the foregoing reasons, defendants' challenged policy was promulgated unlawfully and constitutes arbitrary and capricious agency action contrary to the Medicare Act.

RELIEF

Defendants have interpreted the provision of the statute pertaining to "part-time or intermittent care" in a way that arbitrarily excluded from "part-time or intermittent" coverage part-time care provided to Medicare beneficiaries on more than four days per week.

It is therefore hereby

DECLARED that defendants' "part-time or intermittent" care policy that arbitrarily excluded from its definition part-time care that is needed for more than four days a week is contrary to law, and it is further

DECLARED that home health services that may exceed four days a week and otherwise are eligible for this entitlement satisfy the statutory requirement that they be "part-time or intermittent," *42 U.S.C. § 1395x(m)(1) and (4)*, regardless of how many days per week they are needed, so long as such care otherwise meets the requirements for part-time or intermittent care coverage, and it is further

DECLARED that defendants' interpretation of the "part-time or intermittent" care provision which requires a person otherwise entitled to receive coverage for home health care on a less than full-time basis to establish that such care is both "part-time and intermittent" is contrary to law and that said persons are entitled to coverage if they establish such services are "part-time" or "intermittent."

Having concluded that numerous people were denied and otherwise would be denied their right to home health coverage based on defendants' policy that was contrary to law, it is hereby

ORDERED that a nationwide class be CERTIFIED "consisting of all persons whose claims to reimbursement under Medicare for home health care services have been or will be denied by defendants or their agents based on defendants' unlawful 'part-time or intermittent' care policy interpretation," and it is hereby further

ORDERED that defendants and their agents are enjoined from denying Medicare coverage for "part-time" services on the basis of defendants' unlawful interpretation of that term, and it is further

ORDERED that defendants and their agents are enjoined from excluding from coverage "part-time" care needed more than four days per week even if such care is provided for an indefinite period, and it is further

ORDERED that defendants and their agents are enjoined from interpreting the "part-time or intermittent" care provision to require a person otherwise entitled to receive coverage for home health care provided on a less than full-time basis to establish that such care is both "part-time and intermittent;" and to permit said persons to receive coverage if they establish such services are "part-time" or "intermittent," and it is further

ORDERED that defendants and their agents identify and reopen all Medicare claims pending or submitted at least since the filing of the Complaint in this action on February 17, 1987 which were denied pursuant to defendants' unlawful policy and process those claims in conformity with the Memorandum Opinion issued this day, and it is further

ORDERED that the Secretary shall report what actions he has taken to correct the abuses that have been detailed in this Opinion and to comply with this Order in thirty days, and it is further

ORDERED that this court shall retain jurisdiction to provide whatever additional relief may be required.

Begandy v. Richardson
134 Misc. 2d 357, 510 N.Y.S.2d 984 (1987)

On November 14, 1985, plaintiff commenced this negligence action to recover for injuries sustained on March 21, 1985 while a patient at the defendant Latta Road Nursing Home. The complaint alleges that while unattended, plaintiff wandered down the hallway leading to the cellar stairway, opened the cellar door and fell down the stairs. Plaintiff now moves pursuant to CPLR 3025 (b) for leave to serve an amended complaint to assert an additional cause of action alleging violation of Public Health Law § 2801-d.

Subdivision (1) of section 2801-d states: "1. Any residential health care facility that deprives any patient of said facility of any right or benefit, as hereinafter defined, shall be liable to said patient for injuries suffered as a result of said deprivation, except as hereinafter provided. For purposes of this section a 'right or benefit' of a patient of a residential health care facility shall mean any right or benefit created or established for the well-being of the patient by the terms of any contract, by any state statute, code, rule or regulation or by any applicable federal statute, code, rule or regulation, where noncompliance by said facility with such statute, code, rule or regulation has not been expressly authorized by the appropriate governmental authority."

One advantage a patient bringing suit under section 2801-d derives is that any damages recovered thereby are exempt from consideration with regard to Medicaid eligibility (Public Health Law § 2801-d [5]). In addition, subdivision (2) provides that compensatory damages recovered may be "no * * * less than twenty-five percent of the daily per-patient rate of payment established for the residential health care facility * * * or * * * the average daily total charges per patient for said facility, for each day that such injury exists." Subdivision (2) also permits the recovery of punitive damages "where the deprivation of any such right or benefit is found to have been willful or in reckless disregard of the lawful rights of the patient." In addition, where a judgment is rendered in favor of the patient, the court has the discretion to award attorney fees (§ 2801-d [6]).

In her amended complaint, the plaintiff alleges that a number of regulations and contract provisions were violated by defendants proximately causing her injuries. More specifically, it is alleged that defendants' failure to lock, label or otherwise prevent access to the cellar stairway violated 10 NYCRR 713.15 and paragraph (1) of the defendants' admission agreement; that defendants' failure to have the cellar stairway lighted violated New York State Building Code § 765.1(e) (9 NYCRR), 10 NYCRR 713.19(d), and paragraph (1) of defendants' admission agreement; and that defendants' failure to provide adequate nursing care to prevent plaintiff from wandering, falling and becoming injured violated 10 NYCRR 416.2, 42 CFR 405.1124, 442.340, 442.342 and paragraph (2) of defendants' admission agreement. As a result of the violation of these regulations and the admission agreement, plaintiff contends that she was deprived of a "right or benefit" as defined in section 2801-d, and is entitled to compensatory damages for the personal injuries she sustained as well as punitive damages.

Defendants' position is that section 2801-d has no application under the facts of this case, arguing quite correctly it would seem that the legislative history of the statute reveals that it was enacted as part of a package of legislation dealing with nursing homes and other medical care facilities to insure availability to the court system for patients denied rights of privacy, private communications, civil and religious liberties, financial care, basic medical care, courteous treatment, freedom from mental and physical abuse and other elements of patients' rights set forth in Public Health Law § 2803-c. Because damages resulting from the deprivation of such rights tend to be small, the minimum damages provision was added.

In response, plaintiff refers to the definition of "right or benefit" contained in subdivision (1), previously quoted, as well as subdivision (4) which provides that the remedies provided are "in addition to and cumulative with any other remedies available * * * at law or in equity or by administrative proceedings."

There is, of course, a significant difference in the proof required under each of the theories in which plaintiff has framed her action. In negligence, the plaintiff has the burden of proof on each of the requisite elements; duty, breach of duty, injury and proximate cause (1B Warren's Negligence, Proof of Negligence, ch 9, § 2.01). Where negligence is predicated upon the violation of an agency regulation, such violation is " 'merely some evidence which the jury may consider on the question of defendant's negligence' * * * it does not establish negligence as a matter of law" (*Long v Forest-Fehlhaber, 55 NY2d 154, 160*, quoting *Teller v Prospect Hgts. Hosp., 280 NY 456, 460*; see generally, 1A Warren's Negligence, Statutes and Ordinances § 9 et seq.).

In contrast, under section 2801-d, a patient need only prove deprivation by a residential health care facility of any right or benefit created or established for his or her well-being by a statute, code, rule, regulation or contract. Section 2801-d does not, however, impose absolute liability. By pleading and proving that it "exercised all care reasonably necessary to prevent and limit the deprivation and injury for which liability is asserted" (§ 2801-d [1]), the facility may avoid liability. Nevertheless, interpreted as plaintiff urges, section 2801-d would significantly alter the traditional burden of proof requirements in a negligence action whenever injury is suffered by a patient in a health care facility. It is doubtful that this is what the Legislature intended.

An examination of the definition of "right or benefit" is of little help. The statute defines these terms in a rather circular fashion, stating, "a 'right or benefit' * * * shall mean any right or benefit created or established for the well-being of the patient" (Public Health Law § 2801-d [1]).

The various memoranda which accompanied the enactment of section 2801-d indicate that the rights or benefits referred to by the statute involve certain rights or benefits afforded an individual patient such as the right to privacy, to make decisions regarding medical treatment and financial matters, to be free from mental and physical abuse, to present grievances without fear of reprisal, and those others which are expressly set forth in Public Health Law § 2803-c, entitled "[rights] of patients in certain medical facilities," and elsewhere (e.g., 10 NYCRR 405.25, 730.17, 740.14).

According to the memorandum of the State Executive Department, the bill's purpose was to provide nursing home patients "with increased powers to enforce their rights to adequate treatment and care by providing them with a private right of action" (1975 McKinney's Session Laws of NY, at 1685). In the same context, the Governor's memorandum refers to "the creation of a patient's right of action against a facility which fails to meet required standards of care" (1975 McKinney's Session Laws of NY, at 1764). The State Executive Department's memorandum points out "[several] methods of increasing the protection of nursing home patients can be identified. Some would involve increased governmental supervision by existing agencies or the creation of new protective boards or bodies. Another approach, and the one embodied in the proposed new statute, would be to create incentives which would encourage private non-governmental parties to help protect the rights of nursing home patients." (Op. cit., at 1685–1686.) Reference is then made to the statute's authorization for class actions, a minimum level of compensatory damages, and an award of attorney fees as an inducement to the private bar to bring suits on behalf of the patients, who "have been deprived of adequate food, sanitation, nursing care, therapy, etc.," and who "are largely helpless and isolated * * * [and] cannot afford attorneys." (Op. cit., at 1686.)

These memoranda clearly show that the purpose of section 2801-d was to create a private right of action where no such right previously existed. Obviously, the right of a nursing home patient to bring a personal injury action predicated on the nursing home's negligence existed prior to the passage of section 2801-d. The other objective of section 2801-d, to augment the State's limited ability to police the care afforded nursing home patients by creating incentives to induce the private bar to prosecute claims, is not necessary in a personal injury action; nor, in such an action, would a patient's lack of financial resources be a concern because of the availability of a contingent fee arrangement.

That the statute sets a minimum amount of compensatory damages and permits a class action to be brought lends further support to this view. The inclusion of a minimum damages amount suggests that the monetary damages typically resulting from the deprivation of the "rights and benefits" contemplated by section 2801-d would be small or nonexistent. That others would tend to be similarly situated so as to provide a basis for a class action is also not indicative of a typical personal injury action.

Absent a clear expression of an intention to confer a right not vested by the common law, a statute will not be so construed, since it is presumed that the Legislature intended to make no further innovation upon common-law rights than the particular case requires (McKinney's Cons Laws of NY, Book 1, Statutes § 301 [b]). For instance, the doctrine of implied warranty of habitability legislated in Real Property Law § 235-b has not been construed to extent strict liability thereunder to landlords with regard to derelictions which have traditionally been a matter to tort liability (see, *Segal v Justice Ct. Mut. Hous. Coop., 108 Misc 2d 1074; Curry v New York City Hous. Auth., 77 AD2d 534*).

For the foregoing reasons it would appear that section 2801-d is limited to those instances where the wrong complained of involves a deprivation of a personal right or benefit contemplated by section 2803-c and 10 NYCRR 730.17. Since the regulations and the contract provisions upon which plaintiff seeks to base her claim under section 2801-d pertain not to specific personal rights or benefits but generally to the condition of the building used by the facility, no claim is stated under that section.

Leave to amend pleadings should be freely granted absent significant prejudice or surprise to the other party (*Edenwald Contr. Co. v City of New York, 60 NY2d 957*; CPLR 3025 [b]). Although generally the merits or legal sufficiency of a proposed amendment should not be examined on such motion, where, as here, the proposed amendment is clearly and patently insufficient on its face, leave to amend should be denied (see, *Newton v Aqua Flo Co., 106 AD2d 919, 920*).

Plaintiff's motion for leave to amend is, accordingly, denied.

EMPLOYMENT AND INCOME ISSUES

CHAPTER OUTLINE

INTRODUCTION

Many older Americans continue to work, either out of need or desire, long after they become eligible for Social Security retirement benefits. The continually escalating cost of food, clothing, housing, and medical care have required many persons to keep working after what was formerly considered retirement age simply to maintain an adequate standard of living. Furthermore, due to improved health care, people are remaining vigorous and active for longer periods of time, and many do not wish to stop contributing their experience and expertise to the workplace. As a consequence of the foregoing, many laws affecting employment and income maintenance have a direct impact on the elderly, and the elder law legal assistant should become familiar with the implications of these laws.

The ADEA

In reaction to the civil rights movement of the 1960s, Congress enacted the Civil Rights Act of 1964, designed to protect persons who fall into statutorily enumerated categories from being discriminated against in employment. The categories covered under Title VII of the Civil Rights Act include race, color, national origin, sex, and religious affiliation. Notably absent from this grouping was the category of age. Consequently, in 1967 Congress passed the **Age Discrimination in Employment Act (ADEA)**, 29 U.S.C. § 621(b), to protect all persons over the age of 40 from being discriminated against in hiring, training, promotion, and firing. The ADEA is one of the first pieces of federal legislation, excluding the Social Security Act, that was directly designed to affect older Americans. Pursuant to this act, employees of employers who come within the provisions of the statute (discussed later in this chapter) are protected in securing and maintaining employment based on their abilities, regardless of their chronological age.

Income Maintenance

Many older Americans are unable to work and their major concern is their ability to maintain an adequate income level to support a fair standard of living. The first major legislation directed toward the elderly and designed to provide Americans with an adequate income during retirement was the Social Security Act of 1933. This statute, enacted during the Depression, was intended to provide a minimum level of income to persons who had been wage earners but were considered too old to work. The Social Security Act was designed to free up jobs held by older Americans by guaranteeing older persons a secure income; thus, they could retire and their positions would become available for unemployed younger workers.

However, over the years the income provided by Social Security benefits has become, in many instances, inadequate. Many older Americans are dependent upon both private pension plans and additional government programs that are designed to assist the elderly and disabled to maintain a decent standard of living.

This chapter focuses on the issues of income for the elderly, in terms of both employment protection and income maintenance.

THE AGE DISCRIMINATION IN EMPLOYMENT ACT

Age Discrimination in Employment Act (ADEA) Federal statute protecting persons over the age of 40 from being discriminated against in employment based on age.

History of the ADEA

As stated in the introduction, the purpose behind enactment of the Age Discrimination in Employment Act was to incorporate the concept of age discrimination into the general prohibition against discrimination embodied in Title VII of the Civil Rights Act of 1964. The ADEA applies to all persons who are at least 40 years old and protects them against discrimination based on their age in hiring, firing, promotion, training, and participation in mandatory retirement plans. The act applies to all employers who employ a minimum of 20 employees during the calendar or fiscal year; however, even an employer that falls within the parameters of the act may discriminate by requiring a minimum age for employees. Note that, as a general principle, employers are prohibited from imposing a maximum age limitation.

Example

An employer who comes within the purview of the ADEA operates a long-distance trucking service. Insurance and bonding companies require that long-distance truck drivers be at least 25 yeas old to be insured and bonded. In this instance the employer may discriminate in favor of persons who are at least 25 years old.

Example

The employer from the previous example believes that truck drivers over the age of 50 present risks because of perceived failing eyesight and slowed reflexes. This perception is not necessarily accurate and is a stereotype held by the employer. If the employer refuses to hire truck drivers who are over the age of 50, the refusal would be considered unlawful discrimination under the ADEA.

Who Is Covered

The ADEA applies not to individuals but to "employers." For the provisions of the statute to be applied, the entity being challenged with unlawful discriminatory practices must meet the definition of *employer* in the ADEA.

The ADEA defines **employer** as one who is in an industry that "affects commerce" and employs 20 or more persons. Because almost any business, including a law office, may be deemed to "affect commerce," this provision of the ADEA really concerns the number of persons employed by the entity. To be considered an employee, the person must be employed "each working day for 20 or more calendar weeks in the current or previous year"; the 20 weeks need not be consecutive. In this calculation, all employees are considered, not just permanent staff.

employer Person who meets the ADEA's statutory definition, usually determined by a minimum number of employees.

Example

An employer maintains a permanent workforce of 12 individuals and hires part-time and temporary workers throughout the year. The number of part-time and temporary workers varies between four and seven. This employer does not meet the statutory definition of *employer* under the ADEA.

Example

An employer maintains a permanent workforce of 15 persons and hires between 12 and 15 part-time and temporary workers throughout the year. Provided that the part-time and temporary workers work at least 20 weeks each, this employer would come within the provisions of the ADEA.

The ADEA covers all persons who meet the definition of *employer* with the minimum number of employees, including all federal, state, and local government agencies and religious organizations. However, federal employees are required to follow special procedures in instances of alleged age discrimination.

Certain organizations are exempt from the provisions of the ADEA:

1. Bona fide membership clubs, other than labor organizations, provided that the purpose of the organization is to serve a social, recreational, or charitable purpose, and provided that the club is exempt from federal income taxation.

   Example

   A 50-year-old woman brings a charge of age discrimination in employment against her employer, which is a charitable organization defined under § 501(c)(3) of the Internal Revenue Code. This organization is exempt from the provisions of the ADEA.

2. The United States military is not considered an employer under the ADEA with respect to the members of the Armed Forces; however, the military is considered an employer under the ADEA with respect to its civilian personnel.

   Example

   A civilian paralegal works for the Judge Advocate General's office. She has been denied special training to improve her computer skills because she is 60 years old and her boss does not think such training is worthwhile, because of her age. This paralegal may bring an action against the military organization pursuant to the ADEA.

3. Native American tribes do not come under the provisions of the ADEA, because the tribes are legally deemed to be separate nations.

The ADEA applies to all individuals who are 40 years of age or older. No upper age limit is imposed by the act. However, persons who are considered to be bona fide executives, are in a high policy-making position, or are entitled to a nonforfeitable pension benefit of at least $44,000 per year are not covered by the statute. The burden of proving that the employee falls within one of these exceptions rests with the employer.

Example

The president of a medium-size corporation is 65 years old and is being forced out by the corporation's board of directors, who want a younger person in the office. The corporate president cannot maintain an action under the ADEA because the president is a bona fide executive in a policy-making position.

The ADEA also exempts from its provisions:

1. law enforcement officers and firefighters, for reasons of public safety
2. government appointees and elected officials who are not considered employees
3. participants in bona fide apprenticeship programs, because such programs are deemed to be educational rather than employment-related.

Also, the individual alleging discrimination based on age must be shown to be an actual employee, not an independent contractor hired by the employer.

Example

A company that meets the definition of *employer* under the ADEA has retained an attorney to negotiate various contracts on its behalf over the years. When the company hires a new, younger, attorney, the original lawyer believes she was discriminated against because of her age (57). This attorney is not an employee, but an independent contractor, and therefore has no recourse under the ADEA.

Proving Discrimination

Simply because a person who is over the age of 40 has failed to be hired, promoted, trained, or was fired, does not automatically mean that the individual was the victim of unlawful discrimination. To maintain an action pursuant to the ADEA, the individual must prove discrimination. The legal assistant may be called upon to document the discrimination or lack thereof. Various methods are used to establish the fact of age discrimination:

1. A showing of express discrimination, such as announcing an employment policy based on age. If such a policy can be proven, the burden shifts to the employer to demonstrate that the policy has a bona fide occupational basis (see next sub-section).

   Example

   A 56-year-old employee failed to receive a promotion for which she was qualified. When she questioned her employer as to its reason for not promoting her, the employer told her that she was "too old" and that the company has a policy of placing people in their thirties in the position she wanted. This statement, if documented, constitutes direct evidence of age discrimination.

2. A showing of circumstantial evidence that would cause reasonable persons to believe that the employer did unlawfully discriminate based on age, such as preferential treatment given to persons who perform similar tasks but who are in different age categories.

   Example

   Two employees perform the same job for the same employer. One is 25 years old, the other is 55. During a period of recession, the employer fires the older worker, who earns more money because of his longevity with the company. Unless it can be demonstrated that there was a legitimate reason for discharging the older employee, such as poor job performance, the employer may have engaged in an act of unlawful age discrimination.

3. Statistical records that demonstrate a constant pattern of age discrimination.

   Example

   An employee who was not promoted managed to obtain company records showing that the company has never promoted an employee over the age of 45 to the position the employee in question failed to receive. The employee is 51. The company records cover a 20-year period. These records may constitute statistical evidence of age discrimination.

4. A showing that the employer's policy has a negative impact on persons over the age of 40.

Example

An employer's sales force consists of 20 salespeople and 20 in-house personnel. The 20 salespeople generally have higher incomes because of commissions. The company usually "promotes" salespeople who have sold for the company for 20 years to in-house positions. Although not directly related to age, this policy has a negative impact on all salespersons over the age of 40 because, as a consequence of this policy, they have less earning potential.

Defenses: RFOA and BFOQ

Two categories of defenses are available to an employer who is charged with unlawful age discrimination. The first is known as a **reasonable factor other than age (RFOA)**. These factors may include personality conflicts, health problems, poor job performance, rude conduct, and other circumstances indicating that the employee was fired for reasons not connected with the person's age. Of course, employers may attempt to hide the fact that the person was discriminated against based on age by asserting some other reason, but these are questions of proof for the trier of fact.

Example

An employee in her sixties is constantly late for work and so her employer fires her. The employee claims that she was fired because of her age so that the employer could replace her with a younger, less expensive, employee. The employer claims that the employee was more than 30 minutes late more than 60 percent of the time, which it documents by time cards. The employer may have a legitimate RFOA defense, or it may be hiding the fact that the employee was fired because of her age.

The second category of defense available to an employer is known as the **bona fide occupational qualification (BFOQ)**. A BFOQ means that the employer has instituted an age requirement or qualification with respect to its employees but that there is a bona fide business reason for such age restriction. To prove that the age restriction is a BFOQ, the employer must show that:

1. The group that is excluded cannot perform an essential task required for the position. To maintain this defense, the employer must show that the task is essential to job performance and is

reasonable factor other than age (RFOA) An employer defense to an age discrimination claim under the ADEA.

bona fide occupational qualification (BFOQ) Employer defense to an age discrimination claim, indicating a rational, job-related reason for instituting an age requirement.

not based on stereotyping, custom, or any other reason that does not go to the essence of the position.

Example

A law office refuses to hires people over the age of 40 as receptionists because "clients prefer being greeted by young people." This is not a bona fide occupational qualification because the position of receptionist does not require any age-related skills. This is an example of age discrimination based on stereotyping and will not qualify as a bona fide occupational qualification.

2. All or substantially all persons over a particular age cannot perform the essential tasks of the job. This limitation usually refers to a physical ability.

Example

An employer refuses to hire people of over the age of 60 to work on its loading dock because the average weight of the items that must be loaded exceeds 200 pounds. Although there are many physically fit persons over the age of 60, the employer may be able to demonstrate that most people over the age of 60 generally do have some strength limitations. This may qualify as a BFOQ.

3. Employing older workers may pose substantial risks to third persons. Even if the lack of ability to perform specific tasks would not apply to *all* older workers, this may still qualify as a BFOQ if it can be shown that it would be a hardship for the employer to judge each applicant individually.

Example

The employer from the immediately preceding example could also claim that even if some older workers can handle packages weighing more than 200 pounds, it would be a hardship to attempt to test each applicant because lifting packages once is not determinative— the applicant would be lifting such packages 8 hours a day. If the applicant cannot continue to lift such weight for an entire shift, there may be accidents that injure other workers.

4. The nature of the job is such that it is reasonably necessary to discriminate based on age.

Example

A clothing manufacturer makes clothes for teenagers and employs several persons as fitting models to try on the garments during the design and manufacturing process. Even if an older worker had the physical proportions necessary for the job, the look and movements of the older model would be insufficient for the manufacturer's purposes. In this instance discrimination in favor of teenage models would probably constitute a BFOQ.

An employer may also defend a seniority system if it can show that the system does not reduce benefits as the employee ages, even if it requires retirement at a specified age. However, since 1990, employers are prohibited from refusing to hire older workers because of the increased costs incurred for such workers in the employer's benefit package, pursuant to the **Older Workers' Benefit Protection Act**.

Procedures for Enforcing a Claim

If a client believes that he or she has been the victim of unlawful discrimination, the attorney and the paralegal must assist the client in preparing a claim on the client's behalf. Any claim based on a violation of the ADEA must be commenced within two years of the alleged discriminatory act. Jurisdiction over such claims rests with the **Equal Employment Opportunity Commission (EEOC)**, which was created in 1972 to administer the ADEA and Title VII of the Civil Rights Act of 1964. Once the claim has been filed with the EEOC, the EEOC must investigate the claim and try to settle the matter, or it has the authority to file suit in court; no statutory time limit is imposed for filing pleadings in court for claims brought pursuant to the ADEA.

The person who institutes the claim, known as the **charging party**, may bring suit in either state or federal court, but only 60 days after charges have been filed with the EEOC, provided that the EEOC does not institute its own lawsuit. Any lawsuit instituted by the EEOC precludes the charging party from filing his or her own suit. The **charge** must contain the following information:

1. the name of the person claiming the discrimination
2. the person whom he or she claims is guilty of the discriminatory act
3. the specifics of the discriminatory act
4. the date, place, and nature of the act.

The charge must be in writing and sworn to by the charging party, and must be filed with the regional office of the EEOC or in a state or local government office used as an enforcement agency by the EEOC, known as a **deferral agency**. If there is a deferral agency, the charge must be brought there before it can be brought to the EEOC.

Older Workers' Benefit Protection Act Federal statute providing protection to the elderly with respect to employee benefits.

Equal Employment Opportunity Commission (EEOC) Federal agency that administers the ADEA and other federal statutes prohibiting discrimination in employment.

charging party Person who institutes a claim based on unlawful discrimination.

charge Document used to initiate a claim based on unlawful discrimination.

deferral agency State agency used to investigate ADEA claims.

If a charge has been filed with a deferral agency, the charging party may file suit 60 days after the charge has been filed, if the deferral agency fails to resolve the matter. The charging party must file an EEOC charge within 30 days of notification that the deferral agency has terminated its proceedings. The EEOC charge may be filed prior to, simultaneously with, or within 60 days after filing of the state charge.

The court action must be filed no less than 60 days after filing charges with the deferral agency and the EEOC, but in no event more than 2 years after the alleged discriminatory act, or 3 years if the act was willful. A **willful** act is defined as one done in knowing disregard of the law. If more than this time period has elapsed, the charging party may still file suit if it is within 90 days after the EEOC notified him or her that its proceedings have been terminated. Class actions are not permitted under the ADEA; each individual must file separately.

Example

An employee believes that she was fired because of her age (59). She files charges with both the deferral agency and the EEOC on the same day. She can file her claim in federal court in 60 days if the matter has not been resolved by either the deferral agency or the EEOC.

Remedies

Pursuant to the provisions of the ADEA, a successful claimant may be entitled to one or more of the following remedies:

willful Knowing (usually used in the context of disregard of the law).

injunction Court order to stop engaging in specified activities; a remedy under the ADEA.

back pay Remedy under the ADEA in which the employee may be entitled to pay lost due to the discriminatory act.

consequential damages Monetary award above the normal award due to special circumstances; a remedy permitted under the ADEA.

- Injunction. An **injunction** is a court order that requires the employer to stop the unlawful practice and to restore or hire the claimant. If no position is available, the injured party must be offered the first position that opens up and must be paid *front pay*—wages or salary—until the position becomes available.

- Back pay. **Back pay** is all the pay the injured party has lost because of the unlawful act, and includes the value of all benefits to which the injured party would have been entitled to during the period from the unlawful act until the resolution.

- Interest. The injured party may be entitled to recover interest on the back pay from the employer.

- Consequential damages. **Consequential damages** are money used to compensate an injured party for economic loss the party has suffered as a consequence of the unlawful act, such as premium payments on private health insurance the injured party had to pay because of the loss of company health insurance benefits.

- Punitive damages. **Punitive damages** are monetary awards imposed as a punishment to the employer for malicious or reckless indifference to the employee's rights. Punitive damages can range from $50,000 for employers of fewer than 101 employees to a maximum of $300,000 for employers with more than 500 employees.

- Seniority. The employer may be required by the court to award the injured employee **seniority** rights the person may have lost because of the unlawful act. Seniority awards benefits based on the length of employment.

- Liquidated damages. **Liquidated damages** are additional funds the injured party may be entitled to, equal to the lost back pay, if the injured party can prove that the employer's action was willful.

- Attorneys' fees. The prevailing party in a suit based on employment discrimination may be entitled to reasonable attorneys' fees that are occasioned by the lawsuit; this remedy applies to employers as well if they have successfully defended the suit.

INCOME MAINTENANCE

One of the earliest pieces of federal regulation specifically designed to affect older Americans was the Social Security Act, 42 U.S.C. § 301 *et seq.* This statute was created to ensure that individuals who work all their lives will not find themselves destitute or dependent on the charity of relatives or public institutions in their later years. Social Security provides income to retired persons (and those who are disabled) that is presumably adequate to provide them with the necessities of life.

The purpose of the Social Security Act is to fund a program of retirement and service benefits for persons who have worked a sufficient number of years. Pursuant to the provisions of the act, the government levies a tax on employees' wages. This tax is imposed on both the employee and the employer who collectively contribute to the plan. The law is administered by the **Social Security Administration**, and the funds collected are used to provide retirement and disability benefits, as well as health care benefits in the form of Medicare, Medicaid (see Chapter 2), and certain child health care programs.

To qualify for Social Security retirement benefits, the employee must meet certain requirements:

1. The employee must be "fully insured"
2. The employee must be at least 62 years of age.

punitive damages
Monetary award used as a punishment for willful misconduct under the ADEA.

seniority Employee benefits based on length of employment.

liquidated damages
Monetary remedy under the ADEA that specifies a particular dollar amount pursuant to a contract.

Social Security Administration
Federal agency that administers the Social Security Act.

Fully insured means that the employee has worked a minimum number of quarters during which the Social Security tax was withheld. A quarter consists of a consecutive 3-month period, and the minimum number of quarters necessary to qualify is 40.

Example

A paralegal wishes to retire. She has only worked for 9 years, which equals 36 quarters. This paralegal has not met the requirement of being fully insured, and consequently would not be entitled to Social Security retirement benefits.

The 40 quarters do not have to be consecutive. Periods of unemployment may occur throughout the person's work life. To qualify for Social Security retirement benefits, the employee must simply have worked a *total* of 40 quarters during which the Social Security tax was imposed.

Example

A woman worked for five years and then married a wealthy man. She quit work and spent the next several years raising a family. When her children were grown, she returned to work for an additional five years so as to become eligible for Social Security retirement benefits.

Social Security also provides benefits to the employee contributor's dependents, including a spouse, surviving spouse, children, and dependent parents. A spouse who is supported by a wage earner and who is not entitled to Social Security retirement benefits in his or her own right may be entitled to benefits that supplement the amount the retired wage earner receives. This may be true even if the couple has divorced, provided that the spouse seeking the benefits was not individually insured by Social Security.

Example

A couple had been married for 25 years when they divorced. The wife worked only three years before the marriage, and the couple decided that the wife would stay home while the husband continued to work. The husband was the wife's sole means of support. Now the couple is divorced and the husband is retired. The ex-wife, who has not remarried, may be entitled to spousal Social Security retirement benefits.

fully insured Under Social Security, having worked 40 quarters to be entitled to benefits upon retirement.

Surviving spouses of contributors to Social Security, who were supported by a deceased spouse, are entitled to survivor's benefits under the provisions of the Social Security Act if they were married to the deceased spouse for at least 10 years.

Example

After 35 years of marriage a husband dies, leaving a widow who was supported by him for her entire adult life. The widow may be entitled to Social Security benefits as a surviving spouse of a contributor.

Surviving spouses are entitled to receive benefits once they reach the age of 60 or, if they are disabled, at the age of 50. Children of a deceased contributor to Social Security are entitled to benefits if they are unmarried, under the age of 18, or under the age of 19 if they are students. They may also be entitled to survivors' benefits if they were disabled before they reached the age of 21.

Example

A contributor to Social Security dies leaving a widow and three minor children. The widow and the children are all entitled to Social Security benefits as the survivors of the contributor.

Social Security permits the parents of the contributor to receive benefits as survivors if:

1. the parent is at least 60 years old
2. the parent received at least one-half of his or her support from the deceased contributor
3. the parent does not marry or receive benefits in his or her own right.

Example

A paralegal is the sole support of his single mother. The paralegal predeceases the mother. If the mother is over the age of 60 and does not receive Social Security benefits in her own right, she would be entitled to receive benefits as the surviving dependent parent of a contributor child.

Social Security also applies to persons who are self-employed, provided that they work a sufficient number of quarters and make payments to the plan at the rate determined for self-employed individuals.

Example

An attorney practices as a sole practitioner. Every quarter he contributes into the Social Security fund as a self-employed individual. When he retires he will be entitled to receive Social Security retirement benefits.

To qualify for benefits, the wage-earning contributor must file for benefits with the Social Security Administration and document the history of his or her earnings and contributions (see Exhibit 3-1). The Social Security Administration issues a Social Security number as identification; this number is used on all of the employee's employment records to verify employment income and taxes withheld (see Exhibit 3-2 on page 107).

The exact amount of a person's benefits depends on the person's earnings during his or her work life and the amount of the contributions paid into the plan. These benefits may be increased if the person works beyond the minimum retirement age without receiving benefits and continues to contribute to the Social Security fund. Conversely, if a person works and also collects Social Security benefits, the amount of the benefits will be reduced to reflect the employee's continuing income from employment.

Example

A paralegal retires at age 65 and begins to collect Social Security retirement benefits. The retirement benefits prove to be insufficient for her to maintain the lifestyle she desires, and so she returns to work to produce extra income. If she earns more than the statutory minimum for extra earned income for Social Security benefit recipients, her current benefits will be reduced, but her future benefits, when she eventually stops working, will be higher because of her additional contributions to the plan.

Social Security retirement benefits are one of the primary sources of income for the elderly in the United States. Not only does Social Security provide direct payments to the recipient, but persons who are eligible to receive Social Security are also automatically enrolled for Medicare Part A, and may use the Social Security income to pay for Medicare Part B premiums. However, even though Social Security does provide for *cost-of-living increases*—additional benefits due to the increased cost of goods and services—the actual benefit may still be inadequate to provide the recipient with an adequate standard of living. Nowadays many elderly persons continue to work beyond the Social Security retirement age in order to maintain an adequate income level to support their lifestyles.

VETERANS' BENEFITS

Veterans' benefits are a major source of income for a large number of Americans. At present, more than 70 million Americans qualify to

SOCIAL SECURITY ADMINISTRATION ☐ TEL   TOE 120/145/155

Form Approved
OMB No. 0960-0007

APPLICATION FOR RETIREMENT INSURANCE BENEFITS

(Do not write in this space)

I apply for all insurance benefits for which I am eligible under Title II (Federal Old-Age, Survivors, and Disability Insurance) and part A of Title XVIII (Health Insurance for the Aged and Disabled) of the Social Security Act, as presently amended.

☐ **Supplement.** If you have already completed an application entitled "APPLICATION FOR WIFE'S OR HUSBANDS'S INSURANCE BENEFITS", you need complete only the circled items. All other claimants must complete the entire form.

1. (a) PRINT your name — FIRST NAME, MIDDLE INITIAL, LAST NAME

(b) Enter your name at birth if different from item (a) — FIRST NAME, MIDDLE INITIAL, LAST NAME

(c) Check (✓) whether you are ——————▶   ☐ Male   ☐ Female

2. Enter your Social Security Number ——————▶   _ _ _ / _ _ / _ _ _ _

3. (a) Enter your date of birth ——————▶   MONTH, DAY, YEAR

(b) Enter name of State or foreign country where you were born. ——————▶

If you have already presented, or if you are now presenting, a public or religious record of your birth established before you were age 5, go on to item 4.

(c) Was a public record or your birth made before you were age 5?   ☐ Yes   ☐ No   ☐ Unknown

(d) Was a religious record of your birth made before you were age 5?   ☐ Yes   ☐ No   ☐ Unknown

4. (a) Have you (or has someone on your behalf) ever filed an application for Social Security benefits, a period of disability under Social Security, supplemental security income, or hospital or medical insurance under Medicare? ——————▶

☐ Yes
(If "Yes," answer (b) and (c).)

☐ No
(If "No," go on to item 5.)

(b) Enter name of person on whose Social Security record you filed other application.   (First name, middle initial, last name)

(c) Enter Social Security Number of person named in (b). *(If unknown, so indicate)* ——————▶   _ _ _ / _ _ / _ _ _ _

Do not answer 5 if you are age 66 or older. Go on to question 6.

5. (a) Are you, or during the past 14 months have you been, unable to work because of illnesses, injuries or conditions? ——————▶   ☐ Yes   ☐ No

(b) If "Yes," enter the date you became unable to work. ——————▶   MONTH, DAY, YEAR

6. (a) Were you in the active military or naval service (including Reserve or National Guard *active* duty or active duty for training) after September 7, 1939 and before 1968? ——————▶

☐ Yes
(If "Yes," answer (b) and (c).)

☐ No
(If "No," go on to item 7.)

(b) Enter dates of service. ——————▶   From: (Month, year)   To: (Month, year)

(c) Have you *ever* been (or will you be) eligible for a monthly benefit from a military or civilian Federal agency? (include Veterans Administration benefits *only* if you waived military retirement pay) ——————▶   ☐ Yes   ☐ No

7. Have you or your spouse worked in the railroad industry for 7 years or more? ——————▶   ☐ Yes   ☐ No

Form SSA-1-F6 (6-99)
Destroy prior editions

Page 1

♻ Printed on recycled paper

(Over)

EXHIBIT 3-1   SSA application form (retirement benefits)

8.	(a) Do you have social security credits (for example, based on work or residence) under another country's social security system?_____	☐ Yes (If "Yes," answer (b).)	☐ No (If "No," go on to item 9.)
	(b) If "Yes," list the country(ies). ────────────▶		

9.	Have you ever been married? ────────────▶	☐ Yes (If "Yes," answer item 10.)	☐ No (If "No," go to item 12.)

10.

(a) Give the following information about your current marriage. If not currently married, show your last marriage below.

To whom married		When (Month, day, year)	Where (Name of City and State)
Your current or last marriage	How marriage ended (If still in effect, write "Not ended.")	When (Month, day, year)	Where (Name of City and State)
	Marriage performed by: ☐ Clergyman or public official ☐ Other (Explain in Remarks)	Spouse's date of birth (or age)	If spouse deceased, give date of death
	Spouse's Social Security Number (If none or unknown, so indicate) _ _ _ / _ _ / _ _ _ _		

(b) Give the following information about each of your previous marriages. **(IF NONE, WRITE "NONE")**

To whom married		When (Month, day, year)	Where (Name of City and State)
Your previous marriage (Use a separate statement for information about any other marriages.)	How marriage ended	When (Month, day, year)	Where (Name of City and State)
	Marriage performed by: ☐ Clergyman or public official ☐ Other (Explain in Remarks)	Spouse's date of birth (or age)	If spouse deceased, give date of death
	Spouse's Social Security Number (If none or unknown, so indicate) _ _ _ / _ _ / _ _ _ _		

11.	If you are currently married, answer this question **only** if your spouse is within 3 months of age 62 or older; or has a child-in-care who is eligible on your earnings record. Do you wish this application to protect your spouse's right to Social Security benefits? ☐ Yes ☐ No

12.	List below FULL NAME OF ALL your children (including natural children, adopted children, and stepchildren) or dependent grandchildren (including stepgrandchildren) who are now or were in the past 6 months UNMARRIED and: • UNDER AGE 18 • AGE 18 TO 19 AND ATTENDING SECONDARY SCHOOL • DISABLED OR HANDICAPPED (age 18 or over and disability began before age 22) Also list any student who is between the ages of 18 to 23 if such student was both: 1. Previously entitled to Social Security benefits on any Social Security record for August 1981, and 2. Was also in full-time attendance at a post-secondary school prior to May 1982. **(IF THERE ARE NO SUCH CHILDREN, WRITE "NONE" BELOW AND GO ON TO ITEM 13.)**

13.	(a) Did you have wages or self-employment income covered under Social Security in **all** years from 1978 through last year?	☐ Yes (If "Yes," skip to item 14.)	☐ No (If "No," answer (b).)
	(b) List the years from 1978 through last year in which you did **not** have wages or self-employment income covered under Social Security.		

14. Enter below the names and addresses of all the persons, companies, or government agencies for whom you have worked this year, last year, and the year before last.
IF NONE, WRITE "NONE" BELOW AND GO ON TO ITEM 16.

(a) NAME AND ADDRESS OF EMPLOYER (If you had more than one employer, please list them in order beginning with your last (most recent) employer).	Work Began		Work Ended (If still working, Show "Not ended")	
	Month	Year	Month	Year

(b) Are you an officer of a corporation, or are you related to an officer of a corporation? ────────────▶	☐ Yes	☐ No

Form SSA-1-F6 (6-99)   Page 2

EXHIBIT 3-1   *(continued)*

15	May we ask your employers for wage information needed for process your claim?	☐ Yes	☐ No

16 THIS ITEM MUST BE COMPLETED, EVEN IF YOU ARE AN EMPLOYEE
(a) Were you self-employed this year and/or last year? — ☐ Yes *(If "Yes," answer (b).)*   ☐ No *(If "No," skip to item 17.)*

(b) Check the year or years in which you were self-employed	In what kind of trade or business were you self-employed? *(For example, storekeeper, farmer, physician)*	Were your net earnings from your trade or business $400 or more? *(Check "Yes" or "No")*
☐ This year		
☐ Last year		☐ Yes ☐ No
☐ Year before last		☐ Yes ☐ No

17. (a) How much were your total earnings last year? ▶ $

(b) Place an "X" in each block for EACH MONTH of last year in which you did not earn more than *$ ____ in wages, and did not perform substantial services in self-employment. These months are exempt months. If no months were exempt months, place an "X" in "NONE". If all months were exempt months, place an "X" in "ALL".

*Enter the appropriate monthly limit after reading the instructions, "How Your Earnings Affect Your Benefits".

NONE		ALL	
Jan.	Feb.	Mar.	Apr.
May	Jun.	Jul.	Aug.
Sept.	Oct.	Nov.	Dec.

18. (a) How much do you expect your total earnings to be this year? ▶ $

(b) Place an "X" in each block for EACH MONTH of this year in which you did not or will not earn more than *$ ____ in wages, and did not or will not perform substantial services in self-employment. These months are exempt months. If no months are or will be exempt months, place an "X" in "NONE". If all months are or will be exempt months, place an "X" in "ALL".

*Enter the appropriate monthly limit after reading the instructions, "How Your Earnings Affect Your Benefits".

NONE		ALL	
Jan.	Feb.	Mar.	Apr.
May	Jun.	Jul.	Aug.
Sept.	Oct.	Nov.	Dec.

19. **Answer this item ONLY if you are now in the last 4 months of your taxable year (Sept., Oct., Nov., and Dec., if your taxable year is a calendar year).**

(a) How much do you expect to earn next year? ▶ $

(b) Place an "X" in each block for EACH MONTH of next year in which you do not expect to earn more than *$ ____ in wages, and do not expect to perform substantial services in self-employment. These months will be exempt months. If no months are expected to be exempt months, place an "X" in "NONE". If all months are expected to exempt months, place an "X" in "ALL".

*Enter the appropriate monthly limit after reading the instructions, "How Your Earnings Affect Your Benefits".

NONE		ALL	
Jan.	Feb.	Mar.	Apr.
May	Jun.	Jul.	Aug.
Sept.	Oct.	Nov.	Dec.

"I understand that SSA will use the earnings reported to SSA by my employer(s) and my self-employment tax return (if applicable) as the report of earnings required by law and adjust benefits under the earnings test. I also understand that it is my responsibility to ensure that the information I give SSA concerning my earnings is correct. I also understand that I must furnish additional information as needed when my benefit adjustment is not correct based on the earnings on my record."

20. If you use a fiscal year, that is, a taxable year that does not end December 31 (with income tax return due April 15), enter here the month your fiscal year ends. ▶ (Month) ____

IF YOU ARE AGE 65 AND 6 MONTHS, OR OLDER, DO NOT ANSWER ITEM 21. GO ON TO ITEM 22.

PLEASE READ CAREFULLY THE INFORMATION ON THE OPPOSITE PAGE AND ANSWER ONE OF THE FOLLOWING ITEMS. ▶

21. (a) I want benefits beginning with the earliest possible month that will be the most advantageous. ▶ ☐

(b) I am age 65 (or will be age 65 within 4 months) and I want benefits beginning with the earliest possible month that will be the most advantageous providing there is not permanent reduction in my ongoing monthly benefit. ▶ ☐

(c) I want benefits beginning with ____ . I understand that either a higher initial payment or a higher continuing monthly benefit amount may be possible, but I choose not to take it. ▶ ☐

EXHIBIT 3-1 *(continued)*

If this claim is approved and you are still entitled to benefits at age 65, you will automatically have hospital insurance protection under Medicare at age 65. If you are not also eligible for automatic enrollment in the Supplementary Medical Insurance Plan, this application may be used for voluntary enrollment.

COMPLETE THIS ITEM ONLY IF YOU ARE WITHIN 3 MONTHS OF AGE 65 OR OLDER

ENROLLMENT IN MEDICARE'S SUPPLEMENTARY MEDICAL INSURANCE PLAN: The medical insurance benefits plan pays for most of the costs of physicians' and surgeons' services, and related medical services which are not covered by the hospital insurance plan. Coverage under this SUPPLEMENTARY MEDICAL INSURANCE PLAN does not apply to most medical expenses incurred outside the United States. Your Social Security district office will be glad to explain the details of the plan and give you a leaflet which explains what services are covered and how payment is made under the plan.

Once you are enrolled in this plan, you will have to pay a monthly premium to cover part of the cost of your medical insurance protection. The Federal Government contributes an equal amount or more toward the cost of your insurance. Premiums will be deducted from any monthly Social Security, railroad retirement, or civil service benefit checks you receive. If you do not receive such benefits, you will be notified about when, where, and how to pay your premiums. If you are eligible for automatic enrollment, you will be automatically enrolled unless you indicate, by checking the "NO" block below, that you do not want to be enrolled.

22.	DO YOU WANT TO ENROLL IN THE MEDICARE SUPPLEMENTARY MEDICAL INSURANCE PLAN? ⟶	☐ Yes	☐ No

Answer question 23 ONLY if you were born January 2, 1924, or later. Otherwise, go on to question 24.

㉓	(a)	Are you entitled to, or do you expect to become entitled to, a pension or annuity based on your work after 1956 not covered by Social Security?	☐ Yes (If "Yes," answer (b) and (c).)	☐ No (If "No," go on to item 24.)
	(b)	☐ I became entitled, or expect to become entitled, beginning ⟶	MONTH	YEAR
	(c)	☐ I became eligible, or expect to become eligible, beginning ⟶	MONTH	YEAR

I agree to notify the Social Security Administration if I become entitled to a pension or annuity based on my employment after 1956 not covered by Social Security, or if such pension or annuity stops.

24. Check if applicable:
(   ) I am not submitting evidence of earnings that are not yet on my earnings record. I understand that these earnings will be included automatically within 24 months, and any increase in my benefits will be paid with full retroactivity.

REMARKS *(You may use this space for any explanations. If you need more space, attach a separate sheet.)*

I know that anyone who makes or causes to be made a false statement or representation of material fact in an application or for use in determining a right to payment under the Social Security Act commits a crime punishable under Federal law by fine, imprisonment or both. I affirm that all information I have given in this document is true.

SIGNATURE OF APPLICANT	DATE *(Month, day, year)*
SIGNATURE *(First Name, Middle Initial, Last Name) (Write in ink.)* **SIGN HERE** ▶	Telephone Number(s) at Which You May Be Contacted During the Day _____ *(Area Code)*

	Direct Deposit Payment Address *(Financial Institution)*			
FOR OFFICIAL USE ONLY	Routing Transit Number	C/S	Depositor Account Number	☐ No Account ☐ Direct Deposit Refused

Applicant's Mailing Address *(Number and street, Apt. No., P.O. Box, or Rural Route) (Enter Residence Address in "Remarks," if different.)*

City and State	ZIP Code	County *(if any)* in which you now live

Witnesses are required ONLY if this application has been signed by mark (X) above. If signed by mark (X), two witnesses who know the applicant must sign below, giving their full addresses. Also, print the applicant's name in the Signature block.

1. Signature of Witness	2. Signature of Witness
Address *(Number and Street, City, State and ZIP Code)*	Address *(Number and Street, City, State and ZIP Code)*

Form SSA-1-F6 (6-99)   Page 4

EXHIBIT 3-1   *(continued)*

CHANGES TO BE REPORTED AND HOW TO REPORT
Failure to report may result in overpayments that must be repaid, and in possible monetary penalties

► You change your mailing address for checks or residence. To avoid delay in receipt of checks you should ALSO file a regular change of address notice with your post office.

► You go outside the U.S.A. for 30 consecutive days or longer.

► Any beneficiary dies or becomes unable to handle benefits.

► Work Changes--On your application you told us you expect total earnings for 19___ to be $_____.

You (are) (are not) earning wages of more than $_____ a month.

You (are) (are not) self-employed rendering substantial services in your trade or business.

(Report AT ONCE if above work pattern changes)

► You are confined to jail, prison, penal institution, or correctional facility for conviction of a crime or you are confined to a public institution by court order in connection with a crime.

► You become entitled to a pension or annuity based on your employment after 1956 not covered by Social Security, or if such pension or annuity stops.

► Your stepchild is entitled to benefits on your record and you and the stepchild's parent divorce. Stepchild benefits are not payable beginning with the month after the month the divorce becomes final.

► Custody Change--Report if a person for whom you are filing or who is in your care dies, leaves your care or custody, or changes address.

► Change of Marital Status--Marriage, divorce, annulment of marriage.

HOW TO REPORT

You can make your reports by telephone, mail, or in person, whichever you prefer.

WHEN A CHANGE OCCURS AFTER YOU RECEIVE A NOTICE OF AWARD, YOU SHOULD REPORT BY CALLING THE APPROPRIATE TELEPHONE NUMBER SHOWN NEAR THE TOP OF PAGE 6.

The law requires that a report of earnings be filed with SSA within 3 months and 15 days after the end of any taxable year in which you earn more than the annual exempt amount. You may contact SSA to file a report. Otherwise, SSA will use the earnings reported by your employer(s) and your self-employment tax return (if applicable) as the report of earnings required by law and adjust benefits under the earnings test. It is your responsibility to ensure that the information you give concerning your earnings is correct. You must furnish additional information as needed when your benefit adjustment is not correct based on the earnings on your record.

PLEASE READ THE FOLLOWING INFORMATION CAREFULLY
BEFORE YOU ANSWER QUESTION 21.

If you are under age 65, retirement benefits cannot be payable to you for any month before the month in which you file this claim.

If you are over age 65, retirement benefits may be payable to you for some months before the month in which you file this claim (but not before the month you attain age 65)

If your first month of entitlement is prior to age 65, your benefit rate will be reduced. However, if you do not actually receive your full benefit amount for one or more months before age 65 because benefits are withheld due to your earnings, your benefit will be increased at age 65 to give credit for this withholding. Thus, your benefit amount at age 65 will be reduced only if you receive one or more full benefit payments prior to the month you are 65.

Form SSA-1-F6 (6-99)   Page 5

EXHIBIT 3-1   (*continued*)

RECEIPT FOR YOUR CLAIM FOR SOCIAL SECURITY RETIREMENT INSURANCE BENEFITS

TELEPHONE NUMBER(S) TO CALL IF YOU HAVE A QUESTION OR SOMETHING TO REPORT	**BEFORE** YOU RECEIVE A NOTICE OF AWARD	SSA OFFICE	DATE CLAIM RECEIVED
	AFTER YOU RECEIVE A NOTICE OF AWARD		

Your application for Social Security benefits has been received and will be processed as quickly as possible.

You should hear from us within ____ days after you have given us all the information we requested. Some claims may take longer if additional information is needed.

In the meantime, if you change your address, or if there is some other change that may affect your claim, you— or someone for you—should report the change. The changes to be reported are listed on page 5.

Always give us your claim number when writing or telephoning about your claim.

If you have any questions about your claim, we will be glad to help you.

CLAIMANT	SOCIAL SECURITY CLAIM NUMBER

Collection and Use of Information From Your Application—Privacy Act Notice/Paperwork Act Notice

The Social Security Administration is authorized to collect the information on this form under sections 202(a), 205(a), and 1872 of the Social Security Act, as amended (42 U.S.C. 402(a), 405(a), and 1395(ii). While it is VOLUNTARY, except in the circumstances explained below, for you to furnish the information on this form to Social Security, no benefits may be paid unless an application has been received by a Social Security office. Your response is mandatory where the refusal to disclose certain information affecting your right to payment would reflect a fraudulent intent to secure benefits not authorized by the Social Security Act. The information on this form is needed to enable Social Security to determine if you and your dependents are entitled to insurance coverage and/or monthly benefits. Failure to provide all or part of this information could prevent an accurate and timely decision on your claim or your dependent's claim, and could result in the loss of some benefits or insurance coverage. Although the information you furnish on this form is almost never used for any other purpose than stated in the foregoing, there is a possibility that for the administration of Social Security programs or for the administration of programs requiring coordination with the Social Security Administration, information may be disclosed to another person or to another governmental agency as follows: 1. to enable a third party or an agency to assist Social Security in establishing rights to Social Security benefits and/or coverage; 2. to comply with Federal laws requiring the release of information from Social Security records (e.g., to the General Accounting Office and the Veterans Administration); and 3. to facilitate statistical research and audit activities necessary to assure the integrity and improvement of the Social Security programs (e.g., to the Bureau of the Census and private concerns under contract to Social Security).

The information you provide may also be used without your consent in automated matching programs. These matching programs are computer comparisons of Social Security Administration records with records kept by other Federal agencies or State and local government agencies. Information from these matching programs can be used to establish or verify a person's eligibility for Federally funded or administered benefit programs and for repayment of payments or delinquent debts under these programs.

We may also use the information you give us when we match records by computer. Matching programs compare our records with those of other Federal, State, or local government agencies. Many agencies may use matching programs to find or prove that a person qualifies for benefits paid by the Federal government. The law allows us to do this even if you do not agree to it.

Explanations about these and other reasons why information you provide us may be used or given out are available in Social Security offices. If you want to learn more about this, contact any Social Security office.

PAPERWORK REDUCTION ACT NOTICE

The **Paperwork Reduction Act of 1995** requires us to notify you that this information collection is in accordance with the clearance requirements of section 3507 of the Paperwork Reduction Act of 1995. We may not conduct or sponsor, and you are not required to respond to, a collection of information unless it displays a valid OMB control number. We estimate that it will take you about 10 1/2 minutes to complete this form. This includes the time it will take to read the instructions, gather the necessary facts and fill out the form.

Form SSA-1-F6 (6-99)   Page 6   *U.S. Government Printing Office: 1999 — 454-993/80619

EXHIBIT 3-1   *(continued)*

SOCIAL SECURITY ADMINISTRATION
Application for a Social Security Card

Form Approved
OMB No. 0960-0066

1	**NAME** TO BE SHOWN ON CARD	First	Full Middle Name	Last
	FULL NAME AT BIRTH IF OTHER THAN ABOVE	First	Full Middle Name	Last
	OTHER NAMES USED			

2	**MAILING ADDRESS** Do Not Abbreviate	Street Address, Apt. No., PO Box, Rural Route No.		
		City	State	Zip Code

3 CITIZENSHIP (Check One)
☐ U.S. Citizen   ☐ Legal Alien Allowed To Work   ☐ Legal Alien **Not** Allowed To Work   ☐ Other (See Instructions On Page 1)

4 SEX
☐ Male   ☐ Female

5 RACE/ETHNIC DESCRIPTION (Check One Only—Voluntary)
☐ Asian Asian-American or Pacific Islander   ☐ Hispanic   ☐ Black (Not Hispanic)   ☐ North American Indian or Alaskan Native   ☐ White (Not Hispanic)

6 DATE OF BIRTH _____ Month, Day, Year

7 PLACE OF BIRTH (Do Not Abbreviate)   City   State or Foreign Country   FCI
Office Use Only

8	**A. MOTHER'S MAIDEN NAME**	First	Full Middle Name	Last Name At Her Birth
	B. MOTHER'S SOCIAL SECURITY NUMBER (Complete only if applying for a number for a child under age 18.)	☐☐☐ – ☐☐ – ☐☐☐☐		

9	**A. FATHER'S NAME**	First	Full Middle Name	Last
	B. FATHER'S SOCIAL SECURITY NUMBER (Complete only if applying for a number for a child under age 18.)	☐☐☐ – ☐☐ – ☐☐☐☐		

10 Has the applicant or anyone acting on his/her behalf ever filed for or received a Social Security number card before?
☐ Yes (If "yes", answer questions 11-13.)   ☐ No (If "no", go on to question 14.)   ☐ Don't Know (If "don't know", go on to question 14.)

11 Enter the Social Security number previously assigned to the person listed in item 1.
☐☐☐ – ☐☐ – ☐☐☐☐

12 Enter the name shown on the most recent Social Security card issued for the person listed in item 1.
First   Middle   Last

13 Enter any different date of birth if used on an earlier application for a card.
_____ Month, Day, Year

14 TODAY'S DATE _____ Month, Day, Year

15 DAYTIME PHONE NUMBER ( )   Area Code   Number

DELIBERATELY FURNISHING (OR CAUSING TO BE FURNISHED) FALSE INFORMATION ON THIS APPLICATION IS A CRIME PUNISHABLE BY FINE OR IMPRISONMENT, OR BOTH.

16 YOUR SIGNATURE ▶

17 YOUR RELATIONSHIP TO THE PERSON IN ITEM 1 IS:
☐ Self   ☐ Natural or Adoptive Parent   ☐ Legal Guardian   ☐ Other (Specify)

DO NOT WRITE BELOW THIS LINE (FOR SSA USE ONLY)				
NPN		DOC	NTI	CAN	ITV
PBC	EVI	EVA	EVC	PRA	NWR	DNR	UNIT

EVIDENCE SUBMITTED

SIGNATURE AND TITLE OF EMPLOYEE(S) REVIEWING EVIDENCE AND/OR CONDUCTING INTERVIEW

_____ DATE

DCL   _____ DATE

Form **SS-5** (2-98) Destroy Prior Editions   Page 5

EXHIBIT 3-2   SSA application form (Social Security card)

receive veterans' benefits, either as veterans themselves or as qualifying family members of a veteran. Although not all of these individuals would be considered elderly, many are past that "certain age," and these benefits provide a large percentage of their income maintenance. The paralegal may be called upon to assist the attorney in obtaining veterans' benefits for qualifying clients.

Veterans' benefits are defined under Title 38 of the United States Code and are administered by the **Department of Veterans Affairs**, formerly called the Veterans Administration. To qualify for benefits, an individual must either be a veteran, the spouse or surviving spouse of a veteran, or the child or parent of a veteran (similar to Social Security benefits). To be classified as a veteran, an individual must have served in the active military and have been discharged under conditions other than dishonorable, which means having an honorable or general discharge. An individual will be classified as a veteran regardless of whether the period of service was during wartime or peacetime, but only veterans who served during wartime can qualify for **non-service-connected disability** benefits (see following paragraphs). An individual who has received a dishonorable or bad-conduct discharge may appeal that discharge to the Department of Defense.

To qualify for benefits, if the individual served in the military prior to September 8, 1980, any length of service is permitted; persons who served after that date must have served either 24 months of continuous active duty or the full period for which they were called. The 24-month period does not apply to a person who was discharged after serving fewer months if he or she was discharged because of injury or a disability.

Example

A man enlisted in the Army in the mid-1980s, but was injured during a training exercise after he had been in the service for nine months. The injury caused a permanent disability, and he was discharged. This individual qualifies as a veteran for the purpose of receiving benefits even though his period of service was less than 24 months.

Veterans who are discharged because of a service-connected injury may qualify for **service-connected disability** benefits. To determine that the injury or disability was service-connected:

1. the individual must prove that the condition was diagnosed for the first time during military service
2. the individual must demonstrate that a preexisting condition was aggravated during military service
3. the individual must demonstrate that his or her condition was proximately caused by or was the result of a service-connected occurrence

Department of Veterans Affairs (VA) Federal agency that administers laws relating to veterans.

non-service-connected disability Disability resulting from an occurrence that did not happen during military service.

service-connected disability Disability resulting from participation in the military.

4. the individual must prove that the disease or disability was contracted in a VA medical facility

5. the individual must demonstrate a condition that is legally presumed to be service-connected, such as herbicide or radiation diseases, that was diagnosed within one year of discharge or is a type of disease or injury specific to prisoners of war.

The individual will not be eligible for service-connected disability benefits if the injury was caused by the person's own willful conduct.

Example

After being discharged, a veteran becomes severely ill and is diagnosed with a disease that results from exposure to a certain biochemical agent. These biochemicals were used by the military, and by the veteran in particular, during his period of service. This disability will probably be determined to be service-connected.

Example

An individual wants to get out of military service. During boot camp he shoots a bullet into his foot and the injury necessitates the amputation of his small toe. This injury is not service-connected, because it was the result of the individual's willful misconduct.

A veteran who is diagnosed with a service-connected disability is given a rating on that disability from 10 to 100 percent; the rating determines the amount of the monthly compensation that he or she will receive as a veterans' disability benefit. The amount of these benefits is determined by Congress.

Example

A veteran is diagnosed with an injury that the VA rates as a 40 percent disability. This rating entitles the veteran to a monthly disability benefit of $371.

Veterans may also receive special monthly compensation benefits, in addition to their regular benefits, if the injury results in the loss of an organ or an extremity; or if the veteran has two disabilities, one of which is rated at 100 percent *and* the second disability is rated at 60 percent; or the veteran is permanently homebound because of the disability.

Example

A service-connected disability has caused a veteran to lose his left leg. The loss of this extremity entitles him to additional special monthly benefits in addition to his regular monthly compensation.

Example

A veteran is rated with two service-connected disabilities. One is rated at 100 percent, the other at 50 percent. This veteran is not entitled to the special monthly benefit.

If the service-connected disability is rated at 30 percent or higher, the veteran may also receive additional compensation for dependents, including a spouse, child, and parent.

If a person who served in the military during wartime is totally and permanently disabled from a non-service-connected disability, benefits may be allowed, but only if the veteran meets certain financial requirements. To qualify, the veteran must have served at least 90 days of consecutive or combined duty with at least one day during wartime.

Example

A man was drafted into the Army one day before the end of the Vietnam War. Many years after his discharge, he is severely disabled in a car accident in Wichita. The man is unable to work due to his injuries, and has a low income well within the VA standards. Because he served one day during wartime, he may be entitled to non-service-connected disability benefits.

The benefits for persons with non-service-connected pensions are based on annual **eligibility verification reports (EVRs)**, which are used by the VA to determine the veteran's financial resources. To calculate the veteran's income, all income to the veteran, the veteran's spouse, and the veteran's dependent children are included, except for:

1. income from public or private relief
2. Supplemental Security Income (SSI) benefits
3. VA benefits
4. charitable gifts
5. medical expense payments that exceed 5 percent of the maximum annual pension rate for the veteran.

eligibility verification report (EVR) Annual report to determine a person's continued financial eligibility to receive benefits.

Veterans' Improved Pension Plan (VIPP) Method of reducing a veteran's benefit dollar for dollar based on the amount of the recipient's non-exempt income.

Furthermore, if the combined assets and income of the veteran and the veteran's spouse exceed a certain amount, the benefits are discontinued. Generally, the VA permits the veteran's net worth to reach $10,000 before benefits are terminated.

If the veteran transfers assets to a relation living in the veteran's house, the value of the transferred assets are included to determine eligibility; if the assets are transferred to a non-relation, the value of the transferred assets are not included to determine eligibility.

Under the **Veterans' Improved Pension Plan (VIPP)**, the amount of the prospective pension is reduced dollar for dollar by the amount of the veteran's nonexempt income. Additionally, if the veteran qualifies financially and also requires home health care because the veteran is housebound, the veteran may be entitled to additional monthly benefits to cover this cost.

Example

A veteran is disabled with a non-service-connected disability, and the combined income of the veteran and her spouse is under the eligibility requirements for VA benefits. Under the VIPP, the benefits are determined and then reduced by the amount of her monthly attributed income.

If the veteran is placed in a VA medical facility and has no dependents, the amount of the veteran's benefits will be reduced to $90 per month after 3 weeks of such care, unless the purpose of the care is rehabilitation, in which case the benefits are not reduced. This reduction of benefits to $90 per month also occurs if the veteran has no dependents and is receiving Medicaid-covered care.

Example

A veteran with a non-service-connected disability is placed in a VA hospital, where he suffers a stroke that requires extensive rehabilitation. The veteran is released after two months. In this instance there is no reduction in his benefits.

The surviving spouse and minor children of a veteran who is or was entitled to non-service-connected disability benefits may also receive such benefits based on the financial need of the survivors. The surviving spouse, unmarried children under the age of 18, "helpless" children, children between the ages of 18 and 23 who are attending school, and low-income parents may be entitled to **Dependency and Indemnity Compensation (DIC)** payments for veterans who died as a result of service-connected disabilities or who had service-connected disabilities but died due to other causes, provided that the veteran was rated as having a service-connected disability for at least 10 years prior to death or was rated totally disabled for a period of at least 5 years from the date of discharge.

Example

A veteran has a service-connected disability that was caused by exposure to radiation during his period of service. Thirty years after his discharge he succumbs to the physical problems caused by this disability. His widow and minor children may be entitled to DIC payments.

Dependency and Indemnity Compensation (DIC) Veterans' benefits for survivors.

The benefits for the surviving spouse of a veteran who died with a service-connected disability are not dependent on income and terminate only with the spouse's remarriage. Payments to dependent parents are based on income.

Veterans and qualified dependents and survivors may be eligible for a variety of health care benefits, including care in a VA hospital and/or nursing home, home patient care, outpatient medical treatment, and prescriptions. Veterans are also entitled to various death benefits, such as:

1. burial in a VA cemetery, along with the spouse and minor child

2. a burial allowance of $1,500 if the death is service-connected, along with transfer of the body to a VA cemetery

3. a burial allowance of $300 for non-service-connected death if the veteran was receiving veterans' benefits at the time of death (or had filed for claims prior to death), or if the veteran died in a VA facility

4. a headstone if the veteran is buried in a VA cemetery

5. a plot allowance of $150 if the veteran died from a non-service-connected cause and was either receiving veteran's benefits at the time of death or died in a VA facility.

SUPPLEMENTAL SECURITY INCOME

Since July 1, 1974, the federal government has provided **Supplemental Security Income (SSI)** benefits to very low-income individuals and families who meet specified financial criteria. In addition to the federal payments, almost every state also provides payments to recipients of SSI benefits.

To be eligible for SSI benefits, an individual must be:

1. a United States citizen, a lawful permanent resident, or a qualified alien and

2. 65 years of age or older or

3. blind, which is defined as having eyesight measured at 20/200, or

4. disabled.

Supplemental Security Income (SSI) Government transfer payment to very-low-income individuals.

To meet the financial requirements to receive SSI benefits, the applicant's income and resources are calculated in a manner similar to that used in determining Medicaid benefits. For the income determination, all earned and unearned income is included except for:

1. the first $20 of unearned income each month
2. the first $65 of earned income, plus one-half of the remaining earned income each month
3. the value of food stamps the applicant receives
4. the value of food and clothing the applicant receives from charitable organizations
5. student scholarships
6. the value of any home or health care assistance.

If the applicant is living in a public institution, the applicant is ineligible for SSI benefits, unless Medicaid is paying 50 percent or more of the cost of such residence, in which case the individual would still be eligible to receive SSI payments. Furthermore, all "in-kind" income, except for the excludable items enumerated previously, is includible in determining the applicant's eligibility.

Example

An elderly man does not qualify for Social Security. He works part-time, earning a total of $400 per month. He receives food stamps and takes his midday meal for free at a neighborhood church. The church also occasionally provides him with clothing. For SSI eligibility purposes, this man's monthly income is $167.50 (400 − 65/2).

In addition to income requirements, SSI eligibility is also predicated on the applicant's assets and resources. An individual is permitted to retain up to $2,000 worth of resources; a couple is permitted $3,000 in collective resources. If the applicant's resources exceed this amount, he or she is expected to spend down the additional assets to meet SSI resource eligibility requirements. The following items are not included in the determination of an applicant's total resources:

1. household and personal effects valued at up to $2,000, not including wedding and engagement rings
2. life insurance with a cash surrender value of up to $1,500
3. a car valued at up to $4,500, or the value of any car used for transportation for employment or medical treatment, or a handicapped vehicle
4. the value of a burial plot
5. $1,500 in a separate burial fund
6. $1,500 in a separate burial fund for the applicant's spouse

7. the value of property needed for self-support up to a maximum of $6,000 if it produces income valued at at least 6 percent of the excluded property

8. the value of a personal residence in which the applicant has an ownership interest.

Example

An elderly woman needs to receive dialysis treatment several times each week. To get to the hospital the woman must use her car, which has a fair market value of $9,000. If the woman applies for SSI benefits, the value of her car would not be included as a resource, because she needs it to obtain medical treatment.

Example

The only source of income for an elderly SSI applicant is a part-time electric appliance repair business that he operates out of his house. The value of the equipment he uses to operate this business is not includible as a resource for determining SSI eligibility, because these tools provide 100 percent of the applicant's income.

The benefit amount that eligible SSI recipients receive is adjusted annually to reflect the cost of living. Income that the recipient receives from any other source, including income of a recipient's spouse, is considered to be part of the recipient's income and may reduce the monthly benefit. Furthermore, if the recipient receives food, clothing, or shelter from private individuals rather than from charitable organizations, the value of such items is includible as a part of the recipient's income and may be used to reduce benefits.

Couples do not have to be legally married pursuant to their state's law, but if they hold themselves out as married they are so considered for determining SSI eligibility. Conversely, if a couple has been separated for six months they are considered individuals for the purpose of SSI benefit determinations.

Example

An elderly couple live together. They have not married in any civil ceremony because the woman receives Social Security benefits and a pension from her late husband and does not want to lose that income. The couple is Jewish and were married according to the tenets of their religion, and they hold themselves out as husband and wife. The man is more than 65 years of age and has almost no income or resources. For computing SSI eligibility, the woman's income is included to calculate the man's financial eligibility.

SSI was designed to provide a minimum income to elderly and disabled persons who are not otherwise able to support themselves. It can be considered a form of governmental pension for the very poor.

PRIVATE PENSION PLANS

Many Americans are the recipients of income from private pension plans, which are designed to supplement or supersede any governmental payment an elderly person might receive. Paralegals are often asked to draft initial versions of pension plans to be implemented by an employer-client. Private pension plans fall into three broad categories: those that are maintained and funded by the person himself or herself; those that are maintained and funded, in whole or in part, on behalf of the person by an employer as an employee benefit; or a combination of the first two.

Three types of pension plans may be funded by the recipient himself or herself:

1. **Individual retirement accounts (IRAs).** These accounts, pursuant to federal tax law, permit an individual to place up to $2,000 per year into the account to provide for retirement income. The amount placed in the account constitutes a tax deduction for the calculation of the person's individual income tax, and the interest and appreciation that accrue to these funds are not taxed until the individual starts withdrawing the funds. If the individual starts withdrawing funds before attaining the age of $59\frac{1}{2}$, a tax penalty is imposed on the withdrawal. The rationale behind the creation of these accounts was to give incentives to persons to save for their own retirement, and to tax the money at a time when the individual is no longer working and therefore is in a lower income tax bracket.

   Example

   A woman is 32 years old and employed by a major corporation. In addition to her Social Security contribution and her employer's retirement benefit plan, she puts $2,000 each year into an IRA that she maintains at her local bank. She receives a tax deduction for the $2,000 when she computes her income for income tax purposes and has thus planned for additional retirement income when she no longer works.

individual retirement account (IRA) Private pension plan given favorable tax treatment.

2. **IRA-Plus (Roth).** As of August 5, 1997, individuals may contribute funds to a Roth account, but the contributions to such accounts, unlike regular IRAs, are not tax-deductible; however, after five years earnings from such accounts are income-tax-free. The benefit of a Roth IRA is that the depositor can withdraw funds from such accounts at any time without incurring a tax penalty. Also, unlike regular IRAs, which *require* the depositor to start withdrawing funds at age 70½, there is no withdrawal requirement in a Roth IRA. Individuals may transfer funds from a regular IRA to a Roth IRA, and the taxes are deferred until withdrawal from the Roth IRA.

Example

An individual wishes to establish an individual retirement account, but does not want to suffer any penalties should she need to withdraw the funds prior to attaining a certain age. Furthermore, the $2,000 deduction permitted for IRA contributions does not have a significant effect on her taxes. Under these circumstances, the woman might want to opt for a Roth IRA.

3. **Keogh accounts.** These retirement accounts were established for self-employed individuals. Because these persons are not covered by an employer retirement fund, they may establish one for themselves.

Example

An attorney operates a law office as a sole practitioner. Because she is not employed by anyone, she opens a Keogh account to provide retirement income for herself in addition to Social Security.

IRA-Plus (Roth) Form of IRA that permits withdrawal without tax penalties.

Keogh account Private pension plan for self-employed individuals.

Employee Retirement Income Security Act (ERISA) Federal statute that regulates pension plans.

The second category of private pension plans, those maintained by an individual's employer, are regulated under the provisions of the **Employee Retirement Income Security Act (ERISA) of 1974**. This federal statute was enacted to provide protection for employees whose pension plans are maintained and operated by their employer. Until enactment of ERISA, such plans were subject to little regulation, and many persons, after working all their lives, discovered that their employers had mismanaged the pension fund so that the retirement income they had counted on no longer existed. Although a detailed discussion of employee benefit plans is beyond the scope of this text, a basic discussion of some of the most significant concepts of ERISA, particularly how its provisions affect the elderly, is appropriate.

Pursuant to the provisions of ERISA, there are two categories of employee benefit plans: pension benefit plans and welfare benefit plans. A

pension benefit plan provides for income during retirement or the deferral of income until the employee is no longer employed. A **welfare benefit plan** is designed to provide medical and nonpension benefits to its participants.

Pension benefit plans are further divided into two subcategories:

1. **Defined benefit plans.** These pension benefit plans provide a retirement income by a fixed calculation based on the employee's length of service and annual salary.

    Example

    A man has worked for a company for 40 years, and his salary in the last two years was $63,000. Pursuant to the terms of his company's defined benefit plan, his retirement pension is the average of his last 2 years' salaries ($63,000) times the number of years of employment (40) times 1 percent. This man's pension, under this formula, is $25,200 per year.

2. **Defined contribution plans.** These plans, also referred to as **individual account plans**, operate by the employer, and sometimes the employee, contributing sums to the account. The amount of the individual's pension upon retirement depends on the amount of the contribution and the skill of the plan manager.

    Example

    A company contributes $5,000 per year to a defined contribution plan for all employees who earn more than $40,000 per year (the amount is less for lower salaried employees). A man has worked for the company for 30 years, and his annual salary has been more than $40,000. At his retirement, $150,000 has been placed into the account on his behalf, plus appreciation due to the management of the funds. His pension is based on the income from this amount.

A *welfare benefit plan* is defined by ERISA as any plan that provides an employee with medical care, legal services, severance pay, or the like, on an individual basis. These plans do not provide retirement income, but may provide various health care benefits upon the employee's retirement, thereby assisting the elderly in receiving adequate medical care (see Chapter 2).

ERISA applies only to plans operated by employers engaged in commerce or industry or in an activity that affects commerce, or unions representing employees engaged in commerce or any other activity that affects commerce. It does not cover governmental pension plans,

pension benefit plan Pension plan that provides for retirement income.

welfare benefit plan Employee benefit package that provides for medical care and benefits other than retirement income.

defined benefit plan Pension plan in which the amount of the pension is specifically determined by employee's length of service and salary.

defined contribution plan (individual account plan) Pension plan in which the pension is determined by the amount of the contributions made to the plan during the pensioner's period of employment.

church plans, or plans that provide benefits only to highly compensated employees.

Example

A company maintains an **excess benefit plan** for its employees who earn more than $150,000 per year. This plan is excluded from ERISA regulation.

ERISA also applies to Keogh and IRA plans.

ERISA's provisions protect the potential pensioner by imposing strict fiduciary obligations on the managers of such funds, similar to those imposed under the Investment Advisors' Act; however, the detailed provisions of ERISA are beyond the scope of this text.

For the pensioner, the primary question concerns the distribution of funds upon retirement. Some plans provide exclusively for income during the life of the covered person, whereas others provide survivor benefits for a spouse and/or minor children of the pensioner (usually at reduced annual amounts). The specifics of each plan must be individually scrutinized.

Example

A man is retiring and must make an election with respect to his pension. If he elects a pension based only on his life, the amount of this monthly benefit will be $3,000. If he elects survivor benefits, the monthly pension will be only $2,000, but the payments will be made until both he and his wife have died.

Regardless of whether the retiree opts for an individual distribution of the benefit or for survivor benefits, there are tax consequences when the pension money is received. For the purpose of the receipt of pension income, the IRS recognizes two methods of determining tax liability:

1. The **annuity method**, in which the pension payment is divided proportionally into a portion that reflects the original contribution and a portion that reflects the earnings on the contributions (including interest). The first part is tax-free; any income tax is levied only on the second portion. Pursuant to the Internal Revenue Code, the calculation is based on an **exclusion ratio**, which is in turn based on the person's life expectancy.

Example

A retiree receives an annual pension of $25,000 per year, which is taxed according to the exclusion ratio by attributing 40 percent

excess benefit plan
Retirement plan for highly compensated employees; excluded from ERISA regulation.

annuity method
Method of distributing pension income.

exclusion ratio
Proportion of an annuity that is not subject to income taxation, based on IRS tables.

of the pension as a return on the retiree's contribution and 60 percent to earnings on the contribution (which is therefore taxable as income). Under this formula, the retiree must report income of $15,000.

2. The **safe harbor method**, in which the retiree's life expectancy is not taken into consideration, but the pension is divided by a given factor depending on the retiree's age when the benefit is first received. The current table is as follows:

Age	Factor
Under 56	300
56–60	260
61–65	240
66–70	170
Over 70	120

The taxable amount of the pension payment is that amount left over after deducting the portion determined by the factor.

Example

In the preceding example, assuming the retiree is 71 years old when the pension is first received. The $25,000 per year is divided by 120. That is the taxable amount of each month's pension.

The safe harbor method is beneficial for younger annuitants, because their longer life expectancy does not affect the calculations. It is also advantageous for those who are opting for survivor benefits, because only one life is used for the factor determination.

Occasionally, a participant in a pension benefit plan will receive the entire value of the benefit in one **lump-sum distribution**, rather than receiving periodic income distributions. If the recipient simply keeps this money, the entire amount, less the value of his or her contribution, is taxable in the year in which it is received. The person also has the option of placing these funds into another pension plan; this **rollover** will result in no negative tax consequence if it is done within 60 days of receipt of the distribution.

Example

An employee is changing jobs. Pursuant to his former company's pension plan, because he had not been with the company for a specified number of years, he is to receive the current value of his benefit in a lump sum upon leaving. One month after receiving the distribution, the employee

safe harbor method Method of taxing pension payments based on the person's age when the benefit is first received.

lump-sum distribution Receiving an entire pension benefit in one payment.

rollover Placing a pension distribution into another pension account.

places the funds into his IRA, thereby avoiding having to pay current income tax on the distribution.

If the lump-sum distribution is not rolled over into another retirement account, the recipient may be entitled to **forward average** the distribution to minimize the negative tax consequences of the distribution. Forward averaging permits eligible individuals to average the distribution as though it had been received as a periodic payment, allocating portions of the distribution to future tax years. To take advantage of forward averaging:

1. the individual must be at least 59½ years old
2. the individual must have contributed to the plan for at least five years prior to the distribution
3. the distribution must represent the individual's entire interest in the plan
4. the distribution must be made in one tax year
5. the individual cannot have used forward averaging before; it is only permitted once
6. no part of the distribution can be rolled over.

Under the provisions of forward averaging, the distribution is treated as though it were paid over a five-year period, and is taxed as though this were the recipient's only income. If the recipient was born prior to 1936, the person may forward average for a 10-year period instead of 5 years, which is extremely beneficial for the elderly.

ETHICAL CONSIDERATIONS

Adequate income during the retirement years is a major concern of most individuals. Social Security was enacted to meet this concern, but many problems have arisen with respect to Social Security funding.

First, as evidenced by recent news reports, because of the declining birth rate and increased number of elderly persons, there is the possibility that Social Security could go bankrupt, because there are fewer workers currently contributing to the fund for an ever-increasing number of recipients. Will the government meet the challenge of providing continued benefits, and if so, at the cost of which other government programs?

Second, many younger people resent the fact that their income must be taxed to pay for the retirement of other persons, while there is

forward averaging
Tax break for persons who receive a lump-sum distribution of their pension benefits.

no guarantee that there will be any money left for them when they re-tire. One of the hallmarks of a society is how it provides for its chil-dren, and many people feel that the older generation is simply using the younger generation to finance their enjoyment of retirement. Con-versely, is the younger generation willing to pay for the upkeep of their own parents and other elderly relations if Social Security is repealed?

Because of the problems associated with Social Security in provid-ing an adequate income, and because people are living longer and healthier, many people wish to continue to work as they age; however, not every employer is willing to hire older workers. The ADEA was en-acted to protect older workers from discrimination in employment, but unscrupulous employers may still be able to circumvent the ADEA to rid themselves of older, relatively highly paid employees in favor of younger, less expensive, workers.

CHAPTER REVIEW

Because a greater number of Americans are living longer than ever be-fore, the problem of maintaining an adequate income level has become increasingly pressing. Social Security payments have not truly kept up with the increased cost of living, although such increases are taken into consideration in determining benefits, and many older Americans must look to private pension plans and other governmental transfer pay-ments (such as SSI) to maintain a reasonable standard of living. Fur-thermore, because of improved health care, people are keeping active well into their eighties and nineties, and therefore continue to work to produce an income.

The ADEA provides protection for older Americans—those over the age of 40—against discrimination in employment based on age. Social Security, Supplemental Security Income, and favorable tax treatment for private pension plans assist the elderly in maintaining income suffi-cient to provide a satisfactory standard of living in their older years.

KEY TERMS

Age Discrimination in
    Employment Act (ADEA)

annuity method

back pay

bona fide occupational
    qualification (BFOQ)

charge

charging party

consequential damages

deferral agency

defined benefit plan

defined contribution plan
    (individual account plan)

Department of Veterans
    Affairs (VA)

Dependency and Indemnity
    Compensation (DIC)

eligibility verification report (EVR)

Employee Retirement Income
    Security Act (ERISA)

employer

Equal Employment Opportunity
    Commission (EEOC)

excess benefit plan

exclusion ratio

forward averaging

fully insured

individual retirement
    account (IRA)

injunction

IRA-Plus (Roth)

Keogh account

liquidated damages

lump-sum distribution

non-service-connected
    disability

Older Workers' Benefit
    Protection Act

pension benefit plan

punitive damages

reasonable factor other than age
    (RFOA)

rollover

safe harbor method

seniority

service-connected disability

Social Security Administration

Supplemental Security Income
    (SSI)

Veterans' Improved Pension
    Plan (VIPP)

welfare benefit plan

willful

EXERCISES

1. Contact the Social Security Administration to determine how many quarters you have invested and what your projected Social Security benefits would be.

2. Proving discrimination in employment is very difficult. Discuss in detail the various factors you would use to document an allegation of age discrimination in employment.

3. The income of couples who are not legally married is used to determine SSI benefits. Because neither party is legally responsible for the other, do you think this is fair? Discuss.

4. Obtain a copy of a pension benefit plan and analyze its provisions.

5. Social Security was designed to provide older workers with an income to support themselves during retirement, but in many instances the amount received is inadequate and the recipient must continue to work. Social Security deducts this earned income from the benefits. Do you believe this is fair? What if the additional income is needed to meet ordinary living expenses? How would you improve the system?

EDITED JUDICIAL DECISIONS

Sheffield v. Allstate Life Insurance Co.
756 F. Supp. 309 (S.D. Tex. 1991)

An employee and his wife sued Allstate in state court for the costs of medical treatment, asserting a breach of their insurance contract and the misrepresentation of policy benefits. Allstate removed the case under the Employee Retirement Income Security Act since the Sheffields seek benefits under an employee benefit plan. The case will be remanded because ERISA coverage does not extend to Buford Sheffield's employer, World Houston Management Company. The company's business does not affect interstate commerce to the degree required by ERISA's jurisdictional limit.

Buford Sheffield's wife received treatment from a dentist, for which Allstate refused to pay. The wife was a dependent on her husband's insurance that was obtained from Allstate through his employer. The parties agree that the medical plan at issue is an employee welfare benefit plan as the term is defined in ERISA. *29 U.S.C. § 1002.* ERISA coverage, however, is limited to plans established by employers engaged in an "industry or activity affecting commerce." *29 U.S.C. § 1003(a).* World Houston Management is not engaged in a business whose labor relations affect interstate commerce.

ERISA covers "any business ... in commerce or in which a labor dispute would hinder ... the free flow of commerce, and includes any activity ... 'affecting commerce' within the meaning of the Labor Management Relations Act, 1947, or the Railway Labor Act." *29 U.S.C. § 1002(12).*

ERISA coverage extends to the limit of congressional jurisdiction under the commerce clause, but it is defined by the labor component of the business rather than its use of the instrumentalities of interstate commerce, crossing state lines, national markets, or other criteria of interstate effect. *Winterrowd v. David Freedman & Co., Inc., 724 F.2d 823, 825 (9th Cir. 1984).*

The business of World Houston Management, although substantial, does not directly affect interstate commerce. *See e.g., Burke v. Ford, 377 F.2d 901 (10th Cir. 1967); NLRB v. Bill Daniels, Inc., 202 F.2d 579 (6th Cir. 1953); NLRB v. Shawnee Milling Co., 184 F.2d 57 (10th Cir. 1950).* The company consists of two employees, Buford Sheffield and his assistant, who manage the estates of two families, the principal assets of which are entirely within Texas. The company offers management advice to the individuals whose property is included in the management agreement, but it does not directly control the property.

ERISA addresses those employers whose labor disputes could affect interstate commerce. World Houston Management has only two employees, whose business is not demonstrably interstate. The Supreme Court, in speaking of the scope of congressional power of control over intrastate activities, stated:

Undoubtedly the scope of this power must be considered in the light of our dual system of government and may not be extended so as to embrace effects upon interstate commerce so indirect and remote that to embrace them, in view of our complex society, would effectually obliterate the distinction between what is national and what is local and create a completely centralized government.

NLRB v. Jones & Laughlin Steel Corporation, 301 U.S. 1 at 37, 81 L. Ed. 893, 57 S. Ct. 615 (1937).

This court does not have subject matter jurisdiction over this case.

Signed on February 13, 1991, at Houston, Texas.

ORDER OF REMAND

This case is remanded to the 165th District Court of Texas, Harris County.

Thomas v. Sullivan
922 F.2d 132 (2d Cir. 1990)

Plaintiff Gertrude Thomas appeals from a final judgment of the United States District Court for the Southern District of New York, Leonard B. Sand, Judge, dismissing her complaint for review of a decision of the Secretary of Health and Human Services ("Secretary"), which denied her application for widow's insurance benefits ("widow's benefits") under § 216(h)(1)(B) of the Social Security Act (the "Act"), *42 U.S.C. § 416(h)(1)(B) (1988)*, on the ground that her marriage was invalid and she had not gone through a marriage ceremony. The complaint contended that the distinction drawn in § 416(h)(1)(B) between invalid ceremonial and invalid common-law marriages violates the equal protection component of the Due Process Clause of the Fifth Amendment. The district court dismissed the complaint on the ground that the distinction drawn in § 416(h)(1)(B) has a rational basis. On appeal, plaintiff pursues her constitutional challenge. For the reasons below, we affirm the judgment.

I. BACKGROUND

Gertrude Thomas ("Gertrude") lived with Joseph Thomas ("Joseph") for 47 years, from 1938 until his death in 1985, and they had 10 children together. They lived together in Atlanta, Georgia, for many years until they moved to New York. Georgia law recognizes common-law marriages; though New York law does not, it gives full faith and credit to such marriages that are valid under the laws of other states.

In October 1978, Gertrude applied for wife's insurance benefits ("wife's benefits") under

§ 202(b) of the Act, *42 U.S.C. § 402(b) (1988)*, stating that she and Joseph had married on January 25, 1943. In support of that application, Joseph submitted a signed statement to the Social Security Administration ("SSA"), identifying Gertrude as his wife, certifying that they had been married by a "clergyman or authorized public official," and stating that his previous marriage to one "Janie Mills" had ended with Janie's death in 1940. Thereafter, Gertrude received wife's benefits; these were converted to widow's benefits when Joseph died in May 1985.

In July 1985, a woman identifying herself as Janie Thomas ("Janie") applied for benefits as the widow of Joseph Thomas. In support of her application she submitted a marriage certificate showing that she and Joseph had married in September 1918. Janie stated in her application that although she and Joseph had separated in 1933, they had never been divorced and she had never been notified of any attempt by Joseph to obtain a divorce. SSA notified Gertrude that her widow's benefits might be terminated as a result of Janie's claim and gave her an opportunity to present evidence to prove her own entitlement.

A search by SSA turned up no record of a divorce in any of the places where Joseph or Janie had lived since 1933. As a result, SSA determined that Janie was Joseph's lawful widow and that Gertrude's marriage to Joseph was not valid. It notified Gertrude that she would no longer receive widow's benefits. Gertrude promptly requested reconsideration, contending that she was entitled to those benefits, having been told by Joseph that he was divorced and having gone through a marriage ceremony with him. In support of her request for reconsideration, she submitted a statement that in October 1942 she had obtained a marriage license in Decatur, Georgia, and that, shortly thereafter, she and Joseph had been married by a minister in Atlanta. She also stated, "my husband had told me that he was previously married and divorced. But, he never gave me any details about the first marriage." Gertrude submitted a second statement in which she described having met Joseph's first wife:

> In fact, when Mr. Thomas and I first married, we lived together in Atlanta, Ga. with his mother, his first wife Janie Thomas would come to the house to visit Joseph's mother and she knew Joseph and I married [sic]. She never once expressed the fact that she and Joseph never divorced. I never discussed with Joseph where the divorce was taken out or who took out the divorce. He never wanted to discuss anything about his first marriage.

In a March 1986 "Reconsideration Determination," SSA indicated that it had searched the marriage records of Decatur and had found no record of a marriage of Gertrude and Joseph, and that it had separately searched for any record of issuance to them of a marriage license, also without success. As a result, SSA concluded that "since Gertrude Thomas was not validly married to Mr. Thomas," and since "no evidence of a ceremonial marriage has been submitted or located," Gertrude was not eligible for widow's benefits.

Gertrude timely requested and received a hearing before an Administrative Law Judge ("ALJ"). At the hearing, she testified that she had obtained a marriage license and she and Joseph had been married by a minister in 1938. She said the only witnesses to the wedding had been members of the minister's family, whom she did not know. Her own family was informed of the wedding a few days thereafter; none of the family was still alive at the time of the hearing. Gertrude testified that after the ceremony, the minister "told us that he was going to mail the license in so it could be recorded, and mail us our marriage

certificate, which he never did." She explained that her failure to verify that the marriage had been recorded was a result of her youthful trust in Joseph:

> [Gertrude]: I didn't follow up as I should have, because I was quite young at the time and I just took what he said to be true, and at the time I was 21 and he was 45, so I can see now where I could have been very much easy to lead, to be led by what he said and I was in love with him and I just accepted what he told me, thinking everything was okay.
> ALJ: It happens when you are in love.
> [Gertrude]: Oh, yes Sir. But I can see my mistake now. It's just too late.

After giving Gertrude more time to attempt to produce additional evidence, the ALJ found that because Joseph had remained married to Janie until his death, he "was under a legal impediment preventing him from entering into a valid marriage with Gertrude" and that Gertrude "has not supplied any evidence of a ceremonial marriage with Joseph Thomas and therefore cannot be considered as a deemed widow" within the meaning of § 416(h)(1)(B). ALJ Decision dated September 20, 1986.

Gertrude timely sought review of the ALJ's decision by the SSA Appeals Council. While conceding that she was "unable to prove her assertion that she and the wage earner were ceremonially married," she contended that the Secretary's refusal to grant benefits to her in light of her good-faith belief in the validity of her common-law marriage violated her right to equal protection. Gertrude's request for review was denied, and she brought the present action for review of that denial.

The district court, in an opinion published at *713 F. Supp. 114 (1989),* rejected Gertrude's constitutional challenge to § 416(h)(1)(B), finding that there was a rational basis for the statute's distinction between invalid ceremonial marriages and invalid common-law marriages. Noting that the legislative history of § 416(h)(1)(B) was sparse, the court found principally that Congress might well have considered claims based on invalid marriages to be "inherently suspect," and that it could rationally have decided to exclude such claims as it believed could more easily be falsified:

> The issue, like that in [*Weinberger v.*] *Salfi,* [*422 U.S. 749, 45 L. Ed. 2d 522, 95 S. Ct. 2457 (1975),*] is whether the distinction made by § 416(h)(1)(B)—though less than perfectly tailored to the problem—is based on a rational fear that there is a greater possibility of false claims related to invalid common law marriages as opposed to invalid ceremonial marriages. We think it is.
>
> In the first place, it is easier for a claimant to fake a common law marriage than a ceremonial one. Put another way and seen from the perspective of the Social Security Administration, it is easier to detect a false claim of a ceremonial marriage than a common law marriage. A ceremonial marriage requires documentary proof, such as a marriage license, an official and witnesses to the ceremony, that cannot be faked after the death of one of the parties. Thus, Congress reasonably might have considered an invalid ceremonial marriage to have some indicia of reliability that are not present in invalid common law marriages. Because a common law marriage—and in particular one that is not even valid—does not have the same level of formality, it can be faked more easily.

713 F. Supp. at 118.

Accordingly, the district court upheld the denial of benefits and dismissed the complaint. Gertrude has appealed, pursuing her contention that § 416(h)(1)(B), insofar as it grants rights to invalidly married persons who in good faith went through marriage ceremonies but denies rights to invalidly married persons who in good faith believed that they were married under common law, violates the equal protection component of the Due Process Clause.

II. DISCUSSION

Section 216(h)(1)(A) of the Act provides that for purposes of deciding an application for, inter alia, widow's benefits, the Secretary will recognize as valid a marriage that would be recognized as valid by the courts of the state in which the wage earner was domiciled. *42 U.S.C. § 416(h)(1)(A).*

Where there is no valid marriage, § 216(h)(1)(B) of the Act requires the Secretary to "deem[ ]" the applicant for benefits to be a widow in certain cases where she has in good faith gone through a marriage ceremony. The latter section (the "deeming rule") provides, in pertinent part, as follows:

> in any case where ... an applicant is not the ... widow of an ... insured individual, ... but it is established to the satisfaction of the Secretary that such applicant in good faith went through a marriage ceremony with such individual resulting in a purported marriage between them which, but for a legal impediment not known to the applicant at the time of such ceremony, would have been a valid marriage, and such applicant and the insured individual were living in the same household at the time of the death of such insured individual[,] ... such purported marriage shall be deemed to be a valid marriage. ... For purposes of this subparagraph, a legal impediment to the validity of a purported marriage includes only an impediment (i) resulting from the lack of dissolution of a previous marriage, or (ii) resulting from a defect in the procedure followed in connection with such purported marriage.

42 U.S.C. § 416(h)(1)(B). For the reasons below, we conclude that this provision does not violate principles of equal protection.

There is no fundamental right to the receipt of benefits from the government. See generally *Dandridge v. Williams, 397 U.S. 471, 485–86, 25 L. Ed. 2d 491, 90 S. Ct. 1153 (1970).* In deciding an equal protection challenge to a statute that classifies persons for the purpose of receiving such benefits, we are required, so long as the classifications are not suspect or quasi-suspect and do not infringe fundamental constitutional rights, to uphold the legislation if it bears a rational relationship to a legitimate governmental objective. See *Weinberger v. Salfi, 422 U.S. 749, 769–70, 45 L. Ed. 2d 522, 95 S. Ct. 2457 (1975); Schweiker v. Wilson, 450 U.S. 221, 234–35, 101 S. Ct. 1074, 67 L. Ed. 2d 186 (1981).* In seeking to determine whether there are such a relationship and objective, we consider not only contemporaneous articulations of legislative purpose but also any legitimate policy concerns on which the legislature might conceivably have relied. See, e.g., *Exxon Corp. v. Eagerton, 462 U.S. 176, 196, 103 S. Ct. 2296, 76 L. Ed. 2d 497 (1983); Minnesota v. Clover Leaf Creamery Co., 449 U.S. 456, 464, 101 S. Ct. 715, 66 L. Ed. 2d 659 (1981)*. We will uphold the legislation if we can ascertain that the classifications Congress has created can be explained on the basis of factors relevant to the administration and purposes of the particular benefit program, and are not "merely an unthinking response to stereotyped generalizations" about the excluded group. *Califano v. Jobst, 434 U.S. 47, 54, 98 S. Ct. 95, 54 L. Ed. 2d 228 (1977)*. "As long as the classificatory scheme chosen by Congress rationally advances a reasonable and identifiable governmental objective, we must disregard the existence of other methods of allocation that we, as individuals, perhaps would have preferred." *Schweiker v. Wilson, 450 U.S. at 235.*

Where the legislation grants rights to a segment of a class that as a whole had theretofore been denied benefits, our assessment of the rationality of Congress's scheme should be even more generous. In lifting a barrier to benefits, Congress should not be "required to take an all-or-nothing approach," but should be allowed to "proceed more cautiously" where "it had valid reasons for doing so." *Bowen v. Owens, 476 U.S. 340, 347, 106 S. Ct. 1881, 90 L. Ed. 2d 316 (1986); see also id. at 348* ("A constitutional rule that would invalidate Congress' attempts to proceed cautiously in awarding increased benefits [under the Act] might deter Congress from making any increases at all."); *Mathews v. De Castro, 429 U.S. 181, 185, 97 S. Ct. 431, 50 L. Ed. 2d 389 (1976); Califano v. Jobst, 434 U.S. at 57–58.* Congress is generally entitled to adopt prophylactic rules as a means of reducing the possibility of fraudulent claims upon the public treasury. Though the lines drawn may not perfectly exclude all abusers and include all nonabusers, they are to be upheld if Congress could rationally have concluded (a) that the general classification would provide some protection against abuse, and (b) that the expense and other difficulties of making individual determinations

justified the inherent imprecision of the exclusion of a group:

> the question raised is not whether a statutory provision precisely filters out those and only those, who are in the factual position which generated the congressional concern reflected in the statute. Such a rule would ban all prophylactic provisions. ... Nor is the question whether the provision filters out a substantial part of the class which caused congressional concern, or whether it filters out more members of the class than nonmembers. The question is whether Congress, its concern having been reasonably aroused by the possibility of an abuse which it legitimately desired to avoid, could rationally have concluded both that a particular limitation or qualification would protect against its occurrence, and that the expense and other difficulties of individual determinations justified the inherent imprecision of a prophylactic rule.

Weinberger v. Salfi, 422 U.S. at 777.

In analyzing § 416(h)(1)(B) in the present case, we are aided little by the legislative history. Prior to 1957, social security benefits to spouses were awarded in accordance with state laws of succession. See *42 U.S.C. § 416(h)(1) (1952).* In 1957, Congress enacted § 416(h)(1)(A), which premised rights to such benefits on state laws with respect to marriage. *Pub. L. 85-238, § 3(h)(1), 71 Stat. 518, 519 (1957).* Thus, until 1960, widow's benefits were available only to applicants whose marriages to the wage earner were valid. Section 416(h)(1)(B) was added in 1960 because Congress recognized that it is sometimes difficult for an individual to determine, inter alia, whether or when a prior marriage has been validly ended. See S. Rep. No. 1856, 86th Cong., 2d Sess. 22, reprinted in 1960 U.S. Code Cong. & Admin. News 3608, 3629 ("since the State laws governing marriage and divorce are sometimes complex and subject to differing interpretations, a person may believe that he is validly married when he is not"). Though those who aspire to a common-law marriage may find it equally difficult to determine whether a prior marriage has been validly ended, the legislative history is silent as to why Congress excluded such aspirants from those who should be "deemed" valid widows. See id.; see also H.R. Rep. No. 1799, 86th Cong., 2d Sess. 16 (1960).

Congress may have modeled § 416(h)(1)(B) after the civil-law doctrine of "putative marriages." Under this doctrine, some states recognize an invalid marriage as valid when one or both parties have a good faith belief in the validity of a marriage and were ignorant of the legal impediment that makes the marriage invalid. See generally H. Clark, The Law of Domestic Relations § 2.4, at 55–56 (2d ed. 1988). Traditionally, this recognition was not given unless the participants had gone through a ceremonial marriage, a requirement imposed to demand proof of their good faith, albeit mistaken, belief in the validity of their marriage. See, e.g., *Smith v. Smith, 1 Tex. 621, 628–29 (1846)* (ceremony prerequisite to the granting of relief to a putative spouse is relevant to applicant's good faith); Comment, The Requisite of a Marriage Ceremony for Putative Relationships, 4 *Baylor L. Rev.* 343, 346 (1952). In more recent years, some states have extended the putative-marriage doctrine to recognize common-law marriages. See, e.g., *Hupp v. Hupp, 235 S.W.2d 753 (Tex. Civ. App. 1950); Minn. Stat. § 518.055.*

Though Congress gave no explanation in the legislative history for its decision to limit the deeming rule of § 416(h)(1)(B) to applicants who have gone through ceremonial marriages, it is inferable that the decision to continue to deny benefits to invalidly married persons who had not gone through such ceremonies had two purposes. First, Congress may have sought a means of reducing the incidence of fraudulent claims. In these modern times, many couples, with or without uncertainty as to the dissolution of a prior marriage, decide to cohabit without marrying. Congress may have envisioned the possibility that an unlimited deeming provision would invite fraudulent claims from such persons. Further, Congress may have adopted the more traditional view that a willingness to go through a formal marriage ceremony constitutes some objective evidence of a good-faith belief in the dissolution of any prior marriages. It could rationally have believed that

persons who have doubts about whether a prior marriage has been validly ended will be more reluctant to go through a marriage ceremony than they will to enter into an informal cohabitational relationship, perhaps from fear of public criticism, or from fear of having word get back to the prior spouse, or from fear of violating laws against bigamy.

Second, since § 416(h)(1)(B) requires the applicant to show that but for the unknown impediment there would have been a valid marriage, Congress may have sought to establish a criterion that is entirely objective and normally susceptible to documentary proof in order to limit the administrative cost of determining whether that prerequisite is met. If the deeming rule had been made applicable to invalid common-law marriages, the applicant would have to show that all of the prerequisites to common-law marriage were met. Traditionally, the two fundamental requirements for a common-law marriage imposed by the states that have recognized such marriages were (1) the parties' express agreement to be husband and wife, and (2) their holding themselves out to the world as married. See H. Clark, The Law of Domestic Relations § 2.4, at 48. The first requirement has been eroded somewhat by rulings that have allowed the existence of the required agreement to be inferred from the fact that the couple has lived together "for all intents and purposes" as husband and wife. Id. § 2.4, at 49 & n.31. Whichever test is applied, however, the focus is on the parties' intent. Thus, establishment of a purported common-law marriage would generally require proof of an element that is ultimately subjective.

A ceremonial marriage, on the other hand, is an objectively observable event occurring at a defined place and time. Proof of such a marriage will normally be available through documentary evidence such as the original marriage certificate, a certified copy of a public record of marriage, or a certified copy of a church or synagogue record of marriage. See generally SSA Program Operations Manual System ("Manual") § 00305.075. Such documentary evidence is normally accepted by the Secretary as conclusive proof that there was a marriage ceremony. By extending benefits only to those invalidly married persons who can prove that they went through such a ceremony, Congress has made it possible for the Secretary to make a determination in part on the basis of one objective, rather than subjective, criterion, and on the basis of documentary, rather than testimonial, proof.

To be sure, the marriage ceremony requirement in the deeming rule does not relieve the Secretary of all need to assess subjective factors or testimonial evidence. First, there is the statutory requirement that any applicant demonstrate to the Secretary's satisfaction that she went through the marriage ceremony "in good faith." This element, of course, requires a subjective assessment:

> In determining whether the claimant acted in good faith, the test is the individual claimant's belief at the time of the ceremony. ... The fact that another person might not have had the same belief under the same circumstances ... will not preclude a finding that the claimant acted in good faith. ... Factors which may be helpful in doubtful cases in resolving the question (i.e., whether the claimant's allegation of believing the marriage valid is credible) are the claimant's education, experience in worldly affairs, and age.

Manual § 00305.180. Thus, even where there has been a ceremonial marriage, there remains at least one subjective component to be dealt with by the Secretary.

Further, under the Secretary's procedures, the marriage ceremony itself may be proven by secondary evidence where "primary proof" of a marriage by a certificate or official record is not available. Such secondary proof might consist of the testimony of witnesses who attended the ceremony. Where the claimant relies on secondary evidence, the Secretary will not deem that evidence conclusive but will conduct further inquiry. See Manual § 00305.090 ("Secondary proof of marriage ... cannot be treated as conclusive but must be considered in the light of other information in the file. ... This is particularly significant in claims involving a deemed marriage."). Thus, in some cases even the marriage-ceremony requirement will not spare the Secretary the burden of taking testimony on all of the elements of the applicant's claim.

Nonetheless, in most instances, the ceremonial marriage requirement does lessen the Secretary's administrative burden by eliminating the need to receive and assess testimonial evidence on one element, and it is therefore rationally related to the goal of reducing administrative costs. In these circumstances, the fact that the line drawn does not lessen the burden in all instances is unimportant.

In sum, though the result of the deeming rule structured by Congress may seem harsh in the present case, we conclude that it is rationally related to legitimate governmental objectives and may not be overturned.

CONCLUSION

For the foregoing reasons, we affirm the judgment dismissing the complaint.

HOUSING

INTRODUCTION

The living situations and patterns of the elderly have changed dramatically during the last half of the 20th century. Historically, families lived in multigenerational residences, with grandparents, parents, and children (as well as assembled other relations), cohabiting and contributing to the family unit. Nowadays, either by design or necessity, more and more older Americans are forced to secure adequate housing on their own. Families do not remain in the same geographic location, the way they have since the dawn of recorded history; more and more families consist of single-parent households; and many people are deciding not to marry or to procreate. As a consequence, the elderly must fend for themselves without assistance from families or friends.

This chapter explores the various housing alternatives that are available to the elderly in this country: rental units, ownership of homes or apartments, and retirement communities. It also analyzes the effect of the Americans with Disabilities Act on housing for the elderly, and the growth of retirement communities.

The selection process is rarely just one of choice among various alternatives. Because of reduced retirement incomes and the escalating cost of health care, the decision is often based on financial considerations rather than what may be best for the person involved. According to published statistics, at the end of the 1980s, people over the age of 78 spent, on average, 48 percent of their income on housing alone. Also, a growing number of older Americans find themselves totally homeless, forced to live on the streets and fend for themselves as best they can.

RENTING

For most of the urban elderly, the typical form of housing is the rental unit, either an apartment or a small house. The rights and obligations of the tenant are based on the contractual relationship existing between the lessor and the lessee; except for jurisdictions that statutorily regulate residential rental units, the tenant is on his or her own with respect to negotiating a reasonable rent. The tenant may call upon an attorney and the attorney's paralegal to assist in negotiating a fair rental agreement.

Tenants' Rights

All rights that a tenant may have with respect to a rental contract are defined both in the lease agreement itself and in the specifics of any state statutes guaranteeing certain rights and obligations with respect to leaseholds. Regardless of the statutory base, all jurisdictions provide tenants with certain common-law rights with respect to the lease.

Warranty of Habitability

A **warranty of habitability** is a guarantee that the law mandates from landlords that a tenant's residence is one in which a person is capable of living. This warranty covers the basic condition of the premises, including heat; running hot and cold water; the condition of the walls, windows, ceilings, and stairways; and the existence and function of certain basic appliances, such as a stove and refrigerator. In most instances, air conditioning must be specified in the lease itself to give the tenant rights regarding that appliance. If the landlord fails to provide the tenant with premises that are in a habitable state, or fails to maintain those premises in a habitable condition, the tenant may seek relief for a breach of warranty, which could result in a reduction of the rent, both retroactively and prospectively, until the substandard conditions are repaired.

warranty of habitability Common-law guarantee that a rental unit is fit to live in.

Example

A tenant moves into an apartment. The second day she is there, the bathroom ceiling collapses, exposing electrical wires and plumbing fixtures. This presents a dangerous condition for the tenant. If the landlord does not make speedy repairs, the landlord has breached the warranty of habitability.

Example

A man's apartment is infested with rats because of construction in his neighborhood. The rats are able to enter his apartment because the landlord has failed to maintain the walls of the building properly and there are gaping holes in the brickwork. The landlord may be found to have breached the warranty of habitability.

Right ofs Occupancy

Once a tenant has signed a lease, the tenant has the right to occupy the premises as of the date specified in the agreement. If the landlord, in any way, prohibits the tenant from such occupancy, it is a breach of the **warranty of occupancy**. Conversely, the tenant must permit the landlord to have access to the premises to make repairs and in case of emergencies.

Example

A tenant has complained that her bathroom ceiling has collapsed, but she refuses to let the landlord's repairmen enter the apartment because she mistrusts them. In this instance it is the tenant who is in breach. She is not entitled to any rent modification because the tenant herself has hindered the landlord's ability to make repairs.

Most states have established administrative agencies to handle landlord-tenant disputes, and many states, such as New York, have a specialized court that exclusively adjudicates landlord-tenant problems if the administrative agency fails to reach an adequate solution. However, despite the statutory process that may apply to rental units, it must always be borne in mind that a lease is a contract; provided the agreement does not violate any specific law, the rights and obligations of the lessor and the lessee are determined by the parameters of their agreement. The legal assistant must always check the provisions of the lease before any legal evaluation of the tenant's or landlord's rights can be made.

warranty of occupancy Common-law guarantee that tenants can reside in a unit without interference.

RENT ASSISTANCE

Statistically, most elderly Americans wish to remain in their own homes. However, because the cost of housing usually increases with every new lease, many elderly persons find that they need some form of financial assistance to remain in their rental units. The legal assistant should be familiar with any assistance that might be available for the elderly in his or her community. Generally, three forms of rental assistance may exist:

1. subsidies from the federal government
2. state-guaranteed protection
3. government-subsidized public housing.

Federal Subsidies

The federal government does not provide direct subsidies for privately owned rental units; however, the federal government does provide some assistance for the low-income elderly with respect to meeting utility bills. In 1981 Congress passed the **Low Income Energy Assistance Program**, 42 U.S.C. § 8621 *et seq.,* under which the federal government provides funds so that the states can create and maintain energy assistance programs. Each state has established its own program with its own eligibility requirements. Typical requirements are:

1. having attained a minimum age
2. being the recipient of SSI benefits
3. being the recipient of retirement, survivor, or disability income benefits from the Social Security Administration.

Other restrictions may include the type of housing the candidate for assistance lives in, the type of energy used, and the candidate's resources other than income. Although funded by the federal government, these programs are separately devised and administered by each state.

Low Income Energy Assistance Program Federal and state program designed to help tenants and homeowners to meet energy bills.

Example

An elderly man who receives Supplemental Security Income lives in a one-room apartment. He cannot pay his monthly heating bills. The attorney and paralegal provided to him by his state bar association's pro bono program prepare an application for assistance pursuant to the Low Income Energy Assistance Program. His state agency will evaluate his situation to determine his eligibility for assistance.

These programs also typically provide energy payment if the elderly person is without heat or the heat available is insufficient.

State Government Programs

Many state and local governments regulate the rental housing market, and as a part of such regulation may impose rent increase restrictions for the elderly and the disabled. States such as New York create guidelines limiting the amount of a rent increase a landlord may charge; if the tenant is elderly or disabled with a low income, maximum rents may be mandated as a fixed percentage of the tenant's income.

Example

An elderly tenant lives just on Social Security and her small savings. She cannot afford an increase in her rent. She applies to the state agency that regulates housing in her area. Once it is determined that she meets the age and financial eligibility requirements, the state government will limit the maximum rent that she can be charged.

One problem facing the elderly in rent-regulated communities is the possibility of harassment by the landlord, who may try to force the elderly tenant to vacate the apartment so that a higher rent can be charged to a new lessee. Any action on the part of the landlord or the landlord's agents that constitutes harassment is prohibited, and many states have agencies designed specifically to handle these types of situations.

Example

An elderly tenant has lived in her apartment for 45 years and, consequently, pays a fairly low rent. The landlord wants her to move, so he refuses to provide her with any repair services and the building superintendent continually threatens her verbally. These actions can give rise to a cause of action against the landlord for harassment, and the legal assistant should be prepared to aid the attorney in protecting this person's rights.

cooperative Form of ownership in which a person buys shares that entitle the person to possess a unit in the cooperative.

condominium Form of ownership in which a person owns an individual unit and is a tenant-in-common with other owners for common areas.

Because many people desire to own rather than rent their homes, many rental units have undergone—and continue to undergo—conversion to cooperative or condominium status. A **cooperative** is a form of ownership in which a person purchases shares in cooperative, commonly owned premises; these shares entitle the shareholder to reside in a unit in the premises. With a **condominium**, a person purchases a separate unit that is individually owned, but owns the common areas of the premises along with the other condominium owners as tenants-in-common. Many elderly people cannot afford to purchase these units when the premises are converted. To avoid having them forced out of their homes, many states provide statutory protection for such persons, mandating that they may continue to reside in their units as renters if their building converts to a condominium or cooperative, until they either die or choose to move.

Example

An elderly couple has lived in an apartment for more than 50 years. The owner of the building wants to convert the building into condominiums. The couple cannot afford the purchase price of their unit. Under their state's law, they may continue to live in the building as tenants even if the other units are sold as condominiums.

Government-Subsidized Public Housing

For persons whose income and resources do not permit them to rent units from the private sector, the government provides various forms of public housing. Ever since the Depression, the federal government has recognized the responsibility of government to provide adequate shelter for its poorer citizens. The first federal statute that specifically dealt with this issue was the **United States Housing Act of 1937**, 42 U.S.C. § 1401 *et seq.*

Currently, federally assisted public housing is administered by the **Department of Housing and Urban Development (HUD)**. There are three main programs dealing with low-income housing:

1. Section 8 subsidies
2. Section 202 housing
3. Section 504 of the Rehabilitation Act.

Section 8 subsidies refers to § 8 of the United States Housing Act of 1937. Almost half of the persons who participate in this program are elderly. Section 8 provides subsidies for a qualified low-income individual for the difference between 30 percent of the person's income and the fair market value rent for the person's unit. Under this system, HUD presents the individual with a voucher for this difference, which the landlord must accept; payment for the voucher is made directly to the landlord by HUD.

United States Housing Act of 1937 Early federal statute dealing with housing issues.

Department of Housing and Urban Development (HUD) Federal agency that administers housing laws.

Example

An elderly man's monthly income is $1,000. The fair market value rent for his apartment is $500. Under the Section 8 voucher program, the man must pay the landlord $300 (30 percent of his income) and give the landlord a HUD voucher for $200, the difference between 30 percent of his income and the fair market rent of this unit.

Section 8 also operates what is referred to as **project-based programs**, in which the low-income tenant pays 30 percent of his or her income for rent, but must live in a designated publicly owned property. If the tenant leaves the property, he or she will lose the subsidy, unless the tenant moves to another designated publicly owned property. With the project-based program, the tenant has little or no choice with respect to where he or she lives.

Example

An elderly woman living on a very low income lives in a project-based building. Pursuant to Section 8, she pays only 30 percent of her income for rent. The woman no longer wishes to live in the neighborhood where the building is located, but the area in which she would prefer to live does not have a designated property. If she moves to this new neighborhood, she will lose her subsidy. If she were on the voucher system, she could move and simply give the new landlord the HUD voucher for the difference between 30 percent of her income and the fair rental value of the apartment.

It should be borne in mind that if a Section 8 recipient is moving, rather than remaining in a unit, the new landlord may choose not to rent to a person under circumstances in which HUD determines the fair rental value of the unit.

Section 202 housing is housing created with a government subsidy to give the elderly and the disabled the ability to live independently with necessary support services available. Section 202 also provides subsidies to rehabilitate facilities to accommodate the elderly and disabled. More than 90 percent of the participants in Section 202 housing are elderly. However, due to severe budget cuts, these facilities have been greatly limited and there are long waiting lists for units in such housing. As with the Section 8 program, the participants must pay 30 percent of their income for rent.

HUD mandates certain standards for all projects included in HUD-assisted housing. HUD makes yearly inspections of properties to ensure that tenants are provided with:

- proper sanitary facilities
- adequate security arrangements
- adequate heating and air conditioning
- premises that are free from serious defects.

project-based program Public housing in which the tenant must live in a specified building.

Section 202 HUD program providing subsidies to create housing for the elderly and the disabled.

Owners who fail to meet these standards can be fined and/or barred from HUD-assisted programs.

Section 504 of the Rehabilitation Act of 1973 requires that at least 5 percent of public housing authority units be made accessible to the elderly and the disabled. Accessibility criteria include ramps, doors, and other facilities that are equipped for wheelchair use. These provisions overlap with the provisions of the Americans with Disabilities Act (discussed later in this chapter).

SHARED HOUSING

Because of the ever-increasing cost of housing, many elderly persons have opted for various alternatives in which they share a residence with other elderly persons. In addition to the situation in which a group of elderly people simply rents a unit together (à la the "Golden Girls"), four varieties of shared housing are currently prevalent.

SROs

Single-room occupancies (SROs) are buildings in which persons rent one room and share bathroom facilities. Cooking is usually not permitted in such residences. SROs sprang up after World War II to provide short-term housing during a period of rental shortages; however, they have survived as a form of housing for low-income and poor persons. In most SROs, rooms can be rented on a weekly or monthly basis. They provide a means for the elderly to remain in neighborhoods where regular rental units have become too expensive for their budgets.

> ### Example
> An elderly man wants to live near his friends, but cannot afford the rent on a regular apartment in the neighborhood. He rents a room in a single-room occupancy facility, where he shares a bathroom with other residents on his floor and is precluded from cooking. Although the housing situation is limited, he can still be with his friends.

single-room occupancy (SRO) Living facility in which a person rents a room and shares bathroom facilities with other tenants.

adult home Housing for persons over a certain age.

Adult Homes

An **adult home** is a form of adult care facility that provides basic housing and care for the elderly. It falls somewhere between a retirement community and a nursing home, providing care for persons who cannot manage totally on their own but who do not need constant medical care. The residents in these facilities still maintain independence and mobility.

Example _____

An elderly woman is diabetic and needs assistance in administering her daily insulin injections, but is otherwise healthy, She may opt to live in an adult home in order to receive such help.

Shelters

Shelters are designed to provide temporary emergency housing for persons in distressed situations. Such shelters are maintained by charitable organizations or the local government, and typically provide refuge for the homeless.

Example _____

An elderly man is homeless. During the winter, to get out of the cold, he goes to a shelter run by his municipality to obtain temporary housing.

Enriched Housing

Enriched housing refers to sophisticated housing communities in which housing is integrated with social services and activities. These communities are most often referred to as *retirement communities,* and are designed for the more prosperous and healthy among the elderly. Retirement communities are discussed in detail later in this chapter.

Example _____

A couple retire and move to Hawaii, where they acquire a house in a retirement community because of the community's gym, golf course, and other recreational facilities.

Despite the large number of elderly who rent their housing, there are still many elderly who own their own homes, and these persons face problems unique to homeowners.

OWNING

Leaving a home in which one has lived most of one's life and in which one raised one's family can be an extremely traumatic experience. Therefore, many elderly persons prefer, if possible, to remain in their homes. However, the cost of maintaining and repairing a private home, even if the mortgage has been paid off, can still be a tremendous financial burden

shelter Form of temporary emergency housing.

enriched housing Housing communities that integrate social services and activities.

for older persons on limited incomes and with limited resources. For most people, the primary asset is the home, and losing that asset can have a devastating psychological impact on the homeowner. Consequently, many programs with which the legal assistant should become familiar have been established to assist older Americans to remain in the homes that they own.

Help for the Homeowner

There are three main areas of financial concern facing the elderly homeowner with respect to remaining in the home: property tax assessments; the cost of maintaining and repairing the premises; and utility costs. Various programs exist to ease these financial burdens for the elderly homeowner.

Tax Assessments

Property taxes are governed by individual state law; however, many states have instituted real property tax abatements for the qualifying elderly. Most states with such programs impose the following requirements:

1. The homeowner must be at least 65 years old (in some states this age requirement is 55).
2. The homeowner must have title to the property vested in him or her.
3. The residence must be used exclusively for residential purposes.
4. The income and resources of the homeowner must not exceed statutorily determined levels.

Homeowners who believe they qualify must file with their state tax authority, and typically are required to file each year to document continued eligibility. If determined to be eligible, the homeowner's property tax assessment will be reduced according to schedules established by the state.

Example

An elderly couple (he is 75 and she is 73) have lived in their home for more than 50 years, and have title to the property as tenants by the entirety. The couple live on a modest income, and they cannot afford the increase in the property tax assessment on their house. They are afraid that they will lose their home if they are forced to pay the tax increase. The couple applies to the state tax authority for a tax abatement. If they meet the income and resource requirement, their property tax assessment may be reduced, allowing them to continue to live in their own home.

In addition to tax abatements, some states also provide qualified elderly homeowners with a real property tax credit program in which the elderly homeowner can recover a rebate on previously paid property taxes. This type of program is also state-specific, and each jurisdiction's statute must be analyzed.

Finally, some states provide elderly homeowners with assistance to avoid eminent domain acquisition of their property. **Eminent domain** is the right of the government to buy private property for a governmental use.

Home Repairs

Many municipalities throughout the country offer various forms of assistance to help elderly homeowners meet the cost of repairing and maintaining their homes. The most usual form of such assistance is low or no-interest loans for qualifying homeowners for the purpose of repairing their heating systems, electrical and plumbing equipment, and other general home repairs. Usually, repayment of the loan is not required until sale or transfer of the residence. Elderly homeowners should inquire at local agencies specially dedicated to the aging as to what homeowners assistance programs are available.

Example

An elderly homeowner has just had her boiler break, and she cannot afford to repair or replace the system. Pursuant to the program administered by her city, she applies for a low-interest homeowner repair loan available to elderly homeowners. The woman qualifies with respect to title and income levels, and is granted a loan at a 3 percent interest rate to acquire a new boiler. The loan itself does not have to be repaid until she transfers title to her home.

It must be remembered that these are loans and must, at some point, be repaid. This can reduce the amount the homeowner actually receives when the home is sold. The legal assistant should be careful to alert the client to this fact.

Equity Assistance Program

To help low-income elderly homeowners meet the cost of utilities, in 1981 the federal government passed the Low Income Energy Assistance Program, 42 U.S.C. § 8621 *et seq.*, which provides funds to each state to

eminent domain
The right of the government to acquire private property for a legitimate governmental use.

operate utility assistance programs for the elderly. Each state administers its own plan, but all impose age and income restrictions on potential recipients. If the homeowner qualifies, the government will help pay the cost of his or her utility bills. Be aware that this program applies to elderly low-income renters as well as homeowners.

Example

An elderly homeowner's only income is Social Security Retirement benefits, and he cannot afford to heat his home. He applies to his state agency for assistance under the Low Income Energy Assistance Program and is found eligible. The government helps him pay his gas and electric bills.

Reverse Mortgages

Despite the various assistance programs available, many elderly homeowners still find it difficult or impossible to acquire loans for large-scale repairs. Several decades ago, to meet this type of financial need, many banks and financial institutions developed reverse mortgage programs. A **reverse mortgage**, also known as a **home equity conversion mortgage**, is a form of equity loan, whereby the homeowner uses the equity he or she has in the home to borrow money. Unlike a typical mortgage arrangement, in which the homeowner makes monthly repayments and the lender gives the funds to the seller of the realty, in a reverse mortgage the creditor makes monthly payments to the borrower. The loan is repaid only when the home is sold or the borrower dies.

Reverse mortgages are guaranteed by the Fair Housing Administration (FHA), and each state's banking laws determine the specifics of the program. As a general rule, the homeowner who is seeking a reverse mortgage must be over the age of 60, the term of the loan cannot exceed 30 years, and the amount of the loan cannot exceed 80 percent of the residence's value. Generally, three types of reverse mortgages are generally available.

FHA-Insured Reverse Mortgages

reverse mortgage
Loan made to a homeowner that permits the homeowner to live in the house and receive income payments.

home equity conversion mortgage *See* reverse mortgage.

This program, which is administered through the FHA division of HUD, operates reverse mortgages and home equity reverse mortgages. Because these loans are guaranteed by the government, they are the most attractive to the lender. Also, pursuant to government provisions, the homeowner must receive counseling with respect to the implications of reverse mortgages prior to signing the papers.

Example

An elderly couple's sole asset is their home, and their income is limited to Social Security benefits and a small pension. They need to supplement their income, and apply for an FHA-insured reverse mortgage. The couple qualifies for the loan and receives counseling with respect to the fact that this is a loan, which eventually must be repaid when the home is sold or the couple dies. They agree to the conditions. In this manner they are now able to increase their income.

Privately Insured Mortgages

If the homeowner qualifies, he or she may be able to obtain a privately insured reverse mortgage. Typically, a privately insured program requires greater income and resources on the part of the homeowner, but it also provides a larger loan.

Uninsured Mortgages

Uninsured reverse mortgages are the least favorable because they usually are for fixed terms (specified number of years, typically not exceeding 10), after which the entire loan must be repaid. Note that the loans that are guaranteed usually are not subject to repayment until the death of the borrower or the transfer of the residence.

Example

An elderly woman acquires an uninsured reverse mortgage. She receives payments for 10 years and then must repay the entire loan.

To qualify for a reverse mortgage, the following criteria usually must be met:

1. The homeowner must be at least 62 years old.
2. There must be little or no loan outstanding on the home.
3. The home must be a single-family residence or a separate unit in a multiple dwelling.
4. If the residence is a condominium, the condominium must be FHA-approved.

Once the homeowner is approved for a reverse mortgage, there are four options that may be chosen with respect to receiving the funds:

1. **tenure plan**—the borrower receives monthly lifetime payments calculated on actuarial tables based on the homeowner's age
2. specific monthly payments for a **specified term** ($300 a month for 10 years)
3. **lump sum**—the homeowner receives the entire amount of the loan at once

tenure plan
Method of payment under a reverse mortgage in which the homeowner receives a set monthly payment.

specified-term reverse mortgage
A reverse mortgage with a designated period during which payments will be made.

lump-sum mortgage
A reverse mortgage in which the homeowner receives the entire amount of the loan at once.

4. **credit line**—a line of credit permits the holder to draw on the amount of the loan as needed, but no direct payments are made to the borrower.

When the homeowner dies (or at the death of the survivor, if the home was owned by a couple) or the house is sold, the full amount of the loan becomes due to the lender. It is important to emphasize that reverse mortgages are loans, not sales, and must be repaid eventually. The loan aspect of the reverse mortgage is why the FHA requires homeowners to receive counseling prior to entering into a loan, so that they fully understand its implications. However, reverse mortgages are a viable option for many elderly homeowners, permitting them to increase their monthly income and still remain in their homes.

Sale-Leasebacks

Another option utilized by elderly homeowners to acquire funds and still remain in their homes is the **sale-leaseback**. In this type of arrangement the homeowner actually sells the home, for which the homeowner receives payment and takes a mortgage, but also retains in a life tenancy in the residence, for which rent payments are made to the purchaser. Unlike the reverse mortgage, with the sale-leaseback the home is sold and when the seller dies possession of the residence transfers to the purchaser.

Example

An elderly couple sell their home to their children, from whom they receive a purchase price of $200,000. The couple retains a life tenancy in the house and are obligated to pay the children, the new homeowners, a monthly rent of $500 as long as the couple chooses to remain in the house.

credit line Funds that can be drawn on.

sale-leaseback Arrangement whereby a homeowner sells his or her house but remains in possession as a tenant.

Truth in Lending Act Federal statute mandating that consumers be given certain information before entering into a loan agreement.

Truth in Lending

Whenever a consumer enters into a loan agreement, such as a reverse mortgage or even a sale-leaseback agreement, if payment is not made at once, the provisions of the federal **Truth in Lending Act**, 15 U.S.C. §§ 1601–1667e, become operative. This statute mandates that, prior to entering into a loan contract, the borrower must be made aware of the following terms:

1. the term of the payment schedule
2. the annual interest rate
3. variable interest rates that may attach to the loan

4. credit charges

5. any other fees that may attach to the agreement. (See Exhibit 4-1, pages 146–152.)

Also, a Truth in Lending form spelling out the total cost of the loan must be provided.

Furthermore, if the loan is for a mortgage, the law requires mortgage counseling, which must include:

1. other available options

2. the financial implications of the mortgage

3. the tax consequences of the loan

4. the effect of the loan on the homeowner's eligibility for government benefits.

The homeowner must be informed of his or her rights to reconsider the loan and to opt out of the loan instrument without any negative consequences within three days of signing the agreement.

Example

An elderly woman applies for a reverse mortgage to supplement her income so that she can remain in her home. The financial institution that agrees to the mortgage does not provide her with counseling, information regarding the total cost of the loan, or any other option she may have. Two days after signing the agreement, the woman decides she does not want the loan, but the financial institution tells her that she has signed the instrument and is now obligated. Under the Truth in Lending Act, the woman does have the right to opt out of the agreement, because it is within three days of the signing and several other requirements of the act have not been met.

Selling

At some point the homeowner may decide that he or she wishes to sell the residence. At this point, if the homeowner has taken out a reverse mortgage, the amount of the loan will become due and payable. Furthermore, regardless of whether there are any loans outstanding on the house, whenever a residence is sold certain tax consequences must be addressed.

A residence is considered a **capital asset**, and if it is sold for more than it cost, plus improvements made on the house over the years, the seller/homeowner is liable for taxes on the gain resulting from the sale, known as a **capital gains tax**.

capital asset Property owned for increase in value.

capital gains tax Tax imposed on any increase in value of a capital asset, determined when the asset is sold.

Uniform Residential Loan Application

This application is designed to be completed by the applicant(s) with the lender's assistance. Applicants should complete this form as "Borrower" or "Co-Borrower", as applicable. Co-Borrower information must also be provided (and the appropriate box checked) when ☐ the income or assets of a person other than the "Borrower" (including the Borrower's spouse) will be used as a basis for loan qualification or ☐ the income or assets of the Borrower's spouse will not be used as a basis for loan qualification, but his or her liabilities must be considered because the Borrower resides in a community property state, the security property is located in a community property state, or the Borrower is relying on other property located in a community property state as a basis for repayment of the loan.

I. TYPE OF MORTGAGE AND TERMS OF LOAN

Mortgage Applied for:	☐ VA ☐ FHA	☐ Conventional ☐ FmHA	☐ Other:	Agency Case Number	Lender Case No.

Amount $	Interest Rate %	No. of Months	Amortization Type:	☐ Fixed Rate ☐ GPM	☐ Other (explain): ☐ ARM (type):

II. PROPERTY INFORMATION AND PURPOSE OF LOAN

Subject Property Address (street, city, state, & ZIP) — No. of Units

Legal Description of Subject Property (attach description if necessary) — Year Built

Purpose of Loan	☐ Purchase ☐ Refinance	☐ Construction ☐ Construction-Permanent	☐ Other (explain):	Property will be: ☐ Primary Residence ☐ Secondary Residence ☐ Investment

Complete this line if construction or construction-permanent loan.

Year Lot Acquired	Original Cost $	Amount Existing Liens $	(a) Present Value of Lot $	(b) Cost of Improvements $	Total (a + b) $

Complete this line if this is a refinance loan.

Year Acquired	Original Cost $	Amount Existing Liens $	Purpose of Refinance	Describe Improvements ☐ made ☐ to be made Cost: $

Title will be held in what Name(s) — Manner in which Title will be held — Estate will be held in: ☐ Fee Simple ☐ Leasehold (show expiration date)

Source of Down Payment, Settlement Charges and/or Subordinate Financing (explain)

III. BORROWER INFORMATION

	Borrower		Co-Borrower	
Borrower's Name (include Jr. or Sr. if applicable)		Co-Borrower's Name (include Jr. or Sr. if applicable)		

Social Security Number	Home Phone (incl. area code)	Age	Yrs. School	Social Security Number	Home Phone (incl. area code)	Age	Yrs. School

☐ Married ☐ Separated	☐ Unmarried (include single, divorced, widowed)	Dependents (not listed by Co-Borrower) no. ages	☐ Married ☐ Separated	☐ Unmarried (include single, divorced, widowed)	Dependents (not listed by Borrower) no. ages

Present Address (street, city, state, ZIP) ☐ Own ☐ Rent _____ No. Yrs.		Present Address (street, city, state, ZIP) ☐ Own ☐ Rent _____ No. Yrs.	

EXHIBIT 4-1 Uniform residential loan application

146

If residing at present address for less than two years, complete the following:

Former Address (street, city, state, ZIP)	Own	Rent	No. Yrs.	Former Address (street, city, state, ZIP)	Own	Rent	No. Yrs.
Former Address (street, city, state, ZIP)	Own	Rent	No. Yrs.	Former Address (street, city, state, ZIP)	Own	Rent	No. Yrs.

IV. EMPLOYMENT INFORMATION

Borrower		Co-Borrower	
Name & Address of Employer	Self Employed	Yrs. on this job	Name & Address of Employer	Self Employed	Yrs. on this job
		Yrs. employed in this line of work/profession			Yrs. employed in this line of work/profession
Position/Title/Type of Business	Business Phone (incl. area code)	Position/Title/Type of Business	Business Phone (incl. area code)

If employed in current position for less than two years or if currently employed in more than one position, complete the following:

Name & Address of Employer	Self Employed	Dates (from - to)	Name & Address of Employer	Self Employed	Dates (from - to)
		Monthly Income $			Monthly Income $
Position/Title/Type of Business	Business Phone (incl. area code)	Position/Title/Type of Business	Business Phone (incl. area code)
Name & Address of Employer	Self Employed	Dates (from - to)	Name & Address of Employer	Self Employed	Dates (from - to)
		Monthly Income $			Monthly Income $
Position/Title/Type of Business	Business Phone (incl. area code)	Position/Title/Type of Business	Business Phone (incl. area code)

Freddie Mac Form 65   10/92

PLD 155

Page 1 of 4

Fannie Mae Form 1003   10/92

EXHIBIT 4-1   *(continued)*

V. MONTHLY INCOME AND COMBINED HOUSING EXPENSE INFORMATION

Gross Monthly Income	Borrower	Co-Borrower	Total	Combined Monthly Housing Expense	Present	Proposed
Base Empl. Income *	$	$	$	Rent	$	
Overtime				First Mortgage (P&I)		$
Bonuses				Other Financing (P&I)		
Commissions				Hazard Insurance		
Dividends/Interest				Real Estate Taxes		
Net Rental Income				Mortgage Insurance		
Other (before completing, see the notice in "describe other income," below)				Homeowner Assn. Dues		
				Other:		
Total	$	$	$	Total	$	$

* Self Employed Borrower(s) may be required to provide additional documentation such as tax returns and financial statements.

Describe Other Income   *Notice:* Alimony, child support, or separate maintenance income need not be revealed if the Borrower (B) or Co-Borrower (C) does not choose to have it considered for repaying this loan.

B/C		Monthly Amount
		$

VI. ASSETS AND LIABILITIES

This Statement and any applicable supporting schedules may be completed jointly by both married and unmarried Co-Borrowers if their assets and liabilities are sufficiently joined so that the Statement can be meaningfully and fairly presented on a combined basis; otherwise separate Statements and Schedules are required. If the Co-Borrower section was completed about a spouse, this Statement and supporting schedules must be completed about that spouse also.

Completed ☐ Jointly ☐ Not Jointly

ASSETS	Cash or Market Value	Liabilities and Pledged Assets. List the creditor's name, address and account number for all outstanding debts, including automobile loans, revolving charge accounts, real estate loans, alimony, child support, stock pledges, etc. Use continuation sheet, if necessary. Indicate by (*) those liabilities which will be satisfied upon sale of real estate owned or upon refinancing of the subject property.	Monthly Payt. & Mos. Left to Pay	Unpaid Balance
Description		LIABILITIES		
Cash deposit toward purchase held by:	$	Name and address of Company	$ Payt./Mos.	$
		Acct. no.		
List checking and savings accounts below		Name and address of Company	$ Payt./Mos.	$
Name and address of Bank, S&L, or Credit Union				
Acct. no.	$	Acct. no.		
Name and address of Bank, S&L, or Credit Union		Name and address of Company	$ Payt./Mos.	$

EXHIBIT 4-1 *(continued)*

148

Acct. no.

Name and address of Bank, S&L, or Credit Union | $

Acct. no.

Name and address of Bank, S&L, or Credit Union | $

Acct. no.

Stocks & Bonds (Company name/number & description) | $

Life insurance net cash value | $

Face amount: $

Subtotal Liquid Assets | $

Real estate owned (enter market value from schedule of real estate owned) | $

Vested interest in retirement fund | $

Net worth of business(es) owned (attach financial statement) | $

Automobiles owned (make and year) | $

Other Assets (itemize) | $

Total Assets a. | $

Acct. no.

Name and address of Company | $ Payt./Mos. | $

Acct. no.

Name and address of Company | $ Payt./Mos. | $

Acct. no.

Name and address of Company | $ Payt./Mos. | $

Acct. no.

Name and address of Company | $ Payt./Mos. | $

Acct. no.

Alimony/Child Support/Separate Maintenance Payments Owed to: | $

Job Related Expense (child care, union dues, etc.) | $

Total Monthly Payments | $

Net Worth (a minus b) | $ | **Total Liabilities b.** | $

EXHIBIT 4-1 (*continued*)

149

VI. ASSETS AND LIABILITIES (cont.)

Schedule of Real Estate Owned (If additional properties are owned, use continuation sheet.)

Property Address (enter S if sold, PS if pending sale or R if rental being held for income)	Type of Property	Present Market Value	Amount of Mortgages & Liens	Gross Rental Income	Mortgage Payments	Insurance, Maintenance, Taxes & Misc.	Net Rental Income
		$	$	$	$	$	$
Totals		$	$	$	$	$	$

List any additional names under which credit has previously been received and indicate appropriate creditor name(s) and account number(s):

Alternate Name	Creditor Name	Account Number

VII. DETAILS OF TRANSACTION

a. Purchase price	$
b. Alterations, improvements, repairs	
c. Land (if acquired separately)	
d. Refinance (incl. debts to be paid off)	
e. Estimated prepaid items	
f. Estimated closing costs	
g. PMI, MIP, Funding Fee	
h. Discount (if Borrower will pay)	
i. Total costs (add items a through h)	
j. Subordinate financing	
k. Borrower's closing costs paid by Seller	
l. Other Credits (explain)	
m. Loan amount (exclude PMI, MIP, Funding Fee financed)	
n. PMI, MIP, Funding Fee financed	
o. Loan amount (add m & n)	

VIII. DECLARATIONS

If you answer "yes" to any questions a through l, please use continuation sheet for explanation.

	Borrower Yes	Borrower No	Co-Borrower Yes	Co-Borrower No
a. Are there any outstanding judgments against you?	☐	☐	☐	☐
b. Have you been declared bankrupt within the past 7 years?	☐	☐	☐	☐
c. Have you had property foreclosed upon or given title or deed in lieu thereof in the last 7 years?	☐	☐	☐	☐
d. Are you a party to a lawsuit?	☐	☐	☐	☐
e. Have you directly or indirectly been obligated on any loan which resulted in foreclosure, transfer of title in lieu of foreclosure, or judgment? (This would include such loans as home mortgage loans, SBA loans, home improvement loans, educational loans, manufactured (mobile) home loans, any mortgage, financial obligation, bond, or loan guarantee. If "Yes," provide details, including date, name and address of Lender, FHA or VA case number, if any, and reasons for the action.)	☐	☐	☐	☐
f. Are you presently delinquent or in default on any Federal debt or any other loan, mortgage, financial obligation, bond, or loan guarantee? If "Yes," give details as described in the preceding question.	☐	☐	☐	☐
g. Are you obligated to pay alimony, child support, or separate maintenance?	☐	☐	☐	☐
h. Is any part of the down payment borrowed?	☐	☐	☐	☐
i. Are you a co-maker or endorser on a note?	☐	☐	☐	☐
j. Are you a U.S. citizen?	☐	☐	☐	☐
k. Are you a permanent resident alien?	☐	☐	☐	☐
l. Do you intend to occupy the property as your primary residence? If "Yes," complete question m below.	☐	☐	☐	☐
m. Have you had an ownership interest in a property in the last three years?	☐	☐	☐	☐

EXHIBIT 4-1 (continued)

p. Cash from/to Borrower
(subtract j, k, l & o from i)

(1) What type of property did you own-principal residence (PR), second home (SH), or investment property (IP)?

(2) How did you hold title to the home-solely by yourself (S), jointly with your spouse (SP), or jointly with another person (O)?

IX. ACKNOWLEDGMENT AND AGREEMENT

The undersigned specifically acknowledge(s) and agree(s) that: (1) the loan requested by this application will be secured by a first mortgage or deed of trust on the property described herein; (2) the property will not be used for any illegal or prohibited purpose or use; (3) all statements made in this application are made for the purpose of obtaining the loan indicated herein; (4) occupation of the property will be as indicated above; (5) verification or reverification of any information contained in the application may be made at any time by the Lender, its agents, successors and assigns, either directly or through a credit reporting agency, from any source named in this application, and the original copy of this application will be retained by the Lender, even if the loan is not approved; (6) the Lender, its agents, successors and assigns will rely on the information contained in the application and I/we have a continuing obligation to amend and/or supplement the information provided in this application if any of the material facts which I/we have represented herein should change prior to closing; (7) in the event my/our payments on the loan indicated in this application become delinquent, the Lender, its agents, successors and assigns, may, in addition to all their other rights and remedies, report my/our name(s) and account information to a credit reporting agency; (8) ownership of the loan may be transferred to successor or assign of the Lender without notice to me and/or the administration of the loan account may be transferred to an agent, successor or assign of the Lender with prior notice to me; (9) the Lender, its agents, successors and assigns make no representations or warranties, express or implied, to the Borrower(s) regarding the property, the condition of the property, or the value of the property.

Certification: I/We certify that the information provided in this application is true and correct as of the date set forth opposite my/our signature(s) on this application and acknowledge my/our understanding that any intentional or negligent misrepresentation(s) of the information contained in this application may result in civil liability and/or criminal penalties including, but not limited to, fine or imprisonment or both under the provisions of Title 18, United States Code, Section 1001, et seq, and liability for monetary damages to the Lender, its agents, successors and assigns, insurers and any other person who may suffer any loss due to reliance upon any misrepresentation which I/we have made on this application.

Borrower's Signature	Date	Co-Borrower's Signature	Date
X		X	

X. INFORMATION FOR GOVERNMENT MONITORING PURPOSES

The following information is requested by the Federal Government for certain types of loans related to a dwelling, in order to monitor the Lender's compliance with equal credit opportunity, fair housing and home mortgage disclosure laws. You are not required to furnish this information, but are encouraged to do so. The law provides that a Lender may neither discriminate on the basis of this information, nor on whether you choose to furnish it. However, if you choose not to furnish it, under Federal regulations this Lender is required to note race and sex on the basis of visual observation or surname. If you do not wish to furnish the above information, please check the box below. (Lender must review the above material to assure that the disclosures satisfy all requirements to which the Lender is subject under applicable state law for the particular type of loan applied for.)

BORROWER

I do not wish to furnish this information

Race/National Origin:
- American Indian or Alaskan Native
- Asian or Pacific Islander
- Black, not of Hispanic origin
- White, not of Hispanic Origin
- Hispanic
- Other (specify)

Sex:
- Female
- Male

CO-BORROWER

I do not wish to furnish this information

Race/National Origin:
- American Indian or Alaskan Native
- Asian or Pacific Islander
- Black, not of Hispanic origin
- White, not of Hispanic Origin
- Hispanic
- Other (specify)

Sex:
- Female
- Male

To be Completed by Interviewer

This application was taken by:
- face-to-face interview
- by mail
- by telephone

Interviewer's Name (print or type)

Interviewer's Signature   Date

Interviewer's Phone Number (incl. area code)

Name and Address of Interviewer's Employer

EXHIBIT 4-1 (continued)

Continuation Sheet/Residential Loan Application

Use this continuation sheet if you need more space to complete the Residential Loan Application. Mark **B** for Borrower or **C** for Co-Borrower.

Borrower:

Co-Borrower:

Agency Case Number:

Lender Case Number:

I/We fully understand that it is a Federal crime punishable by fine or imprisonment, or both, to knowingly make any false statements concerning any of the above facts as applicable under the provisions of Title 18, United States Code, Section 1001, et seq.

Borrower's Signature:

X

Date

Co-Borrower's Signature:

X

Date

Freddie Mac Form 65   10/92

Page 4 of 4

Fannie Mae Form 1003   10/92

EXHIBIT 4-1 *(continued)*

The Internal Revenue Service (IRS) provides two forms of relief from imposition of the capital gains tax on the sale of a residence:

1. A **rollover** permits the homeowner to use the proceeds from sale of the home to purchase a new home *within two years* of the sale. If the cost of the new home equals or exceeds the sale price of the old house, no tax is imposed. If the cost of the new house is less than the sale price of the old house, capital gains tax is imposed only on the difference. The tax is not excused with the rollover, just deferred until the eventual final sale of the taxpayer's home.

   Example

   A couple retires and sells their home in Michigan, which originally cost them $45,000, for $300,000. They move to Arizona and buy a new home nine months later. The cost of the new house in Arizona is $250,000. The couple must pay capital gains tax on $50,000.

2. Under the new law, a homeowner who has owned and resided in his or her home for two of the previous five years can exclude up to $250,000 against imposition of the capital gains tax on sale of the home. This option is available every two years to a homeowner. The amount is $500,000 for a couple.

   Example

   A couple retires and decides to sell their home and move to a retirement community. They are going to rent rather than purchase, and have sufficient income from pensions, Social Security, and dividends to meet their rental expense. They sell their house for $300,000. Their original cost was $45,000, and they have made $50,000 worth of improvements on the house over the years. Their gain on the sale is $205,000. Because this is below the $500,000 exclusion, they do not have to pay any tax on this gain.

Fair Housing Laws

The elderly, per se, are not protected against discrimination in housing, but may be protected if they come within the definition of *handicapped* under the provisions of the **Fair Housing Act (FHA)**, 42 U.S.C. § 3601 *et seq.*, which prohibit discrimination in housing against persons who have a physical or mental disability that substantially limits one or more major life activities. As indicated earlier, because many elderly persons have physical problems, they may be covered under the

rollover Process of taking the gain from the sale of a home and putting it into the purchase of a new home; this avoids the capital gains tax.

Fair Housing Act (FHA) Federal statute protecting persons from discrimination in housing.

provisions of the FHA. Pursuant to the FHA, the following actions are prohibited:

- refusing to rent or sell to persons protected under the act

- refusing to negotiate for housing with persons who are protected under the act

- making housing inaccessible to persons who are protected under the act

- setting different terms for the sale or rental of a dwelling to persons who are protected under the act

- providing different housing to persons who are protected under the act

- falsely stating that housing is not available for persons who are protected under the act

- denying access for the sale or rental of housing to persons who are protected under the act.

If a potential purchaser or renter is considered disabled, the owner must make reasonable accommodation to provide the individual with access to the premises (see the following discussion of the Americans with Disabilities Act).

If an individual believes that he or she has been unlawfully discriminated against in housing, he or she can file a complaint with HUD, which will attempt to resolve the issue. HUD can provide a hearing, and may award damages and penalties if the assertion is substantiated.

AMERICANS WITH DISABILITIES ACT

Americans with Disabilities Act (ADA) Federal statute designed to protect persons with physical or mental disabilities from being discriminated against in employment and access to public facilities.

The **Americans with Disabilities Act (ADA)**, 42 U.S.C. § 12100 *et seq.*, was enacted in 1990 to protect disabled Americans against unlawful discrimination. The ADA prohibits discrimination in four main areas:

1. employment
2. public services and transportation
3. public accommodation
4. telecommunication services.

Although the ADA does not prohibit discrimination in housing (which comes under the provisions of the Fair Housing Act), it does affect certain aspects of accommodations.

To fall within the protections of the ADA, a person must either be disabled or perceived to be disabled. Under the act, **disability** is defined as having a mental or physical defect that substantially limits a major life activity. As previously discussed, because many older Americans do suffer physical and mental problems that substantially affect major life functions, the ADA provisions may apply to the elderly under specific circumstances. Note that neither the ADA nor the FHA prohibit discrimination based on age.

If the individual is deemed disabled, **reasonable accommodation** must be made to provide the person with access to the services and accommodations covered by the statute. Accommodation must be made to provide the disabled with access to:

- entrances and exits
- elevators, stairs, and escalators
- parking spaces
- telephones
- restaurants and cafeterias
- hotel rooms
- drinking facilities
- other similar public facilities.

The ADA mandates that such access be made available in all public housing facilities, hotels and motels, and other nonhousing facilities utilized by the disabled.

Example

A municipal government is rehabilitating an abandoned building for public housing. Pursuant to the provisions of the ADA, the building must be made handicapped-accessible with ramps, enlarged doorways, and handrails in the bathrooms. This will give access to persons in wheelchairs and on crutches.

RETIREMENT COMMUNITIES

As they age, many older Americans find that they are more comfortable being surrounded by people of their own age and temperament rather than in an age-integrated community. As a consequence, many areas have developed into **retirement communities**, geographic living facilities designed exclusively for older residents.

disability Physical or mental condition that limits a major life activity.

reasonable accommodation Requirement under the ADA for persons with disabilities.

retirement community Living facility designed for persons who are retired.

Types

Retirement communities fall into three broad categories.

Continuing Care Retirement Communities (CCRC)

Continuing care retirement communities (CCRCs) are designed as living facilities for the older person who requires continual medical supervision but does not require the care that can only be provided at a nursing home. The persons who are attracted to these facilities are those with chronic, although somewhat manageable, medical problems.

Example

An elderly woman is diabetic and must have daily insulin injections, which she cannot manage on her own. Also, she has severe respiratory problems. The woman decides to live in a continuing care retirement community because of the 24-hour, on-site medical staff and facilities that can help her maintain her health without restricting her movements and independence.

Assisted Living Facilities

Assisted living facilities are designed to provide nonmedical supplemental services for persons whose needs are more social than medical.

Example

An elderly man, although generally healthy, is confined to a wheelchair because of some circulatory problems. He needs assistance in cleaning, cooking, and dressing himself, but not necessarily any medical care. He might choose to reside in an assisted living facility that provided such services.

---

continuing care retirement community (CCRC) Living facility that provides certain medical care for persons who do not require nursing home care.

assisted living facility Housing in which certain services are provided to help a person maintain independence.

Retirement Communities

A pure retirement community is simply a facility designed for older persons who are predominantly healthy and independent but who wish to be surrounded by persons of similar ages in a living facility that provides social and recreational services.

Example

An elderly couple decide to retire to the "sun belt" and choose to live in a retirement community because of the golf course, swimming pool, and social club maintained by the community. They live in their own unit and are totally independent.

Contracts

When deciding which type of facility is appropriate for a given individual, among the considerations the legal assistant must look at for the client is the nature of the contractual agreement the elderly person is entering into with a community. Although a detailed discussion of contract law is beyond the scope of this text, certain typical provisions that appear in contracts for retirement communities should be addressed by the legal assistant:

- *Financial soundness of the facility.* Just as when a person purchases a unit in a cooperative or condominium that is managed by an owner or independent management company, the financial resources of the seller are a major factor in the decision as to whether to enter into the agreement. The retiree should look into the financial ability of the owner/manager to cover emergency expenses due to the age of the facility and the cost of making capital improvements; the retiree should also find out who is obligated, and to what extent, to maintain and repair the facility. The purchase price may be low because the maintenance costs are very high, which may be prohibitive for a person on a limited income.

- *Entrance fees and admission procedures.* In addition to the cost of the unit, either by purchase or lease, some communities charge an entrance fee, which may or may not be refundable if and when the retiree moves or dies. A fee may also be charged just for the application, with no guarantee that the application will be approved or that a unit will be available in the immediate future.

  Some facilities require medical evaluation of prospective residents, and some communities even have entrance requirements, refusing to admit persons with certain physical or mental problems or limitations. For persons with physical or mental problems, even if those problems do not disqualify them from admittance, the availability of care at the facility should be investigated.

- *Costs.* In addition to an entrance fee and the cost of renting or purchasing the unit, the community may charge management fees, recreational fees, and so on, which can add substantially to the cost of entering the community. All hidden costs must be discovered and analyzed before the person enters into any agreement with the facility.

- *Services provided.* All retirement communities provide areas for recreation, and the contract should specify the services provided (and not provided; see the following section).

- *Arbitration.* Nowadays many contracts dictate that disputes over the terms of the agreement are to be settled by submitting the dispute to arbitration. Although arbitration procedures are quicker and less expensive than judicial determination, the resident may not wish to submit to arbitration, because the arbitrator's decision cannot be appealed and the resident may have little or no say in the selection of the arbitrator. Such specifics should be detailed in the contract.

- *Term of the contract.* All contracts terminate at some point, and the contract should specify when the contract ends, what conditions could cause termination prior to that date, and the rights of the parties with respect to early termination and renewal. A resident may not be happy to discover that the agreement can be terminated at the will of the owner of the community.

  The retiree must be informed of the community's policies with respect to cancellation and termination of any and all facilities and agreements, as well as any eviction policies. Some communities may require annual financial reports to document that the resident will continue to be able to meet his or her financial obligations of the contract. Conversely, a resident may decide that he or she does not like the facility and wish to leave, and so must be aware of community policy with respect to terminating a contract before the agreed-upon termination date.

- *Liability.* Liability is an extremely important issue for couples who enter into contracts with retirement communities. If one spouse dies, is the surviving spouse liable for the remainder of the contract, or can the survivor terminate early? Furthermore, if one spouse is unable to pay, is the other spouse responsible for the fees?

- *Security deposit.* The contract should indicate whether a security deposit is required and, if so, under what conditions the deposit will or will not be refunded to the resident.

- *Furniture.* Some retirement communities provide units that are completely or partially furnished; they do not expect and are not equipped for residents who bring their own belongings. In other communities, the units are unfurnished and it is the resident's responsibility to furnish his or her own unit. This can be a huge factor in the retiree's decision with respect to entering a particular community.

Services and Support

All retirement communities, by nature, provide certain services to their residents; in fact, these services present the biggest draw for attracting applicants to a facility. The actual services provided by each community should be completely investigated to determine that the services meet the retiree's needs and desires.

One of the major considerations with respect to retirement community services is the cost of such services. In some facilities, the cost of all provided services is included in the cost of the unit, and the retiree does not have to worry about incurring additional expenses for use of the services. Some facilities provide modified services in the contract, in which some services are included and others are not. This is one of the reasons the services provided should be specified in the contract. In a growing number of communities, although services are available, the resident must pay for the service on a per-use basis.

The types of services provided fall into three general categories:

1. Medical services, including medical and nursing care, dental facilities, rehabilitation and therapeutic services, and provision of various medical equipment.
2. Social services, including sports and recreational facilities, entertainment centers, beauty and hairdressing services, gym facilities, and a full range of recreational activities.
3. Assisted living services, including housekeeping, meals, laundry services, and some home health care services.

Residents' Rights

More than 30 states regulate continuing care facilities, but not all retirement communities fall within a particular statutory definition of *continuing health care facility.* Consequently, the rights of the residents are really determined more by the contract signed than by legislative enactment. For this reason, the legal assistant should make sure that certain rights are detailed in the resident's contract:

1. Transfer decisions: under what circumstances may the community transfer a resident to a different unit?
2. Grievance procedures: are any procedures established for the resident to voice complaints against the facility?
3. Management participation: may the residents participate in management decisions to determine policy, or are they subject to management decisions without appeal?
4. Eligibility requirements: must all residents be a minimum age, or may an elderly resident share the unit with a younger family member? Must the resident show evidence of private income to cover the costs of the facility? Will the facility accept Medicaid payments? What happens if the resident no longer meets eligibility requirements?

The answers to these questions may be determined only by reference to the contract in question. Unlike the laws previously discussed, which specify the rights of tenants and homeowners, no specific legal rights are afforded to residents of retirement communities outside of the general laws applicable to all tenants and homeowners.

ETHICAL CONSIDERATIONS

Living arrangements are a primary concern of all individuals, but especially of older persons whose income may be diminished and whose physical condition may be deteriorating. The desire and ability to maintain independence is a general rallying cry for the older American.

Because of the perceived frailty of elderly persons, many individuals may attempt to take advantage of them by subtle harassment, to force the elderly tenant or homeowner to move. Unscrupulous financial institutions may coerce elderly persons into entering into various forms of reverse mortgage commitments without fully explaining the implications to the homeowner, who may not realize that the loan could cause him or her ultimately to lose the house.

Even though there are various laws designed to protect the elderly from certain actions of landlords and financial institutions, many older persons are reluctant to press or fearful of asserting these rights. Legal guarantees on paper do not provide assistance in reality if the individual is too afraid to see that those rights are enforced. The fear of losing one's residence can have a potent chilling effect on the assertion of rights.

CHAPTER REVIEW

Maintaining adequate shelter is one of the primary concerns of the elderly American. All persons either rent or own their apartments or houses, and for the elderly tenant/homeowner on a reduced income, maintenance of the residence is a major financial problem.

The government provides certain limited housing assistance for the elderly. The federal government, pursuant to the Low Income Energy Assistance Program, can help elderly tenants meet utility bills. Many states mandate limits on the amount of rent that may be charged to low-income elderly tenants, and both the federal and state governments provide public housing for the elderly poor.

Elderly homeowners are faced with problems different from those of tenants. The homeowner is personally responsible for maintaining his or her residence, and may be unable to meet these obligations. Many states provide tax abatements for elderly homeowners with low incomes, and municipalities may provide low- or no-interest loans to older homeowners to assist them in maintaining their residences in good repair. Furthermore, the elderly homeowner may use the equity he or she has acquired in the residence to obtain a reverse mortgage to increase his or her monthly income while still remaining in the house.

If and when a person moves or retires, various housing alternatives are available for the elderly resident. The three major categories of such facilities are continuing care communities, which provide medical assistance to their residents; assisted living facilities, which provide limited medical care for their residents; and retirement communities, which exist primarily for healthy and active retirees.

KEY TERMS

adult home

Americans with Disabilities Act (ADA)

assisted living facility

capital asset

capital gains tax

condominium

continuing care retirement community (CCRC)

cooperative

credit line

Department of Housing and Urban Development (HUD)

disability

eminent domain

enriched housing

Fair Housing Act (FHA)

Low Income Energy Assistance Program

lump-sum reverse mortgage

project-based program

reasonable accommodation

retirement community

reverse mortgage (home equity conversion mortgage)

rollover

sale-leaseback

Section 202

shelter

single-room occupancy (SRO)

specified-term reverse mortgage

tenure plan

Truth in Lending Act

United States Housing Act of 1937

warranty of habitability

warranty of occupancy

EXERCISES

1. Check your state statute for its regulatory policies with respect to continuing care facilities.

2. Obtain a copy of a bank's reverse mortgage application and determine whether it meets the requirements of the Truth in Lending Act.

3. Check your state statute for protections afforded to elderly tenants with respect to cooperative and condominium conversions.

4. Does your state regulate residential rental units? If so, determine which, if any, rental protections are designed for elderly tenants.

5. Discuss under what circumstances a reverse mortgage would be a good or bad arrangement for an elderly homeowner.

EDITED JUDICIAL DECISIONS

Senior Civil Liberties Ass'n, Inc. v. Kemp
761 F. Supp. 1528 (M.D. Fla. 1991)

… This Court finds that there is an absence of a genuine issue as to any material fact present in this case. Therefore, this case will be decided as a matter of law.

Plaintiffs filed their complaint on April 28, 1989. The complaint alleged the following facts as relevant to the causes of action asserted:

1. The individual Plaintiffs, at all times material hereto, all have resided in dwelling units encumbered by documentary use restrictions which are covenants running with the land, and which predate the Fair Housing Amendments Act of 1988, *42 U.S.C. § 3601 et seq.,* hereinafter referred to as "Act," which prohibits children from being a permanent resident of their "community," i.e., their respective condominium, subdivision, or mobile home park.

2. Each of the individual Plaintiffs is over 70 years of age, and acquired his dwelling unit as a permanent residence prior to September 13, 1988 with the reasonable expectations:

a. That these documentary restrictions, which violated no statutory or constitutional provisions of the law or Constitutions of the United States or the State of Florida, would continue to be valid and enforceable property and contract rights, free from impairment by any law of the State of Florida so long as they were not arbitrarily and selectively enforced, and that these property and contract rights would not be taken by action of the United States Government.

b. Of privacy in continued peaceful possession of their respective dwelling units without the permanent presence of children under the age specified in their respective documents.

3. Each of the individual Plaintiffs' ownership or leasehold interest in his dwelling unit includes, as an appurtenance thereto, a joint ownership or use interest in the common areas/elements of their community, such as the recreation facilities and open space areas.

4. Each of the individual Plaintiffs purchased or leased his dwelling unit in reliance on advertising or written assurances that his community was an adult retirement community.

5. Each of the individual Plaintiffs resides in a community in which at least 80 percent of the dwelling units are occupied by at least one person 55 years of age or older, and intentionally chose to live in a community with such an age-homogenous environment.

6. Each of the individual Plaintiffs, by virtue of accepting the deed or lease to his property,

agreed to be bound by the documentary restrictions encumbering his community, which documents constitute a mutual agreement among all of the dwelling unit owners or lessees in each community.

7. The Act, in *42 U.S.C. § 3602(k)* defines "familial status" as: "... one or more individuals (who have not attained the age of 18 years) being domiciled with a parent, one having legal custody, or the designee of such parent or other person." The familial status is further bestowed upon pregnant women, and any person in the process of securing legal custody of an individual under 18 years of age.

8. The Act, in § 3604, makes it unlawful to, based upon familial status, refuse to sell or rent, or otherwise make unavailable or deny, a dwelling to any person; to discriminate against any person in the terms, conditions, or privileges of sale or rental, or in the provision or services or facilities in connections therewith; and to make, print, or publish any notice, statements or advertisement with respect to a sale or rental indicating any preference, limitation, or discrimination.

9. By virtue of the aforementioned sections of the Act, enforcement of the documentary restrictions would be violative of the Act, and would subject the individual Plaintiffs, and the members of the Boards of Directors of their respective associations, as well as the associations themselves, to severe penalties for violating the Act.

10. The Act contains two exemptions, for two types of "housing for older persons," hereinafter referred to HFOP, which are material to the privately financed housing communities at issue, as described in §§ 3607(b)(2)(B) and (C). These HFOP exemptions are commonly known as the "62 or older" and the "55 or older" exemptions.

11. Although enacted on September 13, 1988, the Act by its terms did not take effect until March 12, 1989.

12. In order to qualify for the 62 or older exemption, all new occupants of a housing facility after September 13, 1988 must have been aged sixty-two or older. The presence of one underage occupant is fatal to qualification for the exemption.

13. The 62 or older exemption is restrictive in its definition and severely limits the use and marketability of Plaintiffs' dwelling units.

14. The 55 or older exemption requires that the housing facility have:

(i) ... significant facilities and services designed to meet the physical or social needs of older persons, or if the provision of such facilities and services is not practicable, that such housing is necessary to provide important housing opportunities for older persons; and

(ii) that at least 80 percent of the units are occupied by at least one person 55 years of age or older per unit; and

(iii) the publication of, and adherence to, policies and procedures which demonstrate an intent by the owner or manager to provide housing for persons 55 years of age or older.

The Complaint contains the following causes of action against Defendants:

Plaintiffs seek to have this Court declare unconstitutional and enjoin certain provisions of the Fair Housing Amendments Act of 1988 as applied to the Plaintiffs on the grounds that they are violative of the following provisions of the Constitution of the United States:

1. The Act violates Plaintiffs' right to freedom of association guaranteed to them by the First Amendment and their right of privacy as guaranteed to them by the First, Fourth, Fifth and Ninth Amendments.
2. The Act deprives Plaintiffs of equal protection of the laws in that it deprives them of liberty and property rights in violation of the Fifth Amendment with no basis therefor.
3. The Act takes Plaintiffs' liberty and property interests for a private purpose, without compensation, in violation of the Fifth Amendment.
4. The Act deprives Plaintiffs of due process of law, by depriving them of vested property and contractual rights with no basis therefore, and subjects Plaintiffs PRIEL, RIEDEL and SHIPLEY to arbitrary and capricious discrimination without due process of law, in violation of the Fifth Amendment.

5. The Act, and the regulations promulgated thereunder by Defendant, deprive Plaintiffs of due process of law by virtue of the vagueness of the "Housing for Older Persons" exemptions, in violation of the Fifth Amendment.

6. Finally, the Act violates Plaintiffs' property and contract rights guaranteed them by the State of Florida, in violation of both the Tenth Amendment and the principles of federalism embodied in the Constitution. The Act regulates purely local conduct, and is not a proper matter for federal regulation.

THE PLAINTIFFS

The individual Plaintiffs are all residents of Pinellas County, Florida, and are all members of Plaintiff, Senior Civil Liberties Association, Inc. (hereinafter "SCLA").

Plaintiffs MOTYL own a detached single-family home in a subdivision known as Highland Lakes in Palm Harbor. They are retired, are in their seventies and are originally from Detroit. Prior to their retirement, they decided they wanted a quiet place to retire, in a "senior citizen's retirement subdivision," with no children. They found no such facility in Michigan, or in the Atlanta area and eventually came to Florida. After looking at several advertised areas, they decided on a new home in Highland Lakes. Moving to a new state and severing life-long relationships and friendships was very difficult, but their new adopted life-style without children "supersedes all previous sacrifices and hardships encountered so far."

All of the advertising by the developer described Highland Lakes as an "adult retirement community." A sign at the front entrance says "Highland Lakes for the Retirement Time of Your Life."

Highland Lakes is comprised of 2,360 single-family houses and villa units, plus a three-story, thirty-unit condominium apartment building. The entire subdivision is subject to a Declaration of Restrictions, which originally required at least one permanent occupant of a lot to be at least fifty years of age and prohibited permanent occupancy by anyone under sixteen. The common areas of the subdivision, including two clubhouses, two swimming pools and a twenty-seven hole executive golf course are, pursuant to the Declaration, owned and operated by a homeowner's association. The Declaration makes membership in the association mandatory with acquisition of title to an encumbered lot and grants the lot owner the right to use the association properties.

In 1989, the Declaration was amended to raise the minimum age to fifty-five and give the homeowners' association the power to assess for any alterations or improvements in order to provide facilities or services designed to meet the requirements of the Act.

The facilities presently include a twenty-seven hole executive golf course, two swimming pools, two clubhouses (each with a kitchen, auditorium, offices, small meeting rooms, management office and card rooms), tennis courts, shuffleboard courts, exercise classes, swimming classes, aerobics classes, ceramics, dances, entertainment, speakers at association meetings and association sponsorship of various clubs such as the men's club, theater club, travel club and organ club.

Plaintiff PRIEL is the owner of a double-wide, "tied-down" mobile home in Golden Crest Mobile Home Park, in Dunedin. She is seventy-eight. She and her late husband retired from upstate New York to the park in 1971. In 1975 they "traded up" to the present unit. When they purchased, they intentionally chose to live with people of their own age.

The original advertising for the park said it was a "retirement community." The Park Rules, which were part of the only lease she ever signed, in 1975, said it was an "adult park," although children could visit as guests. The Prospectus approved by the Florida Bureau of Mobile Homes in 1985, pursuant to Chapter 723, Florida Statutes, restated the adult-only rule by requiring that every resident shall be eighteen years of age or over.

Golden Crest Mobile Home Park has 176 mobile homes. The present facilities include a swimming pool, shuffleboard courts, pool table, laundry facilities, recreation building (with kitchen, library, piano, television, stereo and large tables), dinners, pot luck coffee hours, meals on wheels, congregate dining and public bus service. Most of the furnishings and equipment have been paid for over the years by the residents, and not the park owner. The recreation facilities are run by a Recreation Board, an unofficial entity created by the park owner. The Board has no assessment powers. There is also an incorporated homeowners' association, created in 1987, pursuant to Chapter 723, Florida Statutes.

The Complaint alleges that shortly after the passage of the Act, the park owner threatened to stop enforcing the no-children rule unless the residents came up with money to pay for the installation of additional facilities and services. This demand was dropped in the face of pressure from the homeowners' association. The park owner amended the rules anyway, in 1989, to require that residents be fifty-five years of age or older.

Plaintiff SHIPLEY is in her seventies and from Virginia. Her husband is in his nineties. Neither of the Shipleys are in good health. They live in the Heather Lake Condominium Community, in Dunedin, comprised of twelve low-rise apartment buildings in ten separately declared condominiums. She purchased a unit in Condo II in 1979 or 1980 where she lived for a year before marrying her husband and moving into his unit in Condo X in 1981. Her husband's unit was purchased in 1979 or 1980 on re-sale from a speculator who had purchased from the developer.

Both of the SHIPLEYS purchased their units because the complex was for adults only. They have raised four children, but now, in their "later years," they cannot tolerate the noise which would be made by children residing in the complex.

All of the Declarations of Condominium in Heather Lake have the same provisions. The originally recorded Rules and Regulations require that each unit shall be used as a single-family residence of persons over the age of sixteen. In 1989, the Declaration was amended, with the expressed intent of qualifying for an exemption under the Act, to require that 80 percent of the units have at least one permanent occupant 55 years or older,

and that all permanent occupants be at least 18 years of age.

The Heather Lake complex contains a recreation clubhouse (with kitchen, library, bathrooms, lounge, pool table, card tables, sofas, chairs, piano, television and tables), swimming pool, shuffleboard courts, entertainment, coffee hours, cookouts, "stitch & chat," card games, bingo, hospital volunteer program, Neighborly Senior Services, Inc., meals on wheels, "walking for fitness," Thanksgiving dinner, Christmas dinner dance, and outings.

In late 1988–1989, Plaintiff SHIPLEY put her unit in Condo II on the market for sale. When the Act took effect in March, 1989, she could not continue advertising the unit as "adults only" or "no children," for fear this would constitute a violation of the Act. Advertising consisted of a notice on the clubhouse bulletin board, and ads in two small local newspapers: the *Palm Harbor Sounder* and the *Dunedin Times.* The unit was eventually sold, in October, 1989. Plaintiff SHIPLEY did not use a real estate broker.

Plaintiffs RIEDEL are in their eighties and retired to Florida from New York City in 1963. They rented in various places, mostly in Clearwater Beach, until purchasing their unit in the Clearwater Point Condominium complex in December, 1982. They never saw any printed advertising materials, as they purchased on resale, but "it was generally known in the area that Clearwater Point was and is an 'adult community.' "

Plaintiffs RIEDEL are not in good health either. The prohibition against children contained in the condominium documents was also an important consideration to them when they purchased because of their age and their health.

Clearwater Point is comprised of eight separately declared condominiums, six of which are three-story town house clusters. The other two condominiums, including theirs, are each comprised of two high-rise apartment buildings. The two buildings which comprise the RIEDELS' condominium contain a total of 137 units. The entire community contains a much greater number of units.

The recreational facilities for the complex are owned by a separate corporation controlled by the eight condominium associations. There are two small heated pools and a large heated pool and jacuzzi, adjacent to which is a small building with showers and toilets, a barbecue area and beachfront. Pursuant to the condominium documents, unit owners (only) may, upon purchasing their units, elect to join the corporation and obtain use rights in the facilities, which Plaintiffs RIEDEL did. Once elected, this right runs with ownership of the unit.

The Declaration of Condominium has, at least since they acquired their unit, prohibited children under sixteen from residing on the premises. Their condominium association has not amended the Declaration since the passage of the Act.

Plaintiffs MOTYL, PRIEL and SHIPLEY make the educated guess that virtually all of the units in their communities are occupied by at least one person over fifty-five. Plaintiffs RIEDEL do not know, knowing only that most residents are retired.

PRELIMINARY ISSUES

Local Rule 3.01 [discussion omitted]

Standing [discussion omitted]

Legislative History

The applicable sections of the Fair Housing Amendments Act of 1988, *42 U.S.C. § 3601 et seq.* (1988), read as follows:

§ 3604. Discrimination in the sale or rental of housing and other prohibited practices

As made applicable by section 3603 of this title and except as exempted by sections 3603(b) and 3607 of this title, it shall be unlawful—

(a) To refuse to sell or rent after the making of a bona fide offer, or to refuse to negotiate for the sale or rental of, or otherwise make unavailable or deny, a dwelling to any person because of race, color, religion, sex, familial status, or natural origin.

(b) To discriminate against any person in the terms, conditions, or privileges of sale or rental of a dwelling, or in the provision of services or facilities in connection therewith, because of race,

color, religion, sex, familial status, or natural origin.

(c) To make, print, or publish, or cause to be made, printed, or published any notice, statement, or advertisement, with respect to the sale or rental of a dwelling that indicates any preference, limitation, or discrimination based on race, color, religion, sex, handicap, familial status, or national origin, or an intention to make any such preference, limitation, or discrimination.

(d) To represent to any person because of race, color, religion, sex, handicap, familial status, or national origin that any dwelling is not available for inspection, sale, or rental when such dwelling is in fact so available.

(e) For profit, to induce or attempt to induce any person to sell or rent any dwelling by representations regarding the entry or prospective entry into the neighborhood of a person or persons of a particular race, color, religion, sex, handicap, familial status, or national origin.

Because the Act itself contains no expressions of congressional purpose or intent, the Court looks to the report of the House Judiciary Committee, H.R. Rep. No. 100-711, reprinted 1988 U.S. Code Cong. & Admin. News 2173, and the floor debates in Congress, where the original bill was amended. 134 Cong. Rec. H4603–4607 (daily ed. June 22, 1988), H4679–4688 (daily ed. June 23, 1988), S10454–20469 (daily ed. Aug. 1, 1988), H6497–6501 (daily ed. Aug. 8, 1988).

Both parties allege that Congress was presented with overwhelming evidence that discrimination against families with children was a major national problem in need of congressional attention and action. There the similarities end.

Plaintiffs further allege that although the House Report states the purpose of the "familial status" portions of the Act was to deal with an increasing difficulty that people with children are having in finding housing, none of the studies cited in the house report attest to any nationwide problem these people are having in finding homes to purchase. Plaintiffs also allege that in the initial presentation of the bill on the House floor, the familial status provisions of the Act were again explained in terms of the problems created by the fact of too much rental housing prohibiting children. Finally, Plaintiffs call this Court's attention to the comments made by Rep. Fish. Rep. Fish described the problem solely in terms of rental housing, and stated that:

> The aim is not to disrupt the lives of senior citizens or the operation of legitimate retirement communities. Rather, we seek to expand the availability of rental units for young families without arbitrary exclusions and limitation. 134 Cong. Rec. H4605.

Plaintiffs conclude by stating that the legislative history does not support Defendant's assertion that Congress was presented with any evidence that documentary age restrictions in ownership housing are a problem.

Defendant alleges that a substantial amount of testimony focused on how discrimination was a problem for families in all types of housing units and transactions. Defendant contends that Congress was presented with evidence that documentary age restrictions were a problem in ownership housing and did in fact intend to alleviate discrimination in ownership housing as well as in rental housing by passing this Act.

Most of the pertinent legislative history is contained in the Hearings before the Subcommittee on Civil and Constitutional Rights of the Committee on the Judiciary, House of Representatives, One Hundredth Congress, First Session on H.R. 1158, Fair Housing Amendments Act of 1987 (hereinafter known as House Hearings), and the Hearings before the Subcommittee on the Constitution of the Committee on the Judiciary, United States Senate, One Hundredth Congress, First Session on S. 558, A Bill to Amend Title VIII of the Act Commonly Called The Civil Rights Act of 1968, to Revise the Procedures for the Enforcement of Fair Housing, and for Other Purposes (hereinafter referred to as Senate Hearings).

After reading all the pertinent legislative history, this Court agrees with Defendant that the Fair Housing Amendments Act of 1988 applies to both rental and ownership housing.

Although nothing in the reports and hearings of both the House and the Senate directly states that this Act includes discrimination in ownership housing, all materials speak to "the housing market" and "housing discrimination" in general.

The Fair Housing Amendments Act of 1988 came before Congress exactly 20 years after the Fair Housing Act of 1968 was passed. Congress stated when they passed the Fair Housing Act of 1968 that they could no longer tolerate discrimination in the sale or rental of housing on the basis of race, color, religion, or national origin. In 1974, sex was added to this list. Twenty years later, with discrimination and segregation well documented, Congress saw the need to add to the list of protected classes, families with children and individuals with handicaps. In short, it was the legislature's intent to open up all forms of housing to parents with children under 18 except those that are designed for older persons and qualify for an exemption.

Defendant also asserts that a substantial amount of the legislative history focuses on criticism of the discrimination laws of other states. According to the statement and testimony of James Morales found at Senate Hearings, pp. 166–210, sixteen states and the District of Columbia currently have laws prohibiting child discrimination. Mr. Morales also testified that many advocates have had a difficult time going against powerful real estate interests who oppose bills that would prohibit housing discrimination against families with children. Mr. Morales further testified that the result of this is that the vast majority of states do not have laws and those that do generally have weak and ineffectual laws that are riddled with exemptions that permit discrimination to continue because they fail to cover all real estate transactions.

Mr. Morales then goes on to give some examples. Illinois, for example, protects families with younger children but does not protect families with older children above the age of fourteen. Also, nine of the sixteen states with housing discrimination laws, Florida incidentally not being one of them, limit their laws to encompass only rental units and thus do not apply to discrimination in the sale of property. Other states do not cover specific types of housing such as mobile home parks and condominiums.

Mr. Morales concludes by stating that amending the Fair Housing Act to protect familial status would obviously not end child discrimination, but it would, with the addition of the strengthening of administrative remedies, become one of the strongest fair housing laws for families in the country. Not only would it provide remedies in those States where none exist, but would also close many of the loopholes that currently exist in the State Laws, such as covering rental, but not ownership housing, and provide further remedies in the Federal Courts. *Id.* at 168.

This Court interprets Mr. Morales' statements to mean that Congress designed the Act to alleviate all the listed forms of discrimination present in all housing arrangements.

The testimony of David S. Liederman found in the House Hearings, pp. 163–72, also addresses this subject matter. Mr. Liederman testified that it is time to establish a national anti-discrimination standard for treatment of families seeking homes anywhere in the United States. He further testified that the existing sixteen state statutes offer varying degrees of fair housing protection to families but none can offer assurance of coverage for all families. Mr. Liederman then asks that the legislature provide a minimum level of fair housing for families with children as part of the overall effectiveness of Title VIII. *Id.* at 170.

Defendant further argues that the Act addresses discrimination that is prevalent in two common types of ownership housing, namely, mobile homes and condominiums. The statement of the American Planning Association, found at House Hearings, pp. 513–20, states that interest in manufactured housing, and mobile homes in particular, has surged greatly in recent years, the greatest attraction being low cost and low maintenance. The statement also refers to a state-wide study of mobile home parks which revealed that 63% expressly stated that they were "adult-only." The Association further states that families with children are encountering extreme difficulties in finding mobile home housing and that their frus-

trations are manifested through a growing number of lawsuits in which current or prospective residents are challenging age-restrictive policies of mobile home parks. Lastly, the statement points out that the increased demand for affordable housing by families, as well as significant changes in the design of mobile homes, make the exclusionary practices of some park owners all the more unfair and detrimental to the welfare of society. *Id.* at 516.

Congress also heard testimony regarding discrimination occurring in condominiums. One report in particular, also from the American Planning Association, states that condominiums traditionally have catered to the elderly or to the young and therefore have age-restrictive rules or covenants. The Association concluded that as a result, families with children have been greatly excluded from this segment of the housing market. *Id.* at 516.

The Court concludes that the purpose of the Fair Housing Amendments Act is to put into effect an overall system that uniformly protects all states and alleviates discrimination against families in all housing markets. Congress was informed and took into consideration the problems occurring in the rental and sales of single-family homes, mobile homes and condominiums.

Plaintiffs did present a thought-provoking argument. Plaintiffs contend that the primary studies were restricted to rental housing and that Congress was not presented with any evidence that discrimination against families with children in the ownership context was a national problem to any extent. Therefore, Plaintiffs contend that applying the Act retrospectively to ownership housing is not rationally related to the problem as perceived by Congress.

The Court concedes that most, but not all, of the testimony brought before Congress concerned the affect that age discrimination was having on rental housing. This Court notes that the reason for this emphasis on rental housing is well documented in the legislative history. The studies and reports consistently stated that over the past ten years more and more Americans have been unable to purchase homes and have been forced into the rental market. Factors that have forced this shift have included high interest rates, and energy and inflation-related increases in land prices, and construction costs, to the point where the average cost of a single-family home is over $100,000. At the same time the supply of affordable rental housing has not expanded to meet the demand. This has been due to cuts in federal funds subsidizing the construction of housing for low and moderate-income people, as well as changes in tax laws and other conditions making multi-family housing less attractive to developers.

Besides these economic factors, the last ten years have seen a shift in demographic factors affecting housing. More and more baby boomers are postponing marriage, delaying having children, and are living alone, or as couples or in other small households. At the same time, more and more people over 55 are enjoying longer life expectancies, also in households of one or two. These two groups, the baby boomer and the seniors are competing with less affluent families with larger households for what is available in the way of rental housing. Landlords prefer to rent to smaller households who are perceived to have larger, or at least steadier, incomes and quieter, less disruptive life-styles.

Upon further examination of the legislative history, the Court notes other items which round out the history. Congress was provided with a nationwide statistic that stated that about 35% of all families depend on the rental market. House Hearings, p. 514 (Statement of the American Planning Association). Second, James Morales' testimony, found at House Hearings, pp. 374–75, extended the above history by further stating that with household size decreasing and childless households increasing, developers and landlords do not have to respond to the demands of families with children to make their businesses financially successful. Mr. Morales' testimony also stated that instead, developers can build houses and apartments with fewer bedrooms and less square footage and landlords can refuse to rent to families with children or impose other policies that severely restrict the number of children in units. Third, the prepared statement of Homer C. Floyd found on pp. 241–42 of the Senate Hearings provides some insight into the economic situation discussed above. Mr. Floyd's statement declares that discrimination against families with children also injures middle and higher income families because even though they may not be trapped in the rental market, they are likely to find that income alone will not necessarily buy them the housing of their choice should that choice include condominiums and other facilities which exclude children.

The legislature was presented with an awesome amount of information concerning the need to alleviate discrimination based on familial status. The Act in question was intended to close all the loopholes and make all the State laws uniform. It is this Court's opinion that the Act was intended to encompass both the sale and rental of single-family dwellings, mobile homes and condominiums. Therefore, this Act would apply to any alleged discriminatory practices of Plaintiffs or their associations, unless their communities qualify for an exemption.

RETROACTIVITY

Plaintiffs insist that the Act applies retrospectively to existing ownership housing and is therefore unconstitutional.

More specifically, Plaintiffs allege that the application of the Act to existing ownership communities creates disparate treatment. Plaintiffs state that while the developer of a new community can, from the outset, plan to include whatever is deemed sufficient to qualify for the "55 or over" exemption, and factor those additional cost into the sales of the units, Plaintiffs do not have that luxury.

Finally, Plaintiffs allege that since it is only the retrospective application of the Act to existing ownership housing that is at issue, there is no rational basis for failing to exempt existing communities from the familial status provisions of the Act, while exempting existing housing facilities from the "building code" provisions of the "handicap" provisions of the Act. § 804(f)(3)(C).

Defendant has not addressed the issue of retroactivity. However, Plaintiffs state that Defendant may respond that exempting existing structures from the building code provisions was a practical necessity in that to require landlords to undertake such major structural renovations would wreak financial havoc on the landlords, while unduly disrupting the lives of their tenants while the renovations are being undertaken.

In seeking justification for retroactive application of the familial status provisions to the Plaintiffs, Plaintiffs argue that the Constitution does not provide greater protection to profit-motivated activities than to the conduct of people's lives.

This Court is not persuaded by Plaintiffs' arguments because it finds that the Act does not apply retrospectively. For this reason, no justification for retroactivity is necessary. In fact, this Court would also be open to the suggestion that the familial status portions of the act are prospective for the very same reasons that Plaintiffs feel the handicap provisions are. Further reasons for this Court's holding are as follows.

This Court would once again address the "Housing For Older Persons" exemptions of the Act set out supra, pp. 38–39.

This Court relies on *White v. U.S., 191 U.S. 545, 24 S. Ct. 171, 48 L. Ed. 295 (1903).* In that case, the Court said:

> Where it is claimed that a law is to have retroactive application such must be clearly the intention, evidenced in the law and its purposes, or the court will presume that the lawmaking power is acting for the future, and not for the past; that it is enacting a rule of conduct which shall control the future rights and dealing of men, rather than review and affix new obligations to that which has been done in the past.

Id. at 552, 24 S. Ct. at 172, 48 L. Ed. at 295.

This Court can find no clear intent expressed in the Act that any of its provisions should act retrospectively. There are, however, certain provisions that clearly express that they are to be applied prospectively. For example, § 807(b)(3)(A) and (B) read as follows:

(3) Housing shall not fail to meet the requirements for housing for older persons by reason of:

(A) persons residing in such housing as of September 13, 1988, who do not meet the age requirements of subsections (2)(B) or (C): Provided, that new occupants of such housing meet the age requirements of subsection (2)(B) or (C); or

(B) unoccupied units: Provided, that such units are reserved for occupancy by persons who meet the age requirements of subsection (2)(B) or (C).

These provisions go a step further and make the age requirement explicitly prospective. If Congress wanted to make the whole Act prospective, Congress could have included a similar provision regarding the other requirements of the exemptions. However, this was not done. This Court speculates that this was not done because Congress presumed that all presently existing facilities were likely to qualify, but could not presume that all current residents met the age requirement; hence, the different treatment.

This idea is also furthered by legislative history. Representative Synar's testimony, found at House Hearings, p. H4681 reads in part that:

> The gentleman from Florida addressed that [retrospective application] and he tried to make the statement that would require expenditures of money in order to qualify. The fact of the matter is if one looks at the report language of the committee we do not require specific facilities to be retrofitted in order to meet this qualification. Second, and most importantly, most of the senior citizen-type housing in this country already meets these types of restrictions and limitations.

Once again this Court finds the whole idea of "significant facilities and services specifically designed to meet the physical or social needs of older persons" is a function of what the older person intended it to be when they chose the place in which they now reside. These facilities need not now be retrofitted to better fit the language of the Act.

This Court speculates that existing older person housing already qualifies for the exemption. For the future, however, Congress has seen fit to give additional guidelines for determination of appropriate older person housing.

CONSTITUTIONAL ISSUES

The Commerce Clause

The Commerce Clause is found in Article I, § 8 of the United States Constitution and reads in part as follows: "Congress shall have the power to regulate commerce with foreign nations and among the several states and with Indian tribes ... ."

The definitions of "commerce" and "commerce among the several states" are set out in *Gibbons v. Ogden, 9 Wheat. 1, 22 U.S. 1, 6 L. Ed. 23 (1824).* In that case, the Court defined "commerce" as commercial intercourse—anything related to buying and selling. The Court defined "commerce among the several states" to mean any commerce (commercial intercourse) that affects more than one state. The Court went on to say that the activity didn't have to cross state lines in order to constitute interstate commerce.

Plaintiffs contend that Congress does not have authority under the Commerce Clause to regulate age-restricted housing as it has done in the Act. In support, Plaintiffs assert that there is "no activity 'in' or 'in the flow of' interstate commerce" due to the fact that "any construction materials which once moved in interstate commerce have long since been affixed to the realty" and "any advertising utilizing instrumentalities of interstate commerce is long over."

Plaintiffs also contend that "they are now home, long retired from their life in commerce. Any further involvement of interstate commerce, when and if it is remotely involved, is separate, distinct, and merely fortuitous."

Plaintiffs further contend "any incidental effect on interstate commerce or interstate travel is also purely speculative." Plaintiffs state that "there is no indication that any parent transferred to Florida from out of state for business reasons has had any problem finding a home or apartment to purchase because of the existence of child restrictions in ownership housing, or even that the documented shortage of rental housing in other parts of the country has anything to do with existing age restrictions in ownership units available for rental."

This Court is not persuaded by Plaintiffs' reasoning, and supports Defendant's position and analysis.

Defendant relies on the recent case of *Preseault v. I.C.C., 494 U.S. 1, 110 S. Ct. 914, 108 L. Ed. 2d 1 (1990)* in which the Supreme Court held that "[courts] must defer to a congressional finding that a regulated activity affects interstate commerce 'if there is *any* rational basis for such a finding' " [emphasis added]. *Id.*

Defendant further cites *Heart of Atlanta Motel, Inc. v. United States, 379 U.S. 241, 85 S. Ct. 348, 13 L. Ed. 2d 258 (1964).* In that case, the appellant challenged the constitutionally of *28 U.S.C. § 2201* which prohibited discrimination against race in public accommodations affecting commerce.

The Court stated that "the determinative test of the exercise of power by the Congress under the Commerce Clause is whether the activity sought to be regulated is 'commerce which concerns more States than one' and has a real and substantial relation to the national interest," which includes the interstate travel of citizens. The Court explained that racial discrimination in the hotel burdened interstate commerce by hindering the interstate mobility of the population. The Court further explained that this discrimination discouraged certain persons from interstate travel.

The above scenario is very close to the scenario in the instant case. With the present mobility of the population in mind, it is certainly foreseeable that if an increasing amount of subdivisions, mobile homes, condominiums and apartments regularly excluded families with children, these same families would be prevented from seeking new housing around the country. The possibility of this discriminatory treatment would most likely prevent such families' interstate travel, and therefore affect interstate commerce. Additionally, the efficient allocation of labor among interstate components of the economy would be hindered, once again affecting interstate commerce.

Therefore, if housing discrimination against families with children occurred a substantial amount of times, it would inhibit the ability and desire of families to travel interstate. Because interstate travel is a form of interstate commerce, this discrimination against families with children could have a far-reaching effect on interstate commerce, and thus would fall within Congress' ambit to regulate.

By using its power to regulate in this sphere and eliminating housing discrimination based on familial status, Congress provided a rational means of removing impediments to the interstate movement of people and commerce.

Defendant further contends that Plaintiffs' argument ignores the reality of ownership housing. Defendant explains that in considering this legislation, Congress reasonably concluded that the fact that construction of a home was complete, or the fact that such a home may be subject to only "occasional resale," does not remove it from the flow of interstate commerce and thereby insulate it from congressional regulation.

Defendant contends that Plaintiffs have not presented a plausible argument that individual sales of their own homes do not affect interstate commerce in some manner under the decisions of the Supreme Court. Real estate concerns do business on an interstate basis. Homes are renovated and improved utilizing instrumentalities and goods in interstate commerce. Most basically, people travel across state lines to purchase homes. Plaintiffs cannot deny that a substantial majority of older persons in Florida moved there from out of state. In fact, all of the individual Plaintiffs did so.

This Court is further persuaded by the reasoning in the *Heart of Atlanta* case wherein the Court stated that "if it is interstate commerce that feels the pinch, it does not matter how local the operation which applies the squeeze." Also, with regard to local action, the *Heart of Atlanta* case held:

> In deciding the constitutional power of Congress ... we do not consider the effect on interstate commerce of only one isolated, individual, local event, without regard to the fact that this single local event when added to many others of a similar nature may impose a burden on interstate commerce by reducing its volume or distorting its flow.

Id. at 275.

Further, in *McLain v. Real Estate Board of New Orleans, 444 U.S. 232, 100 S. Ct. 502, 62 L. Ed. 2d 441 (1980)* the Supreme Court determined that certain aspects of local real estate activity are subject to congressional regulation under the Commerce Clause. The Court finds that Congress has the power to regulate, through the Act, the local real estate activities of the Plaintiffs which includes occasional resale.

The final Commerce Clause contention involves the case of *Goldfarb v. Virginia State Bar, 421 U.S. 773, 95 S. Ct. 2004, 44 L. Ed. 2d 572 (1975).* In that case, the activity at issue was the fixing of prices of title insurance. The Court held that this activity was a commercial service that was an integral part of the financing of the purchase of property, which financing operated in interstate commerce.

Plaintiffs contend that in Goldfarb the minimum fee schedule was a commercial service that affected all sales of property all over the country, whereas, in the instant case, there is no showing of anything other than occasional individual resales of units—an action that does not constitute commercial activity.

Defendant states that this distinction is not persuasive because Plaintiffs' attempt to downplay the degree of commercial action in the ownership of existing housing communities as "occasional resales" is belied by their own actions. This Court is in full agreement with the Defendant because three out of the four individual Plaintiffs admitted in their interrogatories to rental, sale or resale of their housing units since they have been residing in Florida. These actions would not be classified as "occasional resales."

In conclusion, this Court finds that Congress has the power to regulate discriminatory practices that are occurring in all types of housing through the Fair Housing Amendments Act.

Tenth Amendment

Plaintiffs also contend that the Act violates their property and contract rights as guaranteed them by the State of Florida, in violation of both the Tenth Amendment and the principles of federalism embodied in the Constitution. Plaintiffs further contend that the Act regulates purely local conduct and is not a proper matter for federal regulation.

Plaintiffs base their claim on the fact that the people of Florida amended their Constitution in 1980 to add a new, express right of privacy to the Florida Declaration of Rights. Article I, Section 23 of the Florida Declaration of Rights provides:

> Right of privacy—Every natural person has the right to be left alone and free from governmental intrusion into his private life except as otherwise provided herein. This section shall not be construed to limit the public's right of access to public records and meetings as provided by law.

Plaintiffs contend that the Florida Supreme Court has held that, consistent with express invitations to do so by the United States Supreme Court, the citizens of Florida, in adopting this amendment, opted for more protection from governmental intrusion than afforded by the United States Constitution. Plaintiffs rely on *In re T.W., 551 So. 2d 1186 (Fla. 1989).*

Plaintiffs further argue that since the State of Florida has chosen to affirmatively act to grant its citizens greater privacy rights than those granted by the federal government, the Tenth Amendment comes into play to void any attempt to interfere therewith under the guise of the Commerce Clause.

This Court finds Plaintiffs' argument without merit. Plaintiffs are relying on the outdated concept of "dual federalism." Dual federalism stood for the proposition that the Tenth Amendment is a check upon the plenary power of Congress—even if the commerce power is correctly applied. However, the Supreme Court, in *Garcia v. San Antonio Metropolitan Transit Authority, 469 U.S. 528, 105 S. Ct. 1005, 83 L. Ed. 2d 1016 (1985),* sets out the Tenth Amendment limits on Congress' authority to regulate State activities.

Defendant correctly points out that there is no regulation of a state activity present because the Act is directed at private housing conduct that has no relation to the state, and therefore no relation to the Tenth Amendment.

Defendant further argues that the Supreme Court, in *South Carolina v. Baker, 485 U.S. 505, 108 S. Ct. 1355, 99 L. Ed. 2d 592 (1988),* noted that "Garcia holds that the [Tenth Amendment] limits are structural, not substantive—i.e., that states must find their protection from Congressional regulation through the national political process, not through judicially-defined spheres of unregulable state activity." In addition, the South Carolina court reasoned that: "Nothing in *Garcia* or the Tenth Amendment authorizes courts to second-guess the substantive basis for congressional legislation. Where, as here, the political process did not operate in a defective manner, the Tenth Amendment is not implicated." *Id. at 512.*

This Court notes that it is questionable whether Plaintiffs have standing to raise the claims of the State of Florida. However, the Court will not address that issue, in light of the fact that after *Garcia,* it appears that the Tenth Amendment [issue] has been virtually eliminated.

Additionally, as in the *Garcia* case, there is no indication that the political process involved in drafting the Act has not worked properly. This Court finds that the legislative history indicates that Congress gave substantial attention to numerous considerations during its deliberations on the Act.

Plaintiffs also contend that under the federal system, the regulation of the real property rights of its citizens is one of the most important aspects of the sovereignty retained by the States. Plaintiffs further argue that the regulation of how the State's people live is particularly a matter of local concern, especially when the preservation of a way of life involves no invidious discrimination.

Plaintiffs argue that because Florida has chosen to enact a broad state constitutional protection of privacy, the Federal Fair Housing Amendments Act must be struck down. This interpretation blatantly violates the Supremacy Clause contained in Article VI of the United States Constitution. The Supremacy Clause mandates that whenever state and federal law conflict, it is the state, not the federal provision which must be voided. See again, *Garcia, supra.*

For the aforementioned reasons, this Court finds that the Fair Housing Amendments Act does not violate the Tenth Amendment of the United States Constitution.

Rights of Privacy and Association

Plaintiffs have also alleged that the Act violates their right of privacy as guaranteed to them by the First, Fourth, Fifth and Ninth Amendments and their right to freedom of association as guaranteed to them by the First Amendment.

Plaintiffs contend that the right of privacy has both "decisional" and "spatial" aspects, both of which converge in the instant case.

Plaintiffs cite *Thornburgh v. American College of Obstetricians and Gynecologists, 476 U.S. 747, 106 S. Ct. 2169, 90 L. Ed. 2d 779 (1986),* which states that "the Constitution embodies a guarantee that a 'certain private sphere of individual liberty' will be kept largely beyond the reach of government."

Plaintiffs address, in turn, "decisional" and "spatial" privacy. "Decisional" privacy involves privacy in personal living and family arrangements. *Bowers v. Hardwick, 478 U.S. 186, 106 S. Ct. 2841, 92 L. Ed. 2d 140 (1986).* In that case the Court stated that the right of decisional privacy is protected not because these decisions contribute, in some direct and material way, to the general public welfare, but because they form so central a part of an individual's life.

"Spatial" privacy recognizes a privacy interest with respect to places—the very basic right to be free within the privacy of one's own home from "sights, sounds, and tangible matter (one) does not want." *Reeves v. McConn, 631 F.2d 377 (5th Cir. 1980),* quoting *Rowan v. United States Post Office, 397 U.S. 728, 90 S. Ct. 1484, 25 L. Ed. 2d 736 (1970).*

Defendant contends that Plaintiffs claim an alleged right of privacy which extends far beyond any such right carved out by the Supreme Court. The Supreme Court has consistently limited the "private sphere" to highly personal, intimate relationships that are not present in this case. Those protected relationships are best exemplified by marriage and the creation and sustenance of a family. Of the cases addressing intimate relationships, two cases involved contraception, one involved pregnancy, one involved childraising, two involved marriage and one involved marital privacy.

As to "decisional" privacy, Defendant contends that while the dissenting opinion in *Bowers* argued that such a right may exist, the Court in that case did not find a violation of that right in a far more "intimate" setting than the facts in this case. In the *Bowers* case, the Court was asked to extend privacy to include consensual homosexual sodomy—a much more intimate relationship than the one present in the instant case. The Court, however, refused to do so, stating that privacy has been extended as far as it will ever go. As a result of that case, it seems as if the Court is not likely to create more fundamental rights nor expand the definitions of those fundamental rights that already exist.

Moreover, the Act does not involve a breach of the "physical integrity of the home" as referred to in the *Bowers* case and there is no mandated physical invasion of Plaintiffs' private residences which could give rise to a Fourth Amendment claim.

As to "spatial" privacy, Defendant contends that the case relied on by Plaintiffs is inapposite. The *Reeves* case involved a First Amendment challenge to municipal regulation of sound amplification ostensibly designed to protect privacy rights of citizens. This Court agrees with Defendant's argument and finds that although *Reeves* may stand for the proposition that such sound regulation is appropriate in certain circumstances, it certainly does not stand for the proposition that there is a constitutional right to be free from the sounds of children. Furthermore, this Court does not interpret the *Bowers* case to stand for the proposition that there is a fundamental right contained in the Constitution "not to have children around."

Both Plaintiffs and Defendant rely on *Roberts v. United States Jaycees, 468 U.S. 609, 104 S. Ct. 3244, 82 L. Ed. 2d 462 (1984).* In *Roberts,* the Court stated that:

> Family relationships, by their nature, involve deep attachments and commitments to the necessarily

few other individuals with whom one shares not only a special community of thoughts, experiences and beliefs but also distinctly personal aspects of one's life. Among other things, therefore, they are distinguished by such attributes as relative smallness, a high degree of selectivity in decisions to begin and maintain the affiliation, and seclusion from others in critical aspects of the relationship.

The Court finds that Plaintiffs have not demonstrated the existence of such highly personal relationships in the sale or rental of housing units in their respective communities. The Court also notes that all Plaintiffs live in communities ranging from well over one hundred to several thousand housing units. There is no "family" relationship between residents of different units in the development. There is no indication of any relationship other than neighbor. Further, none of the Plaintiffs set forth any facts that speak to the type of relationship necessary to support their privacy and free association claims. Plaintiffs allege that having children in their communities gives rise to detrimental health effects. The Court concludes that the Act neither affects the immediate "family" of any of the Plaintiffs nor requires persons to admit children into their homes. Moreover, what occurs at a neighbor's house obviously does not involve the creation and sustenance of Plaintiffs' families.

Defendant also points out that Plaintiffs' communities are not selective. This Court can find no facts that suggest that potential homeowners in Plaintiffs' communities are screened as to beliefs, life-styles, habits, etc. The facts of this case indicate that the only basis of selection is the age of permanent residents.

Defendant further contends that other undisputed facts dilute even what little selectivity exists. Defendant calls this Court's attention to the fact that three out of four of the Plaintiffs live in communities that prior to the recent change-over to a 55 and older requirement had age restrictions that precluded children as permanent residents, but had no age limit beyond that as to homeowners. This indicates to this Court that before the Act

required residents of certain communities to be a specific age, the only age prohibition was against children as permanent residents. This demonstrates less selectivity than Plaintiffs suggest to this Court to be present.

With the foregoing in mind, it is crucial to note that Plaintiffs' overlapping freedom of association argument concerning this topic is also without merit.

Plaintiffs argue that the legislative history of the Act and the Preamble to the Regulations make it clear that while Congress intended to protect the "legitimate rights of older persons" to live in childless retirement communities, it has unduly restricted that choice to only certain types of housing, containing "significant" facilities and services designed to meet the "physical and social" needs of the residents.

Plaintiffs also contend that the consistently recognized needs and desires of many of the elderly for the quiet companionship of their peers and the psychological support inherent in an age-homogeneous environment are completely ignored.

Plaintiffs further contend that many older people want to live their lives in peace and quiet, without children, and with other older people who share their pleasures and pains, and who understand what it means and feels like to have reached their stage in life.

This Court cannot adopt Plaintiffs' reasoning because communities like the Plaintiffs' have traditionally allowed anyone who can contract and who does not have children to reside there. This Court agrees with Defendant that were Plaintiffs to adopt the Act's familial status provisions exempting housing for older persons, the "right" of older persons to associate with persons their own age would be furthered more than under restrictions previously in effect because then over 80% of the residents would assuredly be over fifty-five.

Plaintiffs also argue that freedom of association for purely social and personal purposes is a separately identified fundamental right which, nonetheless, overlaps with the right of decisional privacy. Plaintiffs rely on *Roberts v. United States Jaycees,* see supra:

> [C]hoices to enter into and maintain certain intimate human relationships must be secured against undue intrusion by the State because of the role of such relationships in safeguarding the individual freedom that is central to our constitutional scheme. In this respect, freedom of association receives protection as a fundamental element of personal liberty.

Id. at 617–18, 104 S. Ct. at 3249.

> [T]he protection of individual liberty includes protection of certain kinds of personal bonds which cultivate and transmit shared beliefs, thereby fostering diversity, and acting as critical buffers between the individual and the power of the state.

Id. at 618–19, 104 S. Ct. at 3250.

> Moreover, the constitutional shelter afforded such relationships reflects the realization that individuals draw much of their emotional enrichment from close ties with others. Protecting these relationships from unwarranted state interference therefore safeguards the ability independently to define one's identity that is central to any concept of liberty.

Id.

Plaintiffs also rely on *Wilson v. Taylor, 733 F.2d 1539 (11th Cir. 1984).* In that case, the Eleventh Circuit applied a right of association to protect a police officer from being fired merely because he was dating the daughter of a reputed organized crime chief. This Court finds, however, that the *Wilson* case involved more of an intimate relationship than that of the ones involved in the instant case.

Additionally, this Court concludes that Plaintiffs' freedom of association claim must fail for the same reason that their privacy right claim failed. Although the Supreme Court held in *Board of Directors of Rotary International v. Rotary Club of Duarte, 481 U.S. 537, 107 S. Ct. 1940, 95 L. Ed. 2d 474 (1987),* that the right of association is not restricted to relationships among family members, the Supreme Court emphasized in the *Roberts* case, supra, that the First Amendment protects only those relationships, including family relationships, that presuppose the "deep attachments and commitments" to "necessarily few" individuals.

The Court finds that no such private or intimate relationship is present in the instant case. Each association of persons who chose to live in Plaintiffs' respective communities is large, and in some cases the association is very large. The residents there constitute less unified and less selective groups than either of the organizations at issue in *Roberts* or *Rotary Club,* supra, both of which were held to lack the distinctive characteristics of the intimate groups entitled to First Amendment protection.

Defendant correctly reiterates that the only characteristic that the residents of Plaintiffs' respective communities may have in common is being over a certain age. Moreover, Defendant is correct in pointing out that persons living in their respective communities have no stated purpose which sets them apart from the millions of other persons, including families with children, seeking an affordable and desirable place to live.

This Court additionally notes that the Act does not in any way prevent Plaintiffs from associating or not associating with whomever they wish in their communities. Plaintiffs are free to ignore families with children who move in next door to them if they so desire.

In conclusion, this Court finds that the Plaintiffs are not involved in the sort of "intimate human relationships" referred to in the case law. Therefore, Plaintiffs have not met their burden of demonstrating facts sufficient to support either the right to privacy or freedom of association claims.

Vagueness [discussion omitted]

Fifth Amendment

Finally, Plaintiffs contend that the Act deprives them of equal protection of the laws because it deprives them of liberty and property rights, in violation of the Fifth Amendment. Plaintiffs also claim that the Act takes their liberty and property interests for a private purpose, without compensation, in violation of the Fifth Amendment. Plaintiffs further contend that the Act deprives them of vested property and contractual rights and subjects Plaintiffs PRIEL, RIEDEL and SHIPLEY to arbitrary and capricious discrimination without due process of law, in violation of the Fifth Amendment.

Equal Protection

Plaintiffs contend that the Act violates their equal protection rights as applied to the federal government through the Fifth Amendment because the discrimination is gross enough to be deemed a confiscation. Plaintiffs argue that the Act discriminates against them by interfering with their choice to live in a community which excludes children. Plaintiffs further argue that the Act discriminates against them because there is no rational basis or justification for application of the Act to Plaintiffs when there is no indication of documentary age restrictions in existing ownership housing in Florida having anything to do with a shortage of rental apartments elsewhere in the country.

Defendant contends that Plaintiffs' claims are without merit. The Court agrees.

It is a fundamental principle that in order to establish a colorable equal protection claim, Plaintiffs must show that the Act has created a classification that violates equal protection principles. This Court does not find that Plaintiffs have met this burden. The Act is designed to prohibit discrimination on the basis of familial status. The Act requires that persons with and without children be treated without distinction in the sale and rental of housing. The only classification created by the statute is one which exempts certain groups of older persons from this prohibition, a classification which Plaintiffs are not challenging on an equal protection basis.

This Court understands that the basis of Plaintiffs' equal protection claim is that the Act is discriminating against a group of people who want to continue to be able to discriminate on the basis of familial status. Even assuming that this is an appropriate basis for an equal protection challenge, this Court agrees with Defendant's contention that Plaintiffs cannot meet their heavy burden of demonstrating that such a "classification drawn by

the statute is not rationally related to a legitimate state interest." This proposition was set out in *Cleburne v. Cleburne Living Center, Inc., 473 U.S. 432, 105 S. Ct. 3249, 87 L. Ed. 2d 313 (1985).*

As to the rational relationship to a legitimate state interest, Plaintiffs never contend that this asserted classification is not rationally related to the primary purpose and basis of the familial status provisions of the Act, which is to provide a remedy for the widespread housing discrimination against families with children. The legislative history is replete with evidence demonstrating that discrimination on the basis of familial status is a severe problem in both rental and ownership housing.

As to the legitimate state interest, Congress also recognized that a prohibition against discrimination based on familial status would reduce barriers to interstate movement of persons and the efficient allocation of labor among interstate components of the economy.

This Court concludes that eliminating discrimination on the basis of familial status is rationally related to a legitimate state interest and is therefore not a violation of equal protection.

Impairment of Vested Contract and Property Rights

Plaintiffs contend that the Act, as it applies retroactively to existing age-restricted housing, violates the Due Process Clause of the Fifth Amendment. Plaintiffs rely on *Pension Benefit Guaranty Corp. v. R.A. Gray & Co., 467 U.S. 717, 104 S. Ct. 2709, 81 L. Ed. 2d 601 (1984).* In that case, the Court held that in order to not be violative of due process, legislation must not be "particularly harsh and oppressive" or "arbitrary and irrational."

Plaintiffs emphasize that, in the Plaintiffs' communities, development is over. Plaintiffs also argue that the business of construction and marketing by the developer is finished. Plaintiffs further argue that while dollars are still spent by the Plaintiffs, they are spent in the form of payment of assessments levied by their not-for-profit associations for the cost of maintenance and repair of the common elements and common areas which are appurtenances to their units. This activity,

Plaintiffs contend, is no more properly viewed as within the scope of "economic regulation" than it is as "commerce." Finally, Plaintiffs contend that because they already own their housing, the Act is "retrospective economic legislation" that violates the Due Process Clause as applied to them.

This Court notes that Plaintiffs admit that the Contract Clause of Article I, § 10 only applies to the states and not to Congress. Plaintiffs challenge this legislation only under the Due Process Clause of the Fifth Amendment. The case of *Pension Benefit,* supra, emphasized that a due process challenge to a federal law must satisfy a higher burden than that necessary to prove a violation of the Contract Clause. *Id.* at 732–33.

Plaintiffs contend that existing case law on the protection of vested contract and property rights from the actions of Congress can only serve as a guide in this case because there is no modern precedent dealing with a life-style decision or the constitutionally protected rights of privacy and association being effectively destroyed by congressional regulation. Plaintiffs then contend that the personal decisions, rights and expectations of the Plaintiffs are entitled to at least as great protection as the economic rights and investment-backed expectations of those in the business world, which are involved in the modern cases.

Plaintiffs rely on the reasoning set out in *Usery v. Turner Elkhorn Mining Co.,* 428 U.S. 1, 96 S. Ct. 2882, 49 L. Ed. 2d 752 (1976). In that case, the Court held that legislation "adjusting the burdens and benefits of economic life come[s] to the Court with a presumption of constitutionality, and the burden is on one complaining of a due process violation to establish that the legislature has acted in an arbitrary and irrational way."

Plaintiffs seem to agree with Defendant that legislation adjusting the burdens and benefits of personal decisions, rights and expectations comes to the Court with a presumption of constitutionality and it is Plaintiffs' burden to establish that the legislature has acted irrationally. This Court finds that Plaintiffs have not met their burden.

Defendant also contends that Plaintiffs' assertion that the Act operates "retroactively" is without merit. The Court agrees with Defendant. Defendant relies on *Pension Benefit Guaranty Corp.,* supra. That Court held in part that:

> The strong deference accorded legislation in the field of national economic policy is no less applicable when the legislation is applied retroactively. Provided the retroactive application of a statute is supported by a legitimate legislative purpose furthered by a rational means, judgments about the wisdom of such legislation remains within the exclusive province of the legislative and executive branches.

Id. at 729.

Defendant argues that according to the above reasoning, even if it is assumed that the provisions of the Act apply retroactively, Plaintiffs cannot meet their burden concerning the rational basis for the Act. This Court agrees. The Act and the rules promulgated thereunder set rules for future use and transfer and interfere with the expectations of past purchasers only regarding the future use of their property by themselves and by others.

Defendant argues that readjustment of such expectations is constitutional and again cites the *Usery* case, supra. In that case, the Court also stated that the "cases are clear that legislation readjusting rights and burdens is not unlawful solely because it upsets otherwise settled expectations." *Id.* at 16.

Taking Without Just Compensation

Plaintiffs allege that a "right to exclude children" from a "buffer zone" around their homes has been taken without compensation. Plaintiffs claim a taking of alleged property rights to exclude children from their communities and to rely on the exercise of those covenants by others in their communities.

Defendant responds that if Plaintiffs' claim is based upon violation of restrictive covenants by others, Plaintiffs have standing to sue those individuals only. This Court agrees. Further, Defendant points out that according to the reasoning in the case of *Hodel v. Irving,* 481 U.S. 704, 107 S. Ct. 2076, 95 L. Ed. 2d 668 (1987), Plaintiffs cannot assert a taking claim against HUD because "the government has considerable latitude in regulating property rights in ways that may adversely affect the owners." *Id. at 713.* For these reasons, this Court finds that Plaintiffs' taking claim is not ripe.

Defendant relies on *Penn Central Transportation Co. v. New York City, 438 U.S. 104, 98 S. Ct. 2646, 57 L. Ed. 2d 631 (1978).* That case held [that] whether or not legislation violates the Fifth Amendment's prohibition against the taking of private property without just compensation depends largely upon the particular circumstances in that case. That Court enunciated certain factors that are considered. One factor is the extent to which the government action diminishes the economic value of property, specifically by interfering with distinct investment-backed expectations. Another factor considers the character of the governmental action. The Court must consider whether the legislation is a physical invasion by the government or if it is part of some public program adjusting the benefits and burdens of economic life to promote the common good.

The Court has weighed the above factors, and finds that Plaintiffs have not suffered a taking adequate to constitute a violation of the Fifth Amendment.

This Court notes that it is difficult to ascertain to what extent the familial status provisions of the Act took anything from Plaintiffs. Plaintiffs claim the taking of all age-restricted ownership housing by the very enactment of the Act. However, Plaintiffs have made no claim for compensation. Plaintiffs stated in their answers to interrogatories that they have suffered no injury to date. Further, Plaintiffs have not presented a concrete controversy concerning the Act's economic effect on "particular parcels of land." Plaintiffs has not established that their property values will be diminished as a result of the Act.

In formulating the Regulations, HUD concluded that while "there are ... aspects of the Amendments Act that have some economic impact and will thus affect property rights ... , none of these impacts ... rises to the level of a 'taking' within the meaning of the Fifth Amendment of the United States Constitution." *54 Fed. Reg. 3232, 3281* (Jan. 23, 1989).

Defendant contends that because there will now be a wider group of potential buyers for Plaintiffs' properties as a result of the Act (if Plaintiffs do not qualify for the "Housing for Older Persons" exemptions of the Act), the resale value of the property may increase, or at least will not be diminished. All but one Plaintiff stated in their interrogatories that either their properties have increased in value since their purchase or have actually resold at a profit. One Plaintiff did state that her property had decreased in value, but it has not been established that the Act is the cause of this decrease in value, especially since the mobile home park has continued to be senior housing since the Act's passage.

Defendant also argues that, assuming that Plaintiffs' property has decreased in value somewhat, the case of *Keystone Bituminous Coal v. DeBenedictis, 480 U.S. 470, 107 S. Ct. 1232, 94 L. Ed. 2d 472 (1987)* made it clear that most diminutions in the economic value of a property will be insufficient to constitute a taking. The Court in *Euclid v. Ambler Co., 272 U.S. 365, 47 S. Ct. 114, 71 L. Ed. 303 (1926)* upheld regulation that diminished property value by 75%. In *Hadacheck v. Sebastian, 239 U.S. 394, 36 S. Ct. 143, 60 L. Ed. 348 (1915),* the Court upheld a regulation that caused a diminution in property value of 87½%.

Defendant asserts that Plaintiffs would be left with viable and other uses of their homes. Defendant states that the Act would not take the use of Plaintiffs' properties as a place to sleep, to eat, to converse privately, to enjoy amenities or any of the things which serve as the core value of a home. Defendant also argues that the Act would not deprive Plaintiffs of the many ways to increase the economic and subjective value of their homes because they will still be allowed to continue to reside and enjoy the many benefits of their homes.

None of the discussion as to Florida's special recognition of the group ownership nature of certain property is relevant to the issues involved in this case. Even when a state recognizes a certain property right as a separate interest, its abrogation is not necessarily a taking. Defendant relies on the aforementioned cases of *Keystone and Penn Central.*

In *Keystone,* supra, the Court recognized that the support estate regulated in the statute could be separately bought and sold. In *Penn Central,* supra, the Court addressed the claim that the law deprived plaintiffs of any gainful use of their air rights. In both cases, the Courts found no taking and instead focused on "the extent of the interference with rights in the parcel as a whole." *Keystone, 480 U.S. at 497; Penn Central, 438 U.S. at 130.*

In conclusion, this Court finds that the Act does not destroy the economic viability of Plaintiffs' property. The Act does not physically invade their property, but instead would adjust the benefits and burdens of economic life to promote the common good.

This Court finds, for the aforementioned reasons, that the Act does not constitute a taking of Plaintiffs' property in violation of the Fifth Amendment of the United States Constitution.

Gonzalez v. St. Margaret's House Housing Development Fund Corp. 668 F. Supp. 187 (S.D.N.Y. 1987)

Plaintiffs are tenants of St. Margaret's House, a low-income congregate care housing facility in lower Manhattan operated by St. Margaret's House Housing Development Fund Corporation. The defendants are St. Margaret's, the United States Department of Housing and Urban Development ("HUD") and HUD Secretary Samuel R. Pierce, Jr. Plaintiffs challenge the lawfulness of the imposition by St. Margaret's House (with approval by HUD) of a mandatory meal charge as a condition of occupancy. St. Margaret's counterclaims under its rental agreements with the plaintiffs for unpaid meal charges to which plaintiffs agreed, but which several plaintiffs have withheld during the course of this action. In defense against the counterclaim, plaintiffs rely on the alleged unlawfulness of the charge and also on the contention that a HUD policy approving the charge was adopted in violation of the Administrative Procedure Act.

Plaintiffs' first and second claims allege that imposing the meal charge as a condition of occupancy violates the "Brooke Amendment" to the Housing Act of 1937, *42 U.S.C. § 1437a(a)(1),* which caps each eligible tenant's "rent" at 30% of the tenant's adjusted gross income. They argue first that the mandatory meal charge constitutes additional rent in excess of the 30% limitation. In

addition, they argue that even if the charge is not rent, it violates the purpose of the Brooke Amendment to provide affordable housing to low-income elderly or handicapped persons. The third claim alleges that the meal plan violates the tenants' rights as third-party beneficiaries of a Regulatory Agreement made between St. Margaret's and HUD, which plaintiffs interpret as barring all supplemental charges for services unless requested by individual tenants.

The fourth claim, directed only against the federal defendants, alleges that HUD's original policy authorizing such mandatory meal plans violated the rulemaking provisions of the APA, and was arbitrary and capricious in failing to require exemptions for medical and other reasons. This claim has been mooted as to future application by HUD's recent promulgation, observing all procedural requirements, of a rule requiring several exemptions in mandatory meal programs.

After a bench trial, I find that the mandatory meal charge does not constitute rent within the meaning of the Brooke Amendment and that St. Margaret's program does not contravene that law as reasonably interpreted by HUD. I also find that the Regulatory Agreement gives plaintiffs no right to be exempted from the meal charge. Finally, I conclude that St. Margaret's is entitled to judgment on its counterclaim, regardless whether HUD violated the APA in the original adoption of its policy.

FINDINGS OF FACT

Background

The construction of St. Margaret's House was financed by a direct loan from HUD pursuant to Section 202 of the National Housing Act of 1959. *12 U.S.C. § 1701q.* It opened in 1981 and currently houses 290 residents in 249 units (not including staff). Under the Section 8 Housing Assistance Program, HUD also supplies an operating subsidy of the difference between the authorized rent for the apartments and the maximum rent chargeable to the tenants under the 30% rent cap. See *42 U.S.C. §§ 1437a(a), 1437f(c)(3).*

In its November 16, 1977 application for a Section 202 loan and Section 8 subsidies, St. Margaret's identified a mandatory meal plan as part of its proposed "core service program." Other core services included an optional housekeeping program, a health maintenance program, and a recreation and creative activity program. The specified purposes of the meal plan were to ensure proper nutrition, encourage social interaction and a sense of community, and allow management to identify residents' health problems as they arise.

The HUD Region II Director approved the mandatory meal plan by letter of June 1, 1981. Each tenant could be charged $110 per month for a daily meal. HUD required, however, that the charge be reduced as necessary in order to leave each resident at least $120 in residual income after paying rent and the meal charge. The other proposed "core services" at St. Margaret's House were to be financed out of the rent payments and subsidies, with no supplemental charge to residents.

HUD and St. Margaret's executed a Housing Assistance Payment ("HAP") contract which incorporates the terms of the Brooke Amendment. They also entered into a Regulatory Agreement, which provides in paragraph 12(c):

Upon prior written approval by the Secretary, Mortgagor may charge to and receive from any tenant such amounts as from time to time may be mutually agreed upon between the tenant and the Mortgagor for any facilities and/or services which may be furnished by the Mortgagor or others to such tenant upon his request, in addition to the facilities and services included in the approved rental schedule.

The plaintiffs were informed before they signed their leases that participation in the meal plan was a condition of occupancy at St. Margaret's House. Each lease specifies that the resident is required to pay $110 per month in return for 30 meals. Each plaintiff signed a lease undertaking the obligation to pay the monthly meal charge before moving into St. Margaret's House. All initially paid the meal charge and all but one at first ate the food. For several years, however, most of the plaintiffs have refused to pay the meal charge and none has taken the daily meal in the St. Margaret's dining room.

Operation of the Meal Plan

Meals at St. Margaret's House are provided by Nutrition Management Services Company ("NMS") under its contract dated January 1, 1984 with St. Margaret's. Residents receive 30 meal tickets a month. The resident may use the ticket at lunch or dinner at her option. The meal ticket entitles the resident to soup or juice, an entree, two vegetables, salad, bread and butter, dessert, milk or punch or soda, and coffee or tea. Foods appropriate for residents on low-salt, low-fat, and diabetic diets are available. Postings and dietary assistance are available to direct residents to such foods. In addition, the kitchen will attempt to accommodate special advance orders.

During the trial, together with counsel, I made an unannounced visit to St. Margaret's House for lunch. I found the meal to be ample, tasty and nutritious and the dining facility clean and pleasant.

Before the commencement of this action, St. Margaret's granted no exemptions from the meal plan. Since May 1985, however, St. Margaret's has permitted credit for missed meals and exemptions for employment, vacations, hospitalization, and medical reasons.

In order to receive a medical exemption from the meal program, a resident must provide St. Margaret's with a doctor's letter explaining the individual's special dietary needs. The individual is then asked to make an appointment with an NMS dietician. If St. Margaret's House, in consultation with the dietician, decides that NMS cannot meet the individual's dietary needs, she is exempted from the program. Five residents are currently exempted from the program pursuant to this policy, and another is partially exempted.

No plaintiff has been given a medical exemption. Plaintiffs contend the exemption procedure is not fairly administered. They argue that St. Margaret's and NMS have a financial interest in denying exemptions. They presented no evidence, however, that the exemption policy is administered unfairly. Indeed, although certain plaintiffs testified that they require a special diet for medical reasons, none has followed the reasonable procedure specified by St. Margaret's for a medical diet exemption. Although several plaintiffs testified they could not eat the meals for medical reasons and some wrote to request exemptions, none presented a doctor's prescription to St. Margaret's.

Several residents asserted that they eat better and more cheaply preparing all their own meals than they would if they participated in the meal plan. Some further assert that they could not afford to remain at St. Margaret's House if they had to pay the meal charge. The plaintiffs did not, however, submit any budgets or analyses showing how they currently spend their money, or how their budgets would be affected if they were required to pay for the mandatory daily meal.

HUD's Policy

Since 1959, HUD and its predecessor, the Housing and Home Finance Agency, have permitted owners of federally-assisted projects for the elderly or handicapped to require their tenants to purchase meals in the project dining facilities. See *52 Fed. Reg. 6,300, 6,300 (Mar. 2, 1987).* HUD maintained this position after the enactment of

the Brooke Amendment and its application to Section 8/Section 202 housing projects in the 1970s. As of 1981, HUD's policy was set forth in its Processing Handbook for Section 202 projects as follows:

> Congregate Housing. Congregate living facilities may be considered by an eligible Borrower. It may propose to supply tenants with food, maid service, or other personal services. However, in determining approvable Contract Rents under Section 8, staffing and other operating costs of such services may not be recognized. Agreement to purchase personal services or food in excess of one meal per day shall not be required as a condition of occupancy. It may be necessary for some services to be covered by tenants outside Section 8 rents or from funds provided by the Borrower from other sources. Where a Borrower proposes to furnish food or other services, the Borrower shall clearly separate such charges from the total charges for shelter and project-supplied utilities which are entered on Form FHA-2013.

Section 202 Direct Loan Program for Housing for the Elderly or Handicapped, Processing Handbook, 4571.1 Rev, § 5-32(c) (Mar. 1978).

In *Birkland v. Rotary Plaza, Inc.,* 643 F. Supp. 223 (1986), Judge Spencer Williams found that HUD had adopted this policy in violation of the publication requirement of the Freedom of Information Act ("FOIA"), *5 U.S.C. § 552,* and in violation of the notice and comment procedures mandated by the APA. *Id. § 553.* On January 10, 1986, he ordered that HUD undertake notice and comment procedures to promulgate a mandatory meal policy as a final rule. In the interim, HUD was to publish the policy set forth in the Processing Handbook, modified by the requirement that medical and employment exemptions be provided to project residents. *Slip op. at 2–4.*

HUD proceeded to publish the specified interim policy and notice of its proposed final rule. See *51 Fed. Reg. 4997 (Feb. 10, 1986); 51 Fed. Reg. 11,483 (Apr. 3, 1986); 51 Fed. Reg. 32,764 (Sept. 1, 1986).* After considering public comments and a March 1985 General Accounting Office report, HUD issued its final rule on March 2, 1987. Mandatory Meals Program in Multifamily Rental or

Cooperative Projects for the Elderly or Handicapped, *52 Fed. Reg. 6,300, 24 C.F.R. Part 278.* The rule became effective on April 1, 1987.

The final rule adopts HUD's interpretation that the term "rent" as used in Section 8 does not include mandatory meal charges. *52 Fed. Reg. at 6,301, 24 C.F.R. §§ 278.1(c), 278.20(c).* The rule authorizes the continuation of current HUD-approved programs, but bars adoption in the future of additional mandatory meal programs. *52 Fed. Reg. at 6,301.* The rule also requires that projects provide exemptions from participation for medical and other reasons. *24 C.F.R. § 278.12.*

HUD concluded that it should authorize the continuation of existing mandatory meal programs:

> because … [the programs] provide nutrition and socialization benefits and because if such programs were required to convert to voluntary participation, project sponsors may not be able to obtain necessary sources of subsidies to fund their programs, and thus might terminate them as financially infeasible. This result would frustrate the reasonable expectations of:
>
> (1) Sponsors who relied on HUD's mandatory meals policy in proposing projects that offered a mandatory meals program, included a central dining facility in their projects' design with specific HUD approval, and established a mandatory program because they had determined that without the mandatory nature of the meals program, attendance would be too unpredictable to ensure a sufficiently steady stream of income to continue the program on a financially sound basis—resulting in the possible economic necessity of terminating the meals programs in that project;
>
> (2) HUD, which approved and funded the inclusion of a central dining facility in the projects' construction, with the expectation that the project and its facilities would be used as the sponsor had intended; and
>
> (3) Tenants who accepted units in a HUD assisted project with a mandatory program because of the availability of a meals service at that project.

52 Fed. Reg. at 6,301.

St. Margaret's House has administered its mandatory meal program in accordance with its stated purposes and HUD's policy. At the time of trial, it was in the process of conforming its program to the final HUD rule.

DISCUSSION

The Brooke Amendment Claims

At the start of this litigation, I denied defendants' motion to dismiss. I observed at the time that "any charge required as a condition of occupancy can be seen as rent, particularly if the charge is attributed to a service that the tenant does not desire and does not use." *620 F. Supp. 806, 808 (1985).* I also noted that such a charge might violate the "purpose of the Brooke Amendment to provide publicly assisted housing for persons of very low income by assuring that the rental charges imposed on them not exceed 30% of their income." *Id.* After trial and further briefing, I conclude that plaintiffs have failed to prove their contention that the meal program violates the statute.

Defendants contend that the statutory cap applies only to "rent" and does not prevent additional charges for other services. The fact that food is outside the normal understanding of the term "rent" is not dispositive. The imposition of substantial mandatory charges for luxuries even less closely associated than food with the common understanding of "rent" (such as charges for flower arrangements, distribution of fancy soaps and fragrances, provision of musical or theatrical entertainments, etc.) would be so clearly incompatible with the purposes of the statute, they would surely be ruled illegal, notwithstanding the correctness of the argument that the word *rent* does not generally include them. This result might be reached by ruling either that, in imposing a 30% rent cap, the statute intended to cover all charges imposed as a condition of occupancy, or that such charges were incompatible with the statute's objective of making subsidized housing more accessible to the poor. I therefore do not find the question satisfactorily answered by the simple proposition that the cap applies only to rent, which does not include food.

At least three questions must therefore be answered: (a) whether any mandatory charge no matter for what purpose must be seen as a violation of the statute if it exceeds the 30% cap; (2) if not, whether a mandatory charge for provision of food can be allowed under the statute; and (3) if so, whether this mandatory meal program in all its details is compatible with the statute.

The most significant factor for resolution of these questions is that Congress entrusted the administration of the program and interpretation of the statute in the first instance to a department of government. HUD is charged with the responsibility of establishing guidelines and passing on the suitability of each project that seeks funding assistance under the statute. Under the Supreme Court's ruling in *Chevron, U.S.A., Inc. v. National Resources Defense Council, Inc., 467 U.S. 837, 843–44, 104 S. Ct. 2778, 81 L. Ed. 2d 694 (1984),* an agency so charged is entitled to substantial deference from the courts as to its interpretation of the governing statute and the policies it devises for carrying out the statute's purposes.

HUD has consistently determined that a mandatory meal participation program imposing charges in excess of the 30% cap does not on its face violate the statute—that such programs could be maintained so long as their terms were found by HUD to be in conformity with the purposes of the statute. In its recently promulgated rule, HUD expressly authorizes the continuation of existing mandatory meal programs (although it bars the adoption of new such programs).

HUD concluded, furthermore, that the particular program administered by St. Margaret's House was acceptable. At all times since its inception the St. Margaret's program has had HUD approval.

The first conclusion, that the "rent" cap does not necessarily bar any mandatory charge exceeding the 30% cap, is consistent with the view that rent is employed in the statute with its conventional meaning. That view is supported by the Senate Report, which stated:

> for purposes of determining the maximum amount of assistance payments with respect to any unit, the "rental" for such unit would be the proportionate share of the total shelter costs to be borne by the low-income tenants of a project attributable to that unit.

S. Rep. No. 392, 91st Cong., 1st Sess. 19, reprinted in 1969 U.S. Code Cong. & Admin. News 1524, 1542.

It is further supported by the statutory scheme. The statute employs the word and concept of "rent" in two complimentary usages—one being to fix the tenant's rent at a maximum of 30% of her adjusted income, see *42 U.S.C. § 1437a(a)(1),* the second being to impose on HUD the duty to pay the remainder of the authorized rent, to the extent it exceeds 30% of the tenant's income. See *id. § 1437f(c)(3).* It is unlikely that the word would be used with different meanings in two such closely related complementary usages. It is also unlikely that, by the second usage, Congress intended to fund payment for food. The most reasonable conclusion is therefore that "rent" in both portions of the statute refers to the charge for shelter, together with closely associated services such as heat, maintenance, refuse disposal, etc., see *24 C.F.R. § 880.203(a),* and not to other types of service charges a facility might impose.

I conclude that HUD's interpretation of "rent" under the Brooke Amendment is a reasonable one. The Supreme Court recently ruled, furthermore, that HUD's interpretation of this statutory term was entitled to deference. *Wright v. Roanoke Housing & Development Authority, 479 U.S. 418, 107 S. Ct. 766, 774, 93 L. Ed. 2d 781 & n.11 (1987).*

As to the second and third questions, the finding of HUD that mandatory meal programs, and in particular this one, are compatible with the purpose of the statute is also reasonable and entitled to deference. Such a program serves a number of valuable goals in a congregate care facility for elderly and disabled persons. It assures that the residents will have access to a nutritious diet; it promotes friendly social interaction among the residents, combating the tendency among many elderly people to withdraw in isolation in their apartments; it also assists the management of the facility to be aware of health problems of residents as they develop. (If an elderly resident made a habit of remaining secluded in her apartment, the management might be quite unaware of the onset of an illness and the need for medical assistance.) Furthermore, mandatory participation in the meal program permits the facility to offer meals at a lower price than would otherwise be the case. The value of these contributions to a congregate care facility is great. The fact that a particular resident may be disadvantaged by the program does not make HUD's approval unreasonable. Food, furthermore, is a necessity which residents would have to acquire elsewhere if it were not provided by the program. The program does not subject them to expenses for a type of service that they could properly forego. All courts that have considered the question have found HUD's approval of such programs to be reasonably compatible with the statute, in spite of the additional charge to the tenants above their maximum rent. *Aujero v. CDA Todco, Inc., 756 F.2d 1374, 1376 (9th Cir. 1985); Mayoral v. Jeffco American Baptist Residences, Inc., 726 F.2d 1361 (10th Cir.),* cert. denied, *469 U.S. 884, 105 S. Ct. 255, 83 L. Ed. 2d 192 (1984); Johnson v. Soundview Apartments Housing Development Fund Co., 585 F. Supp. 559, 560,* reconsideration denied, *588 F. Supp. 1381 (1984),* later opinion, *647 F. Supp. 1410 (S.D.N.Y. 1986); Chambers v. Toledo Jewish Home for the Aged, Inc., No. C 80-575, Memorandum and Order (N.D. Ohio Oct. 23, 1980).*

Nor has HUD given carte blanche to any mandatory program, regardless of its reasonableness. It has imposed a number of requirements designed to keep the programs consistent with the purposes of the statute. The details and price of the mandatory meal were subject to HUD's approval. At the start, HUD required of St. Margaret's that it reduce the charge to the extent necessary to leave the resident a minimum of $120 per month. More recently, other requirements were added including exemptions for work, vacation and medically prescribed diet, all of which are designed to ease any financial burden on the residents.

I cannot conclude that HUD has exceeded reasonable bounds in construing the statute to allow for such a program.

Plaintiffs argue that the plan must be seen as violating the objectives of the Brooke Amendment because, reasonable or not, it increases the cost of residence at the facility and therefore forecloses access to at least some needy people. This argument attributes to the statute an intention that is not reflected by its words or provisions. The argument depends on the proposition that the statute seeks to make every Section 8 facility affordable to every potential applicant. It is true there is language in the legislative history that proclaims such an objective, but it is contradicted by the statute itself.

The statute unquestionably eased access to poor persons by subsidizing their rent, but the subsidy is a limited one. No matter how small the resident's income, she is required to pay 30% of it towards her rent. Thus a resident who has only $100 per month for lodging, food and other necessaries must pay $30 for rent, leaving only $70 for all other necessities. By its own terms the statute rebuts plaintiffs' contention.

The argument might be considerably stronger if the statute were designed to provide full subsidy below a minimum income level. It does not do so.

In this respect the meal plan evinces greater concern for the poverty line than the statute. It fully subsidizes the meals to the extent that payment would take the residents' residual income below $120. The rent subsidy does not. Thus, the hypothetical tenant with a total income of $100 per month is better off with the St. Margaret's program than without, as it gives her 30 free meals per month.

I therefore cannot agree with plaintiffs' contention that the statute seeks to eliminate all financial obstacles to residence in a funded facility. Although the meals program may well add some financial burden for certain residents, depending how little they would otherwise spend on food, it diminishes the burden on others, providing them with free meals. It is within the discretion of HUD to approve such a program.

The reasonableness of HUD's interpretation is further strengthened by the fact that only a small percentage of Section 8 facilities operate with a mandatory meal plan. This means that applicants who consider its provision advantageous can seek admission at facilities where such a plan operates while those who do not can seek admission elsewhere. This distinguishes cases in which courts have struck down the imposition by local authorities of eligibility criteria not authorized by the public housing statute. *Cf. James v. New York City Housing Authority, 622 F. Supp. 1356 (S.D.N.Y. 1985); Fletcher v. Housing Authority of Louisville, 525 F.2d 532 (6th Cir. 1975), reinstating 491 F.2d 793 (6th Cir. 1974); Ferguson v. Metropolitan Development & Housing Agency, 485 F. Supp. 517 (M.D. Tenn. 1980).*

The Regulatory Agreement

Plaintiffs contend that even if the statute does not bar a mandatory meal charge in excess of the 30% rent cap, this is barred by the Regulatory Agreement made between HUD and St. Margaret's House. Plaintiffs claim to be the third-party beneficiaries of this contract.

There are at least two serious flaws in the plaintiffs' argument:

First, each plaintiff agreed to the mandatory meal program upon applying to St. Margaret's House. Plaintiffs did not make out a sufficient showing of duress to nullify their agreement.

Second, it surely misconceives the Regulatory Agreement to describe it as a promise exacted by HUD that St. Margaret's would not operate a mandatory meal program. Although it is possible to find words in the text of the Agreement that seem to support this conclusion, we know it is completely contrary to the contractual relationship between St. Margaret's and HUD. HUD did not exact a promise that there would be no mandatory meal program. To the contrary, HUD expressly approved St. Margaret's plan after careful review of its provisions. The argument is completely inappropriate.

I need not reach the issue that I noted in the motion to dismiss, whether *Reiner v. West Village Associates, 768 F.2d 31, 32 (2d Cir. 1985)* bars suit employing the third-party beneficiary theory under Regulatory Agreements governing Section 8 projects.

St. Margaret's Counterclaim

Since the inception of this lawsuit several plaintiffs have engaged in a strike, refusing to participate in the mandatory meal program. St. Margaret's counterclaims to recover the meal payments that these plaintiffs agreed to pay in their contracts for residency, but did not make. Plaintiffs defend on the grounds of the illegality of the plan under the Brooke Amendment and of the APA deficiencies in HUD's adoption of its policy governing the plan.

I have rejected the plaintiffs' contention under the Brooke Amendment. As to the defenses based on HUD's conduct, although similar claims were sustained against HUD in another lawsuit, it is not clear that the deficiencies in HUD's policy can avail plaintiffs as a defense against St. Margaret's claims for plaintiffs' breach of contract. Plaintiffs entered into voluntary agreements with St. Margaret's to participate in the meal program. The fact that HUD had not conducted a notice and comment procedure prior to the adoption of its policy was no less true when plaintiffs entered the agreement than it was when plaintiffs decided to stop paying.

St. Margaret's planned its financial and physical structure and built its kitchen and dining facilities in justified reliance on HUD's approval. It has borne substantial losses by reason of plaintiffs' refusal to honor their contracts. HUD's procedural deficiencies furthermore played no role in plaintiffs' refusal to honor their contracts. Months ago HUD concluded a new rulemaking process after notice and comment as required by the APA. Plaintiffs brought no amended complaint challenging the new procedure or the adoption of the new rule. They concede that HUD's adoption of the new rule moots their APA claims against HUD. Nonetheless, plaintiffs did not resume participation in accordance with their agreements.

Insofar as HUD's deficiency lay in its earlier failure to require reasonable exemptions, this is not relevant to these plaintiffs' defenses as none of them has shown entitlement to any of the exceptions now available.

I conclude that plaintiffs' claims under the Administrative Procedure Act do not provide a defense against St. Margaret's claim for breach of plaintiffs' contracts. St. Margaret's is entitled to a judgment for damages. St. Margaret's loss, however, is reduced by the savings it realized by not preparing meals for the plaintiffs during the period of their strike.

Judgment is granted to the defendants on each of plaintiffs' claims. St. Margaret's House is entitled to judgment on its counterclaim.

CHAPTER

5

GUARDIANSHIP AND DISABLED CHILDREN

INTRODUCTION

Since earliest Roman times it has been considered the moral and legal responsibility of the government to care for those of its citizens who are unable to care for themselves. This concept, known as *in parens patriae,* passed into modern law under the general concept of guardianship.

Guardianship, broadly speaking, is the appointment of a person to take legal responsibility for the care and management of another person who is unable to care for himself or herself. Historically, the concept of guardianship connoted the stigma of incompetence, when the person cared for was an adult, but nowadays legislative interpretation of guardianship has evolved so that incompetence is neither the sole nor the exclusive criterion for the determination of guardianship. At present, it is simply the factual determination as to whether the person is capable—physically, mentally, or emotionally—of taking care of his or her own financial or personal needs. Modern courts look at the person's capacity to act on his or her own; if it decides that a guardian is appropriate, the court attempts to authorize the person so appointed as the guardian with the least intrusive powers appropriate over the person whose care is under consideration.

in parens patriae
"In place of the parent"; Roman concept that forms the basis of guardianship law.

189

For the elderly individual, the concept of guardianship falls into two main categories: the need for a guardian to take care of the elderly individual if the individual becomes incapacitated, and the need of the elderly person to take care of his or her own children who are disabled and will need care once the elderly parent is no longer capable of caring for the child personally. This chapter explores these two areas of guardianship, indicating the procedures that must be followed to have a guardian appointed or removed, as well as some alternative measures to actual guardianship that still provide the necessary care for the ward.

GUARDIANSHIP

Development of Guardianship Law

As mentioned in the introduction, the concept of guardianship evolved from the Roman concept of the *parens patriae,* the state having the responsibility for the health, welfare, and safety of its citizens who are incapable of caring for themselves. To protect an incapacitated individual from being taken advantage of by unscrupulous relatives and strangers, it is the duty of the state, by means of the judicial system, (1) to determine whether a person does in fact need assistance in caring for himself or herself; (2) if so, to see that an appropriate person is appointed, if necessary; and (3) to supervise the guardianship to protect the person from irresponsible guardians.

Example

An elderly woman is fairly wealthy, and her son wants to make sure that his potential inheritance remains intact. He wants to be appointed the guardian over his mother's property to curtail her spending, so that the money will survive her. The woman is perfectly capable of handling her own affairs. In this instance the court would refuse to appoint a guardian. The woman can care for her own financial needs, and the son's interests are irrelevant.

Example

An elderly man is physically weak and suffers from incontinence, but is otherwise mentally alert. His daughter wants to be appointed his guardian to take care of his physical needs, such as hiring a health care worker and other assistants to care for her father. In this instance the court would probably appoint the daughter as the guardian for the limited purpose of providing physical care for her father—the father does not need assistance in managing his finances.

Historically, the concept of guardianship was divided into two broad categories: a *guardian* was the person responsible for the physical body of the incapacitated person, whereas a **conservator** was the person appointed by the court to handle the property of the incapacitated person. The modern trend is to use the term *guardian* as an umbrella concept; the court's order determines the authority of the guardian to act.

Example———————————————

An elderly man suffers with Alzheimer's disease and cannot manage his personal or financial affairs. Thirty years ago the court would have appointed a conservator to manage his finances and a guardian to take legal responsibility for the man's personal affairs. Nowadays the term *guardian* would be applied to both functions.

The original laws dealing with guardianship mandated that the person who would be subject to the guardianship, known as the **ward**, be shown by appropriate evidence to be "incompetent." The modern trend is away from such stigmatizing determinations, and most current statutes simply require a showing of "incapacity" to deal with personal or financial affairs. The evidence presented to the court to make such a determination must meet the burden of proof of clear and convincing evidence, and it is the function of the court to make the final determination of the potential ward's abilities. Note that the term *ward* has now been replaced by the term **incapacitated person**.

Example———————————————

An elderly man has developed severe arthritis and can no longer take care of himself. His nephew wants to be appointed by the court as his uncle's guardian to assist in providing physical care for him. Before a guardian will be appointed, the court must be convinced that the potential incapacitated person cannot manage his personal affairs himself and that no other, less intrusive method, such as home health care, can provide all that is necessary to meet the needs of the potential ward.

In making its determination, the court looks at the individual's functional level of activity and his or her demonstrable capacity to manage his or her own affairs. The court will always seek the least restrictive alternative available, to keep the individual as independent as possible.

The law of guardianship is primarily state law; there is no specific federal statute dealing with the subject. The only federal legislation in the area comes under Title XX of the Social Security Act, 42 U.S.C. §§ 1397–1397f, which requires protective services to be created by each

conservator Former term for a guardian of the estate.

ward Person who is under guardianship.

incapacitated person Current term for a ward.

state to guard the needs of all persons receiving Social Security benefits. *Protective services* include state assistance for persons who are deemed incapacitated and for whom no one has petitioned for guardianship. Guardians may be appointed for individuals either voluntarily or involuntarily.

Example

An elderly man resides in a nursing home and receives Social Security benefits. The head of the facility believes that the man's condition has so deteriorated that he can no longer manage his own affairs, and petitions the state protective services agency to have a guardian appointed for the man. This is an example of involuntary guardianship.

Example

An elderly man had just been diagnosed with a degenerative liver disease, and he realizes that as time passes he will no longer be able to care for himself. In anticipation of his decline, he petitions to have a guardian of his own choosing appointed. This is an example of voluntary guardianship.

Determination of Competency

Before a court can appoint a guardian, it must determine that the individual cannot manage his or her own affairs. To accomplish this, the court looks at the behavior and functional ability of the potential incapacitated person, and typically appoints an independent person to make an evaluation of the individual, as well as hearing evidence presented to it by the person petitioning for the appointment of the guardian.

The court is primarily interested in ascertaining the degree or severity of the potential incapacitated person's incapacity; the court will try to appoint a guardian in the least restrictive manner that will meet the specific needs of the individual. The court wants to restrict the potential incapacitated person as little as possible under the circumstances. Many attorneys are appointed as guardians by the court and the legal assistant may be required to assist the attorney in fulfilling the court-appointed obligations.

Example

An elderly man suffers from debilitating asthma, and cannot physically manage to care for his person or his home, but his mental facilities are intact. In this instance the court would probably appoint a guardian only for the person of the individual, and still permit the man to manage his own financial and legal affairs, because his incapacity does not affect these functions.

The potential incapacitated person has the right to be represented by counsel at guardianship hearings and may present evidence in his or her own behalf.

Example

A man petitions to be made the guardian of his elderly aunt. The aunt opposes the petition but has no funds to acquire counsel. The court will appoint counsel to help the aunt present evidence of her capacity to continue to act on her own behalf.

If the court determines that the person has capacity, the petition will be denied; conversely, if the person is deemed incapable of acting in his or her own behalf, the court will see that an appropriate guardian is appointed.

Guardian's Powers and Duties

The powers and duties of the guardian appointed by the court are dependent upon the type of authority granted. Generally, guardians fall into four categories:

1. **Guardian of the estate.** This type of guardian is the modern equivalent of the conservator, appointed by the court to deal with the incapacitated person's property and finances. The guardian of the estate has no power over the physical care of the incapacitated person or the incapacitated person's ability to act outside of financial affairs.

   ### Example

   The guardian of the estate of an elderly woman wants to hire live-in help for his incapacitated person, but the woman does not want strangers in her house and prefers to manage on her own. The guardian lacks the legal authority to hire such help, and the incapacitated person's wishes in the matter will prevail.

2. **Guardian of the person.** This type of guardian is only authorized to deal with the physical and legal concerns of the incapacitated person, but has no right to manage the incapacitated person's finances. It is the reverse function of the guardian of the estate.

   ### Example

   An elderly woman lives in a rental unit. The landlord has failed to maintain the premises, in the hopes that the woman will move. The

guardian of the estate Guardian to manage the property of a incapacitated person.

guardian of the person Person legally authorized to manage the personal, nonfinancial affairs of a incapacitated person.

guardian of the person of the woman has the authority to act on the woman's behalf in dealing with the landlord, even to the extent of taking the landlord to court.

3. **Plenary guardian.** A plenary guardian is a guardian over both the person and the property of the incapacitated person. The plenary guardian fulfills the functions of both the guardian of the estate and the guardian of the person.

Example

The plenary guardian of an elderly man who can no longer care for himself has the legal authority, if necessary, to sell the man's house, place him in an assisted care facility, and go to court to assert claims on the incapacitated person's behalf.

4. **Limited guardian.** This last kind of guardian is really a hybrid, a person whose authority to act is specifically limited by the court, in financial and personal matters, to permit the guardian to act in the manner least intrusive to the incapacitated person's ability to maintain independence.

Example

An elderly man is physically incapable of carrying out certain financial transactions that require him to travel on a regular basis. A limited guardian may be appointed by the court to assist the man only in these specific financial transactions.

Regardless of the category, all guardians are required to adhere to general fiduciary standards with respect to the care of their incapacitated persons. Such duties include:

- acting on behalf of the incapacitated person with due care and diligence

- acting on behalf of the incapacitated person in accordance with the incapacitated person's own preferences, whenever possible

- acting with honesty, loyalty, and fidelity to the interests of the incapacitated person

- not acting in any manner that defeats the interests of the incapacitated person, nor acting in any matter on the incapacitated person's behalf if not so authorized by the court

- making regular reports to the court on the state of the incapacitated person and the incapacitated person's affairs, and making

plenary guardian
Guardian over both the person and the property of the incapacitated person.

limited guardian
Guardian appointed with specified powers.

regular visits to the incapacitated person to determine his or her current capabilities.

A guardian who fails to meet these obligations can be removed and disciplined by the court.

Procedure

The paralegal will assist the attorney in preparing the papers to have a client appointed as a guardian. The procedure for having a guardian appointed is a five-step process:

1. *File petition.* A petition must be filed with a court of competent jurisdiction. The petition must be filed either by the person alleged to be incapable (voluntary) or by an interested person or the head of the residence facility where the potential incapacitated person resides (involuntary). The petition must include the following information:

    a. the functional level of the person for whom guardianship is sought

    b. the reasons why the guardianship is sought

    c. a statement that alternative measures have been attempted and have proven unsuccessful

    d. the powers sought by the guardian (type of guardianship sought)

    e. the suitability of the proposed guardian

    f. the nature and value of the property of the person for whom guardianship is sought.

2. *Notice.* Once the petition has been filed, the petitioner must send written notice to the alleged incapacitated person and the person's parents, spouse, children, siblings, and so on—whomever would qualify as the person's next-of-kin.

3. *Court evaluation.* The court will appoint an independent investigator to assess the alleged incapacitated person's functional ability. The potential incapacitated person is entitled to be represented by an attorney during this process and at the eventual hearing.

4. *Hearing.* The court will have a hearing to determine the appropriateness of appointing a guardian. The potential incapacitated person may be present and represented by an attorney and may present evidence to the court regarding his or her capacity to manage his or her own affairs.

5. *Court order.* At the conclusion of the hearing, the court will either deny the petition or appoint a guardian. Some states have

provisions for professional guardians (persons preapproved by the court to be appointed as guardians), and many states require guardians to attend special training courses prior to being appointed.

Before it issues a final order, the court may order certain provisional remedies:

1. *Temporary guardian.* A provisional guardian, a **guardian ad litem**, may be appointed by the court to protect the potential incapacitated person's interests until a final disposition is made.

2. *Injunction.* The court may enjoin any action being taken on behalf of the potential incapacitated person until the conclusion of the hearing.

Function of the Court

The role and function of the court with respect to guardianship does not end with appointment of the guardian. The court supervises the guardianship until such guardianship is terminated, either by the regained capacity or the death of the incapacitated person. At all times the guardian remains accountable to the court.

The court has the power to remove a guardian if he or she fails to comply with the court's order or is found guilty of neglect or a breach of any of the fiduciary obligations listed earlier. If the incapacitated person's condition improves or deteriorates, the court can modify the guardian's powers to reflect the changed state of the incapacitated person.

Example

A guardian has failed to file reports with the court for the past three years and has never visited the incapacitated person. When the situation comes to the court's attention, the court removes the guardian, who is still subject to damages for any injury resulting to the incapacitated person due to this neglect.

Example

An elderly man had a guardian appointed five years ago because of his declining mental functions. Six months ago his doctor began giving him a new drug that has dramatically improved his mind and memory. Under these conditions, if appropriate, the court may modify the guardian's authority to act on behalf of the incapacitated person to reflect the incapacitated person's improved mental condition.

guardian ad litem
Guardian during litigation.

Alternatives to Guardianship

Before a guardian will be appointed by the court, the petitioner must demonstrate that alternative solutions have been sought and found inadequate. There are several alternatives to guardianship that might be appropriate in a given situation, and the paralegal may be required to assist in the preparation of the following documents.

Power of Attorney

A **power of attorney** is a document by which one person, known as the **principal**, authorizes another person, known as the **agent**, to act on the principal's behalf. A **general power of attorney** authorizes the agent to perform the functions specified in the power until the power is revoked by the principal, the principal dies or becomes incapacitated, or the power terminates by its own stated provisions. A general power of attorney may be an appropriate alternative for persons who have moderate physical incapacities. If a principal lacks contractual capacity, he or she cannot execute a valid power of attorney.

> *Example*
>
> An elderly man owns several apartment buildings, but no longer has the physical ability to manage them. He executes a general power of attorney authorizing his nephew to manage the buildings on his behalf.

In addition to a general power of attorney a principal may also execute either a durable or a springing power of attorney. A **durable power of attorney** comes into effect immediately upon execution and, unlike a general power of attorney, permits the agent to act on behalf of the principal even if the principal later becomes incapacitated. It survives the principal's lack of contractual capacity.

> *Example*
>
> In the preceding example, if the uncle had given the nephew a durable power of attorney, the nephew would be able to continue to manage the apartment buildings even if the uncle became mentally incapacitated; with a general power of attorney, such incapacity on the part of the principal automatically revokes the agent's ability to act for the principal.

A **springing power of attorney** does not take effect upon execution but is contingent upon the principal becoming incapacitated in the future. The agent has the authority to act only when the principal can no longer act for himself or herself.

power of attorney Document authorizing one person to act on behalf of another.

principal Person who authorizes another to act on his or her behalf.

agent Person who acts on behalf of another.

general power of attorney Document granting a person the legal ability to act on behalf of another; the power terminates on the death or incapacity of the principal or by completion of its purpose.

durable power of attorney Power of attorney that survives the principal's incapacity.

springing power of attorney Power of attorney that comes into effect only if and when the principal becomes incapacitated.

Example _____

In the previous example, assume that the uncle was capable of managing the buildings but was afraid that, as he aged, his ability would be diminished. He executes a springing power of attorney in the nephew's favor, but continues to manage the buildings. Two years after the springing power of attorney is executed, the uncle is diagnosed with Alzheimer's disease. At this point, upon certification by physicians, the power of attorney would come into effect and the nephew would then manage the buildings on the uncle's behalf. With a general power of attorney, the uncle's incapacity would terminate the nephew's authority.

_____

Representative Payee

The concept of a **representative payee** comes from the Social Security Act. When the Social Security Administration (SSA) determines that it is in the best interests of the payee not to receive benefits directly, another person may be authorized to receive the Social Security benefits on the payee's behalf. (See Exhibit 5-1, pages 199–210.) This person is called the representative payee. To appoint a representative payee, the SSA must determine that the payee is incapable of managing his or her own affairs, either because of a court determination to that effect or because the payee is receiving SSI benefits for drug or alcohol abuse. The representative payee must file annual reports with the Social Security Administration, is subject to all general fiduciary obligations, and also receives a fee for acting in this capacity.

Example _____

An elderly man is receiving SSI benefits because of severe drug addiction. Pursuant to the federal statutes, he is automatically deemed incapable of handling his own affairs and so the Social Security Administration will appoint a representative payee to receive the benefits on the payee's behalf.

_____

representative payee Person authorized by the Social Security Administration to receive benefits on behalf of the recipient of Social Security benefits.

order of protection (protective order) Document issued by a court or protective services agency to remedy family problems.

Orders of Protection

The court may issue **orders of protection (protective orders)** to protect a person from what would be deemed "family offenses": disorderly conduct, harassment, menace, reckless endangerment, and assault. In issuing these orders, the court will look at the dynamics of the family and orders will be issued to protect elderly relatives from elder abuse (see Chapter 7). A protective order may be sufficient to protect an elderly individual from the importuning of family members.

DISABILITY REPORT—ADULT—Form SSA-3368-BK

READ ALL OF THIS INFORMATION BEFORE
YOU BEGIN COMPLETING THIS FORM

IF YOU NEED HELP

If you need help with this form, do as much of it as you can, and your interviewer will help you finish it.

HOW TO COMPLETE THIS FORM

The information that you give us on this form will be used by the office that makes the disability decision on your disability claim. You can help them by completing as much of the form as you can.

- Fill out as much of this form as you can before your interview appointment.
- Print or type.
- **DO NOT LEAVE ANSWERS BLANK.** If you do not know the answers, or the answer is "none" or "does not apply," please write: "don't know," or "none," or "does not apply."
- **IN SECTION 4, PUT INFORMATION ON ONLY ONE DOCTOR/HOSPITAL/ CLINIC IN EACH SPACE.**
- Each address should include a ZIP code. Each telephone number should include an area code.
- **DO NOT ASK A DOCTOR OR HOSPITAL TO COMPLETE THE FORM.** However, you can get help from other people, like a friend or family member.
- If your appointment is for an interview by telephone, have the form ready to discuss with us when we call you.
- If your appointment is for an interview in our office, bring the completed form with you or, mail it ahead of time, if you were told to do so.
- When a question refers to "you," "your," or the "Disabled Person," it refers to the person who is applying for disability benefits. If you are filling out the form for someone else, please provide information about him or her.
- Be sure to explain an answer if the question asks for an explanation, or if you want to give additional information.
- If you need more space to answer any questions or want to tell us more about an answer, please use the "REMARKS" section on Pages 9 and 10, and show the number of the question being answered.

ABOUT YOUR MEDICAL RECORDS

If you have any medical records and copies of prescriptions at home for the person who is applying for disability benefits, send them to our office with your completed forms or bring them with you to your interview. Also, bring any prescription bottles with you. If you need the records back, tell us and we will photocopy them and return them to you.

YOU DO NOT NEED TO ASK DOCTORS OR HOSPITALS FOR ANY MEDICAL RECORDS THAT YOU DO NOT ALREADY HAVE. With your permission, we will do

EXHIBIT 5-1   Social Security Administration's disability report (adult)

that for you. The information we ask for on this form tells us to whom we should send a request for medical and other records. If you cannot remember the names and addresses of any of the doctors or hospitals, or the dates of treatment, you may be able to get this information from the telephone book or from medical bills, prescriptions and prescription bottles.

WHAT WE MEAN BY "DISABILITY"

"Disability" under Social Security is based on your inability to work. For purposes of this claim, we want you to understand that "disability" means that you are unable to work as defined by the Social Security Act. You will be considered disabled if you are unable to do any kind of work for which you are suited and your disability is expected to last (or has lasted) for at least a year or to result in death. So when we ask, "when did you become unable to work," we are asking when you became disabled as defined by the Social Security Act.

The Privacy and Paperwork Reduction Acts

The Social Security Administration is authorized to collect the information on this form under sections 205(a), 223(d) and 1631(e)(1) of the Social Security Act. The information on this form is needed by Social Security to make a decision on the named claimant's claim. While giving us the information on this form is voluntary, failure to provide all or part of the requested informa- tion could prevent an accurate or timely decision on the name claimant's claim. Although the information you furnish is almost never used for any purpose other than making a determination about the claimant's disability, such information may be disclosed by the Social Security Administration as follows: (1) to enable a third party or agency to assist Social Security in estab- lishing rights to Social Security benefits and/or coverage; (2) to comply with Federal Laws requiring the release of information from Social Security records (e.g., to the General Accounting Office and the Department of Veterans Affairs); and (3) to facilitate statistical research and such activities necessary to assure the integrity and improvement of the Social Security programs (e.g., to the Bureau of the Census and private concerns under contract to Social Security).

We may also use the information you give us when we match records by computer. Matching programs compare our records with those of other Federal, State, or local government agencies. Many agencies may use matching programs to find or prove that a person qualifies for benefits paid by the Federal government. The law allows us to do this even if you do not agree to it. Explanations about these and other reasons why information you provide us may be used or given out are available in Social Security offices.

The Paperwork Reduction Act of 1995 requires us to notify you that this information collection is in accordance with the clearance requirements of Section 3507 of the Paperwork Reduction Act of 1995. We may not conduct or sponsor, and you are not required to respond to, a collection of information unless it displays a valid OMB control number. We estimate that it will take you about 30 minutes to complete this form. This includes the time it will take to read the instructions, gather the necessary facts, and fill out the form.

REMOVE THIS SHEET BEFORE RETURNING THE COMPLETED FORM.

EXHIBIT 5-1   *(continued)*

SOCIAL SECURITY ADMINISTRATION

Form Approved
OMB No. 0960-0579

DISABILITY REPORT
ADULT

For SSA Use Only
Do not write in this box.

Related SSN _____

Number Holder _____

SECTION 1 — INFORMATION ABOUT THE DISABLED PERSON

A. **NAME** *(First, Middle Initial, Last)*

B. **SOCIAL SECURITY NUMBER**

C. **DAYTIME TELEPHONE NUMBER** *(If you have no number where you can be reached, give us a daytime number where we can leave a message for you.)*

_____ _____ Your Number ☐ Message Number ☐ None ☐
Area Code   *Number*

D. Give the name of a **friend or relative** that we can contact (other than your doctors) **who knows about your illnesses, injuries or conditions** and can help you with your claim.

NAME _____   RELATIONSHIP _____

ADDRESS _____
          (Number, Street, Apt. No.(if any), P.O. Box, or Rural Route)

_____ _____ _____   DAYTIME _____ _____
City   *State*   *ZIP*   PHONE   *Area Code*   *Phone Number*

E. What is your **height** without shoes?   _____ _____
                                            feet   *inches*

F. What is your **weight** without shoes?   _____
                                            pounds

G. Do you have a **medical assistance card**? (For example, Medicaid or Medi-Cal)   YES ☐   NO ☐
   If "YES," show the **number** here: _____

H. Can you **speak English**? YES ☐   NO ☐   If "NO," what languages can you speak? _____

   If you **cannot speak English,** is there someone we may contact who speaks English and will give you messages? *(If this is the same person as in "D" above, show "SAME" here.)*

NAME _____   RELATIONSHIP _____

ADDRESS _____
          (Number, Street, Apt. No.(if any), P.O. Box, or Rural Route)

_____ _____ _____   DAYTIME _____ _____
City   *State*   *ZIP*   PHONE   *Area Code*   *Phone Number*

I. Can you **read English**? YES ☐   NO ☐   J. Can you **write more than**   YES ☐   NO ☐
                                                  your name in English?

FORM **SSA-3368-BK** (7/98) **DESTROY ALL PRIOR EDITIONS**   PAGE 1

Disability Report - Adult - Form SSA-3368-BK

EXHIBIT 5-1   *(continued)*

SECTION 2
YOUR ILLNESSES, INJURIES OR CONDITIONS AND HOW THEY AFFECT YOU

A. What are the **illnesses, injuries or conditions** that limit your ability to work? _____

_____

B. How do your illnesses, injuries or conditions limit your ability to work? _____

_____

_____

C. Do your illnesses, injuries or conditions cause you **pain**?   YES ☐   NO ☐

D. When did your illnesses, injuries or conditions **first bother you?**

Month	Day	Year

E. When did you become **unable to work** because of your illnesses, injuries or conditions?

Month	Day	Year

F. Have you **ever worked**?   YES ☐   NO ☐   (*If "NO," go to Section 4.*)

G. Did you **work at any time** after the date your illnesses, injuries or conditions first bothered you?   YES ☐   NO ☐

H. If "YES," did your illnesses, injuries or conditions cause you to: (*Check all that apply.*)

☐ **work fewer hours?** (*Explain below.*)
☐ **change your job duties?** (*Explain below.*)
☐ **make any job-related changes such as your attendance, help needed, or employers?** (*Explain below.*)

_____

_____

_____

_____

I. Are you **working now**?   YES ☐   NO ☐

If "NO," when did **you stop working?**

Month	Day	Year

J. Why did you **stop working**? _____

_____

_____

EXHIBIT 5-1   (*continued*)

SECTION 3—INFORMATION ABOUT YOUR WORK

A. List the **jobs** that you have had in the **last 15 years that you worked.**

JOB TITLE (Example, Cook)	TYPE OF BUSINESS (Example, Restaurant)	DATES WORKED (month & year) FROM	TO	HOURS PER DAY	DAYS PER WEEK	RATE OF PAY (Per hour, day, week, month or year)
						$ /
						$ /
						$ /
						$ /
						$ /
						$ /
						$ /

B. Describe the **job above** that you did the **longest.** (What did you do all day in this job?)

_____

_____

C. In **this job**, did you:

Use machines, tools or equipment?	YES ☐	NO ☐
Use technical knowledge or skills?	YES ☐	NO ☐
Do any writing, complete reports, or perform any duties like this?	YES ☐	NO ☐
Did you supervise other people?	YES ☐	NO ☐
If "YES," was this your main duty?	YES ☐	NO ☐

D. In **this job**, how many total hours each day did you:

Walk? _____
Stand? _____
Sit? _____
Climb? _____
Stoop? *(Bend down and forward at waist.)* _____

Kneel? *(Bend legs to rest on knees.)* _____
Crouch? *(Bend legs & back down & forward.)* _____
Crawl? *(Move on hands & knees.)* _____
Handle, grab or grasp big objects? _____
Write, type or handle small objects? _____

E. Lifting and Carrying *(Explain what you lifted, how far you carried it, and how often you did this.)*

_____

_____

F. Check **heaviest** weight lifted:

☐ Less than 10 lbs.   ☐ 10 lbs.   ☐ 20 lbs.   ☐ 50 lbs.   ☐ 100 lbs. or more   ☐ Other_____

G. Check weight **frequently** lifted: *(By frequently, we mean from 1/3 to 2/3 of the workday.)*

☐ Less than 10 lbs.   ☐ 10 lbs.   ☐ 25 lbs.   ☐ 50 lbs. or more   ☐ Other_____

EXHIBIT 5-1   *(continued)*

SECTION 4 — INFORMATION ABOUT YOUR MEDICAL RECORDS

A. Have you been seen by a **doctor/hospital/clinic** or anyone else for the illnesses, injuries or conditions that limit your ability to work?   YES ☐   NO ☐

B. Have you been seen by a **doctor/hospital/clinic** or anyone else for emotional or mental problems that limit your ability to work?   YES ☐   NO ☐

If you answered "NO" to both of these questions, go to Section 5.

C. List **other names** you have used on your medical records. _____

_____

**Tell us who may have medical records or other
information about your illnesses, injuries or conditions.**

D. **List each DOCTOR/HMO/THERAPIST.** Include your **next appointment**.

1.

NAME	DATES
STREET ADDRESS	FIRST VISIT
CITY STATE ZIP	LAST SEEN
PHONE _Area Code_ _Phone Number_ CHART/HMO #	NEXT APPOINTMENT
REASONS FOR VISITS	
WHAT TREATMENT WAS RECEIVED?	

2.

NAME	DATES
STREET ADDRESS	FIRST VISIT
CITY STATE ZIP	LAST SEEN
PHONE _Area Code_ _Phone Number_ CHART/HMO #	NEXT APPOINTMENT
REASONS FOR VISITS	
WHAT TREATMENT WAS RECEIVED?	

FORM **SSA-3368-BK** (7/98)   PAGE 4

EXHIBIT 5-1   (continued)

SECTION 4 — INFORMATION ABOUT YOUR MEDICAL RECORDS

DOCTOR/HMO/THERAPIST

3.

NAME	DATES
STREET ADDRESS	FIRST VISIT
CITY STATE ZIP	LAST SEEN
PHONE _____ _____ Area Code Phone Number CHART/HMO #	NEXT APPOINTMENT
REASONS FOR VISITS	
WHAT **TREATMENT** WAS RECEIVED?	

If you need more space, use Remarks, Section 9.

E. **List each HOSPITAL/CLINIC.** Include your **next appointment**.

1.

HOSPITAL/CLINIC	TYPE OF VISIT	DATES	
NAME	☐ **INPATIENT** STAYS *(Stayed at least overnight)*	DATE IN	DATE OUT
STREET ADDRESS	☐ **OUTPATIENT** VISITS *(Sent home same day)*	DATE FIRST VISIT	DATE LAST VISIT
CITY STATE ZIP PHONE _____ _____ Area Code Phone Number	☐ **EMERGENCY ROOM** VISITS	DATES OF VISITS	

Next **appointment** _____ Your hospital/clinic **number** _____

Reasons for visits _____

What **treatment** did you receive? _____

What **doctors** do you see at this hospital/clinic on a regular basis? _____

EXHIBIT 5-1   (*continued*)

SECTION 4 — INFORMATION ABOUT YOUR MEDICAL RECORDS

HOSPITAL/CLINIC

2.

HOSPITAL/CLINIC	TYPE OF VISIT	DATES	
NAME	☐ **INPATIENT** STAYS *(Stayed at least overnight)*	DATE IN	DATE OUT
STREET ADDRESS	☐ **OUTPATIENT** VISITS *(Sent home same day)*	DATE FIRST VISIT	DATE LAST VISIT
CITY STATE ZIP	☐ **EMERGENCY ROOM** VISITS	DATES OF VISITS	
PHONE *Area Code Phone Number*			

Next **appointment** _____ Your hospital/clinic **number** _____

Reasons for visits _____

_____

What **treatment** did you receive? _____

_____

What **doctors** do you see at this hospital/clinic on a regular basis? _____

_____

If you need more space, use Remarks, Section 9.

F. Does **anyone else have medical records or information** about your illnesses, injuries or conditions (Workers' Compensation, insurance companies, prisons, attorneys, welfare), or are you scheduled to see anyone else?

YES ☐   *(If "YES," complete information below.)*   NO ☐

NAME	DATES
ADDRESS	**FIRST** VISIT
	LAST SEEN
PHONE *Area Code Phone Number*	NEXT APPOINTMENT
CLAIM NUMBER *(If any)*	
REASONS FOR VISITS?	

If you need more space, use Remarks, Section 9.

FORM SSA-3368-BK (7/98)   PAGE 6

EXHIBIT 5-1   *(continued)*

SECTION 5 — MEDICATIONS

Do you currently take any **medications** for your illnesses, injuries or conditions?   YES ☐   NO ☐
If "YES," please tell us the following: *(Look at your medicine bottles, if necessary.)*

NAME OF MEDICINE	PRESCRIBED BY *(Name of Doctor)*	REASON FOR MEDICINE	SIDE EFFECTS YOU HAVE

If you need more space, use Remarks, Section 9.

SECTION 6 — TESTS

Have you had, or will you have, any **medical tests** for your illnesses, injuries or conditions?
YES ☐   NO ☐   If "YES," please tell us the following: *(Give approximate dates, if necessary.)*

KIND OF TEST	WHEN DONE, OR WHEN WILL IT BE DONE? *(Month, day, year)*	WHERE DONE? *(Name of Facility)*	WHO SENT YOU FOR THIS TEST?
EKG (HEART TEST)			
TREADMILL (EXERCISE TEST)			
CARDIAC CATHETERIZATION			
BIOPSY Name of body part_____			
HEARING TEST			
VISION TEST			
IQ TESTING			
EEG (BRAIN WAVE TEST)			
HIV TEST			
BLOOD TEST (NOT HIV)			
BREATHING TEST			
X-RAY Name of body part_____			
MRI/CT SCAN Name of body part_____			

If you have had other tests, list them in Remarks, Section 9.

EXHIBIT 5-1   *(continued)*

SECTION 7 — EDUCATION/TRAINING INFORMATION

A. Circle the highest grade of **school** completed.

0   1   2   3   4   5   6   7   8   9   10   11   12   GED   College: 1   2   3   4 or more

Approximate **date** completed: _____

B. Did you attend **special education** classes?   YES ☐   NO ☐   If "YES,"

NAME OF SCHOOL _____

ADDRESS _____
(Number, Street, Apt. No.(if any), P.O. Box, or Rural Route)

_____
City   State   ZIP

DATES ATTENDED _____ TO _____

TYPE OF PROGRAM _____

C. Have you completed any type of **special job training, trade or vocational school**?   YES ☐   NO ☐

If "YES," what type? _____

Approximate date completed: _____

SECTION 8 — VOCATIONAL REHABILITATION INFORMATION

A. Have you received services from **Vocational Rehabilitation** or any other organization to help you get back to work?   YES ☐   NO ☐   If "YES,"

NAME OF ORGANIZATION _____

NAME OF COUNSELOR _____

ADDRESS _____
(Number, Street, Apt. No.(if any), P.O. Box, or Rural Route)

_____
City   State   ZIP

DAYTIME PHONE NUMBER _____
Area Code   Number

DATES SEEN _____ TO _____

TYPE OF SERVICES OR
TESTS PERFORMED _____
(IQ, vision, physicals, hearing, workshops, etc.)

B. Would you like to receive rehabilitation services that could help you get back to work?   YES ☐   NO ☐

FORM **SSA-3368-BK** (7/98)   PAGE 8

EXHIBIT 5-1   *(continued)*

SECTION 9 — REMARKS

Use this section for any added information you did not show in earlier parts of this form. When you are done with this section (or if you don't have anything to add), be sure to go to the next page and complete the signature block.

_____

_____

_____

_____

_____

_____

_____

_____

_____

_____

_____

_____

_____

_____

_____

_____

_____

_____

_____

_____

_____

_____

_____

_____

_____

EXHIBIT 5-1   (_continued_)

SECTION 9 — REMARKS

_____
_____
_____
_____
_____
_____
_____
_____
_____
_____
_____
_____
_____
_____
_____
_____
_____
_____
_____
_____
_____

ANYONE MAKING A FALSE STATEMENT OR REPRESENTATION OF A MATERIAL FACT FOR USE IN DETERMINING A RIGHT TO PAYMENT UNDER THE SOCIAL SECURITY ACT COMMITS A CRIME PUNISHABLE UNDER FEDERAL LAW.

Signature of **claimant** or person filing on claimant's behalf *(Parent, guardian)*	**Date** *(Month, day, year)*

Witnesses are required **ONLY** if this statement has been signed by mark (X) above. If signed by mark (X), two witnesses to the signing who know the person making the statement must sign below giving their full addresses.

1. Signature of **Witness**	2. Signature of **Witness**
Address *(number and street, city, state, and ZIP code)*	**Address** *(number and street, city state, and ZIP code)*

FORM **SSA-3368-BK** (7/98)   PAGE 10

☆U.S GOVERNMENT PRINTING OFFICE: 1998 443-420

EXHIBIT 5-1   *(continued)*

Example _____

An elderly woman is being harassed by her son to turn her money over to him, and he threatens her with guardianship proceedings. When the woman's daughter learns what is happening, she seeks a protective order on behalf of her mother to see that her brother stops the harassment. The elderly woman is competent and does not need a guardian, but she does need protection from her son.

Joint Ownership

If a property owner is having trouble managing property but is not totally incapacitated, the person may have the title to the property placed in **joint ownership** with the person he or she would wish to inherit the property eventually. The joint owner has the legal ability to manage the property, and the court's jurisdiction does not have to be invoked. Note that joint ownership might affect benefits that may be available to the older person.

Example _____

An elderly man is becoming more and more feeble, and is having trouble managing his business. He changes the title to the business from his name alone to a joint ownership with his adult son. The son now has the legal ability to manage the business, the father still owns half the property, and at the father's death the full title will pass to the son by operation of law. The court never gets involved.

Revocable Trust

A person who has the legal capacity to enter into contracts may place his or her property in trust. A *trust* is a fiduciary relationship in which one person manages property for the benefit of another. In this fashion the property owner may still enjoy the property, but does not have to worry about managing it; management is the responsibility of the trustee. If the creator of the trust retains the power to revoke, he or she can terminate the **revocable trust** and regain full title to the property. For a fuller discussion of trusts, see Chapter 6.

Example _____

A couple place their property in trust and name their daughter as trustee. The daughter manages the property for her parents' benefit. If the couple decide that they do not like the arrangement, provided that they retained the power to revoke, they can terminate the trust and manage their own property again.

joint ownership
Form of title in which two or more persons have equal rights to property with a right of survivorship.

revocable trust
Trust in which the creator reserves the right to terminate the relationship.

Civil Commitment

Civil commitment is usually a last resort, because it is much more severe than guardianship. With civil commitment, which can be either voluntary or involuntary, a person is placed in a mental facility because he or she is likely to do harm to himself or herself or to others. To be admitted, the person must be certified as being likely to do severe harm by a physician, and most facilities require that the person be reexamined by a staff physician within 48 hours of admittance. Civil commitment is not an adjudication of incapacity.

Example

A woman suffers with bipolar disorder and has become increasingly depressed, to the point where she is considering suicide. Her daughter has her committed to a mental health facility, where she is examined and found to be in danger of doing severe harm to herself.

THE DISABLED CHILD

All people eventually become concerned with care for themselves if and when their ability to care for themselves declines. This concern is augmented for elderly parents of children who are physically and/or mentally disabled. Generally, the parent has been the caregiver for the child for the child's entire life, but a problem arises as to who will care for the disabled child when the parents can no longer fulfill this function. Paralegals concerned with elder law must also be concerned about the elder person's disabled child. Furthermore, if the aging parent has been placed under guardianship prior to making suitable arrangements for the disabled child, it becomes the obligation of the guardian to see that the child is provided for.

civil commitment
The voluntary or involuntary confinement of a person in a mental facility because it is determined that the person may do severe harm to himself or to others.

standby guardian
Contingent guardian.

Services

Pursuant to individual state laws, protective services are available for mentally retarded and disabled children; however, typically such services terminate once the child attains the age of 18. Once a person reaches adulthood, the services available for care are the services that have been discussed earlier with reference to the elderly. The parents of a disabled child, as the natural legal guardians of the child, may arrange for a **standby guardian**, a court-appointed individual who will assume the parents' guardianship responsibilities if the parents become disabled or die. The attorney and the paralegal may have to draft the appropriate documents to have this person appointed. This form of guardianship is conceptually similar to a springing power of attorney (discussed earlier in this chapter). Also, Social Security and SSI have provisions to meet the financial needs of the mentally and/or physically disabled, but it is the parent or guardian's responsibility to see that all appropriate documents are prepared and procedures followed to assure that the disabled child will receive the necessary and available governmental financial support. Additionally, state social service agencies may provide certain care for the mentally and physically disabled.

*Example*_____

A couple in their fifties are the parents of a mentally retarded 22-year-old daughter. To provide care for this child, the parents have had their son appointed as their standby guardian, in case they become incapacitated or die. In this fashion they have provided for the guardianship of their disabled child while they are competent to make decisions.

*Example*_____

An elderly man is the guardian of his 50-year-old disabled son. The man has made no arrangements for the son's care should he himself become disabled. The man is eventually diagnosed with Alzheimer's disease and is placed under guardianship by his niece. It is now the niece's obligation to see that guardianship and or other provisions are made for the care of her disabled cousin. It probably would have been better if the elderly man had made these arrangements himself, while he was competent, so that his wishes for the care of his son could have been carried out.

Trusts

As discussed earlier, one alternative to guardianship, at least for the management of assets, is the creation of a trust for the benefit of the incapacitated person. Elder law attorneys are often asked to draw up such trusts, and the elder law paralegal must be ready to assist in their preparation. For the disabled, two special forms of trusts are currently in widespread use.

Supplemental Needs Trust

A **supplemental needs trust** is created to pay for the medical care of the beneficiary when such care is not provided for by other means, such as Medicare, Medicaid, or private insurance. The funds are distributed only to meet these needs. This type of trust may be established by the disabled beneficiary's parents, grandparents, or legal guardian; at the death of the disabled beneficiary, any funds remaining in the trust

supplemental needs trust Trust created to provide medical benefits not otherwise provided for the beneficiary.

are subject to claims by the government and other institutions that have disbursed funds on behalf of the beneficiary during the beneficiary's life.

Example

A child was severely brain damaged as the result of medical malpractice. The parents sue the responsible health care provider and receive a large settlement on behalf of the child. The parents establish a supplemental needs trust for the child's benefit. The funds are distributed to meet medical expenses of the child not otherwise met by governmental benefits. At the child's death, the funds remaining in the trust go to the government to the extent necessary to reimburse the government for the funds expended on the child's behalf during the child's life.

Master Trust

A **master trust** is a form of a pooled supplemental needs trust under Medicaid law. In this form of trust, the child's parents, grandparents, or guardian place funds in a trust in which there are multiple disabled beneficiaries, the guardians of whom have also contributed to the trust. At the death of each beneficiary, the funds remain in the trust to be used for the benefit of the remaining disabled beneficiaries. Beneficiaries can be continually added to the trust, and the trust is required to be managed by a nonprofit charitable institution. With this type of trust, the funds are continually used to benefit disabled individuals rather than being refunded to the government at a beneficiary's death.

Example

The parents from the preceding example, rather than setting up a private supplemental needs trust for their child alone, decide to place their funds in a pooled trust so that other disabled individuals can benefit as well as their own child.

Education and Housing

A detailed discussion of the education and housing programs available to assist disabled children is beyond the scope of this text; however, it should be noted that every state provides special schools and developmental housing facilities for children and adults who are deemed disabled. The determination of disability is made, typically, by medical affidavits of two physicians or one physician and one psychologist. The

master trust
Pooled supplemental needs trust.

provisions of each state's policy must be individually examined by the elder law paralegal.

On the federal level, in addition to the Americans with Disabilities Act (discussed in earlier chapters), there is the **Individuals with Disabilities Education Act (IDEA)** that mandates free education for disabled persons in the least restrictive environment possible, depending on the particular needs of the person in question. Should a person be denied appropriate education, the statute provides the right to an impartial hearing to determine the person's situation and potential needs.

ETHICAL CONSIDERATIONS

The ethical considerations concerned with guardianship of elderly individuals fall into two broad categories: first, the possibility of the guardian breaching one of his or her fiduciary obligations; and second, the possibility of the guardian using that position to abuse the elderly incapacitated person.

All guardians are subject to court scrutiny to assure that they fulfill their fiduciary responsibilities. It is a violation of their obligations to use their authority to benefit themselves, either directly or indirectly, by transferring the incapacitated person's assets. Furthermore, guardians are expected to maintain and file accurate accounts and records of their administration of the incapacitated person's property and assets. In 1998, an independent study concerning the court-appointed guardians in the city of New York discovered that the overwhelming majority of guardians failed to maintain or file any reports, and few of them ever actually visited their incapacitated persons to determine the incapacitated person's current state of capacity. However, most of the guardians did manage to see that they received their fees. Not only can the court remove these persons from their positions of trust, but, if the guardian is an attorney, the court may also institute disciplinary proceedings against the attorney.

A problem that has surfaced over the past few years is the problem of elder abuse, the situation in which the caregiver or presumed confidant of the elderly person uses that position of trust to harass, menace, or psychologically or physically intimidate or harm the elderly person. Because of the dependence of the elderly person on the performance of the guardian, the guardian can use his or her position of trust to abuse the elderly incapacitated person. This problem has become widespread, and a detailed discussion of elder abuse appears in Chapter 7.

Individuals with Disabilities Education Act (IDEA) Federal statute mandating free education for persons with disabilities.

CHAPTER REVIEW

The government has always considered one of its most important responsibilities to be the care of its citizens who are not capable of caring for themselves. Under current legal concepts, this principle falls under the general heading of guardianship.

The modern trend with respect to guardianship is to see that guardianship is made in the least restrictive manner possible, only authorizing a guardian to meet the specific needs of the person who cannot manage for himself or herself. The historic concept of incompetence on the part of the incapacitated person prior to the imposition of guardianship has been replaced by the less stigmatizing requirement of evidencing a "lack of capacity"—which can be physical, mental, or emotional—to handle one's own affairs. The court, acting on behalf of the state, will see that a guardian is appointed with the most limited legal authority necessary to meet the needs of the incapacitated person, while maintaining for the incapacitated person the most personal independence and control possible.

Before the court will appoint a guardian, the person seeking guardianship must prove to the court that other, less restrictive remedies were tried and were unsuccessful. Such alternative measures include powers of attorney, representative payees, joint tenancies, and living trusts. As a last resort, a person may also be civilly committed to confinement if it is shown that the person may do severe harm to himself or herself or to others.

The guardian may be responsible for the care and management of the incapacitated person's person and/or property, depending on the nature of the authority conferred on the guardian by the court. There are four categories of guardian: guardian of the person (acting as the legal decision maker for the incapacitated person); guardian of the estate (conservator for the assets of the incapacitated person); plenary guardian (acting as the guardian of both the person and the estate); and limited guardian, whose actual authority is specified by court order. In all instances the guardian is a fiduciary who is held to the highest standard of care with respect to carrying out the duties of a guardian.

KEY TERMS

agent	general power of attorney
civil commitment	guardian ad litem
conservator	guardian of the estate
durable power of attorney	guardian of the person

in parens patriae

incapacitated person

Individuals with Disabilities
    Education Act (IDEA)

joint ownership

limited guardian

master trust

order of protection (protective
    order)

plenary guardian

power of attorney

principal

representative payee

revocable trust

springing power of attorney

standby guardian

supplemental needs trust

ward

EXERCISES

1. Check your state statutes to ascertain the requirements to be appointed a guardian.

2. Discuss the benefits and detriments of three alternatives to guardianship.

3. Compare and contrast a supplemental needs trust with a master trust and indicate why one might be more preferable in a given situation.

4. Many jurisdictions require guardians to receive special training prior to being appointed. Obtain a copy of such training material and analyze the materials for effectiveness in preparing a person to be a guardian.

5. Discuss some potentials for abuse of trust by a guardian.

EDITED JUDICIAL DECISIONS

In re Boyer
636 P.2d 1085 (Utah 1981)

This appeal is from a district court order appointing a guardian for the appellant, Nelda Boyer. The appointment was based on a jury finding that appellant is an "incapacitated person" in need of a personal guardian to provide her with care and supervision. Appellant contends that the order should be set aside because the standard for determining competency in a guardianship proceeding under Utah Code Ann. (1953), § 75-1-201(1) is unconstitutionally vague and overbroad.

Appellant is a 39-year-old woman who has a mild degree of mental retardation and is a slow learner. She made her home for many years in Reno, Nevada, with her parents. Following her father's death five years ago, she lived with her mother. Turmoil in the home situation led to visits with a family therapist who recommended she be separated from her mother. The family suggested bringing Nelda Boyer to Ogden, Utah, where other members of her family reside. The therapist recommended that she be placed in Jefferson Manor, a nursing home in Ogden, and that a guardian be appointed. Appellant's relatives invited her to Utah and then arranged for her to live at Jefferson Manor.

Her family initiated guardianship proceedings. Appellant requested a jury trial on the issue of her incompetency pursuant to § 75-5-303. An attorney she retained represented her and presented and cross-examined witnesses at the hearing. The jury instructions stated in part:

> "Incapacitated person" means any person who is impaired by reason of mental illness, mental deficiency, physical illness or disability, advanced age, chronic use of drugs, chronic intoxication, or other cause to the extent that he/she lacks sufficient understanding or capacity to make or communicate responsible decisions concerning his or her person.

Mentally retarded citizens are presumed legally competent to manage their personal and financial affairs.

The case was submitted to the jury on special interrogatories, and it found "by a preponderance of the evidence that [appellant] is an 'incapacitated person' ... and that the appointment of a guardian is necessary or desirable as a means of providing continuing care and supervision of [appellant]." Her sister, Naoma Suzie B. Rice, was appointed guardian by order of the court. The Letters of Guardianship set no limits to the powers of the guardian.

Appellant attacks the constitutionality of two sections of the probate code dealing with the appointment of guardians for incapacitated persons. Section 75-1-201(18) defines "incapacitated persons" as:

> any person who is impaired by reason of mental illness, mental deficiency, physical illness or disability, advanced age, chronic use of drugs, chronic intoxication, or other cause (except minority) to the extent that he lacks sufficient understanding or capacity to make or communicate responsible decisions concerning his person.

Section 75-5-304 authorizes appointment of a guardian by the court and provides in part:

> The court may appoint a guardian as requested if it is satisfied that the person for whom a guardian is sought is incapacitated and that the appointment is necessary or desirable as a means of providing continuing care and supervision of the person of the incapacitated person ... . Alternatively, the court may dismiss the proceeding or enter any other appropriate order.

Appellant contends that because a determination of incapacity may result in a deprivation of such fundamental rights as the right of privacy, the right to travel, and the right to make various personal decisions, the statutory provisions must meet due process requirements and contain well-defined standards. Appellant maintains the term "responsible decisions concerning his person," as used in § 75-1-201(18), is unconstitutionally vague and overbroad. She asserts that because of the potential infringement of individual liberties, the statutory scheme is deficient in not incorporating the principle of the "least restrictive alternative." Finally, appellant argues that due process is violated because a finding of incompetency may be based on a preponderance of the evidence rather than clear and convincing proof.

When state action impinges on fundamental rights, strict compliance with due process must be observed. A statute which affects fundamental liberties is unconstitutional if it is so vague that "men of common intelligence must necessarily guess at its meaning." *State v. Packard, 122 Utah 369, 374, 250 P.2d 561, 563 (1952)*, quoting from *Connally v. General Construction Co., 269 U.S. 385, 391, 46 S. Ct. 126, 70 L. Ed. 322 (1926)*. See also *Trade Commission v. Skaggs Drug Centers, Inc., 21 Utah 2d 431, 446 P.2d 958 (1968); State v. Musser, 118 Utah 537, 223 P.2d 193 (1950)*.

A ward in a guardianship case may not, however, be of ordinary intelligence, or even conscious. Nevertheless, intelligible standards must exist both with respect to the determination of incompetency and the powers which a guardian may exercise over the ward. But there must also be flexibility to deal with the infinite variety of problems presented in guardianship cases, and yet sufficient limitations on the discretion of both courts and guardians to insure that the legitimate purposes of the statute will be effectuated without unjustifiable intrusion upon personal liberties.

It is established that a law fails to meet the requirements of the Due Process Clause if it is so vague and standardless that it leaves the public uncertain as to the conduct it prohibits or leaves judges and jurors free to decide, without any legally fixed standards, what is prohibited and what is not in each particular case. [*Giaccio v. Pennsylvania, 382 U.S. 399, 402–03, 86 S. Ct. 518, 15 L. Ed. 2d 447 (1966).*] *See also Grayned v. City of Rockford, 408 U.S. 104, 92 S. Ct. 2294, 33 L. Ed. 2d 222 (1972).*

Of course, "the Constitution does not require impossible standards"; all that is required is that the language convey "sufficiently definite" standards. *United States v. Petrillo, 332 U.S. 1, 7–8, 67 S. Ct. 1538, 91 L. Ed. 1877 (1947).* Vagueness is particularly repugnant if the statute could be construed to permit illegal interference with individual liberties. Facial imprecision in statutory terms, however, is not necessarily, by itself, a reason to hold a statute unconstitutional, *Roth v. United States, 354 U.S. 476, 77 S. Ct. 1304, 1 L. Ed. 2d 1498 (1957),* for it is the duty of this Court to construe a statute to avoid constitutional infirmities whenever possible. Cf. *Munsee v. Munsee, 12 Utah 2d 83, 363 P.2d 71 (1961).*

The statutory definition of an "incapacitated person" focuses on a person's "capacity to make or communicate responsible decisions concerning his person." Utah Code Ann. § 75-1-201(18). The breadth and imprecision of that standard permit the determination of incompetency to be based on factors subjective to the trier of fact and factors extraneous to the legitimate interests of the state and the ward. That standard, standing alone, would allow a guardian to be appointed for a person who makes decisions regarded by some as irresponsible, even though he has sufficient capacity to make personal management decisions which allow him to function in a manner acceptable to himself and without any threat of injury to himself.

One difficulty with the statutory term "responsible decisions" was pointed out by the United States District Court for the District of Utah in a decision holding portions of Utah's involuntary commitment statute (§ 64-7-36) unconstitutionally vague and overbroad. In *Colyar v. Third Judicial District Court, 469 F. Supp. 424, 433 (D. Utah 1979),* the Court stated:

> The use of the word "responsible" focuses the committing authority's attention on the content of the decision rather than on the ability of the individual to engage in a rational decision-making process. The word "responsible", being given no further content, lends itself to a completely subjective and, therefore, potentially arbitrary and nonuniform, evaluation of what is decided rather than an objective evaluation of the method by which the decision is reached.

Prior decisions of this Court have also recognized the importance of examining the decision-making process of an alleged incompetent. In *In re Heath, 102 Utah 1, 61, 126 P.2d 1058, 1061 (1942),* the Court, in dealing with the prior incompetency statute having a different standard, stated:

> The section [dealing with incompetency] implies physical or mental defects which interfere with the rational functioning of the mind. If the mind functions rationally but the individual acts in a way commonly designated as eccentric—that is, his acts deviate from the usual principally because he is less susceptible to public opinion than are many of us—he is not incompetent … . He may be foolish in the eyes of many of us, but he is not incompetent. Competency is not measured by one's ability to accumulate and hold the material things of life. Were it so, there would be many of our ministerial brethren—not to mention some of our learned judicial associates—behind mental bars.

See also *In re Valentine's Guardianship, 4 Utah 2d 355, 362–63, 294 P.2d 696, 701–02 (1956).*

It is also necessary, however, to recognize that the content of an individual's decisions must also on occasion be evaluated, apart from the underlying rationality of the decision-making process. Unusually bad judgment, highly impaired memory, or a severe loss of behavior control may call in question a person's competency. Indeed, psychotic individuals may reason correctly from a premise demonstrably at variance with reality. That the conclusion may follow in a logical sequence from the premise is not necessarily sufficient to compel the conclusion that a person has made a "responsible decision."

Nevertheless, the term "responsible decisions" admits of such a broad interpretation as to raise a serious question of unconstitutional vagueness. But the term may also be construed more narrowly so as to effectuate the statutory purpose and avoid constitutional difficulty, and it is our "duty to adopt that construction which will save the statute from constitutional infirmity." *United States v. Delaware & Hudson Co., 213 U.S. 366, 407, 29 S. Ct. 527, 53 L. Ed. 836 (1909).*

The term "responsible decisions" is reasonably susceptible of a construction giving effect to the statute's basic purpose without improperly impinging on an individual's liberties of self-determination, right of privacy, right to travel, or right to make one's own educational and medical decisions. The basic State interest is in preventing an incapacitated person from causing harm to himself. It has no interest in restricting harmless, unorthodox conduct; indeed, it must be remembered that much human progress resulted from individuals who walked to their own tune and strayed outside usual customs and conventions. The benign purposes of the statute can be effectively accomplished without improperly trenching on those liberties by defining "responsible decisions" in terms of specific, objective standards for determining the ability of one to care for himself.

We hold that under § 75-1-201(18) a determination that a person cannot make "responsible decisions concerning his person," and is therefore incompetent, may be made as to an adult if the putative ward's decision-making process is so impaired that he is unable to care for his personal safety or unable to attend to and provide for such necessities as food, shelter, clothing, and medical care, without which physical injury or illness may occur. See *Fazio v. Fazio, 375 Mass. 394, 378 N.E.2d 951 (1978).*

Appellant next argues that the statutory provision specifying the powers of the guardian is unconstitutionally overbroad because the full scope of powers which may be, and in this case were, conferred on a guardian may not be necessary in specific cases. The latter principle, the least restrictive alternative, is closely allied with the more general overbreadth issue, and, therefore, we address both together. Appellant specifically contends that the State must adopt the alternative least restrictive of the alleged incompetent's liberty and that the Utah procedure sweeps too broadly in permitting a guardian to be invested with wide-ranging powers over the personal decision of one who has no need of complete supervision, although there may be a need for assistance in handling specific aspects of a person's personal affairs.

A legitimate state purpose cannot be accomplished by means that broadly "stifle fundamental personal liberties when the end can be more narrowly achieved." *Shelton v. Tucker, 364 U.S. 479, 488, 81 S. Ct. 247, 5 L. Ed. 2d 231 (1960).* See also *Aptheker v. Secretary of State, 378 U.S. 500, 84 S. Ct. 1659, 12 L. Ed. 2d 992 (1964); Covington v. Harris, 136 U.S. App. D.C. 35, 419 F.2d 617 (D.C. Cir. 1969).* The means adopted must be narrowly tailored to achieve the basic statutory purpose.

The least restrictive alternative standard has been applied in involuntary commitment proceedings. In *Welsch v. Likins, 373 F. Supp. 487, 502 (D. Minn. 1974),* the Court required state officials to make "good faith attempts to place [involuntarily committed] persons in settings that will be suitable and appropriate to their mental and physical conditions while least restrictive of their liberties." See also *Rennie v. Klein, 462 F. Supp. 1131 (D.N.J. 1978); Lynch v. Baxley, 386 F. Supp. 378 (M.D. Ala. 1974).* Cf. *Appeal of Niccoli, 472 Pa. 389, 372 A.2d 749 (1977); State v. Krol, 68 N.J. 236, 344 A.2d 289 (1975).* Compare *Lessard v. Schmidt, 349 F.*

Supp. 1078 (E.D. Wis. 1972) (three-judge court), vacated & remanded on other grounds, *414 U.S. 473, 94 S. Ct. 713, 38 L. Ed. 2d 661 (1974).*

Although the restrictions on, and deprivation of, personal freedom by appointment of a guardian are less in extent and in intrusiveness than by involuntary commitment, nevertheless, the loss of freedom may be substantial. Accordingly, the appointment of a guardian must consider the interest of the ward in retaining as broad a power of self-determination as is consistent with the reason for appointing a guardian of the person.

The nature and extent of the powers conferred on a guardian is for the court to decide. Section 75-5-312(1) provides: "A guardian of an incapacitated person has the same powers, rights, and duties respecting his ward that a parent has respecting his unemancipated minor child ... except as modified by order of the court." Although the powers conferred upon a guardian may be very broad, the court is authorized to tailor the powers of a guardian to the specific needs of the ward. In appointing a guardian, the court should state with particularity the powers granted, unless the full scope of the statutory authorization is called for. The process should be individualized and based upon careful consideration of the particular need for supervision. Cf. *In re Roe, 383 Mass. 415, 421 N.E.2d 40 (1981).*

To enable the court to fashion an appropriate remedy, the parties should submit evidence "showing the proposed ward's inability to think or act for himself as to matters concerning his personal health, safety, and general welfare." *Fazio v. Fazio, 375 Mass. 394, 403, 378 N.E.2d 951 (1978).* Based on this evidence, findings of fact should be made to support the powers conferred on the guardian, and those powers should be as clearly defined as the situation permits. So construed, the guardianship statute is not unconstitutionally overbroad.

The final issue raised by appellant is the standard of proof necessary before a determination of incompetency can be made. The guardianship statute does not deal with the problem. A determination of what standard should govern rests on a weighing of the State's interest and purpose in having a guardian appointed, the interest of the individual for whom a guardian is sought, and the consequences of an erroneous judgment and potential abuse, either wittingly or unwittingly, by third persons. See generally, Note, "We're Only Trying to Help": The Burden and Standard of Proof in Short Term Civil Commitment, *31 Stanford L. Rev. 425 (1979).* The individual interests at stake include loss of personal liberty, stigma, unwanted medical treatment, legal disabilities, and possible imposition by designing individuals. The State's interest is in protecting the individual from injury to himself.

In balancing these competing interests, we conclude that the reasonable doubt standard in the determination of competency is too restrictive and would tend to frustrate the beneficial purposes of the act by making a guardian unavailable to persons needing only a limited degree of supervision. Furthermore, there are other procedures provided which tend to reduce error. The flexibility available to a judge in tailoring a specific remedy to a specific individual, as provided by the statute, lessens the potential for an overly broad deprivation of personal decision-making power. In addition, the trial court's findings will sharpen the effectiveness of appellate review. A reasonable doubt standard in a guardianship case could well frustrate the benign purposes of the guardianship laws.

On the other hand, a preponderance-of-the-evidence standard would provide inadequate protection to an individual's interests. In every case, civil and criminal, courts endeavor to arrive at a conclusion that accurately reflects the facts. Nevertheless, a preponderance of the evidence test allows for considerable doubt in the fact finder's mind as to the correctness of the judgment—a latitude necessary in most civil cases for numerous reasons, not the least of which is the necessity to resolve and conclude disputes. See generally *In re Winship, 397 U.S. 358, 371, 90 S. Ct. 1068, 25 L. Ed. 2d 368 (1970)* (Harlan, J., concurring).

But an erroneous judgment is of greater concern when an individual's liberty is at stake, regardless of the nature of the proceeding, and it is therefore necessary to seek to minimize error to the extent possible without undermining or frustrating the important purposes served by the guardianship statutes. In the absence of a legislative directive on the issue, we think those interests are best accommodated by requiring evidence of incompetency by clear and convincing evidence. A number of courts have imposed that standard in involuntary commitment cases. *Stamus v. Leonhardt*, 414 F. Supp. 439 (S.D. Iowa 1976); *Doremus v. Farrell*, 407 F. Supp. 509 (D. Neb. 1975); *In re Stephenson*, 67 Ill. 2d 544, 367 N.E.2d 1273, 10 Ill. Dec. 507 (1977); *In re Valdez*, 88 N.M. 338, 540 P.2d 818 (1975). We recognize that the deprivation of personal freedoms is greater in commitment cases than in guardianship cases and that, in the latter cases, there will be differences in the extent of curtailment of personal freedoms. Nevertheless, the interests at stake are not so different as to require that a different standard should govern.

The judgment of incompetency is set aside and the case remanded for further proceedings. No costs.

In re Conservatorship of Estate of Martin
228 Neb. 103, 421 N.W.2d 463 (1988)

Donald L. Ellison, conservator for the estate of Elizabeth G. Martin, a protected person, filed a motion for approval of account and resignation as conservator with the county court for Butler County. Elizabeth Martin, the protected person, through her attorney, filed an answer and cross-petition against Ellison and the bond surety company, alleging that Ellison had negligently breached his duties as conservator and that the estate of Martin had been damaged.

An evidentiary hearing was held in the county court, following which the county court found that Ellison had "exercised such care as a prudent man would exercise in dealing with his own property ... ." The county court then approved Ellison's accounting and approved his resignation as conservator.

The district court for Butler County found on appeal that there was no error on the record and affirmed the county court.

Elizabeth Martin appeals the ruling of the district court on the grounds, among others, that the county court applied the wrong standard of care to the performance of Ellison as conservator and that this constituted error on the record, which should have resulted in reversal by the district court.

We review the case, as did the district court, for error on the record. See Neb. Rev. Stat. §§ 30-1601 and 24-541.06 (Reissue 1985).

Prior to 1975, Nebraska statutes defined the standard of care to be that "which men of prudence, discretion, and intelligence acquire or retain for their own account in the management of their own affairs, not in regard to speculation, but in making investment of their own funds with a view to probable income as well as probable safety of the capital involved." Neb. Rev. Stat. § 24-601 (Cum. Supp. 1974). Cf. § 24-601 (Reissue 1975).

With the adoption of the Uniform Probate Code, effective January 1, 1977, the new standard was set out in Neb. Rev. Stat. ch. 30 (Reissue 1985). Section 30-2646 provides: "In the exercise of his powers, a conservator is to act as a fiduciary and shall observe the standards of care applicable to trustees as described by section 30-2813."

Section 30-2813 provides that "the trustee shall observe the standards in dealing with the trust assets that would be observed by a prudent man dealing with the property of another ... ."

Further, the comments under § 30-2813, which were taken directly from the comments to the Uniform Probate Code, state:

This is a new general provision designed to make clear the standard of skill expected from trustees ... . It differs somewhat from the standard stated in § 174 of the Restatement of Trusts, Second, which is as follows:

"The trustee is under a duty to the beneficiary in administering the trust to exercise such care and skill as a man of ordinary prudence would exercise in dealing with his own property ... ."

By making the basic standard align to that observed by a prudent man in dealing with the property of another, the section accepts a standard as it has been articulated in some decisions regarding the duty of a trustee concerning investments. See *Estate of Cook, 20 Del. Ch. 123, 171 A. 730 (1934).* Also, the duty as described by the above section more clearly conveys the idea that a trustee must comply with an external, rather than with a personal, standard of care.

The case of *In re Estate of Wm. H. Cook, Dec'd., 20 Del. Ch. 123, 125–26, 171 A. 730, 731 (1934),* referred to in the comments under § 30-2813, states:

> The rule of a trustee's duty is generally stated to be, that he is under a duty to the beneficiary in administering the trust to exercise such care and skill as a man of ordinary prudence would exercise in dealing with his own property.

When this rule which is applicable to a trustee's duty generally is given specific application to the matter of investments, it needs, for the purposes of the instant case, to be supplemented by at least two observations.

The first is, that the external standard of "such care and skill as a man of ordinary prudence would exercise in dealing with his own property" is not the standard he would use in dealing with his own property if he had only himself to consider; his "duty rather is" (quoting Lindley, L. J., in the case of *In re Whiteley, 33 Ch. Div. 347, 355*) "to take such care as an ordinary prudent man would take if he were minded to make an investment for the benefit of other people for whom he felt morally bound to provide." In other words he must take no risks which would not be taken by an ordinarily prudent man who is trustee of another person's property.

The Supreme Court of New Hampshire, in following the rule set out in the *Cook* case, found that the trial court's finding that the trustee had exercised his best judgment and the care and skill

which a man of ordinary prudence would exercise in dealing with his own property was too liberal. The New Hampshire court found that it was not sufficient that the trustee should use the care and skill of a man in investing his own property, but that there was the additional requirement that he should use the caution exercised by a prudent man in conserving the property. "In making investments the trustee is under a duty not only to exercise such care and skill as a man of ordinary prudence would exercise in dealing with his own property, but he must use the caution of one who has primarily in view the preservation of the estate entrusted to him, a caution which may be greater than that of a prudent man who is dealing with his own property." *Miller v. Pender, 93 N.H. 1, 3, 34 A.2d 663, 665 (1943)* (quoting from 2 A. Scott, The Law of Trusts § 174 (1939)).

Not only must the trustee deal with trust property with ordinary prudence but he is held to two additional standards: (1) since he is dealing with the property of another for whom he is morally bound to provide, he must avoid even those risks which he might take with his own property and (2) he must take no risk which endangers the integrity of the trust corpus. *DuPont v. Delaware Trust Co., 320 A.2d 694, 697 (Del. 1974).* See also, *Wilmington Trust Co. v. Coulter, 41 Del. Ch. 548, 200 A.2d 441 (1964).*

It is apparent that the Legislature, in adopting the Uniform Probate Code, set a different and higher standard of care for a conservator than had previously prevailed in Nebraska.

The order of the county court for Butler County reflects that this standard was not employed by the county court. This constitutes error on the record, which compels reversal. In view of this finding, it is not necessary to, and we do not, consider other grounds for reversal advanced by Martin in this appeal.

The cause is reversed and remanded to the district court for Butler County with directions to remand to the county court for further proceedings in conformance with this ruling.

Reversed and remanded for further proceedings.

ESTATE PLANNING

INTRODUCTION

Probably the most pressing concern of most older Americans, aside from health care, is the problem of planning for the distribution of their property upon their deaths. After a lifetime of accumulating property, most people want to see that property go to their friends and relations and not be subject to excessive estate taxation or lengthy court administration. The purpose of estate planning is to see that, upon a person's demise, his or her property passes to the people and institutions of his or her own choosing with as little administrative fuss and taxation as possible.

This chapter explores the various strategies that have been developed to assist people in the orderly distribution of their property on their deaths. Despite what many people may believe, estate planning is not exclusively concerned with the preparation, drafting, and execution of a will—often it is more complex and involved, using various substitutes for a will that a person may create during his or her lifetime to avoid probate and taxation.

ESTATE PLANNING

Estate planning is primarily a subdivision of general financial planning. The purpose and objective of an effective estate plan is to assist a person in the acquisition and accumulation of property during his or her lifetime in order to meet the person's financial needs and desires, and to see that these assets are appropriately distributed at the person's death according to the person's wishes.

To create an effective estate plan, the planner must be aware of the individual's assets, income, expenses, and familial situation. Of these variables, probably the most important is the person's family situation—the people who are dependent on the individual's financial resources for their support. For the elderly individual, the primary family concern is usually the surviving spouse and dependent children or grandchildren. Conversely, even a young person may need to be concerned with planning for the care of an elderly parent if something should happen to the young person.

Example

An elderly couple have just become the guardians of their three grandchildren because their son and daughter-in-law were killed in a car accident. This couple's estate plan must now be drastically changed. Not only must they be able to provide for themselves and the grandchildren while they are alive, but now they also must plan to provide sufficient funds to maintain the grandchildren should they die before the grandchildren attain adulthood.

Example

The elderly mother of a middle-aged man has become so frail that she can no longer care for herself; she has moved in with him. The man must now make plans for the care of his mother should he become incapacitated or die.

Example

An elderly couple are self-sufficient and self-supporting. Their estate plan concerns making provisions for the survivor and seeing that their assets are appropriately distributed to their children and grandchildren upon the death of the survivor.

estate planning
The process of devising strategies to minimize probate and estate taxes when the client dies and to help the client accumulate property while alive.

To accomplish these various goals, several strategies have been devised with which the paralegal should be familiar: life insurance, inter vivos transfers of property, the creation of trusts, and the execution of valid wills.

INSURANCE

One of the most common and effective methods of providing for the financial needs of one's heirs is the purchase of a life insurance policy that names the heirs as the beneficiaries of the policy. During his or her lifetime, the insured makes premium payments on the policy. When the insured dies, the face value of the policy is distributed directly to the named beneficiary, who receives the entire amount tax-free (although the value may be taxed as part of the deceased insured's estate; see the following sections). Life insurance remains one of the most effective methods of leaving a significant sum of money to care for a survivor even though the insured had few assets while alive.

Example

As part of his employee benefit package, a man was entitled to a $50,000 life insurance policy. The man named his granddaughter as the beneficiary of the policy. Many years later the man died. Although he had few assets to leave as part of his estate, the granddaughter received $50,000 from the insurance company tax-free.

Several different types of life insurance policies are in common use today. The two most popular are term and whole life insurance.

Term life insurance is a life insurance policy whose premiums are based on the age of the insured. The younger the insured, the lower the premium. At regular intervals, usually every five years, the premiums increase because the person has aged into a different premium age bracket (from age 25 to age 30). The insured has no equity in the policy, meaning that if he or she decides to terminate the policy he or she receives no money back. Consequently, the insured can never borrow against the policy.

Example

At age 29 a woman took out a term life insurance policy. She has paid premiums on the policy for the past 30 years, but now needs to cancel the policy and use the premium payments to meet her current expenses. When she cancels the policy she receives no money back.

The second most common life insurance policy is **whole life insurance**, in which the premium, although fairly high, remains constant throughout the insured's lifetime. Unlike term life insurance, with whole life insurance the insured does build up equity in the policy, and if he or she decides to terminate the policy the insured will receive

term life insurance
Form of life insurance in which the insured retains no incidents of ownership.

whole life insurance
Form of life insurance in which the insured retains incidents of ownership.

money back (the *cash surrender value*). Furthermore, the insured may borrow against or pledge this form of life insurance.

Example

A man decided to purchase a whole life insurance policy when he was 29 years old. Although the premium payments were quite high, his income was sufficient to meet this expense. Now, 30 years later, he decides that, because his children are grown, he no longer needs the policy and he terminates the coverage. The man will receive funds back from the company that equal the value of the equity he has built up in the policy over the decades.

In addition to the foregoing, there are two other fairly popular forms of life insurance. An **endowment policy** is a life insurance policy in which premiums are fully paid up within a set period of time, typically 25 years. At the end of this period, if the insured is still alive, the face value of the policy is paid directly to the insured; if the insured has died prior to complete payment, the face value of the policy is paid to the beneficiary named in the policy.

Example

A man purchases an endowment policy with a face value of $100,000. His annual premium payment is $3,000 for a 25-year period. At the end of two years he is killed in a car accident. The full $100,000 is paid to his named beneficiary.

Example

The man from the preceding example lives for the full 25 years of the policy. At the end of this period the insurance company pays him the $100,000.

endowment policy Form of life insurance policy in which the premiums are paid up in a set number of years; if the insured is alive at that date, the insured receives the proceeds.

limited payment life insurance Life insurance with very high premiums that are totally paid up within a short period of time.

Limited payment life insurance is a life insurance policy with an extremely high premium that is fully paid up in a relatively short period of time. Persons who would prefer this type of policy are usually wealthier individuals who do not wish to make premium payments for the rest of their lives.

Example

A young man has just inherited a large sum of money. As part of his estate plan he purchases a limited payment life insurance policy for which the premiums are very high, but it is fully paid up in five years. Although the premiums are high, he can afford them, and at the end of five years he no longer has to make any further life insurance payments to keep his life fully insured.

Life insurance is generally an effective method whereby a person, for a relatively small amount of money, can make quarterly premium payments and leave a large sum of money tax-free upon death.

PROPERTY TRANSFERS AND GIFTS

During a person's lifetime, he or she may decide to transfer assets to children or other potential recipients of the property, rather than waiting to have the recipient receive the property after the property owner's death. This process has several estate planning advantages:

- the property owner can see the recipient enjoy the property

- the transfer can avoid the necessity of having the title transferred pursuant to a court order upon the property owner's death (the **probate** process)

- the transfer may minimize the estate taxes to be paid on property owned by a property owner at death

- the property transfer, depending on the nature of the asset, may operate to transfer income to the recipient, thereby reducing the property owner's income taxes.

Generally, two methods are used to transfer a person's assets: outright gift or changing title to the property to share the title with another person.

A **gift** is a transfer of property from the owner of the property (**donor**) to the recipient (**donee**) without consideration (no payment received by the donor for the transfer). With a gift the donor unconditionally relinquishes all right and title to the property; as a consequence, the property is not considered to be part of the donor's estate at death. The donee always receives the property tax-free, although the donor may be liable for certain transfer, or gift, taxes on the gift (see the following sections).

Example

A father wants to make a gift of an oil painting to his daughter. The painting is valued at $8,000. The father gives the painting to the daughter, who receives the gift tax-free (no income taxes have to be paid upon receipt of the property), and the property is no longer part of the father's taxable

probate The process of either proving a will or having an administrator appointed for an intestate.

gift Transfer of property without consideration.

donor Person who gives a gift.

donee Recipient of a gift.

estate on death. Furthermore, the father gets to see the daughter use and enjoy the painting while he is alive.

Rather than making an outright transfer of property, a property owner may wish to transfer only a portion of the title to another person, thereby retaining some enjoyment and control of the property himself or herself. To effectuate this transfer, a property owner may make use of one of the following titles.

Tenancy in Common

With a **tenancy in common**, two or more persons own a separate but undivided interest in the property, with equal rights of possession and enjoyment. The title does not have to be evenly divided, and this form of title can be created over time.

Example

A father owns a house and has three children. As each child attains the age of 25, the father goes to a law office and has the house title changed to a tenancy in common with the child, giving the child a 25 percent interest in the house. When the first child attained the age of 25, she thereby became a tenant in common with her father, having a 25 percent interest in the house in which her father retained a 75 percent interest.

Each tenant in common is free to alienate his or her portion and may leave his or her portion by will. Also, his or her share is subject to claims by that tenant's creditors.

Joint Tenancy

A **joint tenancy** is distinguishable from a tenancy in common in several ways:

1. A joint tenancy must grant equal title to all joint tenants.
2. The joint tenancy must be created at one time.
3. All joint tenants must have equal rights of enjoyment and possession.
4. There is a right of survivorship in the surviving joint tenants, meaning that a joint tenant may not dispose of his or her portion by will.
5. If a joint tenant alienates his or her portion while alive, that alienation creates a tenancy in common.

tenancy in common Form of multiple ownership of property in which each tenant owns a separate but undivided interest in the whole.

joint tenancy Form of multiple ownership of property with a right of survivorship.

Because of a joint tenancy's right of survivorship, when the first joint tenant dies, his or her portion passes to (devolves upon) the surviving joint tenants. As an estate planning strategy, a person may use a joint tenancy to assure that the property will pass to the surviving joint tenant immediately upon death, by operation of law; the jurisdiction of the probate court need not be invoked. However, for federal estate tax purposes, the entire value of the property is attributed to the estate of the first joint tenant to die, unless the estate can prove that the surviving joint tenants participated in acquiring the property by gift or purchase, in which instance only the portion attributable to the deceased joint tenant is includible in his or her taxable estate.

Example

An elderly woman wants her nurse/companion to inherit her house when she dies. The woman goes to an attorney's office to have her title changed from a sole ownership to a joint tenancy with the nurse. The attorney has her transfer the title to him and he immediately conveys it back to her and the nurse as joint tenants (meeting the requirement that the title be created at the same time). When the woman dies, the title to the house passes completely to the nurse by operation of law. The woman's estate, however, will have to include the value of the entire house as part of her taxable estate, unless she pays a gift tax when she transfers the title to the joint tenancy with the nurse (see the following sections).

Example

Two brothers inherit a house as joint tenants from their grandfather. When the first brother dies, the title vests immediately in the surviving brother. The estate of the deceased brother only has to include the value of one-half of the house, because the brothers participated equally in acquiring the house by inheritance.

Tenancy by the Entirety

A **tenancy by the entirety** is a form of a joint tenancy for legally married couples. It differs from a regular joint tenancy in that the tenants must be legally married and neither one may alienate his or her portion during life without the other's consent. Upon the death of the first spouse, only one-half of the value is attributed to the deceased spouse's taxable estate.

Example

A couple purchases their home as tenants by the entirety. When the husband dies, title immediately vests in the widow, and only one-half of the value is included as part of the husband's taxable estate.

tenancy by the entirety Joint tenancy for legally married couples.

Community Property

Nine jurisdictions mandate **community property** status for property acquired by a married couple during the marriage, unless a different title is specified. With community property, each spouse is deemed to be the outright owner of one-half of the property. Each spouse may will his or her half to whomever he or she wishes.

Example

A couple marry and live in California, a community property state. They purchase a home together. When the husband dies, his one-half of the house passes, by will, to his daughter. The mother and daughter now each have title to one-half of the property.

Title transfers are a viable estate planning strategy to minimize taxes and the administrative probate process. Lawyers and paralegals often assist clients in preparing documents to effectuate these transfers.

INTRODUCTION TO TRUSTS

A **trust** is a legal entity to which property has been transferred to be administered by one person, called the **trustee**, for the benefit of another person, called the **beneficiary**. When the beneficiary dies (or other conditions specified in the trust come to pass), the property passes outright to a person known as the **remainderman**.

A popular estate planning strategy is to have a person transfer his or her property into trust while he or she is alive. This **inter vivos**, or **living trust**, is administered by that person for his or her own benefit for life, and at death the property passes to a named remainderman. In this fashion the property does not have to pass through the probate court, because the property passes to the remainderman automatically by operation of law at the creator-beneficiary's death, and estate tax on the property may be avoided because the property is owned by the trust, not the individual. Furthermore, if done sufficiently in advance, transferring property to a trust may make a person eligible for certain government transfer benefits (see Chapter 2 on Health Care).

Example

An elderly woman places her assets into a trust. She makes her daughter the trustee of the property, but the woman herself is the beneficiary, using and enjoying the property for life. At the woman's death, the property, pursuant to the instrument creating the trust, passes to her daughter as

community property Form of property ownership for married couples in which each spouse owns one-half of the whole.

trust Fiduciary relationship in which title to property is divided into its legal and equitable components.

trustee Person with legal title to trust property.

beneficiary Person who has equitable title to trust property.

remainderman Person in whom the legal and equitable titles merge at the termination of a trust.

inter vivos trust (living trust) Trust created to take effect during the creator's lifetime.

the remainderman. In this manner the woman has avoided the probate process, has minimized her estate tax burden, and may qualify for governmental medical benefits should she need them later on.

A detailed discussion of trusts appears later in this chapter.

INTRODUCTION TO WILLS

A **will** is a formal legal document that, if it meets the statutory requirements, transfers a person's assets on death to the persons and institutions named in the will according to the person's wishes. A will is the most commonly employed estate planning device because it enables the property owner to distribute property according to his or her wishes and according to the needs of the eventual recipients. It provides for an orderly distribution of assets, but it does require administration by the probate court (the court with jurisdiction over decedents' estates), and all property disposed of by will is includible as part of the deceased's taxable estate.

Example

A elderly man has three daughters: the first is married to a millionaire, the second is severely disabled and needs constant medical care, and the third is a woman of average means. By using a will, the man can see that the bulk of his property goes to provide care for the daughter who needs the financial support the most.

A person who dies with a valid will is deemed to have died *testate;* a person who dies without a valid will is deemed to have died *intestate.* If a person dies intestate, all of his or her property is distributed to his or her blood relatives according to the provisions of state statute (called **intestate succession**). This distribution is made equally to all blood relations of the same degree of relationship to the decedent, regardless of the needs of the recipients, and relations of a closer degree of relationship defeat the interests of relatives further removed. Also, friends and in-laws receive nothing under the statutory scheme. Consequently, a will is the most practical method of seeing that the people whom the decedent wishes to receive the property actually receive the property, and in the proportion the deceased deems most appropriate based on the recipients' needs. Furthermore, if there are no blood relatives within the degree of relationship indicated by statute, the person's property will pass to the state in which the property is located, under a process known as **escheating**.

will Formal document that indicates how a person wants his or her property to be distributed at death.

intestate succession Statutory procedure indicating which blood relatives inherit from a person who died without a valid will.

escheat The state's inheritance of the property of an intestate who has no blood relatives.

Example _____

A wealthy woman has no close relatives. Her closest blood relatives are her cousins' grandchildren. However, the woman has several close friends, is very close to the nephew of her deceased husband, and makes significant charitable contributions each year. If this woman were to die without a valid will, all of her property would escheat to the state; if she executes a valid will she can leave her property to her husband's nephew, her friends, and the charitable institutions she supports.

_____

The remainder of this chapter focuses on the two main estate planning strategies generally employed, the will and the trust, and then discusses the estate and gift tax consequences of the various strategies mentioned earlier. In this area of law, the paralegal's role is a dominant one, both in gathering the information necessary to create the appropriate documents and in the actual administration of the wills and trusts that are drawn up.

WILLS

A *will* is a formal legal document that represents the wishes of a testator with respect to the distribution of his or her property upon death. For a will to be deemed legally valid, the form of the will and the manner in which the will is signed and witnessed must adhere to the standards of the state statute in the jurisdiction where the deceased was domiciled at the time the will was executed. The law of wills is state-specific, and although the differences among the states are minimal, the provisions of each statute must be analyzed to determine the validity of the testamentary instrument.

Formation

testator(trix) Person who executes a valid will.

The person whose wishes are specified in the will is known as the **testator (testatrix** for women). To execute a valid will, the testator must be shown to have had testamentary capacity at the moment the will was signed. **Testamentary capacity** refers to a person's legal ability to execute a valid will. Generally, three elements must be evidenced with regard to a person's testamentary capacity.

testamentary capacity The legal ability to execute a will.

Age

Every jurisdiction requires that a person have attained a minimum age in order to execute a valid will (typically the age of 18); however, some jurisdictions make exceptions for younger persons who are either married or in military service. This requirement is conclusively met by anyone who would be considered elderly.

Mental Ability

The only specific requirement with regard to a person's mental ability to execute a valid will is his or her ability to know the nature and extent of his or her property and the natural bounty of his or her affections. A person does not have to know the exact extent of all of his or her property down to the last penny, but he or she must be aware of the nature and type of property owned.

Example

An elderly woman wants to leave her house in Duluth to her niece. The woman executes a will this year, but she has not owned the house in Duluth for more than 20 years. This would indicate a lack of testamentary capacity.

Example

An elderly man wishes to leave all of his corporate bonds to his granddaughter. The man believes the value of the bonds is between $25,000 and $30,000, but he is not sure of the exact amount. The man actually owns corporate bonds at the time he executes the will. In this instance the man probably does have testamentary capacity.

The "natural bounty of one's affection" is deemed to be one's blood relatives. Except for a surviving spouse, a person is not required to leave any other relative property in his or her will, but the person is required to demonstrate a knowledge of who these people are. The blood relatives with whom the state is concerned are those who would be considered the testator's intestate heirs (see preceding sections).

Example

A woman executes a will in which she names her three children but leaves property to only two of them, because she has had a falling-out with the youngest child. On its face, this will indicates testamentary capacity, because the woman knew who her heirs were—she just did not want to leave anything to the youngest child.

When dealing with an elderly testator, challenges are often made to the person's ability to execute a valid will.

Intent

For a will to be deemed legally valid, the proponent of the will must demonstrate that the testator freely and voluntarily executed the will. This means that the person was not defrauded, harassed, coerced, or in any other way forced or tricked into signing the document. This element of testamentary capacity and the validity of the will is the basis for one of the most common challenges to an elderly person's will. Many people believe that the elderly, because of their age, are susceptible to harassment or manipulation with respect to the execution of a will. However, courts have uniformly and conclusively stated that a person's advanced age or physical frailty alone does not negate the person's legal ability to execute a valid will. All of the surrounding circumstances must be analyzed to determine whether the individual executed the will of his or her own free will.

Example

An elderly woman is threatened by her daughter, who wants her to execute a will in the daughter's favor. The daughter says that if the woman does not sign the will, she will have the mother put in a nursing home. The elderly woman does not want to live in a home, and consequently signs the will. This would be an example of a will signed under duress.

One of the most commonly adjudicated issues with respect to a person's intent to execute a will is the question of undue influence. *Undue influence* exists when a person who is in a close and confidential relationship to the testator uses that relationship in an unwarranted manner to cause the testator to make a particular testamentary disposition. The person exerting the influence does not have to benefit personally, either directly or indirectly, but must use his or her position to cause a particular testamentary gift. Persons who are presumptively in such confidential relationships are:

- spouses
- children
- lovers
- doctors
- lawyers
- ministers
- caregivers
- heads of nursing homes.

With the elderly testator, it is necessary to be sure that a person in such a relationship did not unduly influence the testamentary wishes of the testator.

Example

An elderly man lives in a nursing home. The head of the nursing home coerces the man, who has no close relatives, to leave all of his money to the home to provide better care for future residents. This would be an example of undue influence.

Example

An elderly woman has two children—a son who is a lawyer and a daughter who is a stockbroker. The son drafts a will for his mother in which he is given control over all of her money. This may be an example of undue influence.

Another question may arise with respect to an elderly individual who is taking certain forms of medication, some of which may temporarily affect the individual's mental ability. For a will to be deemed valid, it must only be shown that the person had sufficient capacity at the moment of signing the will. If the person is temporarily incapacitated, the signature may be acknowledged within a statutory period of time when the person's legal capacity returns.

Example

An elderly man is taking a prescription drug for lupus. The drug is a strong painkiller, and for several hours after taking the medication the man's mind wanders until the drug takes effect. The man signs his will while under the influence of this medication. Two days later, when the effects have worn off, the man acknowledges that he signed the instrument as his last will and testament. This acknowledgment will validate his signature.

There are many good reasons why an elderly individual should execute a will. First, it avoids the problems of intestacy, discussed earlier. Second, through a will the person's property can be distributed to friends and institutions as well as blood relatives. Third, certain tax advantages can be gained, as discussed later in this chapter. Fourth, the person can determine who will be responsible for administering his or her estate.

The person who is responsible for administering the estate of a decedent is known generically as the **personal representative**. If the person is named in a will, he or she is called the **executor(trix)**; if a person dies intestate, the personal representative is called the **administrator(trix)**. In any instance, it is the court that officially appoints the

personal representative Individual responsible for administering a decedent's estate.

executor(trix) Personal representative named in a will.

administrator(trix) Personal representative of an intestate.

representative, but a testator can indicate who he or she would prefer to be appointed and the court will generally follow the testator's wishes. To be a personal representative, most jurisdictions require the person to be a competent adult who is not a convicted felon and who resides in the state where the property is located (or be able to post a bond with the court if a nonresident). Personal representatives must post bond unless that requirement is waived by the court or the testator in the will, and personal representatives receive a statutorily dictated fee for administering the estate. The testator can vary the fee by testamentary directive.

Example

An elderly woman executes a will in which she appoints her daughter as her executrix and states that her daughter is to serve without bond even if she is not resident in the state at the time of the woman's death. The court will, if at all possible, adhere to the testatrix's wishes.

It is beyond the scope of this text to detail all of the law and procedure incident to the creation of a valid will; however, it is one of the most frequently utilized legal documents prepared by law offices that represent elderly clients.

Execution

Execution of a will refers to the actual signing and witnessing of the document. To be valid, the will must be signed by the testator (or someone who signs at the testator's direction, if the testator is physically incapable of signing) in the presence of competent witnesses or acknowledged before competent witnesses within a statutorily prescribed period of time after the signing. Most jurisdictions require a minimum of two competent witnesses, although a few states still require three witnesses. To be considered a competent witness, the person must be an adult and not have an interest, either directly or indirectly, in the will. A will is not notarized, it is merely witnessed.

Example

An elderly woman comes to her attorney's office to execute her will. The lawyer calls in the office's paralegal and secretary, and the woman signs the will in their presence, after stating that it is her will which she is freely signing. After the woman signs, the paralegal and the secretary sign as attesting witnesses. The will is now executed.

The circumstances surrounding the execution must be proved to the court when the will is presented for probate. The term *probate* means to prove the validity of a document as a person's last will and testament, and the term is used generically to refer to all courts that have jurisdiction over a decedent's estate. To prove the will, the witnesses must appear before the court to be examined regarding the circumstances of execution of the will. To avoid the necessity of having the witnesses come to the court, all jurisdictions now permit the use of **self-proving affidavits**, which are affidavits signed by the witnesses and notarized; this affidavit documents all the circumstances of the execution of the will. In most instances this avoids the necessity of locating witnesses many years after a will was executed when the testator eventually dies.

If the court decides that the will was not validly executed, the decedent is deemed to have died intestate. Some jurisdictions apply the doctrine of *dependent relative revocation,* which holds that if the most recent will executed by the decedent is deemed invalid but an early will exists or can be proven that is valid, the earlier will takes effect. This may create problems for certain elderly individuals who execute wills on a regular basis. Only the last valid will is effective, and if a person continually changes his or her will it may add confusion and difficulty to the administration of the estate. Consequently, it may be best to destroy any old wills each time a new one is executed.

Changing a Will

A will may be amended by the execution of a legal document known as a **codicil**, which is an amendment to a will. To be valid, the codicil must itself meet all of the legal requirements of a full will, including execution. A codicil is used to make minor changes in a will.

Example

A woman has left a sum of money to one of her friends in her will. Several years later the friend dies and the woman executes a codicil to leave the money to a different friend. She did not need to execute an entirely new will, because all of the other provisions remained intact.

A will is also considered to be revoked whenever a person executes a new, later will. A will can be revoked by a physical act of destruction, too.

Example

A woman decides that she does not like the provisions of a will she executed several years ago, and would rather have her property pass according to the laws of intestate succession. She takes her will and tears it up. The will is revoked.

self-proving affidavit Affidavit signed by the attesting witnesses to a will.

codicil Formal amendment to a will.

A will may also be partially revoked by a change in family circumstances, such as a marriage, a divorce, or the birth or adoption of a child.

Example

An elderly widower executed a will dividing his property up equally among his grandchildren. Several months later he meets a widow and they marry. In some states, the marriage acts to revoke the entire will; in other states, the new wife is entitled to a statutory share of the estate and the remaining property passes according to the will.

A law office should always advise a client that any change in family circumstances may require the review of all or part of the client's estate plan.

Will Contests

Once a will has been submitted to probate, the proponent of the will is required to notify all persons who have an interest in the estate; these persons have the right to challenge the will. The people who have such standing are:

1. all intestate heirs
2. all persons named in earlier wills, in jurisdictions that apply the doctrine of dependent relative revocation
3. all persons named in later wills who claim that the will submitted to probate is not the *last* will
4. creditors if the estate is heavily in debt.

If the **will contest** is successful, the decedent is deemed to have died intestate, or an earlier will may take effect.

Despite the formalities surrounding the execution and proving of a will, a will continues to be one of the most effective estate planning devices to assure the orderly distribution of a person's assets according to the person's wishes upon death.

TRUSTS

will contest Challenge to the validity of a document presented to the court as a will.

A *trust* is a fiduciary relationship in which one person, known as the *creator,* transfers property to one or more other persons, known as trustees, who hold the legal title to the property. Legal title enables the trustee to manage and control the property, subject to certain fiduciary obligations, for the benefit of another person, called the *beneficiary*. The beneficiary holds the equitable title to the property, which enables the beneficiary to enjoy the property subject to limitations on such enjoyment imposed by the creator. Once established, a trust is a legal entity separate and distinct from its participants.

Trusts may be established as part of the creator's will, in which case they are called **testamentary trusts**; or they may created to take effect during the creator's lifetime, in which case they are called *inter vivos (living) trusts*. After wills, trusts are probably the most common estate planning device employed by the elderly.

Requisite Elements

There are five requisite elements to create a valid trust.

Creator

The creator of a trust must be a person who has a transferable interest in property and sufficient contractual capacity to effectuate a transfer of that title to the trustee. If property is held as a joint tenancy, the joint tenant, during life, may transfer his or her portion of the property to a trust, thereby destroying the joint tenancy (see preceding sections); or the joint tenants may join to transfer the entire property to the trust. If a married couple hold title to the property as tenants by the entirety, both parties must agree to transfer the property to the trust; one spouse is legally incapable of transferring his or her interest in a tenancy by the entirety.

Example

A woman wishes to create a supplemental needs trust for the benefit of her disabled granddaughter. The woman wants to transfer to the trust certain shares of stock that she owns in her own right. She can transfer such property to create the trust.

Example

An elderly couple want to transfer all of their assets to a living trust in anticipation of their needing governmental medical assistance. Because their property is held as a tenancy by the entirety, both must participate in the transfer of the property.

If the person who has title to the property is under guardianship, the guardian of the estate has the legal authority to transfer the ward's property to a trust.

testamentary trust
Trust created in a will.

Example

An elderly man was placed under the plenary guardianship of his daughter. The daughter, in her capacity as guardian, places the man's property in trust for his benefit during his lifetime, with herself as the trustee; at the man's death the property is to be distributed equally to his grandchildren. His daughter may create such a trust for her father's benefit with her father's funds.

Trust Property

Basically, any property can be made the subject of a trust. The main exceptions to this general statement are governmental transfer payments, tort claims, and any property that has a restriction on transferability. Note that although the rights to governmental transfer payments and tort claims are not transferable, once the recipient actually has the funds the funds may then be transferred to a trust; it is the right itself that is not transferable.

Example

An elderly man wants to place his house and furniture in trust for his benefit during his lifetime. This property may be transferred to a trust.

Example

An elderly man owns shares of stock in a closely held corporation that restricts the transferability of the shares. These shares may not be transferred to a trust.

Valid Trust Purpose

A trust may be created for any lawful purpose. Typically trusts are created to provide benefits to family members, friends, and charitable institutions. A trust will not be deemed valid if it violates any civil or criminal law, or violates public policy. The purpose for which the trust is created must be specifically stated in the instrument creating the trust.

Example

An elderly man wishes to create a trust to provide income to his wife for her life after his death; at the death of the wife, the trust property is to be distributed to their children. This is a valid trust purpose.

Example

A woman is heavily in debt. To avoid losing her property to her creditors, she wants to place her assets into a trust. This would act as a fraud on her creditors and is invalid as against public policy.

Trustee

A *trustee* is the person who is given the legal title to the trust property and who must manage the property for the benefit of the beneficiary according to the purpose for which the trust was created, subject to duties imposed by the creator. Furthermore, a trustee is a fiduciary, meaning that he or she is also subject to general fiduciary obligations imposed on all fiduciaries.

Basically, any person who is capable of holding title to property may be a trustee, but the courts will require that the trustee have contractual capacity so that he or she can actually manage the trust property. Each state has statutorily enacted the qualifications for a person to be appointed as a trustee, and therefore each state's statute must be individually analyzed.

The state and federal governments are precluded from being trustees, but a municipality may be the trustee of a **charitable**, or **public**, **trust** (one that is designed to serve a charitable rather than a private purpose).

Example

An elderly man wants to create a supplemental needs trust for his disabled son, and appoints his attorney as the trustee. The attorney would be an appropriate trustee.

Example

An elderly man wants to create a trust to maintain the public parks in his city. He names the city council as the trustees. In this instance, because the purpose of the trust is charitable, the city council may serve as trustees.

The trustee is liable to the beneficiary for any mismanagement of the trust property and for any diminution in the value of the trust property due to poor investments or breach of a fiduciary obligation.

Beneficiary

All trusts must have a beneficiary who is clearly identified, either by name or by class. Any person who is legally capable of taking title to property may be a beneficiary and, unlike the trustee, the beneficiary need not have contractual capacity. The beneficiary enjoys the trust property subject to any restrictions on such enjoyment imposed by the creator.

Example

An elderly man creates a trust for the benefit of his mentally retarded granddaughter. The granddaughter qualifies as a beneficiary—contractual capacity is not necessary.

charitable (public) trust Trust that serves a public rather than a private purpose.

At the termination of the trust—and all trusts except for charitable trusts must terminate at some point—the property is distributed to a person (or persons) known as the *remainderman*. Complete title vests in this person, meaning that he, she, or they have both legal and equitable title to the property. If the trust is an inter vivos trust that is designed to complete its purpose during the creator's lifetime, the creator may make himself or herself the remainderman; this is known as a **reversion** or **reversionary interest**.

Types of Trusts

Several types of trust are commonly created. The most frequently created are:

1. **Totten trusts.** A Totten trust, or **tentative trust**, is exemplified by a bank account that reads "John Jones in trust for Jane Jones." This type of situation, colloquially referred to as a "poor person's trust," is not really a trust at all, but is given a special status under the law. The depositor may add to or withdraw funds during his or her lifetime, and upon the death of the depositor any remaining funds pass directly to the person named as the beneficiary unless: (a) the funds are needed to discharge debts of the depositor; or (b) the depositor has specifically made a testamentary disposition of the funds. This type of account is used by persons who wish to avoid the probate process so that the beneficiary can have immediate access to the funds upon the depositor's death.

2. **QTIP trusts.** *QTIP* stands for *qualified terminable interest property*. Such a trust is used as part of the marital deduction for estate tax purposes (see following sections). With a QTIP trust, one spouse creates the trust in his or her will, making the surviving spouse the beneficiary of all the income with the right to use the trust property itself upon a showing of financial need. (See Exhibit 6-1.) Upon the death of the second spouse, the property is distributed to remaindermen named by the spouse who created the trust. In this manner the property placed in trust passes free of estate tax when the first spouse dies and is taxed only at the death of the beneficiary spouse (see following sections).

3. Supplemental needs trusts. These trusts (discussed in Chapter 5) are designed to provide medical care for the beneficiary that is not otherwise provided by insurance or the government. For persons receiving Medicaid, upon the death of the beneficiary the government may attach the trust property,

reversion (reversionary interest) Term indicating that the creator of the trust is the remainderman.

Totten trust (tentative trust) Bank account "in trust for"; not a real trust.

qualified terminable interest property (QTIP) trust Trust that qualifies for the marital deduction, created for a surviving spouse.

EXHIBIT 6-1

Sample wording for a QTIP trust

QTIP Trust

Should my said spouse survive me, I hereby give the sum of _____ to my Trustees, to hold the same in trust, to invest and reinvest the same and to pay the net income to my said spouse at least quarterly during his/her life. My Trustees may, at any time or from time to time, pay to my said spouse, or apply for his/her benefit, so much of the principal, whether the whole or a lesser amount, as my Trustees may in their sole, absolute, and uncontrolled discretion deem necessary, advisable, or expedient.

Upon my said spouse's death, my Trustees shall pay all or the principal of the trust, as then constituted, to my issue surviving my said spouse per stirpes. Should none of my issue survive my said spouse, the principal shall be given to my then living heirs-at-law per capita.

---

claiming reimbursement for funds expended for the care of the deceased beneficiary.

4. **Charitable remainder annuity trusts.** This type of trust has certain tax advantages. The trust is established to provide income to a private beneficiary (such as a spouse, child, etc.) during the beneficiary's life. Upon the death of the beneficiary, the trust property passes to a charitable organization.

5. **Charitable remainder unitrusts.** This type of trust, which also has certain tax advantages, divides income from the trust property between private beneficiaries and charitable organizations.

6. **Life insurance trusts.** Rather than name an individual as the beneficiary of a life insurance policy, the insured may use the policy as the creating instrument for a trust. The beneficiary of the policy is a trust, so when the insured dies the trust is created and funded with the proceeds from the policy, which passes to the trust tax-free.

7. **Spendthrift trusts.** A spendthrift trust is established to protect the beneficiary from himself or herself. The creditors of the beneficiary are prohibited from attaching the trust assets, and the beneficiary is precluded from alienating his or her interest in the trust. This type of trust is invalid if its purpose is to defraud creditors; that is, the creator may not establish a spendthrift trust in himself or herself when he or she is heavily in debt so as to avoid having his or her property attached by the creditors to satisfy the debts. However, a person may create a spendthrift trust in himself or herself at a time when he or she is not in debt.

charitable remainder annuity trust
Trust that provides income to a private beneficiary for life, with a charity as the remainderman; provides certain favorable tax treatment for the trust income.

charitable remainder unitrust
Trust that divides income between a charity and a private individual; has favorable tax treatment.

life insurance trust
Trust created with the proceeds of a life insurance policy, usually established by the policy itself.

spendthrift trust
Trust designed to keep the trust property from the creditors of the beneficiary.

Execution

As a general rule, trusts must be created by a written instrument (there are minor exceptions for custodial trusts of personal property). The trust must be signed and may be witnessed. Most importantly, once the trust is created the creator must take all legal steps necessary to see that the property is transferred to the trustee. If the property is not transferred, no trust is created.

Example

An elderly woman goes to a law office to create a living trust of all her assets. She is doing this as part of an estate plan, to avoid probate and to divest herself of property should she require Medicare in the future. The law office's paralegal drafts the trust instrument and the woman signs the instrument at the direction of the attorney. Once the trust is signed, the woman has the office execute a deed to convey title to her house to the trust, affidavits to the stockbroker to have her investments transferred to the trust, letters to her bank to have her accounts transferred, and documents to see that all of her other property is transferred to the trust. Once the property has been transferred, the trust actually exists.

ESTATE TAXES

Scope

A complete discussion of estate taxes is beyond the scope of this text, as is a discussion of state estate and inheritance tax policies. This section focuses only on the most important of the federal tax considerations involved in estate planning for the elderly.

Gift Taxes and the Unified Credit

As mentioned earlier, one of the most common estate planning strategies, to minimize both the administrative probate process and taxes, is divesting one's property while one is alive, in the form of a gift. When a person transfers property as a gift, that property is no longer part of his or her estate at death, and therefore it is not subject to probate or estate taxation. However, the government does not permit the free transfer of property without some taxation, and therefore a gift tax is imposed by the taxing authorities.

gift tax Transfer tax imposed on gifts.

A **gift tax** is the transfer tax imposed on the donor when property is transferred as a gift. The donee, or recipient, of the property *always* receives the property tax-free. However, the federal government does permit a certain amount of property to pass totally tax-free. Each year the Internal Revenue Service permits a donor to give up to $10,000 worth of property *per donee* tax-free. A married couple may combine this amount to give up to $20,000 a year tax-free per donee. Also, certain interfamily gifts, between spouses or to pay for children's education, are also not subject to the federal gift tax.

Example

An elderly man decides to divest himself of his assets to reduce probate and estate taxes. In the current tax year, he gives $10,000 worth of corporate stock to each of his four grandchildren. In this manner he has transferred $40,000 out of his estate tax-free.

Example

An elderly couple, as part of their estate plan, start to divest themselves of their property. They join to give $20,000 to each of their three children, plus $20,000 to each of their children's spouses, and another $20,000 to each of their two grandchildren. The couple has divested themselves of $160,000 tax-free.

However, what happens if the individual wishes to give property valued at more than $10,000 to a particular donee in a given year? The donor has two options: either the donor can pay a gift tax on the amount of the gift that exceeds $10,000, or the donor can have the excess amount deducted from his or her lifetime exclusion pursuant to the Unified Estate and Gift Tax Credit.

The **Unified Estate and Gift Tax Credit** combines inter vivos and testamentary transfers for a maximum amount of property that can be transferred tax-free. When a person dies, all property left to a surviving spouse passes free of estate tax; in addition, a federal tax credit is given in an amount that would pass the following amount of property estate-tax-free to a nonspouse:

Year of Death	Amount of Estate That Passes Tax-Free
Through 1998	$625,000
1999	$650,000
2000	$675,000
2001	$675,000
2002	$700,000
2003	$700,000
2004	$850,000
2005	$950,000
2006	$1,000,000

Unified Estate and Gift Tax Credit
Federal tax credit permitting a certain amount of property left to a nonspouse to pass free of estate tax.

If the donor so desires, the value of an inter vivos gift that exceeds the $10,000-per-year per-donee tax exemption can be deducted from the amount of the donor's estate that can pass tax-free.

> ### Example
>
> An elderly man gives his daughter a painting worth $18,000. The man decides to pay a gift tax on the $8,000 excess and maintain his full lifetime exclusion.

> ### Example
>
> The man from the preceding example decides that his estate will not exceed the lifetime exclusion amount, and therefore completes the appropriate forms from IRS to have the $8,000 deducted from the amount of his estate that can pass tax-free.

Using the estate planning strategy of an inter vivos gift, a person may be able to reduce his or her estate to an amount that will be beneath the tax-free exclusion amount, thereby avoiding all estate taxes.

QTIP and Credit Shelter Trusts

As stated earlier, all property that passes to a surviving spouse passes tax-free. When the surviving spouse dies, all of his or her property is then taxed, unless he or she has remarried, in which case the property passes to another surviving spouse (this is, of course, exclusive of the amount that passes tax-free to a nonspouse because of the unified credit).

Historically, to take advantage of this tax preference for surviving spouses, known as the **marital deduction**, the surviving spouse must have inherited the property free and clear. If any restriction was placed on the surviving spouse's ability to use the property, the marital deduction did not apply. In the mid-1980s, this was amended to permit, under certain circumstances, the property left to a surviving spouse to be placed in a trust created by the deceased spouse and still pass tax-free to the surviving spouse. This type of trust is known as a *qualified terminable interest property (QTIP) trust*. The surviving spouse is entitled to income for life, and has the ability to use the trust property itself upon a showing of financial need. At the surviving spouse's death, the property would pass to the persons named as remaindermen under the first-deceased spouse's will. This type of trust was created to avoid a situation in which the surviving spouse remarries, or squanders the money, thereby leaving few assets for the children or grandchildren.

marital deduction
Tax rule that permits all property inherited by a surviving spouse to pass free of estate tax.

The deceased spouse could restrict the surviving spouse's use of the funds by creating a QTIP trust.

Example

A man created a QTIP trust in his will for the benefit of his wife, and at her death the property is to go to their children. The husband's estate has the advantage of the marital deduction and the children have some assurance that they will eventually inherit property from their father.

Example

A man left his entire estate outright to his wife, expecting her to take care of their children upon her death. Instead, the surviving spouse started gambling, and lost all her inheritance. The children received nothing because the wife had total control over the funds, which she could not manage.

Once the concept of the QTIP trust was established, a secondary estate planning device was created, called the **credit shelter**, or **A-B, trust**. In this situation the testator creates two trusts, one being the QTIP trust and the second being the "B" trust funded with the maximum amount of property that can pass free of estate tax to a nonspouse in the year of the testator's death. The spouse is entitled to the income from both trusts for life, but at the death of the surviving spouse the property in the QTIP trust pours over into the B trust. At the death of the second spouse, the children of the testator are entitled to the income from the B trust for life, and the testator's grandchildren are the remaindermen. In this fashion the testator can make sure that twice the tax-free amount passes to the children and grandchildren, and the entire estate passes tax-free to the surviving spouse.

Example

A man created a credit shelter trust in his will. In the year of his death, $675,000 could pass tax-free to a nonspouse, and this is the amount of his estate that is used to fund the B trust. The rest of his property is placed in the QTIP trust, which passes tax-free. His estate has paid no estate tax. Upon his wife's death, the property in the QTIP trust passes to the B trust. Assume that in the year of her death, $1 million can pass tax-free to a nonspouse. In this situation, $1 million is added to the B trust tax-free—the B trust has received a total of $1,675,000 free of estate tax.

credit shelter (A-B) trust Two trusts created to take advantage of the marital deduction and the unified estate and gift tax credit.

When considering any estate planning strategy, the law office or financial planner must be aware of both the probate process and the tax consequences of each strategy employed.

ETHICAL CONSIDERATIONS

Certain ethical problems may arise with respect to creating an estate planning strategy for an elderly client. First and foremost is the perceived ability of the elderly client to understand the nature of the devices being created. Living wills and powers of attorney (see Exhibits 6-2 and 6-3), though not necessarily part of the estate planning process, are often executed at this time, along with wills and trust documents. Obviously, not every older American suffers from diminished mental ability, but as a person ages, his or her mental facilities do decline, and a person's physical impairments (due to age, disease, or disability) can have a dramatic effect on his or her comprehension. The legal professional involved in estate planning for the elderly must be

EXHIBIT 6-2

Sample living will

Living Will

To my family, my physician, lawyer, clergyman, any medical facility in whose care I happen to be, and any individual who may become responsible for my health, welfare, or affairs:

If the time comes when I can no longer take part in decisions concerning my life, I wish and direct the following:

If a situation should arise in which there is no reasonable expectation for my recover by extreme physical or mental disability, I direct that I be allowed to die and not be kept alive by medications, artificial means, life support equipment, or heroic measures. However, I do request that medication be administered to me to alleviate suffering even though this may shorten my remaining life.

This statement is made after careful consideration and is in accordance with my convictions and beliefs.

If any of my tissues or organs are sound and would be of value as transplants to other people, I freely give my permission for such donation.

In witness whereof, I state that I have read this, my living will, know and understand its contents, and sign my name below.

Dated: _____

Witness:

Witness:

EXHIBIT 6-3

Sample springing power of attorney

Springing Power of Attorney

KNOW ALL MEN BY THESE PRESENTS THAT I, _____[name]_____, of _____, in the County of _____, State of _____, do hereby constitute and appoint _____[name]_____ of _____ to be my true and lawful attorney-in-fact with full power to act in my name and stead and on my behalf to do in my name, place, and stead in any way in which I myself could do, if I were personally present, with respect to the following matters, to the extent that I am permitted by law to act through an agent:

Real estate transactions;
Chattel and goods transactions;
Bond, share, and commodity transactions;
Banking transactions;
Business operating transactions;
Insurance transactions;
Estate transactions;
Claims of any type or nature;
Records, reports, and statements;
Access to safe deposit boxes;
Ability to sign tax returns;
The power to settle, prepare, or in any other way arrange tax matters;
The power to deal with retirement plans;
The power to fund inter vivos trusts;
The power to borrow funds;
The power to enter buy/sell agreements;
The power to forgive and collect debts;
The power to complete charitable pledges;
The power to make statutory elections and disclaimers;
The power to pay salaries and fees;
The power to settle, pursue, or appeal litigation;

Full and unqualified authority to my attorney-in-fact to delegate any or all of the foregoing powers to any person or persons whom my attorney-in-fact shall select;

The power to take any steps and do any acts that my attorney-in-fact may deem necessary or convenient in connection with the exercise of any of the foregoing powers.

This power of attorney shall be binding on me and my heirs, executors and administrators, and shall remain in force up to the time of the receipt by my attorney-in-fact of a written revocation signed by me.

I hereby agree that any third party receiving a duly executed copy or facsimile of this instrument may act hereunder, and that revocation or

EXHIBIT 6-3

(*continued*)

termination hereof shall be ineffective as to such third party unless and until actual notice or knowledge of such revocation or termination shall have been received by such third party, and I, for myself and for my heirs, executors, legal representatives and assigns, hereby agree to indemnify and hold harmless any such third party by reason of such third party having relied on the provisions of this instrument.

This power of attorney shall not be affected by my disability or incompetence, and shall only become effective upon my disability or incapacity. I shall be deemed disabled or incapacitated upon written certification of two independent physicians who have examined me and who believe that I am incapacitated, mentally or physically, and am therefore incapable of attending to my personal business and affairs.

IN WITNESS WHEREOF I have hereunto set my hand and seal this _____ day of _____, 20_____.

_____
Principal

State of _____)
) ss:
County of _____)

On the _____ day of _____, 20_____, before me personally came _____ to me known, and known to me to be the individual described in, and who executed the foregoing instrument, and he/she acknowledged to me that he/she executed the same.

_____
Notary Public

The following represents the signature of my attorney-in-fact:

_____
Attorney-in-fact

State of _____)
) ss:
County of _____)

On the _____ day of _____, 20_____, before me personally came _____, to me known, and known to me to be the individual described in the foregoing instrument as the attorney-in-fact, and who signed the foregoing instrument, and he/she acknowledged to me that he/she signed the same.

_____
Notary Public

acutely aware of these factors to make certain that the client does appreciate the purposes of the strategies employed.

An elderly client may be acting under the influence of close family members or confidants, and may choose a particular estate plan because of the influence exerted by this person rather than because of the client's own free will. Recall from Chapter 1 the problem of deciding who the client is. The problem is particularly evident in the estate planning phase of representing the elderly client because a given plan will have the effect of benefiting or excluding certain family members; the members of the law office must be certain that the client is acting independently. If the elderly individual has been placed under guardianship, the guardian may have the legal authority to create an estate plan for the ward. In this instance it behooves the office to determine that the plan devised is actually for the benefit of the client and not for the benefit, direct or indirect, of the guardian.

Finally, because one objective of an effective estate plan is to minimize probate and estate taxes, some of the strategies may leave the client without sufficient assets to maintain his or her lifestyle, or may work to the disadvantage of persons the client would wish to benefit from his or her estate. In devising an estate plan, the legal professional must be concerned with the totality of the client's existence, not merely the financial aspect of his or her life.

CHAPTER REVIEW

The purpose of estate planning is to minimize both the administrative aspects of the probate process and the amount of estate taxes imposed on the decedent's property. To accomplish these objectives, various strategies are generally employed:

- Gifts—a person may divest himself or herself of property while alive, thereby avoiding probate of those assets and taking advantage of the annual gift tax exemption, which minimizes eventual estate taxation.

- Insurance—by maintaining life insurance, the insured can leave a large sum of money to the named beneficiary, tax-free. Although this strategy avoids probate, because the assets (the policy proceeds) never belong to the deceased, it does not avoid estate taxation; the IRS includes the value of the policy in the decedent's taxable estate if the deceased maintained any incident of ownership over the policy.

- Title transfer—by transferring title to property to a form of joint ownership, the title will pass to the surviving joint tenant automatically at the death of the other joint tenant(s) by operation of law. This property therefore does not pass through the probate court, but is subject to estate taxation.

- Trusts—With an inter vivos trust, the title to the property passes to the trust and therefore is not part of the creator's estate at death. Furthermore, the creator may retain the use of the property during life as the beneficiary. Because the trust owns the property, it may not be included as an asset of the beneficiary for determining Medicare benefits. However, a transfer tax may be imposed on the creator of the trust.

- Wills—by executing a valid will, a person can determine who will receive his or her property, and in what proportion, as well as determining who will be responsible for administration of the estate. Although a will provides for the orderly distribution of an estate, it does not avoid probate or estate taxation. However, it still may be effective for the creation of a QTIP or credit shelter trust to pass property tax-free to a surviving spouse.

In each area of estate planning, the legal assistant plays a critical role. The legal assistant will gather family, income, and asset information from the client; assist in drafting initial documents; and review contracts and deeds to help the attorney meet the estate needs of the client.

KEY TERMS

administrator(trix)

beneficiary

charitable (public) trust

charitable remainder annuity trust

charitable remainder unitrust

codicil

community property

credit shelter (A-B) trust

donee

donor

endowment policy

escheat

estate planning

executor(trix)

gift

gift tax

inter vivos trust (living trust)

intestate succession

joint tenancy

life insurance trust

limited payment life insurance

marital deduction

personal representative

probate

qualified terminable interest property (QTIP) trust

remainderman

reversion

self-proving affidavit

spendthrift trust

tenancy by the entirety

tenancy in common

term life insurance

testamentary capacity

testamentary trust

testator(trix)

Totten trust

trust

trustee

Unified Estate and Gift Tax
   Credit

whole life insurance

will

will contest

EXERCISES

1. Create a questionnaire that could be used to gather information to create an effective estate plan.

2. What factors should be considered in determining whether a person should create an inter vivos or testamentary trust?

3. Obtain sample wills and discuss which provisions would be most appropriate for an elderly client.

4. Discuss which factors must be considered to determine whether an elderly client is acting under the undue influence of another person.

5. Obtain a sample copy of a trust and analyze its provisions.

EDITED JUDICIAL DECISIONS

In re Estate of Maheras
897 P.2d 268 (Okla. 1995)

The dispositive issue presented on certiorari is whether a third party, who receives no personal benefit from a decedent's will, may be regarded in law as capable of unduly influencing a will's procurement or its making? We answer in the affirmative.

I: THE ANATOMY OF LITIGATION

Evelyn Afton Maheras [Maheras or decedent] died testate on January 16, 1991 at the age of 96.

She left the bulk of her estate to the First Baptist Church of Bartlesville [First Baptist], whose pastor, William H. Cook [appellant or Cook], is named co-executor of the will. The decedent's sole heir is her nephew, Richard H. Suagee [appellee or Suagee]. Suagee, as contestant in this proceeding to admit the will to probate, urged at nisi prius that (1) Maheras did not have testamentary capacity, (2) her will's procurement and making had been unduly influenced by Cook, and (3) the subscribing witnesses were interested parties. The district court found that, although the decedent had testamentary capacity and the subscribing witnesses were disinterested, she had been unduly influenced by Cook.

The record documents a history of interaction among Maheras, Cook and First Baptist dating back to 1970. Maheras suffered from alcoholism and during the 1970's her health and living conditions deteriorated. From 1980 to 1983 Cook became closely acquainted with Maheras and visited in her home several times. By 1984 all of Maheras' friends were First Baptist members. Cook arranged for several of them to regularly assist Maheras by cleaning her home. Through this process the decedent became very dependent upon Cook and reposed great trust in him.

Although in 1983 Maheras attended several sessions of an estate planning seminar at First Baptist, she failed to make the last session where a "Will Information Guide" was distributed. In January 1984 Cook brought her a copy of the missed "Will Information Guide" and spent several hours assisting Maheras in cataloging her assets. Later Cook requested Jesse J. Worten, III [Worten]—a lawyer and First Baptist member—to contact Maheras and discuss her will's preparation. Worten had not represented Maheras in any other legal matters. He was recommended by Thomas Preston after Preston declined Maheras' request to prepare her will, stating he no longer practiced law. Before Worten drafted Maheras' will he had one fifteen-minute telephone conversation with her in which he discussed the contents of her estate using the "Will Information Guide" provided him by Cook. After the will was drafted, it was sent to Cook. He then delivered it to Maheras and discussed its terms with her. Worten subsequently discussed the will's provisions in a second ten to fifteen-minute telephone conversation with her.

On February 4, 1984 Maheras was taken to Worten's office by a First Baptist member where after reviewing the will's terms a second time she executed her will. All of the subscribing witnesses were First Baptist members chosen by Cook. They testified at trial that Maheras understood the provisions of her will, appeared normal, and was aware of her nephew's [Suagee] existence. Worten sent to Cook his bill for the preparation of Maheras' will, which was presented to and paid by Maheras.

After the trial court ruled that Cook's actions had overborne Maheras' free agency, Cook appealed and Suagee counter-appealed for review of the nisi prius testamentary-capacity finding. The Court of Appeals concluded (1) that the decedent had testamentary capacity and (2) that because Cook personally received nothing by the will's terms, he was in contemplation of law incapable of unduly influencing Maheras. On certiorari previously granted, the Court of Appeals' opinion is now vacated and the trial court's probate order affirmed.

II: THE STANDARD OF REVIEW [OMITTED]

III: IN THE ABSENCE OF MITIGATING CIRCUMSTANCES, UNDUE INFLUENCE IS PRESENT IF (1) A CONFIDENTIAL RELATIONSHIP EXISTED BETWEEN THE WILL'S MAKER AND ANOTHER PARTY AND (2) THAT OTHER PARTY ASSISTED IN THE PREPARATION OR PROCUREMENT OF THE WILL

If a will is found to have been affected by undue influence, the district court may declare it void in whole or in part. The burden of persuasion in a will contest based on undue influence rests on the contestant. A two-prong test is used to determine whether undue influence taints the procurement or preparation of a will. First, the court must search for the presence of a relationship which would induce a reasonably prudent person to repose confidence and trust in another—i.e., a confidential relationship. Second, the court must decide that the stronger party in the relationship assisted in the preparation or procurement of the weaker person's testamentary instrument. Factors to be considered in applying this two-prong test include:

1. Whether the person charged with undue influence was not a natural object of the maker's bounty;

2. Whether the stronger person was a trusted or confidential advisor or agent of the will's maker;
3. Whether he/she was present and/or active in the procurement or preparation of the will;
4. Whether the will's maker was of advanced age or impaired faculties;
5. Whether independent and disinterested advice regarding the testamentary disposition was given to its maker.

When assaying the nature of a relationship to determine if it was confidential, the court's probe is not confined to instances where there was an interaction of persons who stand vis-à-vis one another in certain limited classes—e.g., familial relationships—since dependent relations may occur in any number of different settings. Upon finding that a confidential relationship existed between the will's maker and another and ascertaining that the stronger party actively assisted in the preparation or procurement of the will, a rebuttable presumption of undue influence will at once arise. The person who desires to overcome this presumption must then go forward to produce evidence showing either that (a) the confidential relationship had been severed before the critical events in controversy or (b) the will's maker actually received independent and competent advice about the disposition of his/her estate.

The existence of a confidential relationship between Maheras and Cook is clearly shown by the record. Cook was Maheras' spiritual advisor and a close personal friend for more than the last fourteen (14) years of her life. First Baptist, the recipient of the bulk of Maheras' estate under her will, was not a natural object of her bounty. She obviously placed great trust in Cook. It is unquestionable that he actively participated in securing the will which was economically beneficial to First Baptist. Maheras had suffered from alcoholism and was of advanced age at the time she executed her will. The record does not disclose that she ever received from any person independent and disinterested advice regarding her will. Upon finding that Cook stood in a confidential relationship with Maheras and that he had unduly influenced her in

the procurement and making of the will in contest, the district court properly shifted to Cook the burden of producing evidence which would rebut the presumption of undue influence.

IV: A PERSON WHO IS NOT A BENEFICIARY UNDER A WILL'S TERMS MAY BE REGARDED AS LEGALLY CAPABLE OF OVERBEARING THE WILL-MAKER'S FREE AGENCY

At common law as well as under our statutory law a will which is the product of an influence brought to bear against the maker in any manner which overcomes his/her free agency cannot be sustained. Whether the person exerting the overbearing influence actually benefits personally under the will's terms is immaterial. A person's lack of beneficiary status under the will's terms does not render one legally incapable of, or excuse him/her from, exerting undue influence.

When a decedent's spiritual advisor procures a will that benefits his/her church, a court may find the will-maker's free agency overborne by the advisor's act if the law's criteria for establishing undue influence are met. While religious institutions are not factually capable of unduly influencing one's will, individuals acting on their behalf can. The gravamen of undue influence is legal harm from the wrongful exertion of power over the will's maker rather than the receipt of personal benefit from the offending act of influence.

The extant jurisprudence Cook offered here and below and which the Court of Appeals found controlling is factually distinguishable from the case under review. In neither of the two cases relied upon by the appellate court—*In re Heitholt's Estate* and *Kindt v. Parmenter*—was there proof of undue influence that would satisfy the criteria articulated in Section III of this opinion. To the extent our pronouncements in *Heitholt* and *Kindt* may be perceived as holding that a person standing in a confidential relationship with a will's maker is legally incapable of exerting undue influence unless he/she receives a benefit under the testamentary instrument's terms, *Heitholt* and *Kindt* may no longer be regarded as a correct exposition of Oklahoma's common law in will contests.

V: SUMMARY

Where a will-maker and another are shown to have stood in a confidential relationship and the stronger person, who actively participated in the procurement and preparation of the testamentary document, overbore the maker's free agency, a nisi prius order denying a will's admission because of the presence of undue influence will be sustained in the absence of proof that either (1) the confidential relationship had been severed before the critical events in question or (2) independent advice was given to the will-maker. Cook's receipt of some personal benefit (or interest) under Maheras' will is not a sine qua non for a judicial finding of undue influence. Upon showing that

the will-maker's free agency was overborne by anyone standing in a confidential (or fiducial) relationship, a presumption of undue influence arises. The will's proponent must then come forward with evidence to overcome this presumption. When that burden is not met, a nisi prius order based upon a finding of undue influence is sustainable. The trial court's decision that denies the Maheras will admission to probate is neither clearly contrary to the weight of the evidence nor to the applicable principles of equity jurisprudence. Today's holding makes Maheras' testamentary capacity a moot issue. On certiorari previously granted,

THE COURT OF APPEALS' OPINION IS VACATED; THE DISTRICT COURT'S PROBATE ORDER IS REINSTATED AND AFFIRMED; AND THE CAUSE IS REMANDED FOR PROCEEDINGS NOT INCONSISTENT WITH TODAY'S PRONOUNCEMENT.

Duggan v. Keto
554 A.2d 1126 (D.C. 1989)

Mary Lemp died on October 2, 1981, leaving the bulk of an estate worth over $1.1 million to her brother, William Stroman, rather than to her stepchildren, James Lemp, Helena Lemp, and John Lemp, Jr. The stepchildren had expected to be the primary beneficiaries under Mary Lemp's will and so brought suit against her estate, alleging that Mary had breached a reciprocal wills agreement which she had made with their late father. The estate filed a counterclaim against James Lemp when it learned that he had removed several bonds from Mary's safe deposit box shortly after her death. The trial court granted summary judgment in favor of the estate on both the original claim and the counterclaim.

In a related action, the stepchildren sued Arthur Peter, Jr., and the partners in his law firm, Hamel & Park, for malpractice and breach of fiduciary duty. Mr. Peter had drafted wills for Mary Lemp and her husband, Colonel John Lemp. The trial court granted summary judgment for the defendants on these claims as well. The stepchildren now appeal from all the awards of summary judg-

ment and from an order authorizing the estate to pay $222,261 in attorney's fees.

I. FACTUAL BACKGROUND

A. The Claim against the Estate

Appellants are the children of Colonel John Lemp and Helena Lemp. John divorced Helena in 1957 and married Mary Lemp. Mary never bore any children.

In May 1973, John and Mary Lemp consulted Arthur Peter, Jr., a member of the law firm of Hamel & Park, about drafting a will for each of them. After discussing their assets and testamentary goals, Mr. Peter wrote separate wills for the Lemps; the terms of the wills, however, were largely reciprocal. Colonel Lemp bequeathed his residuary estate to Mary if she survived him for thirty days. If she did not survive him, his estate would go to his three children (appellants), except for certain property in Texas, which would be left to Mary's brother and sister, William Stroman and Gusta Mae Brewton. Similarly, Mary bequeathed her residuary estate to John should he survive her by thirty days, and, if not, then to appellants except for the property in Texas left to her brother and sister.

Despite their overall similarity, neither will referred to the other, and some provisions in the two wills differed. Mr. Peter testified that he had no knowledge of any agreement between the Lemps to make the wills irrevocable. James Lemp testified, however, that his father had told him that his property would eventually descend to his three children.

Colonel Lemp died on October 25, 1974. Three days before his death, he executed a new will which left his entire estate to his wife Mary, except for some small bequests to his children of personal items, stock which had only a nominal value, and a few thousand dollars in life insurance proceeds. Mary, however, elected not to receive anything under the will. See D.C. Code § 19-113(a) (1973). With the exception of a bank account containing $211.71, Colonel Lemp and his wife had owned all their property jointly, so that she became the sole owner of everything after his death. Mary therefore had the colonel's estate administered as a small estate and received the money in the bank account as her statutory allowance under D.C. Code § 19-101(a) (1973).

After her husband's death, Mary Lemp executed three new wills on November 22, 1974, October 25, 1978, and November 7, 1979. Although the 1974 will has never been produced, the 1978 and 1979 wills were substantially different from Mary's original 1973 will, leaving the bulk of her estate to her own relatives rather than to her stepchildren.

Mary Lemp died on October 2, 1981, leaving an estate valued at $1,126,673.11. Although her will (the 1979 will) bequeathed some property, worth about $208,000, to her three stepchildren, the lion's share of her estate, valued at almost $920,000, went to her own relatives, primarily to her brother William Stroman, the residuary legatee. Appellants thereafter filed suit against George Keto, as personal representative of Mary's estate, alleging that John and Mary Lemp had entered into an agreement not to revoke their 1973 wills and that Mary had breached that agreement. They sought damages for that alleged breach or, alternatively, specific performance of it. As a third alternative, appellants claimed that John and Mary had formed a trust for their benefit.

During discovery, appellants moved to compel Hamel & Park to disclose certain communications made by John and Mary Lemp with the firm. Hamel & Park opposed the motion, asserting Mary's attorney-client privilege. Judge Pratt ruled that the privilege did not apply to those communications made by the Lemps when they sought joint counsel. However, he upheld the claim of privilege as to those communications which Mary made both in her capacity as personal representative of her husband's estate and with regard to her own affairs.

Judge Pratt initially denied the estate's motion for summary judgment on appellants' claims, but without prejudice. After further filings, the estate moved again for summary judgment, which was granted by Judge Barnes.

B. The Estate's Counterclaim

A few hours after Mary's death on October 2, 1981, James Lemp went to a branch of the First American Bank on Wisconsin Avenue, N.W., and removed eleven bearer bonds from a safe deposit box which he held jointly with Mary. These bonds had a face value of $55,000. James did not tell the bank officials about his stepmother's death, nor did he tell anyone about his taking the bonds until December 1983. The estate first learned about the removal of the bonds during discovery proceedings in August 1984, and shortly thereafter it filed a counterclaim against James for conversion.

James claimed as a defense that he and his wife Susan had received the bonds as a gift from Mary before her death or, alternatively, that they were the subject of an informal inter vivos trust under which title to the bonds had vested in James and his wife upon Mary's death. In support of this claim, James produced a letter from Mary dated February 25, 1976, which he offered as proof of her donative intent. The letter stated in part:

Enclosed is the form, Jim, to sign where the "X" is in both places. Although this form states that both of us will be responsible for the rent, etc., I'm writing a letter to accompany it saying that I alone am responsible. Today I put a rubber band around those papers with a small tan envelope on top, and this is what you are [to] remove, if and when it looks as if my time here is ending, for safe keeping for you and Susan.

The form mentioned in the letter was a lease for safe deposit box No. 692 in the main office of the First American Bank on 15th Street, N.W., in downtown Washington. In July 1979 Mary moved the contents of this box to another one located in the Wisconsin Avenue branch of the First American Bank. Mary and James were joint lessees of both boxes.

James testified that Mary gave him a key to the new box in 1979. Additionally, James said that on August 13, 1979, Mary took him to the Wisconsin Avenue branch, where together they opened the box and Mary pointed to the packet of papers to which she had referred in her letter. Although he did not unwrap the packet, James could see that it contained municipal bonds.

The trial court noted in its opinion that only four of the eleven bonds in the packet were purchased before the date of the letter, February 25, 1976, implying that Mary could not have referred to the remaining seven in her letter. The court also observed that all matured coupons except the most recent one on each bond had been removed and redeemed before James took the bonds from the safe deposit box, and that James had stated he never used the box as his own. The court then granted the estate's motion for summary judgment on the counterclaim.

The parties were in further disagreement about the proper calculation of damages. Generally adopting the formula proposed by the estate, the court awarded damages for the present market value of the six bonds still in James' possession, the coupon interest that he had received, the proceeds from the sale of the other five bonds, and pre-judgment interest at eight percent per annum on the sale proceeds and coupon interest. Appel-

lants contend on appeal that both the award of summary judgment and the measurement of damages were erroneous.

The trial court also authorized Mr. Keto, the personal representative, to pay $222,261.00 from the estate's assets for attorney's fees and other costs resulting from the litigation of appellants' claims against the estate. In making this award, the court noted that it constituted only a partial payment (Mr. Keto had petitioned for over $360,000). Appellants now challenge the award as excessive and premature.

C. The Malpractice and Breach of Fiduciary Duty Claims

By 1978 John Lemp, Jr., noticed that his stepmother's attitude toward her stepchildren had begun to change, and he suspected that she might have done something with the property she had inherited from her late husband. John decided to investigate. On July 3, 1979, he went to the Superior Court to review the records pertaining to his father's estate. What he discovered aroused his suspicions even further. First, his father's signature on the will did not look authentic, and the will had been executed at a time when his father was gravely ill and, in John's view, his testamentary capacity was doubtful. Further, the will did not even mention any of Colonel Lemp's three children, nor did it dispose of various personal items mentioned in his previous will. Finally, John discovered that, despite his father's wealth, the estate had been handled as a small estate. John discussed his misgivings with an attorney standing nearby, who coincidentally had some recollection of the small-estate proceedings. The attorney remarked that John would have to take legal action if he wanted to question the administration of his father's estate.

Despite John's doubts, which he shared with his brother and sister, about Mary's inheritance of all the Colonel's estate, the stepchildren chose not to challenge Mary while she was alive. Because they fully expected to receive their father's estate by bequest from Mary, they did not perceive Mary's possible wrongdoing as detrimental to their interests. Consequently, they did not file any malpractice action until after Mary died, when they discovered to their astonishment that she had left the bulk of what she had inherited from the Colonel to her own relatives.

Appellants' claim against Mr. Peter and his law firm was in two parts. First, they alleged that Mr. Peter had committed malpractice in 1973 by negligently failing to explore means by which they would receive most of the Colonel's assets. Second, they claimed that Hamel & Park had breached their fiduciary duty to the Colonel and to them, his children and the natural objects of his bounty, by preparing two subsequent wills for Mary which substantially disinherited them.

The trial court ruled that both the malpractice claim and the breach of fiduciary duty claim were barred by the statute of limitations. The court reasoned that the statute began to run as to each claim upon John's review of his father's will in July 1979, and accordingly it granted summary judgment for Mr. Peter and Hamel & Park. Appellants appeal from this ruling as well.

II. STANDARD OF REVIEW [OMITTED]

III. THE CLAIM AGAINST THE ESTATE

A. Irrevocable Mutual Wills

Appellants first maintain that John and Mary Lemp entered into an oral contract not to revoke their 1973 wills. There can be no doubt that the two instruments are mutual wills, separate instruments containing reciprocal or substantially similar terms. 1 W. BOWE & D. PARKER, PAGE ON THE LAW OF WILLS § 11.1, at 553 (1960) (hereinafter PAGE ON WILLS). But that does not mean that they were irrevocable. The mere fact that mutual wills exist is insufficient proof of an accompanying contract not to revoke. *Coveney v. Conlin, 20 App. D.C. 303, 329 (1902);* accord, e.g., 1 PAGE ON WILLS, supra, § 11.1, at 554. To prove that the mutual wills were made irrevocable by an oral or written contract, District of Columbia law requires that such a contract "be complete, definite in its terms, and proved with clearness and certainty."

Coveney v. Conlin, supra, 20 App. D.C. at 328 (citations omitted).

Acknowledging that this is the law, appellants contend that the evidence necessary to prove a contract may be found in the circumstances surrounding the execution of the mutual wills. Specifically, appellants claim that the purpose of the mutual wills was to provide first for the surviving spouse and then for Colonel Lemp's children. The Lemps stated this twofold intention to Mr. Peter, who drafted the wills, and Colonel Lemp later repeated it to his son James. Appellants reason that, in order to ensure that their goals would be realized, their father and stepmother must have entered into an agreement to make the wills irrevocable.

We cannot agree. Although this evidence may be persuasive to prove a common testamentary scheme, it does not establish the existence of a contract. The court in *Coveney v. Conlin, supra,* did not state exactly what kind of evidence would be sufficient to prove an agreement not to revoke, but it did make clear that evidence of a common testamentary scheme was insufficient. *20 App. D.C. at 329.* Most courts which have been directly faced with the issue have required some independent evidence that the testator actually entered into a contract. E.g., *In re Estate of Moore, 137 Ariz. 176, 669 P.2d 609, 612 (1983); Woll v. Dugas, 104 N.J. Super. 586, 250 A.2d 775, 783–84 (1969), aff'd, 112 N.J. Super. 366, 271 A.2d 443 (1970); Oursler v. Armstrong, 10 N.Y.2d 385, 389, 179 N.E.2d 489, 490, 223 N.Y.S.2d 477, 479 (1961);* see also *Notten v. Mensing, 20 Cal. App. 2d 694, 67 P.2d 734, 735 (1937); Neipp v. Toolen, 313 Ill. App. 28, 38 N.E.2d 980, 981–82 (1942); Neff v. Poboisk, 281 Minn. 475, 161 N.W.2d 823, 824–25 (1968); Willbanks v. Goodwin, 300 Or. 181, 709 P.2d 213, 225 (1985); Fanning v. Fanning, 111 R.I. 116, 302 A.2d 299, 301 (1973); Kirk v. Beard, 162 Tex. 144, 345 S.W.2d 267, 272 (1961).*

Appellants have presented no evidence of an agreement to make irrevocable wills; indeed, Mr. Peter, the draftsman of the wills, testified that the Lemps did not make such an agreement. In *Oursler v. Armstrong, supra, 10 N.Y.2d at 392–93,*

179 N.E.2d at 492, 223 N.Y.S.2d at 482, similar testimony from the drafting attorney helped to persuade the court that evidence of an agreement was lacking. In this case all that appellants have proven is that their father and stepmother executed mutual wills and intended common testamentary goals. This evidence, in our view, is legally insufficient to prove the existence of a contract not to revoke either will. Viewed in the light most favorable to appellants, the evidence shows nothing more than that "the reciprocity or similarity in the dispositive provisions of the two wills results from similar tastes and affections that have resulted from years of living together, and [that] the making of identical or similar wills was a spontaneous thing unaccompanied by even so much as a thought on the part of either husband or wife that they should enter into a contract with each other." 1 PAGE ON WILLS, supra, § 11.1, at 554.

B. Oral or Constructive Trust

Alternatively, appellants claim that they have raised a triable issue of fact on their right to their stepmother's estate under the principles governing oral or constructive trusts. We reject this argument for essentially the same reason that we have rejected their claim of irrevocable mutual wills, namely, that the record contains no evidence of any intent on the part of either John or Mary Lemp to create a trust or of a promise to make any particular disposition of their property.

The elements of a trust include a trustee, who holds the trust property and is subject to equitable duties to deal with it for the benefit of another; a beneficiary, to whom the trustee owes such duties; and the trust property, which is held by the trustee for the beneficiary. *Cabaniss v. Cabaniss, 464 A.2d 87, 91 (D.C. 1983)*. Additionally, there must be proof of the settlor's intention to create a trust, which may be manifested "by written or spoken language or by conduct, in light of all surrounding circumstances." *Id.* (citations omitted).

On the element of intent, courts are properly hesitant to create implied testamentary trusts, i.e., trusts which are not readily apparent from the face

of the will. 5 PAGE ON WILLS, supra, § 40.9, at 128–29. Moreover, "oral instructions should not be used to show that a gift is in trust, and a number of courts have reached this result, even if the will refers expressly to such oral instructions and attempts to incorporate them." *Id.* § 40.11, at 130–31 (footnotes omitted). The test for proving an intent to create a testamentary trust from oral evidence is essentially the same as that for proving an oral agreement not to revoke reciprocal wills: clear and convincing evidence of a promise to dispose of assets by testamentary disposition in favor of one or more specific beneficiaries. See *Levin v. Smith, 513 A.2d 1292, 1296 (Del. 1986); Dougherty v. Dougherty, 175 Md. 441, 2 A.2d 433, 436 (1938); In re Irrevocable Inter Vivos Trust Agreement of Hanley, 307 Pa. Super. 153, 452 A.2d 1360, 1371 (1982)* (Johnson, J., dissenting), aff'd sub nom. *Siebert v. Bird, 503 Pa. 119, 468 A.2d 1093 (1983)*.

Thus appellants' assertion of an oral trust must fail. Neither Colonel Lemp's will nor Mary's will provides for the creation of a trust, and there is no other evidence that either of them ever intended to create a trust for appellants' benefit. Indeed, appellants have failed to prove even that the Colonel and Mary had an oral agreement for the survivor of them to hold the estate, or any part of it, in trust for anyone.

Appellants' argument that the court should establish a constructive trust is also without merit. A constructive trust is fundamentally a remedy to prevent unjust enrichment. D. DOBBS, HANDBOOK ON THE LAW OF REMEDIES § 4.3, at 246 (1973) (hereinafter DOBBS ON REMEDIES). When someone is lawfully entitled to possession of certain property, there is no reason to impose a constructive trust on that property for the benefit of someone else. See, e.g., *Oursler v. Armstrong, supra, 10 N.Y.2d at 391, 179 N.E.2d at 491, 223 N.Y.S.2d at 480*. Mary received no benefits under the Colonel's will because she was already the joint owner of almost all the property at issue. She was fully entitled to all of that property, as well as her statutory allowance. See *Willbanks v. Goodwin, supra, 300 Or., 709 P.2d at 223–24*. Therefore,

Mary was not unjustly enriched, and a constructive trust is not warranted.

IV. THE ESTATE'S COUNTERCLAIM

Mary's estate filed a counterclaim against James Lemp, alleging that he had converted eleven bearer bonds by removing them from the safe deposit box a few hours after Mary's death. James asserted that these bonds were an inter vivos gift from Mary, or, in the alternative, that they were the corpus of a trust of which he was the beneficiary. The trial court ruled that James was liable for conversion. We affirm this ruling because James has not presented sufficient evidence to raise a material issue of fact under either of the two theories on which he bases his claim of entitlement to the bonds.

A. Inter Vivos Gift

"The requisites of a valid gift inter vivos are delivery, intention on the part of the donor to make a gift, and absolute disposition of the subject of the gift." *Murray v. Gadsden, 91 U.S. App. D.C. 38, 49, 197 F.2d 194, 205 (1952)* (citations omitted). The evidence must show that the gift took effect immediately; a gift intended to take effect in the future is not an inter vivos gift. *Lust v. Miller, 55 App. D.C. 217, 219, 4 F.2d 293, 295 (1925);* 38 AM. JUR. 2D Gifts §§ 18, 81 (1968). If the donor retains the right to receive income for life, the inter vivos gift is not necessarily invalidated. But such a retention may become a decisive factor if there are other factors which tend to negate a finding of absolute disposition. *Id.* § 26.

The burden of proving that a transfer was an inter vivos gift falls upon the person asserting the gift, in this instance James Lemp. Because his allegation of an inter vivos gift followed the death of the alleged donor, James must prove the gift by clear and convincing evidence. *Estate of Presgrave v. Stephens, 529 A.2d 274, 280 (D.C. 1987); Davis v. Altmann, 492 A.2d 884, 885 (D.C. 1985).*

We agree that James Lemp at least raised a factual issue as to whether his stepmother intended to make an inter vivos gift or a future gift. The letter of February 25, 1976, quoted at page 6, supra, is ambiguous on this question. It does not refer specifically to the bearer bonds, most of which did not even exist at the time Mary wrote the letter, nor does it explain what Mary meant by "safe keeping." It does appear that James was not to remove the papers from the box until Mary's death was imminent ("when it looks as if my time here is ending"). On the other hand, Mary placed the bonds in a safe deposit box that she leased jointly with James, and James testified that Mary opened the box and showed him a bundle containing some municipal bonds, telling him that they were his. Mary may very well have intended to make an inter vivos gift at that moment, retaining only a right to the interest payments during her lifetime.

We need not rule on the issue of intent, however, for it is clear from the undisputed evidence that there was neither delivery nor absolute disposition, and for that reason the estate was entitled to summary judgment on its counterclaim. Mary kept a key to the safe deposit box and continued to have access to the bonds throughout her lifetime, clipping the coupons from them for her own benefit. Hence she never made an absolute disposition of the bonds. Likewise, James did not produce sufficient evidence of delivery to raise a triable issue of fact. An inter vivos gift can be made by either actual delivery (physically handing over the chattel) or constructive delivery (handling over some type of formal instrument purporting to pass title to the donee). See 38 AM. JUR. 2D Gifts §§ 20, 32 (1968). The evidence here shows neither.

James argues that Mary made actual delivery by placing the bonds in the safe deposit box which she leased jointly with him. Case law in this and other jurisdictions, however, requires that the donor part with all dominion and control of the property to effect actual delivery. *Casey v. Topliffe, 65 App. D.C. 100, 101, 80 F.2d 543, 544 (1935)* (no inter vivos gift of bonds because alleged donor, although an invalid, retained key to safe deposit box containing the bonds); *Lee v. Lee, 55 App. D.C. 344, 345, 5 F.2d 767, 768 (1925)* (no gift of property in trunk because alleged donor retained right to remove trunk's contents); see also *Murray v. Gadsden, supra, 91 U.S. App. D.C. at 49, 197 F.2d at 205* (no gift because alleged donor retained control over joint savings account);

Annotation, Joint Lease of Safe-Deposit Box as Evidence in Support or Denial of Gift Inter Vivos of Contents Thereof, *40 A.L.R.3d 462, 465 (1971)*; Annotation, Necessity of Delivery of Stock Certificate to Complete Valid Gift of Stock, *23 A.L.R.2d 1171, 1184 (1952)*. Because she had continued access to the bonds and clipped coupons for her own benefit, Mary did not part with dominion and control of the property; hence there was no actual delivery. *Casey v. Topliffe, supra,* is dispositive on this point.

The record also fails to support James' theory that Mary constructively delivered the bonds by sending him the February 25 letter. A written instrument may be used to effect delivery of personal property in some cases. E.g., *Smith v. Acorn, 32 A.2d 252, 254 (D.C. 1943)* (automobile effectively delivered when donee received certificate of title even though donor retained possession); see 38 AM. JUR. 2D Gifts § 32 (1968). But the letter written by Mary does not contain the necessary formalities, such as those found in a certificate of title or a bill of sale, to effect constructive delivery of the bonds. Unless physical delivery is impossible or impracticable, an informal writing is generally deemed insufficient to prove a valid gift. See *id.* § 33.

James relies on *Conlon v. Turley, 56 App. D.C. 95, 10 F.2d 890 (1926),* in which the court found constructive delivery of some bonds even though the donor had retained access to them and continued to collect the interest. The donor in *Conlon* told a bank official to place the bonds "in safe-keeping for my daughter, and I want a receipt made out in her name." The official prepared and signed such a receipt on bank stationery, which the father then handed to the daughter. Thereafter she placed the receipt in her father's safe, and the father continued to collect the interest on the bonds, which the bank held as bailee, until his death. The court held that the written receipt, coupled with "the repeated declarations of the donor that he had given the bonds to the donee," were sufficient to prove a gift. *Id. at 97, 10 F.2d at 892.* Mary Lemp's letter of February 25 has none of the formal attributes of the bank

receipt, nor is there anything in this case comparable to "the repeated declarations of the donor" in *Conlon.* Moreover, Mary's letter was, at best, ambiguous as to what property she intended for "safe keeping" when her death became imminent. Finding *Conlon* readily distinguishable, we hold that the February 25 letter is insufficient on its face even to raise a factual issue of constructive delivery.

Thus we conclude that the evidence before the trial court failed to raise a material issue of fact as to absolute disposition and delivery, two of the three elements necessary to prove an inter vivos gift. Accordingly, we affirm the trial court's grant of summary judgment to the estate on its counterclaim.

B. Express Trust

Alternatively, James contends that he rightfully acquired the bonds as the beneficiary of a trust created by Mary. We hold that the trial court properly awarded summary judgment for the estate on this issue as well.

In *Cabaniss v. Cabaniss, supra, 464 A.2d at 91–92,* this court reiterated the requirements for proving a valid trust. There must, of course, be a trustee, a beneficiary, and trust property. Most important for this case is the requirement that the settlor manifest his or her intention to create a trust. That intention may be proved either by words or by conduct, which must be considered in light of all the surrounding circumstances. "No particular form of words or conduct is necessary to manifest an intention to create a trust." *Id. at 91* (citations omitted). Rather, the courts will look to several "evidentiary factors" in determining that intent:

(1) the imperative, as distinguished from precatory, nature of the words used by the settlor to create a trust; (2) the definiteness of the trust property; (3) the certainty of the identity of the trust beneficiaries; (4) the relationship between and financial position of the parties; (5) the motives which may reasonably be supposed to have influenced the settlor in making the disposition; and (6) whether the result reached in construing

the transaction as a trust would be such as a person in the situation of the settlor would naturally desire to produce.

Id. at 92 (citations omitted). Finally, as is the case with gifts, the settlor of a trust may reserve the right to receive income from the trust property for life, thereby postponing the beneficiary's enjoyment. 1 A. SCOTT & W. FRATCHER, THE LAW OF TRUSTS § 26.1, at 293 (4th ed. 1987) (hereinafter SCOTT ON TRUSTS).

In *Moore v. Layton, 147 Md. 244, 127 A. 756 (1925),* the testator owned some bonds that were placed in a vault accessible to him and his nephew. The testator also said that "if anything happened" to him, he wanted his nephew to have the bonds. Until his death, the testator clipped the coupons from the bonds and collected the income himself. On these facts the court found insufficient evidence of a trust for the nephew. Noting that "the intention to create a trust should be clearly manifested," *id., 127 A. at 757,* the court found "no indication of any design by [the testator] to create a trust. No present interest was transferred, and no fiduciary relation was defined by word or conduct." *Id., 127 A. at 758.*

Although *Moore* is not binding on us, we find it persuasive here because its facts are very similar to the facts in the instant case. The only evidence offered by James to prove the existence of a trust was the February 25 letter from Mary. Even when that letter is read in the light most favorable to James, it is insufficient to prove any intent on Mary's part to establish a trust. The meaning of her instructions was extremely vague, as was the identification of the alleged corpus. Although it is arguable that Mary may have intended to transfer to James a present interest in the bonds which existed as of February 25, 1976, i.e., to make an inter vivos gift, the letter simply cannot be read more broadly than that. Neither her words nor her conduct provided any evidence stronger than what was held to be inadequate in *Moore.* Guided by *Moore,* we hold that there was no evidence before the trial court sufficient even to raise an issue as to the existence of a trust.

V. DAMAGES [OMITTED]

VI. ATTORNEY-CLIENT PRIVILEGE

The trial court ruled that Mary Lemp's attorney-client privilege applied against appellants in their litigation with Mary's estate. Appellants argue that the privilege cannot be invoked against them because they are Mary's heirs and legatees. This argument is without merit.

Appellants, as Mary's stepchildren, are not her heirs, but they are legatees because they are designated to receive property under Mary's will. See 26A C.J.S. Descent and Distribution § 34 (1956); 1 PAGE ON WILLS, supra, § 1.3. Nevertheless, their status as legatees does not override Mary's attorney-client privilege in an action brought by appellants against her estate.

The Supreme Court held in *Glover v. Patten, 165 U.S. 394, 17 S. Ct. 411, 41 L. Ed. 760 (1897),* that the attorney-client privilege does not apply in disputes between beneficiaries claiming under a will or heirs claiming through the decedent. However, when an heir or legatee makes a claim adverse to the estate, the estate may defend itself by invoking the privilege. See *id. at 406.* Appellants do not dispute their bequests among themselves in this action, nor do they claim under Mary's will. Rather, they allege that Mary breached a contract not to revoke an earlier will and seek damages for that breach. Their claim, under *Glover v. Patten,* is clearly adverse to the estate, and thus the estate may invoke the attorney-client privilege on behalf of Mary in defending against that claim. See also *DeLoach v. Myers, 215 Ga. 255, 109 S.E.2d 777, 780–81 (1959); Runnels v. Allen's Adm'r, 169 S.W.2d 73, 76 (Mo. Ct. App. 1943); In re Smith's Estate, 263 Wis. 441, 57 N.W.2d 727, 730 (1953).*

VII. ATTORNEY'S FEES [OMITTED]

VIII. THE CLAIMS AGAINST THE LAWYERS

The trial court granted summary judgment in favor of Arthur Peter and his law firm, Hamel & Park, on appellants' claims of malpractice and breach of fiduciary duty. In pertinent part, the court's order reads as follows:

The only acts and omissions complained of by the plaintiffs for which the plaintiffs have proffered any evidence and which might possibly be actionable are those acts and omissions occurring on or about May 30, 1973; however, the consequences of those acts and omissions were fully known to and appreciated by all the plaintiffs on or about July 3, 1979. In view of the fact that the plaintiffs purposely delayed bringing this action until September 26, 1984, it is barred by the applicable Statute of Limitations.

We hold that the trial court erred in concluding that the statute of limitations began to run on July 3, 1979, and accordingly we reverse the grant of summary judgment to Mr. Peter and his partners in Hamel & Park.

A. The Malpractice Claim

The statute of limitations applicable to this case requires that an action be brought within three years from the date on which the claim accrues. D.C. Code § 12-301(8) (1981). A cause of action usually accrues at the time of injury, but if "the relationship between the fact of injury and the alleged tortious conduct is obscure when the injury occurs, we apply a 'discovery rule' to determine when the statute of limitations commences." *Bussineau v. President & Directors of Georgetown College, 518 A.2d 423, 425 (D.C. 1986)* (citations omitted); accord, *Knight v. Furlow, 553 A.2d 1232, slip op. at 5 (D.C. 1989)*. Under the discovery rule, "the statute of limitations begins to run when the facts which form the basis of the claim are discovered, or reasonably should be discovered in the exercise of due diligence." *Interdonato v. Interdonato, 521 A.2d 1124, 1135 (D.C. 1987)* (citations omitted).

The trial court held that appellants "fully [knew] ... and appreciated" the alleged wrongdoing by Mr. Peter and his colleagues on July 3, 1979, when John Lemp, Jr., reviewed the file on his father's estate in the Probate Division of the Superior Court. On that occasion John noticed some peculiarities in his father's 1974 will and learned, to his surprise, that his wealthy father's estate had been administered as a small estate.

John talked briefly with a lawyer present in the room, who advised him to take legal action. From these circumstances the trial court reasoned that appellants knew or should have known of their claimed injury.

The evidence does not support the court's reasoning. The discoveries made by John Lemp in July 1979 do not indicate any malpractice by Mr. Peter or his colleagues in May 1973. There is no dispute that appellants did in fact expect their father's estate to pass to Mary; at most, John may have wondered why his father's personal effects had not been bequeathed to him and his brother and sister. The only possible impropriety uncovered by John in July 1979 was that his father might have lacked testamentary capacity to make his 1974 will, a matter of little or no importance to a claim of malpractice in 1973.

Appellants could not have learned of any possible malpractice by Mr. Peter until Mary died and left the bulk of her estate to her brother. Until then, appellants assumed that Mary would leave most of her estate to them, as they allege their father had intended. Only when appellants learned of their disinheritance, after Mary's death, could they have brought an action for malpractice.

Therefore, we hold that the earliest date upon which appellants could have discovered their alleged injury was October 2, 1981, the date of Mary's death. Since the action against Mr. Peter and his partners at Hamel & Park was filed within three years after that date, the statute of limitations does not bar their malpractice claim.

B. The Breach of Fiduciary Duty Claim

The same reasoning applies to appellants' claim that Mr. Peter and Hamel & Park breached their fiduciary duty. As to this claim also, we hold that the statute did not begin to run until October 2, 1981, at the earliest. We treat the fiduciary duty claim separately here only because appellees make an additional argument which is not supported by the record.

Appellees assert that the trial court made two separate rulings on appellants' claims. In their brief they refer to (and rely on) the trial court's "first ruling, which disposed of Count II of the Amended Complaint alleging a breach of fiduciary duties owed Colonel Lemp when Hamel & Park prepared a new will for Mary Lemp following Colonel Lemp's death." Appellants state in their reply brief that "it is by no means clear" that the court made such a ruling. We agree with appellants.

The only order in the record which purports to address either of appellants' claims on the merits is the one we have quoted at slip op. page 38, supra. That order grants appellees' motion for summary judgment on the sole ground that the statute of limitations began to run more than three years before the filing of the complaint. We find it significant that the reference in appellees' brief to the court's "first ruling" is not accompanied by a citation to the record, as our rules require, although the rest of their brief is replete with such citations. Notwithstanding this lapse, we have combed the voluminous record for some indication of this "first ruling," but we have found no evidence of it. We can only conclude that appellees are mistaken in their recollection of what the trial court did.

Appellees raise certain questions relating to the evidence offered in support of appellants' breach of fiduciary duty claim. Since it does not appear that the trial court ever ruled on these questions, we refrain from considering them here, leaving them for the trial court to resolve in the first instance on remand. Two preliminary issues which the court on remand will have to address are, first, whether appellees Peter and Hamel & Park owed any fiduciary duty to these appellants, as distinct from their father and stepmother (who were the law firm's actual clients), and second, whether these appellants have standing to sue for an alleged breach of fiduciary duty to their father and stepmother. We express no view on either issue.

IX. CONCLUSION

In No. 86-352 we affirm the trial court's grant of summary judgment in favor of the estate on appellants' claim against the estate. We also affirm the trial court's grant of summary judgment on the estate's counterclaim against James Lemp to the extent that it holds him liable for conversion, but we reverse in part the award of damages against James Lemp and remand the case for recalculation of that award. In No. 86-727 we remand the case to the trial court for further proceedings with respect to the award of attorney's fees. In No. 86-1274 we reverse the grant of summary judgment to appellees Peter, et al., and remand the case for further proceedings.

CHAPTER

7

ELDER ABUSE

INTRODUCTION

According to a report of the United States House of Representatives Committee on Aging, 5 percent of all Americans aged 65 or older are victims of elder abuse. The committee report speculated that this percentage represents only the portion of older Americans whose abuse is actually discovered, but that in fact approximately only 12 percent of all elder abuse activity is actually reported. The implication of this statistic is staggering; it indicates that about a third of all older Americans are the victims of abuse.

Elder abuse is considered one of the fastest growing areas of concern for the elderly, not only because of the increasing number of persons who are aging into this category, but also because methods of discovering and reporting such abuse have become more effective. This may indicate that the elderly have always been subject to abuse by close family members, friends, and caregivers, but only recently has the problem been identified and some solutions to the problem formulated. For the attorney or paralegal working with and for the elderly client, the problem can be even more acute, because the legal professional may be in a position not only to discover such abuse, but also to cause such abuse.

This chapter explores the definition of elder abuse, the causes of such abuse, and the types of enactments made in response to this growing problem affecting older Americans.

ELDER ABUSE DEFINED

Elder abuse is generally defined by statute as any act of neglect or physical or mental infliction of injury that harms an older person, or the financial exploitation of the older individual. Elder abuse can take many forms and have various manifestations, but the ultimate result is harm—physical, psychological, emotional, or legal—to the older individual.

Neglect

Neglect is the willful or negligent failure to provide a person with necessary service or care. Neglect is the most common form of reported elder abuse. If the neglect is sufficiently serious, it may engender criminal liability for the person who caused the neglect; however, to be liable for the neglect of another person, the individual so charged must have a duty of care with respect to the person neglected. If no legal duty of care exists, there is no liability.

Example

A woman is the caregiver for her elderly aunt. The aunt suffers from asthma and other respiratory problems and is supposed to be on a fairly strict diet and take medication. The woman is aware of the medication, and makes sure that the aunt takes her pills and uses her inhalator at the appropriate intervals; however, she is totally ignorant of the aunt's special dietary needs. The food she gives her aunt is actually causing greater physical problems for the aunt. This would be an example of negligent neglect—the woman should be made aware of all of her aunt's needs.

Example

A middle-aged man is the legal guardian of his elderly mother. The mother is incontinent, suffers from rashes, and is generally immobile. The man has always resented his mother's bossy attitude, so he lets her lie in her own urine, which aggravates her rashes. This is an example of willful neglect.

elder abuse The willful or negligent causing of physical or psychological harm to an older person.

neglect The willful or negligent failure to provide necessary care or services to another by a person who has a legal duty to provide such care to the other person.

Exploitation

Exploitation is the improper or illegal use of another's property. Some elderly persons are the victims of confidence schemes by strangers, but many are victims of financial exploitation by their own family members and caregivers.

Example

A man calls on an elderly woman and tells her that he is from the government. He explains that the government is going to take her house, under the right of eminent domain, to build a new road. The woman is then visited by another man who represents himself as a real estate agent who is willing to buy the woman's house. The woman, afraid that she will lose her house, agrees to sell her house at a bargain price to the second man. The two men are working together on a confidence scheme—the government was never going to take the woman's home at all.

Example

A woman coerces her father to give her a power of attorney over his assets so that she can "take care of all his bills for him so that he will be relieved of all of his financial worries." Once the woman has the power of attorney, she empties all her father's accounts. This is an example of exploitation.

Physical Abuse

Physical abuse means the actual physical infliction of harm to an elderly person, and can take any form. Any action that results in physical injury to another individual is physical abuse.

Example

A man resides in a nursing home. The staff are overworked and the man has motor problems as well as other ailments. The staff ties the man down so that they do not have to keep constant watch over him. This restraint is physical abuse.

Example

A couple has been married for more than 50 years. The husband has a problem with alcohol, and whenever he is drunk he beats his wife. This is physical abuse.

Psychological Abuse

Psychological abuse can take the form of exerting control over the individual, thereby restricting or removing the person's free will, as well as

exploitation The unlawful taking of another's property.

name-calling or other forms of degrading the individual without actually inflicting physical harm.

Example

An elderly man is fairly wealthy, and his closest relative is his daughter. The daughter is afraid that her father will give his money to charity, so she threatens him into signing over the bulk of his property to her. She continually calls him old and stupid, and does not let him have more than a few dollars at a time, so that he is virtually a prisoner in his house. The woman is exercising abusive psychological and financial control over her father.

Self-Abuse

Many elderly persons are the victims of self-imposed abuse, because they are unable to provide care for themselves or are unwilling or unable to seek aid. This may be one of the saddest forms of abuse, where the victim is also the abuser, because he or she is no longer capable of caring for himself or herself and there is no one who is able or willing to provide such care.

Example

An elderly woman is widowed. She never had any children, and her closest relatives are distant cousins who live 2,000 miles away. The woman has few financial resources. Her funds are too limited to provide food every day, so she only eats every second day. She is also too afraid to leave her apartment to seek medical care. She feels totally isolated, and does not believe anyone cares about her. The woman is the victim of her own lack of care—of **self-abuse.**

Violation of Rights

Any time a person infringes upon another person's rights, it is a form of abuse. With an older person, caregivers may feel that the older person no longer matters and that therefore they can infringe with impunity on the rights of the elderly individual.

Example

self-abuse Abuse caused by the victim to himself or herself by the failure to provide needed care.

An elderly man is the ward of his son, who has been given authority over his father as a limited guardian. Although the son's legal ability to act is circumscribed, he no longer bothers to limit his actions or determine the father's wishes. The son simply does whatever he wants with respect to his father. This is an infringement of the father's legal rights.

CAUSES OF ABUSE

Various reasons why a person would abuse an older individual have been speculated upon, especially in response to the House committee report mentioned in the introduction. Psychologists, sociologists, and legal professionals have all attempted to analyze the causes of the problem, but no definite answer can be found. However, certain common characteristics have been discerned with respect to such abusers. Note that not all of these characteristics will appear in any one person, and there may be many other causes of abuse that have not yet been identified, or appear so infrequently that they are considered statistically insignificant. The most common identified causes are:

1. The abuser has an innate pathological need to harm others. This is a psychological trait of certain individuals, and the causes of such pathological need are as varied as the individuals with this trait.

2. The caregiver simply breaks down under the strain of caring for the elderly person, and that breakdown results in the abuse of the older individual. This situation occurs most frequently when the caregiver is the only caregiver, and the needs of the elderly person are particularly severe, such as the needs of a person with Alzheimer's disease. If the caregiver does not have periodic relief, the strain may cause him or her to lash out at the subject of the care.

3. The caregiver seeks revenge against the victim for injustice, actual or perceived, that the caregiver believes the victim inflicted on the caregiver in the past. Situations such as a parent bullying or controlling a child may cause the child to bully or control the parent when the child becomes the caregiver.

4. The caregiver may be a substance abuser, and when under the influence of alcohol or drugs may abuse the subject of his or her care.

5. The caregiver may feel isolated and unappreciated, and so manifests his or her frustration by abusing the older person who is in his or her care.

6. The person providing the care may still be under the financial control of the older person, and anger and resentment at this financial dependency may result in an abusive situation. This may arise when the caregiver is an adult child who still resides with the elderly parent and the child has no personal financial resources.

7. Institutional caregivers may have insufficient funds or personnel to provide the necessary care that the institution is required to provide. As more and more older Americans seek residence in managed care facilities, the strain on the facilities' resources may result in willful or negligent neglect.

Simply identifying causes of abuse does not justify that abuse. However, such identification provides help in analyzing situations in which elder abuse is or may become a problem. If the caregiver demonstrates one or more of the listed characteristics, it may be a warning sign that the elderly person is or may become the victim of elder abuse.

LEGISLATIVE RESPONSE TO ELDER ABUSE

The statutory responsibility for the problems of elder abuse lies primarily with the states. In 1987 the federal government passed the **Older Americans Act Amendments**, which required state area agencies on aging to determine the need in the state for protective services to assist the elderly—but Congress provided no funds to accomplish this goal. The federal government has provided only limited funds to the states to combat elder abuse, and although many bills have been introduced into Congress dealing with the situation, they have uniformly failed to pass.

The state response to the problem has also been limited. Most legislatures believe, rightly or wrongly, that problems of elder abuse can be absorbed into other statutes that deal with abuse generally. The most typical state enactments dealing with this area are:

1. Power of attorney statutes. Specific legislation attempts to tighten up the requirements for being given a power of attorney, so that the older individual will have some safeguards against being coerced into signing over authority to another.

2. Guardianship reform. As discussed in preceding chapters, many states have modernized guardianship proceedings, and require the potential ward to appear and be examined by the court before a guardian is appointed. Furthermore, the current trend is to limit the guardian's authority as much as possible, so that the ward can maintain as much control over his or her life as is consistent with maintaining the individual.

3. Protective services. All states have protective services agencies to safeguard persons from "familial" abuse, and elderly persons subject to abuse may apply to these agencies. However, these agencies can only issue injunctions against the abuser or take

Older Americans Act Amendments of 1987 Federal statute requiring state agencies to investigate problems affecting older Americans.

the victim away, which may have little effect in many situations (see following material).

4. Patient's Bill of Rights. This statute, designed to protect persons receiving health care, was discussed in detail in Chapter 2. This law affects elderly patients receiving care in an institutional setting.

5. Domestic violence acts. These acts are designed to protect spouses and lovers from abuse by their partners, and include domestic violence committed between elderly couples.

6. Professional reporting of abuse. Many states require certain professionals to report suspected elder abuse to state agencies. Such reporting requirements apply to health care workers and legal professionals, which can include paralegals. However, although many states grant immunity to the "whistleblower," provided that the report was made in good faith, many professionals, especially employees of managed care facilities, are unwilling to make such reports for fear of reprisal.

7. Civil and criminal statutes. General state laws provide for civil and criminal penalties against persons who are found to have committed abuse, but elderly individuals rarely, if ever, seek redress by this means. Many elderly persons are afraid of initiating criminal charges against the abuser, and many cannot afford or are unaware of civil remedies available to them.

ELDERLY VICTIMS OF CRIME

In 1987, the United States Department of Justice published a report on elderly crime victims. According to the report, elderly crime victims tend to share the following characteristics:

1. They are less likely to defend themselves than are younger victims of crime.

2. They generally suffer greater losses due to fraud than younger fraud victims (the average loss at that date was $250).

3. They are African-American, male, separated or divorced, and city dwellers.

4. They are more likely than younger victims to be attacked by total strangers.

Six percent of all elderly crime victims were victims of violent crimes; 4 percent of this number involved robberies.

In another report, a 1990 Senate committee identified several characteristics typical of the elderly victims of abuse:

1. The most likely elderly victim was a woman over the age of 75 (this differs from the Justice Department report cited at the beginning of this section).
2. The victim was dependent on the abuser for care and protection.
3. The victim was more likely to be abused if the caregiver was addicted to drugs or alcohol.
4. The victim demonstrated "provocative" behavior, such as being extremely overbearing or controlling.

The problem associated with identifying victim characteristics is that many people tend to believe that the victim caused the problem: if the victim simply changed his or her behavior, he or she would no longer be victimized. This argument is totally specious. A victim is *never* to blame; the problem lies with the abuser.

ELDERLY CRIMINALS

On the other side of the coin, it is very rare for an elderly person to be the criminal or the abuser. According to FBI statistics, persons over the age of 65 account for less than 1 percent of all arrests. Of this number, the elderly criminal falls into one of the following categories:

1. The elderly criminal is a recidivist who has committed crimes all of his or her life and simply continues to commit crimes as he or she ages.
2. The elderly criminal is a relapsed offender; someone who committed a crime years ago, but has not done so on a continual basis, who simply commits a crime again.
3. The elderly criminal is a first offender.

Sociologists have speculated that older individuals may commit crimes because of poverty, feelings of neglect, or senility, but no definite reasons have been found.

Example

An elderly woman has very limited income and cannot afford clothing. When her only good pair of shoes falls apart, she shoplifts a new pair because she cannot afford to buy them.

Example
An elderly man feels isolated—his family rarely calls or visits. The man goes to a store to shoplift so that he can get some attention from his family.

Most recently, a new area of concern has been the focus of media attention. Several elderly individuals have been charged and convicted of assisting their spouses, who were suffering from terminal illnesses, to commit suicide. For an elderly individual, even a conviction of manslaughter may carry what is in effect a life sentence. As more and more people demand the right to terminate a painful life, this problem may become more acute. Who is the victim and who is the criminal? (See Chapter 8.)

PROTECTIVE SERVICES

As stated earlier, protective services are rendered by state-supported agencies that receive little federal funding. For the elderly individual to come within the auspices of the protective services agencies, the individual must fall within the particular requirements enacted by his or her state.

All states have defined *elder abuse* as physical detriment or harm caused to an older person, but not every state includes the concept of psychological abuse within its definition. Sexual abuse is usually covered by the protective services statutes, but only a few states consider confinement of the individual to be abuse. Almost every state considers neglect to be covered by the protective services law, and many states require mandatory reporting of any suspected abuse.

The major problem with protective services agencies is the effectiveness of their enforcement remedies. Most state agencies can issue injunctions and orders of protection, but are unable to institute any criminal proceedings against the abuser. Any criminal action, whether for violation of the protective services agency order or for the actual abuse, remains the responsibility of the victim; as previously discussed, many victims are afraid to institute criminal proceedings against the abuser, who is usually the caregiver.

Several states have starting keeping lists of all reports of elder abuse, but these lists are confidential. A majority of the states allow protective services to be provided for an elderly individual even if that person has not consented to such action; this in itself may be considered a form of state-inflicted elder abuse if the older individual is still legally competent to act on his or her own behalf.

ETHICAL CONSIDERATIONS

The legal professional is faced with many ethical considerations when presented with potential elder abuse. All codes of professional conduct require that the legal professional report suspected abuse, but it is not always easy to determine when actual abuse is occurring and when the suspected abuse is merely the result of the person's aging pattern and no abuse is occurring at all. Furthermore, the law office is totally prohibited from acting on behalf of a client who is acting under the influence of another person—the client lacks the requisite free will.

Because legal professionals are automatically deemed to be in a confidential relationship with their clients, it is possible that the legal professional may in fact be the abuser. Law offices can easily influence a client to make particular legal choices. Even if the legal professional believes it is in the best interest of the client, the client may in fact be unduly influenced by the relationship that exists between the client and the office's legal team. The legal assistant must be wary of exerting undue influence over the choices of an elderly client, and must also be alert to any misconduct on the part of the attorney in influencing the client.

Finally, what are the consequences of a being a whistleblower? Even though several states grant immunity from prosecution for whistleblowing, what might be the noncriminal consequences of such action? In many instances people let elder abuse continue because they fear the reprisals resulting from reporting such abuse, such as losing jobs (both current and potential) and the odium that may attach if the suspected abuse does not actually exist.

CHAPTER REVIEW

Elder abuse has become one of the most significant problems affecting the elderly in this country. It is suspected that such abuse has always existed, but only recently has it been identified and reported.

Elder abuse occurs whenever anyone willfully or negligently causes physical or psychological harm to an older individual. Such abuse can take the form of neglect (if the abuser has a legal duty of care with respect to the victim), exploitation, violation of rights, physical harm, or self-abuse by the victims themselves. The causes of abuse are varied, but the legislative response to the problem is minimal at present. There is no federal law specifically addressing the problem of elder abuse, and most state laws simply include older Americans in other statutes, with no specific provisions for the special problems of the elderly.

As more and more Americans fall into the category of elderly, the problem of elder abuse will become an increasingly prevalent problem and area of concern.

KEY TERMS

elder abuse

exploitation

neglect

Older Americans Act
    Amendments of 1987

self-abuse

EXERCISES

1. Discuss what you believe should be the federal response to the problem of elder abuse.

2. An elderly individual who is legally competent refuses to take her prescription medication. Is it elder abuse to force her to take her medicine? Discuss.

3. Give examples of and discuss several forms of elder abuse caused by neglect.

4. Discuss the role of the legal assistant with respect to reporting the suspected abuse of an elderly client.

5. Analyze the characteristics of elderly victims of crime (listed in the chapter) and discuss why you think they share these characteristics.

EDITED JUDICIAL DECISIONS

In re Guardianship/Conservatorship of Denton
190 Ariz. 152, 945 P.2d 1283 (1997)

FACTS AND PROCEDURAL HISTORY

At the age of seventy-four, Frances Louise Denton ("Frances") suffered from a multitude of ailments, including coronary heart disease, congestive heart failure, pericardial effusion, mitral and aortic regurgitation, progressive Alzheimer's-type senile dementia, allergies, incoherence, hallucinations, and incontinence. As Frances' condition worsened, her husband, Fred C. Denton ("Fred"), became unable to care for her, and on August 8, 1993, she was admitted to Paradise Homes # 4 (the "Home"), a licensed adult care home. American Family Care Corporation owned the Home, which held itself out as "Specializing in Long Term Alzheimer's Care" and as "Arizona's leader in Alzheimer's Care."

During her six weeks at the Home, Frances developed several serious conditions allegedly resulting from abusive and negligent treatment by the Home's employees. She fell four or five times; suffered from dehydration, malnutrition, and lanoxin toxicity; and endured a stage four decubitus ulcer, otherwise known as a bed sore. The extent of this sore was so great that surgeons had to use a 20 x 30 centimeter skin graft to cover the exposed bone of her coccyx. After she recuperated, Frances was released from the hospital and transferred to Life Care Center of Paradise Valley. She resided there until her death on November 16, 1995.

During Frances' lifetime, Fred filed a complaint against American Family Care Corporation and others ("defendants"). The complaint contained three counts: negligence, breach of contract, and a statutory cause of action under Arizona's elder abuse statute, A.R.S. § 46-455(B) (1989). Frances died while the complaint was pending, and defendants moved for partial judgment on the pleadings on the claim for damages for pain and suffering. Fred did not contest defendants' assertion that the claim for pain and suffering did not survive on the negligence and contract claims. However, he argued that the claim for pain and suffering did survive under the statutory cause of action for elder abuse. The trial court granted defendants' motion. Fred then filed a petition for special action in the court of appeals, which declined to accept jurisdiction. Fred filed a petition for review, which we granted.

ISSUE

Whether a representative of a victim of elder abuse may recover damages for the victim's pain and suffering pursuant to the elder abuse statute, A.R.S. § 46-455, notwithstanding the death of the victim.

JURISDICTION

Ordinarily we do not accept special action jurisdiction to review the propriety of a pretrial ruling granting partial judgment. See *Munroe v. Galati, 189 Ariz. 113, 938 P.2d 1114, 1116, 1997 Ariz. LEXIS 55 (1997)*. We generally prefer to wait until after final judgment because an interlocutory appeal "often frustrates the expeditious resolution of claims, unnecessarily increases both appellate court caseload and interference with trial judges, harasses litigants with prolonged and costly appeals, and provides piecemeal review." *City of Phoenix v. Yarnell, 184 Ariz. 310, 315, 909 P.2d 377, 382 (1995)*. In exceptional circumstances, however, this court will accept special action jurisdiction to review pretrial partial judgments. See *Munroe, 938 P.2d at 1116; Bledsoe v. Goodfarb, 170 Ariz. 256, 258, 823 P.2d 1264, 1266 (1991)*.

We believe the nature of the present case merits our acceptance of special action jurisdiction prior to final judgment. The elder abuse statute is relatively new, and the issue presented is one of first impression in Arizona. See *Sanchez v. Coxon, 175 Ariz. 93, 94, 854 P.2d 126, 127 (1993)* (holding that special action jurisdiction is appropriate for issues of first impression before this court). Trial courts are unclear as to how to decide this issue, which has resulted in contrary rulings in courts in the same county. The issue in this case is of statewide significance, affecting not just the parties involved, but all incapacitated and vulnerable adults and all adult care homes in our state. See *Bledsoe, 170 Ariz. at 258, 823 P.2d at 1266*. Further, the issue presented here is purely a question of law. See *Cardon v. Cotton Lane Holdings, Inc., 173 Ariz. 203, 210, 841 P.2d 198, 205 (1992)* (factor in court's decision to accept special action jurisdiction was that issue was question of law).

The advancing age of petitioner and others similarly situated also militates in favor of a speedy remedy. Finally, in many elder abuse actions, the claim for pain and suffering will often be the most significant element of damages. Persons bringing such cases usually will not have claims for lost earnings or diminution of earning capacity. Their medical and other special damages will usually be covered by Medicare or other insurance. As a result, an elder abuse case that proceeds to trial without damages available for pain and suffering will often be senseless and futile. In this case, reasonably prompt justice can be satisfactorily obtained only through special action relief. See *Cardon, 173 Ariz. at 210, 841 P.2d at 205*. Accordingly, we granted review and have jurisdiction pursuant to Arizona Constitution article VI, section 5(3) and Arizona Rules of Procedure for Special Action 8(b).

DISCUSSION

Fred contends that the elder abuse statute, A.R.S. § 46-455, expressly provides to victims of elder abuse and their representatives the right to recover damages for pain and suffering, even after the death of the abused victim. In support, Fred cites the wording of the statute, legislative intent, principles of statutory construction, and other states' similar statutes. In contrast, defendants contend that the survival statute, A.R.S. § 14-3110 (1974) (formerly A.R.S. § 14-477), explicitly precludes victims of elder abuse and their representatives from recovering damages for pain and suffering after the death of the abused victim. Like Fred, defendants rely on the wording of the statutes, legislative intent, and principles of statutory construction to support their position. We agree with Fred's reading of the statutes.

Our ultimate goal in statutory interpretation is to discern the intent of the legislature. *State v. Williams, 175 Ariz. 98, 100, 854 P.2d 131, 133 (1993)*. To accomplish this, we look first to the statute's words. *Mail Boxes v. Industrial Comm'n of Ariz., 181 Ariz. 119, 121, 888 P.2d 777, 779 (1995)*.

In 1988, the legislature enacted A.R.S. § 46-455 which criminalized abuse of an incapacitated or vulnerable adult. The legislature clearly perceived elder abuse as a very serious problem, justifying legislative intervention and designated elder abuse a class 5 felony. The next year, the legislature expanded the elder abuse statute by creating a statutory civil cause of action for elder abuse. The legislature thereby distinguished civil actions for elder abuse from other personal injury actions and created a statutory civil cause of ac-

tion for elder abuse. 1989 Ariz. Sess. Laws, ch. 118, § 1. This statutory cause of action is set forth in subsection B of A.R.S. § 46-455:

> B. An incapacitated or vulnerable adult whose life or health is being or has been endangered or injured by neglect, abuse or exploitation may file an action in superior court against any person or enterprise that has been employed to provide care, that has assumed a legal duty to provide care or that has been appointed by a court to provide care to such incapacitated or vulnerable adult for having caused or permitted such conduct.

A.R.S. § 46-455(B).

We believe the plain wording of A.R.S. § 46-455 allows the trial court to award damages for pain and suffering. If the trial court finds liability under this statute, it may order the tortfeasor to pay "actual and consequential damages, as well as punitive damages, costs of suit and reasonable attorney fees, to those persons injured by the conduct described in this section." A.R.S. § 46-455(F)(4). Actual damages are synonymous with compensatory damages. 25 C.J.S. Damages § 2, at 615 (1966); *Arizona Copper Co., Ltd., v. Burciaga, 20 Ariz. 85, 94–95, 177 P. 29, 32–33 (1918)*, overruled in part on other grounds, *Consolidated Ariz. Smelting Co. v. Egich, 22 Ariz. 543, 199 P. 132 (1920)*. Compensatory damages include damages for pain and suffering. *Myers v. Rollette, 103 Ariz. 225, 231, 439 P.2d 497, 503 (1968)*. Thus, actual damages include damages for pain and suffering, and the elder abuse statute affirmatively permits the trial judge to award such damages.

Defendants contend, however, that pain and suffering damages awarded after the victim's death are not compensatory because the person whom the damages would compensate is unable to receive the benefit of the compensation. In support, defendants point out that A.R.S. § 46-455(F)(4) permits the trial court to order damages paid "to those persons injured by the conduct described in this section." However, subsection F is merely a nonexclusive list of orders the trial court may issue. The statute does not purport to prohibit a court from ordering damages to be paid to the representatives of the injured victims, whether or not the victim is deceased.

Defendants further argue that because damages for pain and suffering paid after the victim's death are non-compensatory, they are, in effect, quasi-punitive. Thus, according to Defendants, damages for pain and suffering contravene subsection M of A.R.S. § 46-455, which provides that "[a] civil action authorized by this section is remedial and not punitive." Defendants fail to note, however, that subsection (F)(4) expressly allows trial courts to award punitive damages. A.R.S. § 46-455(F)(4). In any event, as previously discussed, pain and suffering damages are compensatory, not punitive.

Defendants' primary contention is that the survival statute prevents recovery of pain and suffering damages after the death of the victim. The survival statute provides:

> Every cause of action ... shall survive the death of the person entitled thereto or liable therefor, and may be asserted by or against the personal representative of such person, provided that upon the death of the person injured, damages for pain and suffering of such injured person shall not be allowed.

A.R.S. § 14-3110.

The legislature amended the elder abuse statute in 1989. Laws 1989, ch. 118, § 3. In so doing, the legislature included two subsections which we believe resolve all doubt as to whether pain and suffering damages survive the death of a victim of elder abuse. The subsections provide in pertinent part:

> M. A civil action authorized by this section ... is not limited by any other ... provision of law. Civil remedies provided under this title are supplemental and not mutually exclusive.

> * * *

> O. The cause of action or the right to bring a cause of action pursuant to subsection B or C of this section shall not be limited or affected by the death of the incapacitated or vulnerable adult.

A.R.S. §§ 46-455(M) and (O).

We can conceive of no reason for the legislature to include these two subsections, particularly subsection (O), other than to exclude the elder abuse statute from the survival statute's limitations. Application of the survival statute here would contravene the express provision in A.R.S. § 46-455(O) that the cause of action shall not be "limited or affected" by the victim's death.

The legislature's intent and the policy behind the elder abuse statute are clear. Arizona has a substantial population of elderly people, and the legislature was concerned about elder abuse. In civil actions for elder abuse, pain and suffering may be the only compensable damages the victim may recover. Because incapacitated or vulnerable adults are not employed, they cannot recover damages for lost earnings or diminished earning capacity. Because incapacitated or vulnerable adults generally have Medicare, Medicaid coverage, or other insurance, they may not recover for medical expenses. Property damage is generally not an issue in elder abuse cases. As a result, the most likely form of damages recoverable in these cases are for pain and suffering. See generally Susan J. Hemp, Note, The Right to a Remedy: When Should an Abused Nursing Home Resident Sue?, 2 *Elder L.J.* 195, 214 (Fall 1994).

Furthermore, most vulnerable or incapacitated adults are near the end of their lives. Under defendants' theory, the tortfeasor would have a great incentive to delay litigation until the victim dies. If we were to ascribe to defendants' theory, the policy of the elder abuse statute would not be furthered.

Moreover, Arizona is not alone in enacting this type of legislation. In 1991, California passed legislation preserving an elder abuse victim's right to recover pain and suffering damages, despite the victim's death. See Cal. Welf. & Inst. Code § 15657(b) (West Supp. 1997); *ARA Living Centers—Pacific, Inc. v. Superior Ct.*, 18 Cal. App. 4th 1556, 23 Cal. Rptr. 2d 224 (1993).

Because the language of the statute is clear and unambiguous, we need not delve into rules of statutory construction to resolve this case. *State v. Reynolds*, 170 Ariz. 233, 234, 823 P.2d 681, 682 (1992). We do note, however, that when there is conflict between two statutes, "the more recent, specific statute governs over the older, more general statute." *Lemons v. Superior Ct. of Gila County, 141 Ariz. 502, 505, 687 P.2d 1257, 1260 (1984).* The elder abuse statute covers a limited class (incapacitated or vulnerable adults) and limited causes of action (abuse, neglect, or exploitation). In contrast, the survival statute applies to all causes of action and all parties injured. Furthermore, the provisions of the elder abuse statute under consideration here were enacted twenty-four years after the survival statute took effect. Thus, under traditional rules of statutory construction, the newer, specific elder abuse statute governs over the older, general survivor statute.

CONCLUSION AND DISPOSITION

The legislature intended to provide victims of elder abuse or their representatives with the ability to recover damages for pain and suffering even if the victim dies prior to judgment. This intent is evident from the plain words and the underlying policy of the elder abuse statute. We hold that representatives of elder abuse victims may recover damages for pain and suffering endured by the victims, notwithstanding the death of the victims. The partial judgment on the pleadings in favor of defendants is reversed, and this case is remanded to the trial court for further proceedings consistent with this opinion.

Boyce v. Fernandes
77 F.3d 946 (7th Cir. 1996)

Claudine Boyce appeals from the dismissal, on summary judgment, of a damages suit for false arrest that she brought against Vera Fernandes, a Peoria police officer, and the City of Peoria. The suit against Fernandes is based exclusively on *42 U.S.C. § 1983* and was dismissed on the ground of public officers' immunity. A supplemental state law claim naming both Fernandes and the City as defendants was also dismissed.

Where the only issue bearing on immunity is whether the defendant had probable cause to make the search or arrest that is challenged, merits and immunity merge; the dispositive question is simply whether the defendant did have probable cause. So at least we held in *Mahoney v. Kesery, 976 F.2d 1054, 1057–58 (7th Cir. 1992),* and implied in *Maxwell v. City of Indianapolis, 998 F.2d 431, 435–36 (7th Cir. 1993).* But *Maltby v. Winston, 36 F.3d 548, 554–55 and n.7 (7th Cir. 1994),* suggests, in great tension with these decisions and in reliance on dicta in *Hunter v. Bryant, 502 U.S. 224, 227, 112 S. Ct. 534, 116 L. Ed. 2d 589 (1991) (per curiam); Malley v. Briggs, 475 U.S. 335, 106 S. Ct. 1092, 89 L. Ed. 2d 271 (1986), and Jones v. City of Chicago, 856 F.2d 985, 994 (7th Cir. 1988) (all cases discussed, however, in Mahoney, 976 F.2d at 1059),* that the immunity doctrine may give public officers an additional layer of protection beyond what is implicit in the right to arrest on probable cause that may well turn out to be mistaken. This is a surprising suggestion. The modern conception of public officers' immunity is that it is designed to protect public officers from their failures to anticipate changes in the law, *Harlow v. Fitzgerald, 457 U.S. 800, 102 S. Ct. 2727, 73 L. Ed. 2d 396 (1982); Jones v. City of Chicago, supra, 856 F.2d at 994,* and the concept of probable cause has not changed in a great many years. In addition, we suspect that the additional layer of protection implied by the concept of probable cause to believe one has probable cause to arrest or search someone may have a merely metaphysical or conceptual existence; human ability to make fine distinctions is limited. But we need not attempt to sort out the tangle in this case—and indeed if we are right about the merely conceptual significance of the additional layer the tangle may never have to be sorted out because no case may ever turn on its untangling. It is apparent that Fernandes had probable cause to make the arrest, and this makes the issue of immunity academic.

Elder abuse is a growing problem in this country because of the growing number of elderly people. Like child abuse, elder abuse is a difficult crime to detect and prosecute. In both types of case the victim is often an unreliable witness because of limited mental capacity—undeveloped in the case of the child, impaired by old age in the case of the elder. Claudine Boyce was employed by a woman of 75 named Auda Tunis who was afflicted by senile dementia caused either by alcoholism or by Parkinson's disease. Detective Fernandes began her investigation of Boyce at the instance of Tunis's granddaughter, who told the detective that she thought Boyce might be stealing from her grandmother. The granddaughter had discovered that all the furniture had been removed from Tunis's home and that she had been placed in a nursing home. The granddaughter had visited her grandmother in the nursing home and found that she seemed confused at first but later recognized the granddaughter and her husband. Tunis told them she did not know why she was there, that Boyce had badgered her into signing what she thought was a document that said merely that she would think about signing a power of attorney, and that she was ashamed of the situation she was in and had not wanted to complain to the granddaughter.

The nursing home had told the granddaughter that Tunis had granted Boyce (who had signed Tunis into the nursing home) both a general power of attorney and a health-care power of attorney. Detective Fernandes therefore called the lawyer who had prepared the powers of attorney. He expressed surprise that Tunis had a granddaughter—he had thought she had no living relatives. Fernandes interviewed employees of the nursing home. They told her that Tunis had been in a shocking condition when admitted to the home, with multiple bruises and lacerations, and that the jewelry Tunis had worn on her previous admission to the nursing home was gone. Fernandes reported that the staff had told her that "Tunis seemed to be in a state of shock and her condition was completely opposite of the first time she had been admitted to the home several weeks prior. She now appeared confused and withdrawn and her clothing was unkempt and old appearing." The staff suspected elder abuse and

decided to institute proceedings to obtain a new power of attorney, in which the nursing home would be the power holder.

Fernandes then spoke to Tunis herself, who in this interview and a subsequent one on December 26 told Fernandes that Boyce had threatened, slapped, and shoved her, had plied her with liquor, and might have (subsequent investigation revealed that she had) deposited her social security checks, without her authorization, in a joint checking account in Boyce's and her name; that Boyce had taken Tunis's furniture and other personal property without her authorization and Tunis did not know what she had done with it. Two days later, December 28, Fernandes learned that Tunis's Cadillac was parked in Boyce's driveway and that the car, formerly registered to Tunis's deceased husband, was now registered to Boyce. A few days later Fernandes arrested Boyce, without a warrant, for the theft of the Cadillac, a felony. Boyce was held in the county jail for 42 hours before being released on bond. Subsequent investigation brought to light that Boyce had in all likelihood forged a bill of sale of the Cadillac to herself for $100. Nevertheless, she has not been prosecuted.

Accusations by demented persons must always be viewed with a certain skepticism, especially since paranoid suspicions are a common incident of dementia. It would have been imprudent for the detective to have reposed automatic, unquestioning credence in Tunis's accusations against Boyce. She did not. Tunis's accusations were corroborated by the granddaughter, by the staff of the nursing home, and by the lawyer, who was upset to learn that Tunis had granted a power of attorney to her housekeeper when (as Boyce well knew) she had an adult granddaughter. Further corroboration came from the fact that Boyce, though knowing of Tunis's granddaughter, had never informed her that Boyce had a power of attorney, that she was managing Tunis's affairs, and that she was preparing Tunis's property for sale. There thus were grounds for suspicion that Boyce was trying to conceal what she was doing from Tunis's only relative.

Tunis's accusations themselves, moreover, had a degree of particularity that reduced the likelihood that they were merely senile fantasies. It is a common mistake to exaggerate the degree to which senile dementia renders an individual mentally incompetent. There are different types and severities of dementia. The most serious—senile dementia of the Alzheimer's type—is progressive. Some persons afflicted with it exhibit only short-term memory loss and occasional disorientation, while others are so far demented as to have forgotten their own name, to have lost the power of speech, and to be unable to recognize their spouse or their children. See generally Fred Plum, "Dementia," in 1 Encyclopedia of Neuroscience 309 (George Adelman ed. 1987). A further complication is that, until the terminal stage that we have just described is reached, the severity of the dementia varies from day to day, even from hour to hour. Mrs. Tunis apparently had good days and bad days. The second interview with Fernandes evidently took place on a good day, because she spoke coherently and precisely, exhibiting a good memory, and nothing she said was bizarre or seemed delusional. Contract law, property law, and criminal law alike have rejected a per se rule that demented persons are legally incompetent. See, e.g., *United States v. Rainone, 32 F.3d 1203, 1208 (7th Cir. 1994); In re Estate of Peterson, 77 Nev. 87, 360 P.2d 259, 267 (1961); In re Will of Wicker, 15 Wis. 2d 86, 112 N.W.2d 137, 139 (1961); O'Brien v. Belsma, 108 Or. App. 500, 816 P.2d 665 (1991); Feiden v. Feiden, 151 A.D.2d 889, 542 N.Y.S.2d 860, 862 (1989); Weir by Gasper v. Ciao, 364 Pa. Super. 490, 528 A.2d 616 (1987); Wright v. Kenney, 746 S.W.2d 626, 631 (Mo. Ct. App. 1988).* We do not think there should be a different rule for witnesses.

To all this Boyce replies that she had a power of attorney and thus was authorized to take and sell Tunis's personal property. She says that she had stored the furniture in her own garage in preparation for sale, and that if she sold the Cadillac to herself at its market value and gave the proceeds to Tunis she was doing nothing more than transforming Tunis's property into a more convenient

form. She adds that if the power of attorney was invalid because Tunis was incompetent at the time she signed it, or even if it was abused, these things would not in themselves convict the power holder of theft in exercising it. And this of course is true. But this is just to say that Fernandes did not have conclusive proof of the theft of the Cadillac. She had a strong, reasonably grounded suspicion and that is all that is required for probable cause. The intimation that a power of attorney immunizes the power holder from a charge of conversion is nonsense. The power creates a fiduciary relation, *In re Estate of Rybolt, 258 Ill. App. 3d 886, 631 N.E.2d 792, 795, 197 Ill. Dec. 570 (1994),* and thus an opportunity for abuse by the power holder that is at best tortious and at worst criminal. We were disturbed by the insistence by Boyce's lawyer at argument that the power holder is authorized to convert to her own use any of the grantor's property that has no market value. Although market value is relevant to the gravity of a theft and therefore the length of the thief's sentence, the theft of an item that has no market value is still theft, *Hessel v. O'Hearn, 977 F.2d 299, 303 (7th Cir. 1992),* and neither explicitly nor implicitly does a power of attorney authorize the power holder to steal from his grantor. *In re Estate of Rybolt, supra, 631 N.E.2d at 795; People v. Wright, 239 Ill. App. 3d 738, 607 N.E.2d 355, 180 Ill. Dec. 461 (1993); Walch v. State, 909 P.2d 1184, 1996 Nev. LEXIS 4, 1996 WL 5200 (Nev. 1996); Dayton Bar Ass'n v. Gross, 62 Ohio St. 3d 224, 581 N.E.2d 520 (1991), reinstated, 651 N.E.2d 1298 (Ohio 1995); State v. Hunt, 75 Wash. App. 795, 880 P.2d 96 (1994).* Indeed, the breach of a fiduciary obligation to an elderly person is explicitly a crime in Illinois. 720 ILCS 5/16-1.3(a), (c). No doubt this sort of thing is common, which may be why the legislature decided to single it out for specific prohibition, but crime does not become legal by being widespread.

The lawyer also disparaged the evidence of physical abuse on the ground that his client had not been arrested for such abuse. But the evidence of abuse, like the evidence of the unexplained disappearance of the jewelry and Boyce's failure to disclose to the lawyer that Mrs. Tunis had an adult granddaughter, cast light on Boyce's probable intentions in registering the Cadillac in her own name. The facts turned up in the investigation that preceded her arrest, when they are taken as a whole, would have indicated to a reasonable police officer that Boyce was trying to despoil a vulnerable old woman. The protection of the vulnerable is a noble duty of government. Fernandes is rather to be commended for the speed and thoroughness of her investigation than condemned for having acted before she had assembled conclusive proof of criminal misconduct. The fact that in the end Boyce was not prosecuted does not establish the absence of probable cause, and not only because the legal standard and the evidentiary requirements for probable cause are more stringent at the preliminary hearing than at the arrest stage, the point emphasized in *Williams v. Kobel, 789 F.2d 463, 469 (7th Cir. 1986)*. The majority of lawfully arrested persons are not prosecuted. Prosecutors' time and other resources are severely limited in relation to the amount of crime in this country, and prosecution may be declined merely because the evidence of guilt is not overwhelming. The State's Attorney may have believed this to be such a case or may have thought that Boyce's arrest would suffice to deter her and perhaps other caretakers of the elderly from abusing their positions. Boyce is herself an elderly woman and prosecuting her for elder abuse might strike a jury as an uncomfortable irony.

It is unfortunate that Boyce, herself a woman of 63 when arrested, was kept in jail for 42 hours. Fernandes cannot be criticized for this sequel to the arrest, however, for she was required to hand Boyce over to the sheriff, and he administers the county jail. Given the overcrowding of American jails, we venture to suggest that a practice of automatic incarceration of all arrested persons, regardless of circumstances, is as wasteful as it is uncivilized. Which is not to say that it entitles the plaintiff to any relief—and certainly not against Detective Fernandes.

We turn last and briefly to the supplemental claim, a claim for false arrest under state law that was dismissed on the ground that Fernandes had not acted willfully and wantonly. 745 ILCS 10/2-202. The normal practice of course is to relinquish jurisdiction over a supplemental claim when the main claim is dismissed before trial, but if the supplemental claim is easily shown to have no possible merit, dismissing it on the merits is a time saver for everybody. *Korzen v. Local Union 705, 75 F.3d 285, slip op. at 4–5, 1996 U.S. App. LEXIS 1037 (7th Cir. 1996)*. That is the case here. The same evidence that shows beyond any possibility of doubt that Fernandes acted reasonably in arresting Boyce shows that the arrest was not willful and wanton. True, the precise force of the term "willful and wanton" in the law of Illinois is unclear. It may be little stronger than negligence. *Davis v. United States, 716 F.2d 418, 425–26 (7th Cir. 1983)*. But there is no evidence even of negligence here. See *Gordon v. Degelmann, 29 F.3d 295, 299 (7th Cir. 1994)*, applying the Illinois public officers' tort immunity statute in a false arrest case such as this. And the state law claim against the City, which is based on respondeat superior, falls with the claim against Fernandes.

AFFIRMED.

CHAPTER

8

ASSISTANCE FOR THE ELDERLY

INTRODUCTION

The law office provides various services with respect to assisting the elderly client. Of course, the office may provide general legal counsel, but the legal professional, in many instances, is also the first resource an elderly client seeks out to determine what federal and state programs exist to assist in various areas of the client's life. It is important that the paralegals in a law office familiarize themselves with the various organizations that can provide guidance and assistance, both to the legal team and to the elderly client.

This chapter references various resources that are available to the legal professional and the elderly individual to assist in obtaining all rights to which the elderly American may be entitled, as discussed in the previous chapters in this text.

FEDERAL AND STATE ASSISTANCE

Except for the specifically enumerated federally operated programs, such as Medicare, Medicaid, Social Security, and so on, the majority of assistance available to the older American lies at the state and private level. Even the various federal statutes previously discussed simply create or define the rights of the elderly, and mandate implementation of their provisions at the state level. However, several federal agencies do provide "hotlines" to guide persons with inquiries to the appropriate agencies to handle their questions. These hotlines are listed later in this chapter.

Most governmental agencies that can provide assistance to the elderly are at the state level. Each state agency can provide assistance only to persons who are within its jurisdiction (state) or who are receiving services from organizations within its jurisdiction. Consequently, the specific agencies operating in each state must be individually investigated. Later in the chapter a listing of the various state agencies on aging is given.

On the local level, there are several resources that should be noted:

- banks and financial institutions that can arrange for mortgages for the elderly

- ambulance services for emergency situations

- local programs such as "Meals on Wheels" that can assist elderly individuals in receiving proper nutrition

- local agencies that can provide day health care workers on a permanent or temporary basis

- insurance providers that can assist in determining and acquiring appropriate life and health insurance policies

- church and other organizations that provide various services for the elderly

- local offices of federal and state agencies that provide services and benefits for the elderly

- local protective services agencies

- law offices that specialize in elder law, as well as legal clinics associated with local law schools that can provide no- or low-cost legal services to the elderly

- local offices of various organizations that provide services and information for persons with various diseases and disabilities, such as Alzheimer's, cancer, and the like.

The law office that provides legal counseling for the elderly should maintain a current listing of all such organizations in the area.

THE OLDER AMERICANS ACT

As previously discussed, in 1965 the federal government promulgated the Older Americans Act, which authorizes federal grants to state agencies that provide specific services for the elderly. The types of services so funded include community planning, legal assistance, and advocacy for the rights of elderly Americans.

Pursuant to this act, each state is required to create a program that provides for legal assistance regarding elder law rights. However, the funding for these programs has been cut back. The state agencies on aging created pursuant to this statute are listed in the next section.

ORGANIZATIONS AND RESOURCES

The following compilation is a basic list of resources that provide assistance to the elderly.

Health Care (Chapter 2)

    Medicare Hotline: 800-638-6833

    Medicare Fraud Hotline: 800-368-5779

    Medicare-Medicaid Assistance Program, AARP:
        1909 K Street, NW
        Washington, DC 20049
        202-729-4143

    Medicare Supplemental (Medigap) Insurance:
        National Insurance Consumer Helpline: 800-942-4242
        American Board of Medical Specialists (Doctor
            Certification):   800-776-2378
        Community Heath Assessment Program: 800-847-8480

Employment (Chapter 3)

    Discrimination Complaints:
        EEOC
        1801 L Street, NW
        Washington, DC 20507
        800-669-EEOC

Americans with Disabilities Act:
United States Department of Justice
Civil Rights Division
Coordination & Review Section
P.O. Box 66118
Washington, DC 20035-6118
202-544-0301

National Association of Protections & Advocacy Agencies
900 Second Street, NE, Suite 211
Washington, DC 20002
202-408-9514

Social Security and Disability Hotline: 800-772-1213

Housing (Chapter 4)

Reverse Mortgages:
National Committee for Home Equity Conversion
7373 147th Street West, Suite 115
Apple Valley, MN 55124
612-953-4474

AARP Home Equity Conversion Service
1909 K Street, NW
Washington, DC 2004
202-434-6030

Federal National Mortgage Association: 800-7-FANNIE

Fair Housing and Discrimination Complaints:
United States Department of Housing and
    Urban Development
Office of Fair Housing & Equal Opportunity, Rm. 5204
Washington, DC 20410
800-669-977

Regional Disability & Business Technical Assistance
Center: 800-949-4232

Shared Housing Resource Center
136½ Main Street
Montpelier, VT 08602
802-223-2627

Guardianship and Disabled Children (Chapter 5)

Children of Aging Parents:
1609 Woodburne Road, Suite 302A
Levittown, PA 199057
215-945-6900

National Information Center for Children & Youth with
Disabilities: 800-628-1696

Health Resource Center for People with
Disabilities: 800-544-3284

American Bar Association
Committee on Legal Problems for the Elderly
1800 M Street, NW
Washington, DC 20036
202-331-2297

Estate Planning (Chapter 6)

Choice in Dying
200 Varick Street
New York, NY 10014
212-366-5540
800-989-WILL

Legal Counsel for the Elderly/AARP
1909 K Street, NW
Washington, DC 20049
202-833-6720

National Academy of Elder Law Attorneys
1604 North Country Club Road
Tucson, AZ 8571
602-881-4005

Elder Abuse (Chapter 7)

National Aging Resource Center on Elder Abuse (NARCEA)
810 First Street, NE, Suite 500
Washington, DC 20002
202-682-2470

State Offices on Aging (by State)

Commission on Aging
136 Catona Street
Montgomery, AL 36103
205-261-5743

Older Alaskans Commission
Department of Administration, Pouch C
Juneau, AK 99811-0209

Aging and Adult Administration
Department of Economic Security
1400 West Washington Street
Phoenix, AZ 85007
602-542-4446

Division of Aging, Adult Services
Department of Social Rehabilitative Service
Donaghey Building, Suite 1417
7th and Main Street
Little Rock, AR 72201
501-682-8500

Department on Aging
1600 K Street
Sacramento, CA 95814
916-322-5290

Aging and Adult Services Division
2200 West Alameda Street
Denver, CO 80223
303-936-3666

Department on Aging
175 Main Street
Hartford, CT 06106
203-566-3238

Division on Aging
Department of Health and Social Services
1901 North Dupont Highway
New Castle, DE 19720
302-421-6791

Office on Aging
1424 K Street, NW
Washington, DC 20005
202-724-5625

Program Office of Aging and Services
Department of Health and Rehabilitation Services
1317 Winewood Boulevard
Tallahassee, FL 32399-0700
904-488-8922

Office of Aging
Room 632
878 Peachtree Street, NE
Atlanta, GA 30309
404-894-5333

Executive Office on Aging
Office of the Governor, Room 241
335 Merchant Street
Honolulu, HI 96813
808-548-2593

Office on Aging
   Room 108, Capitol Building
   Boise, ID 82720
   208-334-3833

Department on Aging
   421 East Capitol Avenue
   Springfield, IL 62701
   217-785-2870

Department of Aging and Adult Community Services
   251 North Illinois Street
   PO Box 7083
   Indianapolis, IN 46207-7083
   317-232-7006

Department of Elder Affairs
   Jewett Building, Suite 236
   914 Grand Avenue
   Des Moines, IA 50309
   515-281-5187

Department on Aging
   Docking State Office Building, Room 122-S
   915 SW Harrison Street
   Topeka, KS 66612-1500
   913-296-4986

Division for Aging Services
   Department of Human Resources
   CHE Building, 6th Floor
   275 East Main Street
   Frankfort, KY 40621
   502-564-6930

Office of Elderly Affairs
   PO Box 80374
   Baton Rouge, LA 70898-0374
   504-925-1700

Bureau of Maine Elderly
   Department of Human Services
   State House-Station #11
   1 Amherst Street
   Augusta, ME 04333
   207-289-2561

Office on Aging
   State Office Building
   301 West Preston Street, Room 1004
   Baltimore, MD 21201
   301-225-1100

Executive Office of Elder Affairs
38 Chauncy Street
Boston, MA 02111
617-727-7750

Office of Services to the Aging
PO Box 30029
Lansing, MI 48909
517-373-8230

Board on Aging
444 Lafayette Road
St. Paul, MN 55155-3843
612-296-2544

Council on Aging
421 West Pascagoula Street
Jackson, MS 39203
601-949-2070

Division on Aging Department
PO Box 1337
2701 West Main Street
Jefferson City, MO 65102
314-751-3082

Community Services Division
PO Box 4210
Helena, MT 59604
800-332-2272

Department on Aging
301 Centennial Mall South
PO Box 95044
Lincoln, NE 68509
402-471-2306

Division on Aging
Department of Human Resources
505 East King Street, Room 101
Carson City, NV 89710
702-885-4210

Council on Aging
6 Hazen Drive
Concord, NH 03301
603-271-4680

Division on Aging
Department of Community Affairs
101 South Broad Street CN807
Trenton, NJ 08625-0807
609-292-4833

State Agency on Aging
    224 East Palace Avenue, 4th Floor
    La Villa Rivera Building
    Santa Fe, NM 87501
    505-827-7640

Office for the Aging
    Empire State Plaza
    Agency Building #2
    Albany, NY 12223
    518-474-4425

Division on Aging
    1985 Umpstead Drive
    Raleigh, NC 27603
    919-733-3983

Aging Services
    State Capitol Building
    600 East Boulevard Avenue
    Bismarck, ND 58505-0250
    701-224-2577

Department on Aging
    50 West Broad Street, 9th Floor
    Columbus, OH 43215
    614-466-5500

Special Unit on Aging
    Department of Human Services
    PO Box 25352
    Oklahoma City, OK 73125
    405-521-2281

Senior Services Division
    313 Public Service Building
    Salem, OR 97310
    503-378-4728

Department on Aging
    231 State Street
    Harrisburg, PA 17101-1195
    717-783-1550

Department of Elderly Affairs
    160 Pine Street
    Providence, RI 02903
    401-277-2858

Commission on Aging
400 Arbor Lake Drive
Columbia, SC 29223
803-735-0210

Office of Adult Services
700 Governors Drive
Pierre, SD 575011-2291
605-773-3656

Commission on Aging
706 Church Street, Suite 201
Nashville, TN 37219-5573
615-741-2056

Department on Aging
PO Box 12786 Capitol Station
Austin, TX 78711
512-444-2727

Division of Aging and Adult Services
Department of Social Services
120 North 200 West, Room 401
Salt Lake City, UT 841103
801-538-3910

Office on Aging
103 South Main Street
Waterbury, VT 05676
802-241-2400

Department on Aging
700 East Franklin Street, 10th Floor
Richmond, VA 23219
804-225-2271

Aging and Adult Services Administration
Department of Social and Health Services
Mail Stop OB-44A
Olympia, WA 98504
206-586-3768

Commission on Aging
Holly Grove-State Capitol
Charleston, WV 25305
304-348-3317

Commission on Aging
217 South Hamilton, Suite 300
Madison, WI 53703
608-266-2536

Commission on Aging
139 Hathaway Building
Cheyenne, WY 82002
307-777-7986

ETHICAL CONSIDERATIONS

Recently, considerable media attention has focused on the ethical and legal problems associated with assisted suicide. An elderly individual whose physical state has so deteriorated that he or she has a poor or nonexistent quality of life may wish to terminate his or her existence. First and foremost, it must be determined that the individual is mentally competent to make such a choice, or, if a guardian has been appointed for the person, that the guardian would have legal authority to perform such an act (highly unlikely). Once the individual's mental condition has been determined, moral, ethical, and legal decisions must still be made to determine whether assisted suicide is appropriate. Several judicial decisions have addressed this issue (see the edited judicial decisions at the end of this chapter). Assisted suicide may not be appropriate assistance for the elderly client, and most legal professionals would strongly counsel against it.

CHAPTER REVIEW

This chapter is designed to provide some preliminary and basic resources to assist the law office in providing adequate and appropriate counsel for the elderly client. The list is, of necessity, only partial, and each law office should compile a list appropriate for its client base and locality.

EXERCISES

1. Locate the addresses and telephone numbers of organizations in your area that provide services for the elderly.

2. What is your opinion of assisted suicide? Should an individual who is mentally competent have the legal right to terminate his or her life if he or she is suffering with a terminal illness? Discuss.

3. What is your opinion of the federal government's lack of funding for agencies that assist the elderly? Discuss.

4. Create a list of organizations that lobby for the rights of the elderly.

5. Discuss some of the benefits and detriments of a law office specializing in elder law.

EDITED JUDICIAL DECISIONS

Washington v. Glucksberg
521 U.S. 702, 117 S. Ct. 2258, 138 L. Ed. 2d 772 (1997)

OPINION BY: REHNQUIST

The question presented in this case is whether Washington's prohibition against "causing" or "aiding" a suicide offends the Fourteenth Amendment to the United States Constitution. We hold that it does not.

It has always been a crime to assist a suicide in the State of Washington. In 1854, Washington's first Territorial Legislature outlawed "assisting another in the commission of self-murder." Today, Washington law provides: "A person is guilty of promoting a suicide attempt when he knowingly causes or aids another person to attempt suicide." Wash. Rev. Code 9A.36.060(1) (1994). "Promoting a suicide attempt" is a felony, punishable by up to five years' imprisonment and up to a $10,000 fine. §§ 9A.36.060(2) and 9A.20.021 (1)(c). At the same time, Washington's Natural Death Act, enacted in 1979, states that the "withholding or withdrawal of life-sustaining treatment" at a patient's direction "shall not, for any purpose, constitute a suicide." Wash. Rev. Code § 70.122.070(1).

Petitioners in this case are the State of Washington and its Attorney General. Respondents Harold Glucksberg, M.D., Abigail Halperin, M.D., Thomas A. Preston, M.D., and Peter Shalit, M.D., are physicians who practice in Washington. These doctors occasionally treat terminally ill, suffering patients, and declare that they would assist these patients in ending their lives if not for Washington's assisted-suicide ban. In January 1994, respondents, along with three gravely ill, pseudonymous plaintiffs who have since died and Compassion in Dying, a nonprofit organization that counsels people considering physician-assisted suicide, sued in the United States District Court, seeking a declaration that Wash Rev. Code § 9A.36.060(1) (1994) is, on its face, unconstitutional. *Compassion in Dying v. Washington, 850 F. Supp. 1454, 1459 (W.D. Wash. 1994).*

The plaintiffs asserted "the existence of a liberty interest protected by the Fourteenth Amendment which extends to a personal choice by a mentally competent, terminally ill adult to commit physician-assisted suicide." *Id., at 1459.* Relying primarily on *Planned Parenthood v. Casey, 505 U.S. 833 (1992),* and *Cruzan v. Director, Missouri Dept. of Health, 497 U.S. 261 (1990),* the District Court agreed, *850 F. Supp., at 1459–62,* and concluded that Washington's assisted-suicide ban is unconstitutional because it "places an undue burden on the exercise of [that] constitutionally protected liberty interest." *Id., at 1465.* The District Court also decided that the Washington statute violated the Equal Protection Clause's requirement that " 'all persons similarly situated . . . be treated alike.' " *Id., at 1466* (quoting *Cleburne v. Cleburne Living Center, Inc., 473 U.S. 432, 439 (1985)).*

A panel of the Court of Appeals for the Ninth Circuit reversed, emphasizing that "in the two hundred and five years of our existence no constitutional right to aid in killing oneself has ever been asserted and upheld by a court of final jurisdiction." *Compassion in Dying v. Washington, 49 F.3d 586, 591 (1995)*. The Ninth Circuit reheard the case en banc, reversed the panel's decision, and affirmed the District Court. *Compassion in Dying v. Washington, 79 F.3d 790, 798 (1996)*. Like the District Court, the en banc Court of Appeals emphasized our *Casey* and *Cruzan* decisions. *79 F.3d, at 813–16.* The court also discussed what it described as "historical" and "current societal attitudes" toward suicide and assisted suicide, *id., at 806–12,* and concluded that "the Constitution encompasses a due process liberty interest in controlling the time and manner of one's death—that there is, in short, a constitutionally-recognized 'right to die.'" *Id., at 816.* After "weighing and then balancing" this interest against Washington's various interests, the court held that the State's assisted-suicide ban was unconstitutional "as applied to terminally ill competent adults who wish to hasten their deaths with medication prescribed by their physicians." *Id., at 836, 837.* The court did not reach the District Court's equal-protection holding. *Id., at 838.* We granted certiorari, and now reverse.

I

We begin, as we do in all due-process cases, by examining our Nation's history, legal traditions, and practices. See, e.g., *Casey, 505 U.S. at 849–50; Cruzan, 497 U.S. at 269–79; Moore v. East Cleveland, 431 U.S. 494, 503 (1977)* (plurality opinion) (noting importance of "careful 'respect for the teachings of history'"). In almost every State—indeed, in almost every western democracy—it is a crime to assist a suicide. The States' assisted-suicide bans are not innovations. Rather, they are longstanding expressions of the States' commitment to the protection and preservation of all human life. *Cruzan, 497 U.S. at 280* ("The States—indeed, all civilized nations—demonstrate their commitment to life by treating homicide as a serious crime. Moreover, the majority of States in this country have laws imposing criminal penalties on one who assists another to commit suicide"); see *Stanford v. Kentucky, 492 U.S.*

361, 373 (1989) ("The primary and most reliable indication of [a national] consensus is … the pattern of enacted laws"). Indeed, opposition to and condemnation of suicide—and, therefore, of assisting suicide—are consistent and enduring themes of our philosophical, legal, and cultural heritages. See generally, Marzen, O'Dowd, Crone & Balch, Suicide: A Constitutional Right?, *24 Duquesne L. Rev. 1, 17–56 (1985)* (hereinafter Marzen); New York State Task Force on Life and the Law, When Death Is Sought: Assisted Suicide and Euthanasia in the Medical Context 77–82 (May 1994) (hereinafter New York Task Force).

More specifically, for over 700 years, the Anglo-American common-law tradition has punished or otherwise disapproved of both suicide and assisting suicide. *Cruzan, 497 U.S. at 294–95* (SCALIA, J., concurring). In the 13th century, Henry de Bracton, one of the first legal-treatise writers, observed that "just as a man may commit felony by slaying another so may he do so by slaying himself." 2 Bracton on Laws and Customs of England 423 (f. 150) (G. Woodbine ed., S. Thorne transl., 1968). The real and personal property of one who killed himself to avoid conviction and punishment for a crime were forfeit to the king; however, thought Bracton, "if a man slays himself in weariness of life or because he is unwilling to endure further bodily pain . . . [only] his movable goods [were] confiscated." *Id., at 423–24 (f. 150).* Thus, "the principle that suicide of a sane person, for whatever reason, was a punishable felony was … introduced into English common law." Centuries later, Sir William Blackstone, whose Commentaries on the Laws of England not only provided a definitive summary of the common law but was also a primary legal authority for 18th and 19th century American lawyers, referred to suicide as "self-murder" and "the pretended heroism, but real cowardice, of the Stoic philosophers, who destroyed themselves to avoid those ills which they had not the fortitude to endure … ." 4 W. Blackstone, Commentaries * 189. Blackstone emphasized that "the law has … ranked [suicide] among the highest crimes," *ibid.,* although, anticipating later developments, he conceded that the harsh and shameful punishments imposed for suicide "border a little upon severity." *Id.,* at * 190.

For the most part, the early American colonies adopted the common-law approach. For example, the legislators of the Providence Plantations, which would later become Rhode Island, declared, in 1647, that "self-murder is by all agreed to be the most unnatural, and it is by this present Assembly declared, to be that, wherein he that doth it, kills himself out of a premeditated hatred against his own life or other humor: ... his goods and chattels are the king's custom, but not his debts nor lands; but in case he be an infant, a lunatic, mad or distracted man, he forfeits nothing." The Earliest Acts and Laws of the Colony of Rhode Island and Providence Plantations 1647–1719, p. 19 (J. Cushing ed. 1977). Virginia also required ignominious burial for suicides, and their estates were forfeit to the crown. A. Scott, Criminal Law in Colonial Virginia 108, and n.93, 198, and n.15 (1930).

Over time, however, the American colonies abolished these harsh common-law penalties. William Penn abandoned the criminal-forfeiture sanction in Pennsylvania in 1701, and the other colonies (and later, the other States) eventually followed this example. *Cruzan,* 497 U.S. at 294 (SCALIA, J., concurring). Zephaniah Swift, who would later become Chief Justice of Connecticut, wrote in 1796 that

> there can be no act more contemptible, than to attempt to punish an offender for a crime, by exercising a mean act of revenge upon lifeless clay, that is insensible of the punishment. There can be no greater cruelty, than the inflicting [of] a punishment, as the forfeiture of goods, which must fall solely on the innocent offspring of the offender. ... [Suicide] is so abhorrent to the feelings of mankind, and that strong love of life which is implanted in the human heart, that it cannot be so frequently committed, as to become dangerous to society. There can of course be no necessity of any punishment.

2 Z. Swift, A System of the Laws of the State of Connecticut 304 (1796).

This statement makes it clear, however, that the movement away from the common law's harsh sanctions did not represent an acceptance of suicide; rather, as Chief Justice Swift observed, this change reflected the growing consensus that it was unfair to punish the suicide's family for his wrongdoing. *Cruzan, supra,* at 294 (SCALIA, J., concurring). Nonetheless, although States moved away from Blackstone's treatment of suicide, courts continued to condemn it as a grave public wrong. See, e.g., *Bigelow v. Berkshire Life Ins. Co.,* 93 U.S. 284, 286 (1876) (suicide is "an act of criminal self-destruction"); *Von Holden v. Chapman, 87 A.D.2d 66, 70–71, 450 N.Y.S.2d 623, 626–27 (1982); Blackwood v. Jones, 111 Fla. 528, 532, 149 So. 600, 601 (1933)* ("No sophistry is tolerated ... which seeks to justify self-destruction as commendable or even a matter of personal right").

That suicide remained a grievous, though nonfelonious, wrong is confirmed by the fact that colonial and early state legislatures and courts did not retreat from prohibiting assisting suicide. Swift, in his early 19th century treatise on the laws of Connecticut, stated that "if one counsels another to commit suicide, and the other by reason of the advice kills himself, the advisor is guilty of murder as principal." 2 Z. Swift, A Digest of the Laws of the State of Connecticut 270 (1823). This was the well-established common-law view, see *In re Joseph G., 34 Cal. 3d 429, 434–35, 667 P.2d 1176, 1179 (1983); Commonwealth v. Mink, 123 Mass. 422, 428 (1877)* (" 'Now if the murder of one's self is felony, the accessory is equally guilty as if he had aided and abetted in the murder' ") (quoting Chief Justice Parker's charge to the jury in *Commonwealth v. Bowen, 13 Mass. 356 (1816)*), as was the similar principle that the consent of a homicide victim is "wholly immaterial to the guilt of the person who caused [his death]," 3 J. Stephen, A History of the Criminal Law of England 16 (1883); see 1 F. Wharton, Criminal Law §§ 451–452 (9th ed. 1885); *Martin v. Commonwealth, 184 Va. 1009, 1018–19, 37 S. E. 2d 43, 47 (1946)* (" 'The right to life and to personal security is not only sacred in the estimation of the common law, but it is inalienable' "). And the prohibitions against assisting suicide never contained exceptions for those who were near death. Rather, "the life of those to whom life had become a burden—of those who [were] hopelessly diseased or fatally wounded—nay, even the lives of criminals condemned to death, [were] under the protection of law, equally as the lives of those who [were] in the full tide of life's enjoyment, and anxious to continue to live." *Blackburn v. State, 23 Ohio St. 146, 163 (1872); see Bowen, supra, at 360* (prisoner who persuaded another to commit suicide could be tried for murder, even though victim was scheduled shortly to be executed).

The earliest American statute explicitly to outlaw assisting suicide was enacted in New York in 1828, Act of Dec. 10, 1828, ch. 20, § 4, 1828 N.Y. Laws 19 (codified at 2 N.Y. Rev. Stat. pt. 4, ch. 1, tit. 2, art. 1, § 7, p. 661 (1829)), and many of the new States and Territories followed New York's example. Marzen 73–74. Between 1857 and 1865, a New York commission led by Dudley Field drafted a criminal code that prohibited "aiding" a suicide and, specifically, "furnishing another person with any deadly weapon or poisonous drug, knowing that such person intends to use such weapon or drug in taking his own life." *Id.,* at 76–77. By the time the Fourteenth Amendment was ratified, it was a crime in most States to assist a suicide. See *Cruzan, supra,* at 294–95 (SCALIA, J., concurring). The Field Penal Code was adopted in the Dakota Territory in 1877, in New York in 1881, and its language served as a model for several other western States' statutes in the late 19th and early 20th centuries. Marzen 76–77, 205–06, 212–13. California, for example, codified its assisted-suicide prohibition in 1874, using language similar to the Field Code's. In this century, the Model Penal Code also prohibited "aiding" suicide, prompting many States to enact or revise their assisted-suicide bans. The Code's drafters observed that "the interests in the sanctity of life that are represented by the criminal homicide laws are threatened by one who expresses a willingness to participate in taking the life of another, even though the act may be accomplished with the consent, or at the request, of the suicide victim."

American Law Institute, Model Penal Code § 210.5, Comment 5, p. 100 (Official Draft and Revised Comments 1980).

Though deeply rooted, the States' assisted-suicide bans have in recent years been reexamined and, generally, reaffirmed. Because of advances in medicine and technology, Americans today are increasingly likely to die in institutions, from chronic illnesses. President's Comm'n for the Study of Ethical Problems in Medicine and Biomedical and Behavioral Research, Deciding to Forego Life-Sustaining Treatment 16–18 (1983). Public concern and democratic action are therefore sharply focused on how best to protect dignity and independence at the end of life, with the result that there have been many significant changes in state laws and in the attitudes these laws reflect. Many States, for example, now permit "living wills," surrogate health-care decisionmaking, and the withdrawal or refusal of life-sustaining medical treatment. See *Vacco v. Quill, post,* at 9–11; *79 F.3d,* at 818–20; *People v. Kevorkian, 447 Mich. 436, 478–80, and nn.53–56, 527 N.W.2d 714, 731–32, and nn.53–56 (1994).* At the same time, however, voters and legislators continue for the most part to reaffirm their States' prohibitions on assisting suicide.

The Washington statute at issue in this case, Wash. Rev. Code § 9A.36.060 (1994), was enacted in 1975 as part of a revision of that State's criminal code. Four years later, Washington passed its Natural Death Act, which specifically stated that the "withholding or withdrawal of life-sustaining treatment ... shall not, for any purpose, constitute a suicide" and that "nothing in this chapter shall be construed to condone, authorize, or approve mercy killing ... ." Natural Death Act, 1979 Wash. Laws, ch. 112, §§ 8(1), p. 11 (codified at Wash. Rev. Code §§ 70.122.070(1), 70.122.100 (1994)). In 1991, Washington voters rejected a ballot initiative which, had it passed, would have permitted a form of physician-assisted suicide. Washington then added a provision to the Natural Death Act expressly excluding physician-assisted suicide. 1992 Wash. Laws, ch. 98, § 10; Wash. Rev. Code § 70.122.100 (1994).

California voters rejected an assisted-suicide initiative similar to Washington's in 1993. On the other hand, in 1994, voters in Oregon enacted, also through ballot initiative, that State's "Death With Dignity Act," which legalized physician-assisted suicide for competent, terminally ill adults. Since the Oregon vote, many proposals to legalize assisted-suicide have been and continue to be introduced in the States' legislatures, but none has been enacted. And just last year, Iowa and Rhode Island joined the overwhelming majority of States explicitly prohibiting assisted suicide. See Iowa Code Ann. §§ 707A.2, 707A.3 (Supp. 1997); R. I. Gen. Laws §§ 11-60-1, 11-60-3 (Supp. 1996). Also, on April 30, 1997, President Clinton signed the Federal Assisted Suicide Funding Restriction Act of 1997, which prohibits the use of federal funds in support of physician-assisted suicide. Pub. L. No. 105-12, 111 Stat. 23 (codified at *42 U.S.C. § 14401 et seq.*).

Thus, the States are currently engaged in serious, thoughtful examinations of physician-assisted suicide and other similar issues. For example, New York State's Task Force on Life and the Law—an ongoing, blue-ribbon commission composed of doctors, ethicists, lawyers, religious leaders, and interested laymen—was convened in 1984 and commissioned with "a broad mandate to recommend public policy on issues raised by medical advances." New York Task Force vii. Over the past decade, the Task Force has recommended laws relating to end-of-life decisions, surrogate pregnancy, and organ donation. *Id.*, at 118–19. After studying physician-assisted suicide, however, the Task Force unanimously concluded that "legalizing assisted suicide and euthanasia would pose profound risks to many individuals who are ill and vulnerable. ... The potential dangers of this dramatic change in public policy would outweigh any benefit that might be achieved." *Id.*, at 120.

Attitudes toward suicide itself have changed since Bracton, but our laws have consistently condemned, and continue to prohibit, assisting suicide. Despite changes in medical technology and notwithstanding an increased emphasis on the importance of end-of-life decisionmaking, we have not retreated from this prohibition. Against this backdrop of history, tradition, and practice, we now turn to respondents' constitutional claim.

II

The Due Process Clause guarantees more than fair process, and the "liberty" it protects includes more than the absence of physical restraint. *Collins v. Harker Heights, 503 U.S. 115, 125 (1992)* (Due Process Clause "protects individual liberty against 'certain government actions regardless of the fairness of the procedures used to implement them' ") (quoting *Daniels v. Williams, 474 U.S. 327, 331 (1986)*). The Clause also provides heightened protection against government interference with certain fundamental rights and liberty interests. *Reno v. Flores, 507 U.S. 292, 301–02 (1993); Casey, 505 U.S. at 851*. In a long line of cases, we have held that, in addition to the specific freedoms protected by the Bill of Rights, the "liberty" specially protected by the Due Process Clause includes the rights to marry, *Loving v. Virginia, 388 U.S. 1 (1967)*; to have children, *Skinner v. Oklahoma ex rel. Williamson, 316 U.S. 535 (1942)*; to direct the education and upbringing of one's children, *Meyer v. Nebraska, 262 U.S. 390 (1923); Pierce v. Society of Sisters, 268 U.S. 510 (1925)*; to marital privacy, *Griswold v. Connecticut, 381 U.S. 479 (1965)*; to use contraception, *ibid.; Eisenstadt v. Baird, 405 U.S. 438 (1972)*; to bodily integrity, *Rochin v. California, 342 U.S. 165 (1952)*; and to abortion, *Casey, supra*. We have also assumed, and strongly suggested, that the Due Process Clause protects the traditional right to refuse unwanted lifesaving medical treatment. *Cruzan, 497 U.S. at 278–79*. But we "have always been reluctant to expand the concept of substantive due process because guideposts for responsible decisionmaking in this [uncharted] area are scarce and open-ended." *Collins, 503 U.S. at 125*. By extending constitutional protection to an asserted right or liberty interest, we, to a great extent, place the matter outside the arena of public debate and legislative action. We must therefore "exercise the utmost care whenever we are asked to break new ground in this field," *ibid.*, lest the liberty protected by the Due Process Clause be subtly transformed into the policy preferences of the members of this Court, *Moore, 431 U.S. at 502* (plurality opinion). Our established method of substantive-due-process analysis has two primary features: First, we have regularly observed that the Due Process Clause specially protects those fundamental rights and liberties which are, objectively, "deeply rooted in this Nation's history and tradition," *id., at 503* (plurality opinion); *Snyder v. Massachusetts, 291 U.S. 97, 105 (1934)* ("so rooted in the traditions and conscience of our people as to be ranked as fundamental"), and "implicit in the concept of ordered liberty," such that "neither liberty nor justice would exist if they were sacrificed," *Palko v. Connecticut, 302 U.S. 319, 325, 326 (1937).* Second, we have required in substantive-due-process cases a "careful description" of the asserted fundamental liberty interest. *Flores, supra, at 302; Collins, supra, at 125; Cruzan, supra, at 277–78.* Our Nation's history, legal traditions, and practices thus provide the crucial "guideposts for responsible decisionmaking," *Collins, supra, at 125,* that direct and restrain our exposition of the Due Process Clause. As we stated recently in *Flores,* the Fourteenth Amendment "forbids the government to infringe ... 'fundamental' liberty interests at all, no matter what process is provided, unless the infringement is narrowly tailored to serve a compelling state interest." *507 U.S. at 302.*

JUSTICE SOUTER, relying on JUSTICE HARLAN's dissenting opinion in *Poe v. Ullman,* would largely abandon this restrained methodology, and instead ask "whether [Washington's] statute sets up one of those 'arbitrary impositions' or 'purposeless restraints' at odds with the Due Process Clause of the Fourteenth Amendment," *post, at 1* (quoting *Poe, 367 U.S. 497, 543 (1961)* (HARLAN, J., dissenting)). In our view, however, the development of this Court's substantive-due-process jurisprudence, described briefly above, has been a process whereby the outlines of the "liberty" specially protected by the Fourteenth Amendment—never fully clarified, to be sure, and perhaps not capable of being fully clarified—have at least been carefully refined by concrete examples involving funda-

mental rights found to be deeply rooted in our legal tradition. This approach tends to rein in the subjective elements that are necessarily present in due-process judicial review. In addition, by establishing a threshold requirement—that a challenged state action implicate a fundamental right—before requiring more than a reasonable relation to a legitimate state interest to justify the action, it avoids the need for complex balancing of competing interests in every case.

Turning to the claim at issue here, the Court of Appeals stated that "properly analyzed, the first issue to be resolved is whether there is a liberty interest in determining the time and manner of one's death," *79 F.3d, at 801,* or, in other words, "is there a right to die?," *id., at 799.* Similarly, respondents assert a "liberty to choose how to die" and a right to "control of one's final days," Brief for Respondents 7, and describe the asserted liberty as "the right to choose a humane, dignified death," *id.,* at 15, and "the liberty to shape death," *id.,* at 18. As noted above, we have a tradition of carefully formulating the interest at stake in substantive-due-process cases. For example, although *Cruzan* is often described as a "right to die" case, see *79 F.3d, at 799; post, at 9* (STEVENS, J., concurring in judgment) (*Cruzan* recognized "the more specific interest in making decisions about how to confront an imminent death"), we were, in fact, more precise: we assumed that the Constitution granted competent persons a "constitutionally protected right to refuse lifesaving hydration and nutrition." *Cruzan, 497 U.S. at 279; id., at 287* (O'CONNOR, J., concurring) ("[A] liberty interest in refusing unwanted medical treatment may be inferred from our prior decisions"). The Washington statute at issue in this case prohibits "aiding another person to attempt suicide," Wash. Rev. Code § 9A.36.060(1) (1994), and, thus, the question before us is whether the "liberty" specially protected by the Due Process Clause includes a right to commit suicide which itself includes a right to assistance in doing so.

We now inquire whether this asserted right has any place in our Nation's traditions. Here, as discussed above, we are confronted with a consistent and almost universal tradition that has long rejected the asserted right, and continues explicitly to reject it today, even for terminally ill, mentally competent adults. To hold for respondents, we would have to reverse centuries of legal doctrine and practice, and strike down the considered policy choice of almost every State. See *Jackman v. Rosenbaum Co., 260 U.S. 22, 31 (1922)* ("If a thing has been practiced for two hundred years by common consent, it will need a strong case for the Fourteenth Amendment to affect it"); *Flores, 507 U.S. at 303* ("The mere novelty of such a claim is reason enough to doubt that 'substantive due process' sustains it").

Respondents contend, however, that the liberty interest they assert is consistent with this Court's substantive-due-process line of cases, if not with this Nation's history and practice. Pointing to *Casey* and *Cruzan*, respondents read our jurisprudence in this area as reflecting a general tradition of "self-sovereignty," Brief of Respondents 12, and as teaching that the "liberty" protected by the Due Process Clause includes "basic and intimate exercises of personal autonomy," *id.*, at 10; see *Casey, 505 U.S. at 847* ("It is a promise of the Constitution that there is a realm of personal liberty which the government may not enter"). According to respondents, our liberty jurisprudence, and the broad, individualistic principles it reflects, protects the "liberty of competent, terminally ill adults to make end-of-life decisions free of undue government interference." Brief for Respondents 10. The question presented in this case, however, is whether the protections of the Due Process Clause include a right to commit suicide with another's assistance. With this "careful description" of respondents' claim in mind, we turn to *Casey* and *Cruzan*.

In *Cruzan*, we considered whether Nancy Beth Cruzan, who had been severely injured in an automobile accident and was in a persistent vegetative state, "had a right under the United States Constitution which would require the hospital to withdraw life-sustaining treatment" at her parents' request. *Cruzan, 497 U.S. at 269*. We began with the observation that "at common law, even the touching of one person by another without consent and without legal justification was a battery." *Ibid.* We then discussed the related rule that "informed consent is generally required for medical treatment." *Ibid.* After reviewing a long line of relevant state cases, we concluded that "the common-law doctrine of informed consent is viewed as generally encompassing the right of a competent individual to refuse medical treatment." *Id., at 277*. Next, we reviewed our own cases on the subject, and stated that "the principle that a competent person has a constitutionally protected liberty interest in refusing unwanted medical treatment may be inferred from our prior decisions." *Id., at 278*. Therefore, "for purposes of [that] case, we assumed that the United States Constitution would grant a competent person a constitutionally protected right to refuse lifesaving hydration and nutrition." *Id., at 279; see id., at 287* (O'CONNOR, J., concurring). We concluded that, notwithstanding this right, the Constitution permitted Missouri to require clear and convincing evidence of an incompetent patient's wishes concerning the withdrawal of life-sustaining treatment. *Id., at 280–81*.

Respondents contend that in *Cruzan* we "acknowledged that competent, dying persons have the right to direct the removal of life-sustaining medical treatment and thus hasten death," Brief for Respondents 23, and that "the constitutional principle behind recognizing the patient's liberty to direct the withdrawal of artificial life support applies at least as strongly to the choice to hasten impending death by consuming lethal medication," *id.*, at 26. Similarly, the Court of Appeals concluded that "*Cruzan*, by recognizing a liberty interest that includes the refusal of artificial provision of life-sustaining food and water, necessarily recognized a liberty interest in hastening one's own death." *79 F.3d, at 816*.

The right assumed in *Cruzan*, however, was not simply deduced from abstract concepts of personal autonomy. Given the common-law rule that forced medication was a battery, and the long legal tradition protecting the decision to refuse unwanted medical treatment, our assumption was entirely consistent with this Nation's history and constitutional traditions. The decision to commit suicide with the assistance of another may be just as personal and profound as the decision to refuse unwanted medical treatment, but it has never enjoyed similar legal protection. Indeed, the two acts are widely and reasonably regarded as quite distinct. See *Quill v. Vacco, post,* at 5–13. In *Cruzan* itself, we recognized that most States outlawed assisted suicide—and even more do today—and we certainly gave no intimation that the right to refuse unwanted medical treatment could be somehow transmuted into a right to assistance in committing suicide. *497 U.S. at 280.*

Respondents also rely on *Casey.* There, the Court's opinion concluded that "the essential holding of *Roe v. Wade* should be retained and once again reaffirmed." *Casey, 505 U.S. at 846.* We held, first, that a woman has a right, before her fetus is viable, to an abortion "without undue interference from the State"; second, that States may restrict post-viability abortions, so long as exceptions are made to protect a woman's life and health; and third, that the State has legitimate interests throughout a pregnancy in protecting the health of the woman and the life of the unborn child. *Ibid.* In reaching this conclusion, the opinion discussed in some detail this Court's substantive-due-process tradition of interpreting the Due Process Clause to protect certain fundamental rights and "personal decisions relating to marriage, procreation, contraception, family relationships, child rearing, and education," and noted that many of those rights and liberties "involve the most intimate and personal choices a person may make in a lifetime." *Id.,* at 851. The Court of Appeals, like the District Court, found *Casey* " 'highly instructive' and 'almost prescriptive' for determining 'what liberty interest may inhere in a terminally ill person's choice to commit suicide' ":

> Like the decision of whether or not to have an abortion, the decision how and when to die is one of "the most intimate and personal choices a person may make in a lifetime," a choice "central to personal dignity and autonomy."

79 F.3d, at 813–14.

Similarly, respondents emphasize the statement in Casey that:

> "At the heart of liberty is the right to define one's own concept of existence, of meaning, of the universe, and of the mystery of human life. Beliefs about these matters could not define the attributes of personhood were they formed under compulsion of the State." *Casey, 505 U.S. at 851.*

Brief for Respondents 12. By choosing this language, the Court's opinion in *Casey* described, in a general way and in light of our prior cases, those personal activities and decisions that this Court has identified as so deeply rooted in our history and traditions, or so fundamental to our concept of constitutionally ordered liberty, that they are protected by the Fourteenth Amendment. The opinion moved from the recognition that liberty necessarily includes freedom of conscience and belief about ultimate considerations to the observation that "though the abortion decision may originate within the zone of conscience and belief, it is more than a philosophic exercise." *Casey, 505 U.S. at 852* (emphasis added). That many of the rights and liberties protected by the Due Process Clause sound in personal autonomy does not warrant the sweeping conclusion that any and all important, intimate, and personal decisions are so protected, *San Antonio Independent School Dist. v. Rodriguez, 411 U.S. 1, 33–35 (1973),* and *Casey* did not suggest otherwise.

The history of the law's treatment of assisted suicide in this country has been and continues to be one of the rejection of nearly all efforts to permit it. That being the case, our decisions lead us to conclude that the asserted "right" to assistance in committing suicide is not a fundamental liberty interest protected by the Due Process Clause. The Constitution also requires, however, that Washington's assisted-suicide ban be rationally related to legitimate government interests. See *Heller v. Doe, 509 U.S. 312, 319–20 (1993); Flores, 507 U.S. at 305.* This requirement is unquestionably met here. As the court below recognized, *79 F.3d, at 816–17,* Washington's assisted-suicide ban implicates a number of state interests. See *49 F.3d, at 592–93;* Brief for State of California et al. as Amici

Curiae 26–29; Brief for United States as Amicus Curiae 16–27.

First, Washington has an "unqualified interest in the preservation of human life." *Cruzan, 497 U.S. at 282.* The State's prohibition on assisted suicide, like all homicide laws, both reflects and advances its commitment to this interest. See *id., at 280;* Model Penal Code § 210.5, Comment 5, at 100 ("The interests in the sanctity of life that are represented by the criminal homicide laws are threatened by one who expresses a willingness to participate in taking the life of another"). This interest is symbolic and aspirational as well as practical:

> "While suicide is no longer prohibited or penalized, the ban against assisted suicide and euthanasia shores up the notion of limits in human relationships. It reflects the gravity with which we view the decision to take one's own life or the life of another, and our reluctance to encourage or promote these decisions." New York Task Force 131–32.

Respondents admit that "the State has a real interest in preserving the lives of those who can still contribute to society and enjoy life." Brief for Respondents 35. The Court of Appeals also recognized Washington's interest in protecting life, but held that the "weight" of this interest depends on the "medical condition and the wishes of the person whose life is at stake." *79 F.3d, at 817.* Washington, however, has rejected this sliding-scale approach and, through its assisted-suicide ban, insists that all persons' lives, from beginning to end, regardless of physical or mental condition, are under the full protection of the law. See *United States v. Rutherford, 442 U.S. 544, 558 (1979)* ("... Congress could reasonably have determined to protect the terminally ill, no less than other patients, from the vast range of self-styled panaceas that inventive minds can devise"). As we have previously affirmed, the States "may properly decline to make judgments about the 'quality' of life that a particular individual may enjoy," *Cruzan, 497 U.S. at 282.* This remains true, as *Cruzan* makes clear, even for those who are near death. Relatedly, all

admit that suicide is a serious public-health problem, especially among persons in otherwise vulnerable groups. See Washington State Dept. of Health, Annual Summary of Vital Statistics 1991, pp. 29–30 (Oct. 1992) (suicide is a leading cause of death in Washington of those between the ages of 14 and 54); New York Task Force 10, 23–33 (suicide rate in the general population is about one percent, and suicide is especially prevalent among the young and the elderly). The State has an interest in preventing suicide, and in studying, identifying, and treating its causes. See *79 F.3d, at 820; id., at 854* (Beezer, J., dissenting) ("The state recognizes suicide as a manifestation of medical and psychological anguish"); Marzen 107–46.

Those who attempt suicide—terminally ill or not—often suffer from depression or other mental disorders. See New York Task Force 13–22, 126–28 (more than 95% of those who commit suicide had a major psychiatric illness at the time of death; among the terminally ill, uncontrolled pain is a "risk factor" because it contributes to depression); Physician-Assisted Suicide and Euthanasia in the Netherlands: A Report of Chairman Charles T. Canady to the Subcommittee on the Constitution of the House Committee on the Judiciary, 104th Cong., 2d Sess., 10–11 (Comm. Print 1996); cf. Back, Wallace, Starks, & Pearlman, Physician-Assisted Suicide and Euthanasia in Washington State, *275 JAMA 919, 924 (1996)* ("Intolerable physical symptoms are not the reason most patients request physician-assisted suicide or euthanasia"). Research indicates, however, that many people who request physician-assisted suicide withdraw that request if their depression and pain are treated. H. Hendin, Seduced by Death: Doctors, Patients and the Dutch Cure 24–25 (1997) (suicidal, terminally ill patients "usually respond well to treatment for depressive illness and pain medication and are then grateful to be alive"); New York Task Force 177–78. The New York Task Force, however, expressed its concern that, because depression is difficult to diagnose, physicians and medical professionals often fail to respond adequately to seriously ill patients' needs. *Id., at 175.* Thus, legal physician-assisted suicide could make it more difficult for the State to protect depressed or mentally ill persons, or those who are suffering from untreated pain, from suicidal impulses.

The State also has an interest in protecting the integrity and ethics of the medical profession. In contrast to the Court of Appeals' conclusion that "the integrity of the medical profession would [not] be threatened in any way by [physician-assisted suicide]," *79 F.3d, at 827,* the American Medical Association, like many other medical and physicians' groups, has concluded that "physician-assisted suicide is fundamentally incompatible with the physician's role as healer." American Medical Association, Code of Ethics § 2.211 (1994); see Council on Ethical and Judicial Affairs, Decisions Near the End of Life, *267 JAMA 2229, 2233 (1992)* ("The societal risks of involving physicians in medical interventions to cause patients' deaths is too great"); New York Task Force 103–09 (discussing physicians' views). And physician-assisted suicide could, it is argued, undermine the trust that is essential to the doctor-patient relationship by blurring the time-honored line between healing and harming. Assisted Suicide in the United States, Hearing before the Subcommittee on the Constitution of the House Committee on the Judiciary, 104th Cong., 2d Sess., 355–56 (1996) (testimony of Dr. Leon R. Kass) ("The patient's trust in the doctor's wholehearted devotion to his best interests will be hard to sustain").

Next, the State has an interest in protecting vulnerable groups—including the poor, the elderly, and disabled persons—from abuse, neglect, and mistakes. The Court of Appeals dismissed the State's concern that disadvantaged persons might be pressured into physician-assisted suicide as "ludicrous on its face." *79 F.3d, at 825.* We have recognized, however, the real risk of subtle coercion and undue influence in end-of-life situations. *Cruzan, 497 U.S. at 281.* Similarly, the New York Task Force warned that "legalizing physician-assisted suicide would pose profound risks to many individuals who are ill and vulnerable. ... The risk of harm is greatest for the many individu-

als in our society whose autonomy and well-being are already compromised by poverty, lack of access to good medical care, advanced age, or membership in a stigmatized social group." New York Task Force 120; see *Compassion in Dying, 49 F.3d, at 593* ("An insidious bias against the handicapped—again coupled with a cost-saving mentality—makes them especially in need of Washington's statutory protection"). If physician-assisted suicide were permitted, many might resort to it to spare their families the substantial financial burden of end-of-life health-care costs.

The State's interest here goes beyond protecting the vulnerable from coercion; it extends to protecting disabled and terminally ill people from prejudice, negative and inaccurate stereotypes, and "societal indifference." *49 F.3d, at 592.* The State's assisted-suicide ban reflects and reinforces its policy that the lives of terminally ill, disabled, and elderly people must be no less valued than the lives of the young and healthy, and that a seriously disabled person's suicidal impulses should be interpreted and treated the same way as anyone else's. See New York Task Force 101–02; Physician-Assisted Suicide and Euthanasia in the Netherlands: A Report of Chairman Charles T. Canady, at 9, 20 (discussing prejudice toward the disabled and the negative messages euthanasia and assisted suicide send to handicapped patients).

Finally, the State may fear that permitting assisted suicide will start it down the path to voluntary and perhaps even involuntary euthanasia. The Court of Appeals struck down Washington's assisted-suicide ban only "as applied to competent, terminally ill adults who wish to hasten their deaths by obtaining medication prescribed by their doctors." *79 F.3d, at 838.* Washington insists, however, that the impact of the court's decision will not and cannot be so limited. Brief for Petitioners 44–47. If suicide is protected as a matter of constitutional right, it is argued, "every man and woman in the United States must enjoy it." *Compassion in Dying, 49 F.3d, at 591;* see *Kevorkian, 447 Mich., at 470, n.41, 527 N.W.2d, at 727–28, n.41.* The Court of Appeals' decision, and its expansive reasoning, provide ample support for the State's concerns. The court noted, for example, that the "decision of a duly appointed surrogate decision maker is for all legal purposes the decision of the patient himself," *79 F.3d, at 832, n.120;* that "in some instances, the patient may be unable to self-administer the drugs and ... administration by the physician ... may be the only way the patient may be able to receive them," *id., at 831;* and that not only physicians, but also family members and loved ones, will inevitably participate in assisting suicide. *Id., at 838, n.140.* Thus, it turns out that what is couched as a limited right to "physician-assisted suicide" is likely, in effect, a much broader license, which could prove extremely difficult to police and contain. Washington's ban on assisting suicide prevents such erosion.

This concern is further supported by evidence about the practice of euthanasia in the Netherlands. The Dutch government's own study revealed that in 1990, there were 2,300 cases of voluntary euthanasia (defined as "the deliberate termination of another's life at his request"), 400 cases of assisted suicide, and more than 1,000 cases of euthanasia without an explicit request. In addition to these latter 1,000 cases, the study found an additional 4,941 cases where physicians administered lethal morphine overdoses without the patients' explicit consent. Physician-Assisted Suicide and Euthanasia in the Netherlands: A Report of Chairman Charles T. Canady, at 12–13 (citing Dutch study). This study suggests that, despite the existence of various reporting procedures, euthanasia in the Netherlands has not been limited to competent, terminally ill adults who are enduring physical suffering, and that regulation of the practice may not have prevented abuses in cases involving vulnerable persons, including se-

verely disabled neonates and elderly persons suffering from dementia. *Id.,* at 16–21; see generally C. Gomez, Regulating Death: Euthanasia and the Case of the Netherlands (1991); H. Hendin, Seduced By Death: Doctors, Patients, and the Dutch Cure (1997). The New York Task Force, citing the Dutch experience, observed that "assisted suicide and euthanasia are closely linked," New York Task Force 145, and concluded that the "risk of ... abuse is neither speculative nor distant," *id.,* at 134. Washington, like most other States, reasonably ensures against this risk by banning, rather than regulating, assisting suicide. See *United States v. 12 200-ft Reels of Super 8MM Film, 413 U.S. 123, 127 (1973)* ("Each step, when taken, appears a reasonable step in relation to that which preceded it, although the aggregate or end result is one that would never have been seriously considered in the first instance"). We need not weigh exactly the relative strengths of these various interests. They are unquestionably important and legitimate, and Washington's ban on assisted suicide is at least reasonably related to their promotion and protection. We therefore hold that Wash. Rev. Code § 9A.36.060(1) (1994) does not violate the Fourteenth Amendment, either on its face or "as applied to competent, terminally ill adults who wish to hasten their deaths by obtaining medication prescribed by their doctors." *79 F.3d, at 838.*

* * *

Throughout the Nation, Americans are engaged in an earnest and profound debate about the morality, legality, and practicality of physician-assisted suicide. Our holding permits this debate to continue, as it should in a democratic society. The decision of the en banc Court of Appeals is reversed, and the case is remanded for further proceedings consistent with this opinion.

It is so ordered.

Legal Services of Northern California, Inc. v. Arnett
114 F.3d 135 (9th Cir. 1997)

We must determine whether a community legal services provider suffered a deprivation of federal statutory rights under the Older Americans Act when a State agency awarded a grant to a rival applicant.

I

Legal Services of Northern California, Inc. ("LSNC") is a non-profit California corporation whose mission is to provide civil legal services without charge to the disadvantaged throughout Northern California.

The Older Americans Act of 1965 ("OAA" or "the Act") established a program of federal grants for State and community social services designed to assist needy older persons. *42 U.S.C. § 3001 et seq.* A State is eligible for federal funding under the OAA if it designates an agency to develop and to administer a statewide plan for the provision of social services to the elderly. California designated its Department of Aging ("CDA") to meet this requirement, which, as further mandated, divided the State into distinct planning areas. The Area II Agency on Aging ("Agency") is CDA's designated sub-state agency for the local administration and distribution of OAA funds for most of northern California, including Lassen, Modoc, Shasta, Siskiyou and Trinity counties.

Under the Act the State and the area agencies are required to develop plans which assure that legal services will be provided to the elderly. *42 U.S.C. §§ 3027(a)(15); 3026(a)(2)(C).* The Act further specifies the kinds of legal services to be given priority in the plans, and requires assurances that no legal assistance will be furnished with OAA funds unless the "grantee administers a program designed to provide legal assistance to older individuals with social or economic need." *42 U.S.C. § 3027(a)(15)(B).* In addition, the plan must include assurances that services will be provided to low-income minority seniors "to the maximum extent feasible ... in accordance with their need for such services," *42 U.S.C. § 3026(a)(5)(A)(ii)(II),* and that the grants will be awarded to the agency "best able" to provide the services, *42 U.S.C. § 3027(a)(15)(B).*

In December 1993, the Agency published a request for proposals for the provision of legal services to the elderly with OAA funds. Two applicants responded with proposals: LSNC and the Senior Legal Center of Northern California. The Agency awarded the grant to the Senior Legal

Center. LSNC appealed this decision through administrative procedures to both the Agency and CDA. Both appeals were denied.

In December 1994, LSNC filed a complaint in federal district court under *42 U.S.C. § 1983,* alleging that the Director of CDA had deprived it of federal rights under the OAA. Specifically, LSNC alleged that the Agency and CDA had violated the OAA by failing to choose LSNC as the grantee on the grounds that it was "best able" to provide the services, and because its proposal included the provision of services to low-income minority elders "to the maximum extent feasible." The complaint sought an injunction ordering the Director to award the grant to LSNC and to take all reasonable and necessary steps to ensure that grants are awarded in accordance with the provisions of the OAA. LSNC further sought a declaration that the Director of CDA violated the OAA by failing to select LSNC for the grant.

The parties filed cross motions for summary judgment and the district court granted summary judgment against LSNC. The district court held that the OAA did not create any enforceable federal rights in unsuccessful applicants for grants. It based its holding on a determination that applicants such as LSNC are not intended beneficiaries of the OAA, and that the statutory terms LSNC sought to have enforced are too vague and amorphous to provide a judicially manageable standard. LSNC timely appealed.

II

Does the OAA create enforceable rights in grant applicants? Section 1983 provides a cause of action against a State actor for the "deprivation of any rights, privileges or immunities secured by the Constitution and laws of the United States." *42 U.S.C. § 1983.* It is well established that § 1983 provides a private right of action for violations of federal statutes in some instances. *Maine v. Thiboutot, 448 U.S. 1, 4, 100 S. Ct. 2502, 65 L. Ed. 2d 555 (1980).* However, § 1983 relief is available only if the statute creates enforceable rights and if Congress has not foreclosed such enforcement in the statute itself. *Wilder v. Virginia Hosp. Ass'n, 496*

U.S. 498, 508, 110 S. Ct. 2510, 110 L. Ed. 2d 455 (1990).

In order to determine whether a particular statute creates rights enforceable in a § 1983 suit, we scrutinize the terms of the statute under a three part test. A statute creates a right enforceable under § 1983 if: (1) the statute was intended to benefit the plaintiffs; (2) the statute imposes a binding obligation on the government unit rather than merely expressing a congressional preference for a certain kind of conduct, and; (3) the interest asserted by the plaintiff is not so vague or amorphous that it is beyond the competence of the judiciary to enforce. *Wilder, 496 U.S. at 509.*

In carrying out this inquiry, we are to examine whether particular statutory provisions create specific enforceable rights, rather than considering the statute and purported rights on a more general level. *Blessing v. Freestone, ___ U.S. ___, 117 S. Ct. 1353, 137 L. Ed. 2d 569, 1997 WL 188396, *8–9 (1997).* LSNC argues that statutory provisions of the OAA which provide direction for selecting grantees create an enforceable right in the "best" applicant to be awarded the grant. It argues that these provisions meet the three-part *Wilder* test and thus create a right in grant applicants which is enforceable under § 1983.

A

LSNC first argues that it is among the intended beneficiaries of the statute's provisions for the selection of service providers because it will benefit from a "proper" enforcement of the Act by being awarded a grant and having access to a network of other grantees. Courts have indeed found service providers to be among the intended beneficiaries of statutes which establish reimbursement rates. *Id. at 510* (finding that medical services providers are among intended beneficiaries of the Boren Amendment requiring States to pay reasonable reimbursements for Medicaid patients); see also *Arkansas Medical Society, Inc. v. Reynolds, 6 F.3d 519, 526 (8th Cir. 1993)* (holding that service providers may challenge State's decision to lower Medicaid reimbursement rates under § 1983); *Little Rock Family Planning Services v. Dalton, 60 F.3d*

497, 502 (8th Cir. 1995), rev'd in part on other grounds, 116 S. Ct. 1063, 134 L. Ed. 2d 115 (1996) (concerning reimbursement for abortion services under the Hyde Amendment to the Medicaid Act).

However, LSNC cites to no authority holding that unsuccessful applicants for federal grants may be considered among the intended beneficiaries of a statute. LSNC contends it was included when Congress expressed its hope that the OAA would create a partnership of groups working towards the common goal of providing services to older Americans. *42 U.S.C. § 3003(4).* Since grantees would benefit from this network and from federal funding, LSNC argues that those seeking the grants are among the intended beneficiaries of the statute.

It may be that the grantee service providers will benefit from being selected for inclusion in the OAA grants program. But it is clear that Congress intended the statutory provisions at issue here to be for the benefit of elders in need of services rather than for the benefit of each group which competes for a grant. Nor does the fact that the OAA conveys benefits on selected grantees indicate a congressional intent to benefit rejected grantees. Furthermore, it is not at all clear that LSNC would necessarily benefit from the injunction it seeks requiring the agencies to comply with the OAA selection criteria. See *Blessing, ___ U.S. at ___, 117 S. Ct. 1353, 137 L. Ed. 2d 569, 1997 WL 188396 at *9* (finding support for its conclusion that individuals are not intended beneficiaries of a provision calling for "substantial compliance" with a statute when individuals are not assured of benefit from such compliance). We therefore decline LSNC's invitation to extend the scope of intended beneficiaries of the OAA to potential service providers who have been rejected from inclusion in the program.

B

We likewise reject LSNC's contention that the statutory and regulatory provisions it seeks to have enforced under § 1983 provide sufficient guidance to allow judicial enforcement, the third factor specified in *Wilder*. Statutory provisions are not judicially manageable when they are "vague and amorphous such that it is beyond the competence of the judiciary to enforce." *Wilder, 496 U.S. at 509* (internal citation omitted).

LSNC points to two sections of the OAA and its implementing regulations which it argues create a judicially manageable standard. First, the OAA requires each area agency to submit a plan assuring that it will "include in each agreement made" a requirement that the chosen service provider will "to the maximum extent feasible, provide services to low-income minority individuals in accordance with their needs for such services." *42 U.S.C. 3026(a)(5)(A)(ii)(II)*. Secondly, the State is required to submit a plan which contains assurances "that any grantee selected is the entity best able to provide the particular service." *42 U.S.C. § 3027(a)(15)(B)*. LSNC argues that the terms requiring services to the needy to the "maximum extent feasible" by the applicant "best able to provide" them are sufficiently defined in the statute and regulations so as to rescue the terms from vagueness. The district court, however, found that the additional definitions merely recast the statute's general goals without providing guidance to courts in determining which applicant's proposal must be selected as a matter of law.

LSNC now asks us to use these statutory and regulatory provisions to declare that CDA has violated the OAA by awarding a grant to the Senior Legal Center rather than to LSNC because it is "best able" to provide services to low-income minority elders "to the maximum extent feasible." We respectfully decline this request. The cited provisions describe obligations to be imposed on the chosen service providers, not criteria which courts may employ to determine as a matter of law which applicant for a grant is "best."

For instance, LSNC argues that its proposal was clearly better than the Senior Legal Center's because it proposed to offer more of the services which the OAA described as priorities, and to provide services to more clients with social needs. Senior Legal Center chose to concentrate its services in the areas of greatest demand by local seniors.

Its proposal included an estimate of fewer clients to be served because it concentrated on face-to-face meetings with seniors, which the Center found to be preferable to the telephone screening procedure favored by LSNC.

We are ill-equipped by the statute's terms to determine which of these two applicants is best able to provide the services or which will provide services to low-income minorities to the maximum extent feasible. While the statute does include a list of priorities, it does not require that each priority must be given the same emphasis. Nor does the term "maximum extent feasible in accordance with their need" indicate whether the term refers exclusively to quantitative measurements. It is at least arguable that fewer clients being served on a face-to-face basis would better fulfill the statute's goal than many clients served on a more superficial phone-in basis.

The statutory terms which LSNC would have us enforce are far different from the kinds of standards which courts have previously found to be judicially manageable. *See e.g., Loschiavo v. City of Dearborn, 33 F.3d 548, 553 (6th Cir.)*, cert. denied, *513 U.S. 1150, 115 S. Ct. 1099, 130 L. Ed. 2d 1067 (1994)* (finding "unreasonable limitations" on satellite dish reception creates a workable standard); *Lampkin v. District of Columbia, 307 U.S. App. D.C. 155, 27 F.3d 605, 612 (D.C. Cir.)*, cert. denied, *513 U.S. 1016, 115 S. Ct. 578, 130 L. Ed. 2d 493 (1994)* (finding "best interest" of homeless children to be manageable where statute defines specific, detailed criteria); *Miller by Miller v. Whitburn, 10 F.3d 1315, 1319–20 (7th Cir. 1993)* (finding that court is competent to determine whether operation is an "experimental procedure" and therefore excluded from Medicaid coverage); *Marshall v. Switzer, 10 F.3d 925, 929 (2d Cir. 1993)* (holding that court may determine whether a statute requires State to pay for particular piece of automotive equipment because it will make a handicapped individual employable). Generally, these judicially manageable standards require the court to determine whether a specified standard has been satisfied in a particular instance.

In contrast, LSNC asks the courts to use the OAA's provisions to determine which member of a pool of applicants is "best" at satisfying the statute's goals. It also argues that every applicant for an OAA grant has the right to mount a similar challenge under § 1983 to the decisions of State and area agencies in selecting grantees. In practice federal courts would replace congressionally designated agencies as decision makers under the Act. Nothing in the statute indicates that Congress intended such a result.

C

Finally, LSNC argues that the statute's terms create a binding obligation on the CDA and the Agency. See *Wilder, 496 U.S. at 512.* Since LSNC is not among the intended beneficiaries of the OAA, and since the terms it seeks to enforce are vague and amorphous, it follows that Congress did not intend the State and area agencies to owe a binding obligation under such provisions to all applicants for grants.

The Supreme Court has held that an ambiguous statutory term precludes a finding that Congress intended to create an enforceable right which would be binding on the States. *Suter v. Artist M., 503 U.S. 347, 363, 112 S. Ct. 1360, 118 L. Ed. 2d 1 (1992).* In *Suter,* the Court held that a term in the Adoption Assistance and Child Welfare Act requiring the States to make "reasonable efforts" to maintain family unity did not "unambiguously confer an enforceable right upon the Act's beneficiaries." *Id.* Since "reasonable efforts" would necessarily vary depending on the circumstances, the court held that the statute gave the States broad discretion as to how the goal was to be pursued. *Id. at 360.* See also *Blessing, ___ U.S. ___, 117 S. Ct. 1353, 137 L. Ed. 2d 569, 1997 WL 188396, at *10* (holding provision requiring "sufficient" staffing to fulfill specific functions is not judicially manageable).

Similarly, the OAA specifies many goals to be pursued in the provision of services to the elderly, but delegates to the designated agencies broad discretion as to how those goals may best be accomplished. Oversight of these efforts is left to the Assistant Secretary on Aging, who is given authority to withhold funding if the State's plan is inadequate. *42 U.S.C. § 3024.* There is nothing in the statute to suggest that Congress has "unambiguously" conferred an enforceable right against the States by the terms LSNC seeks to enforce.

We therefore conclude that the OAA creates no rights which are enforceable under § 1983 by LSNC.

III

The CDA has requested attorneys' fees under *42 U.S.C. § 1988.* Authorization for attorneys' fees under § 1988 is different for prevailing defendants in a civil rights action than for prevailing plaintiffs. *Vernon v. City of Los Angeles, 27 F.3d 1385, 1402 (9th Cir. 1993),* cert. denied, *513 U.S. 1000, 115 S. Ct. 510, 130 L. Ed. 2d 417 (1994).* A prevailing defendant is awarded attorneys' fees only where the action is found to be "unreasonable, frivolous, meritless or vexatious." *Id.* (internal citation omitted). An appeal is considered frivolous when the result is obvious or the appellant's arguments of error are wholly without merit. *Id.*

While LSNC must have known that their position was unsupported by existing precedent, we cannot say that the action was frivolous. It is likely that LSNC was launching a good faith effort to advance a novel theory under our § 1983 jurisprudence. While we have rejected this attempt, LSNC's arguments were not wholly without merit. We therefore decline to award attorneys' fees to the prevailing defendants under § 1988.

The judgment of the district court is AFFIRMED. CDA's request for attorneys' fees is DENIED.

GLOSSARY

A

accelerated death benefit   Portion of the face value of a life insurance policy paid to the insured, the remainder of the face value remaining in effect for the named beneficiaries.

acute ailment   Physical problem of a temporary nature.

administrator(trix)   Personal representative of an intestate.

adult home   Housing for persons over a certain age.

advance directive   Document that expresses the future health care wishes of the signatory.

Age Discrimination in Employment Act (ADEA)   Federal statute protecting persons over the age of 40 from being discriminated against in employment based on age.

agent   Person who acts on behalf of another.

alternative dispute resolution   Nonjudicial method of resolving legal problems, such as arbitration or mediation.

Americans with Disabilities Act (ADA) Federal statute designed to protect persons with physical or mental disabilities from being discriminated against in employment and access to public facilities.

annuity method   Method of distributing pension income.

Area Agency on Aging   Division of the Legal Services Corporation, specializing in the needs of the elderly.

assignment   Under Medicare, a physician's agreement to accept whatever payment Medicare provides.

assisted living facility   Housing in which certain services are provided to help a person maintain independence.

autonomy   The ability to make decisions for oneself.

B

back pay   Remedy under the ADEA in which the employee may be entitled to pay lost due to the discriminatory act.

beneficiary   Person who has equitable title to trust property.

bona fide occupational qualification (BFOQ) Employer defense to an age discrimination claim, indicating a rational, job-related reason for instituting an age requirement.

C

capital asset   Property owned for increase in value.

capital gains tax   Tax imposed on any increase in value of a capital asset, determined when the asset is sold.

charge   Document used to initiate a claim based on unlawful discrimination.

charging party   Person who institutes a claim based on unlawful discrimination.

charitable (public) trust   Trust that serves a public rather than a private purpose.

charitable remainder annuity trust   Trust that provides income to a private beneficiary for life, with a charity as the remainderman; provides certain favorable tax treatment for the trust income.

charitable remainder unitrust   Trust that divides income between a charity and a private individual; has favorable tax treatment.

chronic ailment   Continuous and persistent physical problem that cannot be cured.

civil commitment   The voluntary or involuntary confinement of a person in a mental facility because it is determined that the person may do severe harm to himself or to others.

codicil   Formal amendment to a will.

community property   Form of property ownership for married couples in which each spouse owns one-half of the whole.

competency   The legal ability to make decisions for oneself.

condominium   Form of ownership in which a person owns an individual unit and is a tenant-in-common with other owners for common areas.

consequential damages   Monetary award above the normal award due to special circumstances; a remedy permitted under the ADEA.

conservator   Former term for a guardian of the estate. *See also* guardianship.

conservatorship   Court authorization to have one person make decisions for another who is deemed incompetent.

continuing care retirement community (CCRC)   Living facility that provides certain medical care for persons who do not require nursing home care.

cooperative   Form of ownership in which a person buys shares that entitle the person to possess a unit in the cooperative.

co-payment   Portion of a medical bill that is not reimbursed or covered by insurance and remains the responsibility of the patient.

cost-basis HMO   Form of managed care in which the insured may use various facilities but must pay a small fee for each service received.

credit line   Funds that can be drawn on.

credit shelter (A-B) trust   Two trusts created to take advantage of the marital deduction and the unified estate and gift tax credit.

D

deductible   Percentage of a medical bill for which the patient remains responsible and must pay before insurance coverage takes over.

deferral agency   State agency used to investigate ADEA claims.

defined benefit plan   Pension plan in which the amount of the pension is specifically determined by employee's length of service and salary.

defined contribution plan (individual account plan)   Pension plan in which the pension is determined by the amount of the contributions made to the plan during the pensioner's period of employment.

Department of Housing and Urban Development (HUD)   Federal agency that administers housing laws.

Department of Veterans Affairs (VA) Federal agency that administers laws relating to veterans.

Dependency and Indemnity Compensation (DIC)   Veterans' benefits for survivors.

disability   Physical or mental condition that limits a major life activity.

donee   Recipient of a gift.

donor   Person who gives a gift.

do-not-resuscitate (DNR) directive Document indicating that the signatory does not wish to be resuscitated or maintained on life support equipment.

durable power of attorney   Power of attorney that survives the principal's incapacity.

E

elder   Anyone over a certain age; not universally defined by the law.

elder abuse   The willful or negligent causing of physical or psychological harm to an older person.

elder law   Area of law concerned with the legal problems of persons deemed to be elderly.

eligibility verification report (EVR) Annual report to determine a person's continued financial eligibility to receive benefits.

eminent domain   The right of the government to acquire private property for a legitimate governmental use.

Employee Retirement Income Security Act (ERISA)   Federal statute that regulates pension plans.

employer   Person who meets the ADEA's statutory definition, usually determined by a minimum number of employees.

employer group health plan (EGHP) Health insurance coverage maintained by an employer.

endowment policy   Form of life insurance policy in which the premiums are paid up in a set number of years; if the insured is alive at that date, the insured receives the proceeds.

enriched housing   Housing communities that integrate social services and activities.

Equal Employment Opportunity Commission (EEOC)   Federal agency that administers the ADEA and other federal statutes prohibiting discrimination in employment.

escheat   The state's inheritance of the property of an intestate who has no blood relatives.

estate planning   The process of devising strategies to minimize probate and estate taxes when the client dies and to help the client accumulate property while alive.

excess benefit plan   Retirement plan for highly compensated employees; excluded from ERISA regulation.

exclusion ratio   Proportion of an annuity that is not subject to income taxation, based on IRS tables.

executor(trix)   Personal representative named in a will.

exploitation   The unlawful taking of another's property.

F

fair hearing   Administrative hearing to which a Medicaid recipient is entitled if benefits are denied.

Fair Housing Act (FHA)   Federal statute protecting persons from discrimination in housing.

forward averaging   Tax break for persons who receive a lump-sum distribution of their pension benefits.

fully insured   Under Social Security, having worked 40 quarters to be entitled to benefits upon retirement.

G

general enrollment period   Yearly period during which persons may enroll in Medicare Part B if they did not do so during their initial enrollment period.

general power of attorney   Document granting a person the legal ability to act on behalf of another; the power terminates on the death or incapacity of the principal or by completion of its purpose.

generational justice   Younger generations paying for the needs of older generations.

gift   Transfer of property without consideration.

gift tax   Transfer tax imposed on gifts.

guardian ad litem   Guardian during litigation.

guardian of the estate   Guardian to manage the property of a incapacitated person.

guardian of the person   Person legally authorized to manage the personal, non-financial affairs of a incapacitated person.

guardianship   Court authorization for someone to act on behalf of an incompetent.

H

Health Care Finance Administration (HCFA)   Federal agency that administers government health care programs.

health care proxy   Legal document authorizing someone other than the principal to make health care decisions for the principal should the principal become incapable of speaking for himself or herself.

health maintenance organization (HMO)   A managed health care provider.

home equity conversion mortgage   *See* reverse mortgage.

hospice   Facility designed to provide care to the terminally ill.

I

in parens patriae   "In place of the parent"; Roman concept that forms the basis of guardianship law.

incapacitated person   Current term for a ward.

individual account plan   *See* defined contribution plan.

individual retirement account (IRA)   Private pension plan given favorable tax treatment.

Individuals with Disabilities Education Act (IDEA)   Federal statute mandating free education for persons with disabilities.

initial enrollment period   Period during which an eligible person can enroll in Medicare.

injunction   Court order to stop engaging in specified activities; a remedy under the ADEA.

inter vivos trust (living trust)   Trust created to take effect during the creator's lifetime.

intestate succession   Statutory procedure indicating which blood relatives inherit from a person who died without a valid will.

IRA-Plus (Roth)   Form of IRA that permits withdrawal without tax penalties.

J

joint ownership   Form of title in which two or more persons have equal rights to property with a right of survivorship.

joint tenancy   Form of multiple ownership of property with a right of survivorship.

K

Keogh account   Private pension plan for self-employed individuals.

L

life insurance trust   Trust created with the proceeds of a life insurance policy, usually established by the policy itself.

limited guardian   Court-appointed representative charged with making decisions in a limited area for an incapacitated person.

limited payment life insurance   Life insurance with very high premiums that are totally paid up within a short period of time.

liquidated damages   Monetary remedy under the ADEA that specifies a particular dollar amount pursuant to a contract.

living will   Document indicating the signatory's wishes with respect to life support should the signatory become incompetent.

long-term care insurance   Form of health insurance that provides benefits for extended health care.

look-back period   Period of time the government will review to determine whether an applicant has improperly divested himself or herself of property to become entitled to receive Medicaid.

Low Income Energy Assistance Program   Federal and state program designed to help tenants and homeowners to meet energy bills.

lump-sum distribution   Receiving an entire pension benefit in one payment.

lump-sum reverse mortgage   A reverse mortgage in which the homeowner receives the entire amount of the loan at once.

M

managed care   Health care rendered through an HMO arrangement.

marital deduction   Tax rule that permits all property inherited by a surviving spouse to pass free of estate tax.

master trust   Pooled supplemental needs trust.

Medicaid   Federally funded program providing medical care to low-income persons.

Medical Assistance Utilization Threshold Program (MUTS)   Federal program designed to limit the use of Medicaid benefits.

Medicare   Federally funded health insurance for persons who receive Social Security benefits.

Medi-gap insurance   Form of supplemental insurance designed to provide payment for items not covered by Medicare.

N

neglect   The willful or negligent failure to provide necessary care or services to another by a person who has a legal duty to provide such care to the other person.

non-service-connected disability   Disability resulting from an occurrence that did not happen during military service.

nursing home   Health care facility designed for long-term care for persons who do not need to be in a hospital but who cannot manage their health care on their own.

Nursing Home Reform Act (NHRA) Federal statute affecting the rights of nursing home patients.

O

Older Americans Act Amendments of 1987 Federal statute requiring state agencies to investigate problems affecting older Americans.

Older Americans Act of 1965   First federal statute specifically addressing the needs of the elderly.

Older Workers' Benefit Protection Act Federal statute providing protection to the elderly with respect to employee benefits.

Omnibus Budget Reconciliation Act (OBRA) Federal statute, enacted in 1993, that affects Medicaid recipients.

open enrollment   General period during which a person may enroll for Medicare.

order of protection (protective order) Document issued by a court or protective services agency to remedy family problems.

override application   Request for additional care over and above that permitted pursuant to MUTS.

P

Patient Self-Determination Act   Federal statute requiring Medicare and Medicaid recipients to be given written statements regarding their health care rights.

pension benefit plan   Pension plan that provides for retirement income.

personal representative   Individual responsible for administering a decedent's estate.

plenary guardian   Guardian over both the person and the property of the incapacitated person.

power of attorney   Document authorizing one person to act on behalf of another.

principal   Person who authorizes another to act on his or her behalf.

pro bono legal services   Free legal services provided by law offices and bar associations to low-income individuals.

probate   The process of either proving a will or having an administrator appointed for an intestate.

project-based program   Public housing in which the tenant must live in a specified building.

protective order   *See* order of protection.

public interest law clinic   Government-funded office providing legal services to low-income persons.

punitive damages   Monetary award used as a punishment for willful misconduct under the ADEA.

Q

qualified terminable interest property (QTIP) trust   Trust that qualifies for the marital deduction, created for a surviving spouse.

qualified viatical settlement company Person or company that is licensed by a state or meets the requirements of the Viatical Settlement Model Act; payments received by the insured from such companies exempt from federal income tax.

R

reasonable accommodation Requirement under the ADA for persons with disabilities.

reasonable factor other than age (RFOA) An employer defense to an age discrimination claim under the ADEA.

remainderman Person in whom the legal and equitable titles merge at the termination of a trust.

representative payee Person authorized by the Social Security Administration to receive benefits on behalf of the recipient of Social Security benefits.

retirement community Living facility designed for persons who are retired.

reverse mortgage Loan made to a homeowner that permits the homeowner to live in the house and receive income payments.

reversion (reversionary interest) Term indicating that the creator of the trust is the remainderman.

revocable trust Trust in which the creator reserves the right to terminate the relationship.

risk HMO Managed care that provides all services to enrollees in its geographic area.

rollover (1) Placing a pension distribution into another pension account. (2) Process of taking the gain from the sale of a home and putting it into the purchase of a new home; this avoids the capital gains tax.

S

safe harbor method Method of taxing pension payments based on the person's age when the benefit is first received.

sale-leaseback Arrangement whereby a homeowner sells his or her house but remains in possession as a tenant.

Section 202 HUD program providing subsidies to create housing for the elderly and the disabled.

self-abuse Abuse caused by the victim to himself or herself by the failure to provide needed care.

self-proving affidavit Affidavit signed by the attesting witnesses to a will.

seniority Employee benefits based on length of employment.

service-connected disability Disability resulting from participation in the military.

shelter Form of temporary emergency housing.

single-room occupancy (SRO) Living facility in which a person rents a room and shares bathroom facilities with other tenants.

Social Security Administration Federal agency that administers the Social Security Act.

special enrollment period Time period during which the working elderly can enroll in Medicare.

specified-term reverse mortgage A reverse mortgage with a designated period during which payments will be made.

spend-down program Method whereby a person divests himself or herself of assets in order to qualify for Medicaid.

spendthrift trust   Trust designed to keep the trust property from the creditors of the beneficiary.

springing power of attorney   Power of attorney that comes into effect only if and when the principal becomes incapacitated.

standby guardian   Contingent guardian.

supplemental insurance   Health care coverage designed to provide benefits for care not covered by other policies or programs.

supplemental needs trust   Trust created to provide medical benefits not otherwise provided for the beneficiary.

Supplemental Security Income (SSI)   Government transfer payment to very-low-income individuals.

surplus income   Income above the limit to qualify for Medicaid.

T

tenancy by the entirety   Joint tenancy for legally married couples.

tenancy in common   Form of multiple ownership of property in which each tenant owns a separate but undivided interest in the whole.

tentative trust   *See* Totten trust.

tenure plan   Method of payment under a reverse mortgage in which the homeowner receives a set monthly payment.

term life insurance   Form of life insurance in which the insured retains no incidents of ownership.

testamentary capacity   The legal ability to execute a will.

testamentary trust   Trust created in a will.

testator(trix)   Person who executes a valid will.

Totten trust (tentative trust)   Bank account "in trust for"; not a real trust.

trust   Fiduciary relationship in which title to property is divided into its legal and equitable components.

trustee   Person with legal title to trust property.

Truth in Lending Act   Federal statute mandating that consumers be given certain information before entering into a loan agreement.

U

undue influence   Using a confidential relationship to influence another person's actions in an unwarranted manner.

Unified Estate and Gift Tax Credit   Federal tax credit permitting a certain amount of property left to a nonspouse to pass free of estate tax.

United States Housing Act of 1937   Early federal statute dealing with housing issues.

V

Veterans' Improved Pension Plan (VIPP)   Method of reducing a veteran's benefit dollar for dollar based on the amount of the recipient's nonexempt income.

viatical settlement   Agreement whereby a terminally ill insured person accepts a lump sum from a purchaser who becomes the beneficiary of the insured's life insurance policy.

Viatical Settlement Model Act   Model act designed to regulate viatical settlements.

W

ward Person who is under guardianship.

warranty of habitability Common-law guarantee that a rental unit is fit to live in.

warranty of occupancy Common-law guarantee that tenants can reside in a unit without interference.

welfare benefit plan Employee benefit package that provides for medical care and benefits other than retirement income.

whole life insurance Form of life insurance in which the insured retains incidents of ownership.

will Formal document that indicates how a person wants his or her property to be distributed at death.

will contest Challenge to the validity of a document presented to the court as a will.

willful Knowing (usually used in the context of disregard of the law).

INDEX